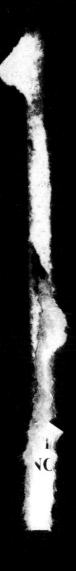

POP AND ROCK

WORLD RECORDS

2011

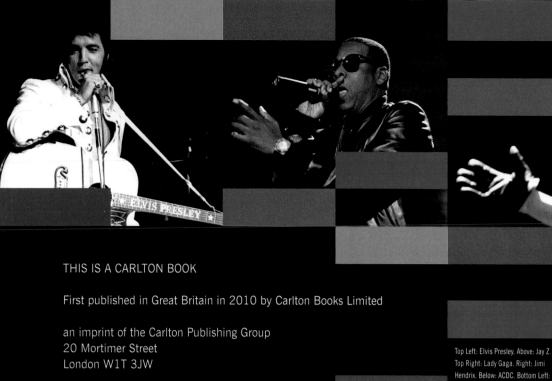

Top Left: Elvis Presley. Above: Jay Z. Top Right: Lady Gaga. Right: Jimi Hendrix. Below: ACDC. Bottom Left: The Beatles. Bottom Right: Britney Spears and Madonna.

MUSIC TELEVISION™

POP AND ROCK

WORLD RECORDS

2011

LUKE CRAMPTON AND DAFYDD REES

CARLTON
BOOKS

CONTENTS

Rock and Pop unite: Slash and Michael Jackson at the 1995 MTV Video Music Awards.

INTRODUCTION

Who, what, when, where? Reliable statistics and accurate facts about the glorious history of rock and roll have remained an inglorious mess throughout much of its evolution. Historically, some of the confusion and lack of coherent data resulted from inflated, self-heralding claims by record labels and publicists, conversely mixed with a cloak of secrecy and poor record-keeping by the very same parties.

Although the compilation of weekly singles and albums charts – which began in the United States and the United Kingdom in the early 1950s – are now regularly compiled in dozens of other countries around the world, a detailed appraisal of the biggest hits, artists, compositions, music genres, tours, triumphs and tragedies over the past 50-plus years has remained elusive – until now. Never before has such a complete, historic accounting on so many different areas of rock history been collected in one place.

With this first edition of this book, we present a unique compendium of crucial rock stats, charts, facts, lists and trivia – which collectively offer a fascinating rock 'n' roll call of the greatest songs and performers of the past 60 years. With a truly global perspective – and research gathered from hundreds of authoritative sources including the authors' own Music Information Database – the following pages are stuffed with informative, comprehensive and fun lists on all manner of rock-related topics: from the best-selling digital downloads of the Internet era to the very first Grammy and BRIT winners.

This book includes definitive data on all things music: from the earliest television shows through Eurovision to *American Idol*, music films and musicals, top-selling singles and albums from dozens of countries and different eras, individual artist best-sellers, the most-played songs on radio, the most expensive music videos, top-grossing tours, iconic music festivals, all major music award winners from around the globe, music milestones, different genre best-sellers, Oscar-winning songs, memorable reunions, *Desert Island Disc* selections, legendary benefit concerts, all-time chart champs, tragic misadventures, wealthist stars, final gigs, gold and platinum disc awards, rock reunions, seminal songwriters and producers, music memorabilia and hundreds of other illuminating rankings from the timeless to the trivial.

Added to these fascinating and indispensable snapshots of rock history past and present, each page is jammed with the backstory behind the numbers, brief artist bios and photos, all combining to tell the complete, real story of rock and pop through the ages. Who, what, when, where: musicians, facts, then-to-now, here.

Luke Crampton and Dafydd Rees

ABOUT THE AUTHORS:

Dafydd Rees and Luke Crampton co-founded the Media Research & Information Bureau (MRIB) in London in the 1980s, which became the largest chart-compiling and music research agency in Europe. Previously the official adjudicators for the Ivor Novello awards and the World Music Awards, Dafydd and Luke are currently voting members for the Grammy Awards, the Rock and Roll Hall of Fame and the Songwriters Hall of Fame.

Now based in the USA, they also create and produce music television series including CNN's *World Beat* and *The Music Room* and continue to develop their Music Information Database, the world's largest research resource on popular music.

Acclaimed authors of more than 30 music books including the *Q Magazine Encyclopedia of Rock Stars*, *Rock and Roll Year By Year*, *The Guinness Book of Rock Stars*, *Billboard's Rock Movers and Shakers*, they have also written biographies on Bob Dylan, Jimi Hendrix, Michael Jackson, John Lennon and Bob Marley.

Since the dramatic arrival of Napster, the illegal MP3 file sharing service, in June 1999, the record industry has seen a momentous shift in the way consumers buy, don't buy and share music. In 2003 there were less than 50 legitimate music-downloading services available worldwide on the Internet – there are now more than 500. At that time only 1 million tracks were available for streaming/downloading; today it's more than 12 million. The worldwide percentage of revenue derived from all digital music sales platforms has gone from zero in the year 2000 to 30% in 2010.

THE BEST-SELLING DIGITAL ARTISTS OF 2009 IN THE US

1	Lady Gaga	15,297,000
2	The Black Eyed Peas	12,988,000
3	Michael Jackson	12,355,000
4	Taylor Swift	12,302,000
5	Beyoncé	9,261,000
6	Flo Rida	8,402,000
7	Miley Cyrus	8,327,000
8	Britney Spears	7,424,000
9	Eminem	6,283,000
10	T.I.	6,277,000

The rapid rise of digital downloading as the new retail model can be illustrated by Rihanna – the best-selling artist of 2008 – selling 9.9 million tracks compared with Lady Gaga's haul of more than 15 million in 2009.

Above: Lady Gaga's "Poker Face" gave her a winning hand in the US.

Above right: The Black Eyed Peas had a good feeling in 2009.

THE TOP 10 BEST-SELLING DOWNLOADS OF 2009, WORLDWIDE

1	Poker Face	Lady Gaga	9.8m
2	Boom Boom Pow	The Black Eyed Peas	8.5m
3	I'm Yours	Jason Mraz	8.1m
4	Just Dance	Lady Gaga featuring Colby O'Donis	7.7m
5	I Gotta Feeling	The Black Eyed Peas	7.1m
6	Love Story	Taylor Swift	6.5m
7	Single Ladies (Put A Ring On It)	Beyoncé	6.1m
8	Kiss Me Thru The Phone	Soulja Boy Tell 'Em	5.7m
9	Heartless	Kanye West	5.5m
10	Circus	Britney Spears	5.5m

THE BEST-SELLING DIGITAL SONGS OF 2009 IN THE US

1	Boom Boom Pow	The Black Eyed Peas	4,762,000
2	I Gotta Feeling	The Black Eyed Peas	4,426,000
3	Poker Face	Lady Gaga	4,381,000
4	Right Round	Flo Rida featuring Ke$ha	4,135,000
5	Just Dance	Lady Gaga featuring Colby O'Donis	3,200,000
6	Party In The U.S.A.	Miley Cyrus	3,165,000
7	Down	Jay Sean featuring Lil Wayne	3,052,000
8	Gives You Hell	The All-American Rejects	2,880,000
9	Fireflies	Owl City	2,748,000
10	Whatcha Say	Jason DeRülo	2,712,000

Total global sales of individual tracks topped 1.5 billion for the first time on 2009. The best-seller in 2008 was 'Lollipop' by Lil Wayne with 9.1 million downloads, with Avril Lavigne's 'Girlfriend' topping the 2007 list with 7.3 million units.

Flo Rida's 'Right Round' was the first song to sell 500,000 in one week – 636,000 downloads in the week to February 15, 2009. A record 31 songs notched up US sales of more than two million each in 2009, compared to 19 in 2008 and 9 in 2007.

THE BEST-SELLING DIGITAL ALBUMS OF 2009 IN THE US

1	Fame	Lady Gaga	461,000
2	Only By The Night	Kings of Leon	428,000
3	Twilight (Soundtrack)	Various Artists	350,000
4	Fearless	Taylor Swift	343,000
5	The E.N.D. (The Energy Never Dies)	The Black Eyed Peas	309,000
6	Blueprint 3	Jay-Z	308,000
7	Big Whiskey and the GrooGrux King	Dave Matthews Band	286,000
8	Relapse	Eminem	277,000
9	No Line on the Horizon	U2	261,000
10	The Fray	The Fray	259,000

Digital music accounted for 40% of all music purchases in 2009 in the US, up from 32% in 2008. Digital album sales in 2009 reached a record 76 million sales rising from 65 million in the previous year.

Right: Taylor Swift cleaned up at the 2009 Grammys.

THE BEST-SELLING INTERNET ALBUMS OF 2009 IN THE US

1	I Dreamed A Dream	Susan Boyle	405,000
2	My Christmas	Andrea Bocelli	151,000
3	Fearless	Taylor Swift	121,000
4	Thriller	Michael Jackson	110,000
5	Crazy Love	Michael Bublé	106,000
6	Big Whiskey And The GrooGrux King	Dave Matthews Band	98,000
7	The Beatles in Stereo	The Beatles	95,000
8	No Line On The Horizon	U2	79,000
9	Off The Wall	Michael Jackson	75,000
10	Fame	Lady Gaga	74,000

This list reflects retail sales of physical albums – CDs, etc. – from mail-order Internet sites such as Amazon.

THE MOST INTERNET-STREAMED SONGS OF 2009 IN THE US

1	You Belong To Me	Taylor Swift	10,651,000
2	You Found Me	The Fray	10,446,000
3	Use Somebody	Kings of Leon	9,390,000
4	Poker Face	Lady Gaga	9,271,000
5	Gives You Hell	The All-American Rejects	9,242,000
6	Love Story	Taylor Swift	9,172,000
7	I'm Yours	Jason Mraz	8,456,000
8	Just Dance	Lady Gaga featuring Colby O'Donis	7,850,000
9	Halo	Beyoncé	7,840,000
10	Second Chance	Shinedown	7,557,000

Below: Ke$ha (Kesha Rose Sebert) in New York in 2009.

THE BEST-SELLING DIGITAL SONGS OF THE CHRISTMAS SEASON OF 2009 IN THE US

1	TiK ToK	Ke$ha	1,634,000
2	Bad Romance	Lady Gaga	1,553,000
3	Empire State Of Mind	Jay-Z & Alicia Keys	1,279,000
4	Fireflies	Owl City	1,241,000
5	Replay	Iyaz	1,191,000
6	Whatcha Say	Jason DeRülo	899,000
7	Meet Me Halfway	The Black Eyed Peas	825,000
8	Down	Jay Sean featuring Lil Wayne	795,000
9	Sexy Chick	David Guetta featuring Akon	774,000
10	Party In The U.S.A.	Miley Cyrus	765,000

THE MOST INTERNET-STREAMED ARTISTS OF 2009 IN THE US

		Streams
1	Taylor Swift	46,135,000
2	Beyoncé	42,962,000
3	Michael Jackson	39,358,000
4	Nickelback	35,290,000
5	Mariah Carey	33,696,000
6	Britney Spears	32,381,000
7	P!nk	28,925,000
8	Lady Gaga	27,580,000
9	Kelly Clarkson	26,204,000
10	Ne-Yo	24,624,000

MTV MUSIC TELEVISION

YOUTUBE'S MOST WATCHED MUSIC CLIPS OF 2009 WORLDWIDE

The Internet's most popular video streaming website, YouTube, spun off Vevo, a music video only streaming service, in 2009.

			Views in Millions
1	I Know You Want Me (music video)	Pitbull	86+
2	Britain's Got Talent (TV clip)	Susan Boyle	82+
3	Jizz In My Pants (music video)	The Lonely Island	73+
4	Guitar (home video)	funtwo	67+
5	The Climb (music video)	Miley Cyrus	66+
6	Party In The U.S.A. (music video)	Miley Cyrus	59+
7	Beat It (music video)	Michael Jackson	56+
8	I'm On A Boat (music video)	The Lonely Island featuring T-Pain	39+
9	Fly On The Wall (music video)	Miley Cyrus	38+
10	Best Ever Moonwalk (TV clip)	Michael Jackson	38+

Above: Pitbull's success in video was not matched by download sales in 2009.

Internet measurement agency, Visible Measures, regularly updates its own "100 Million Viewers Club" - which ranks the most-watched, accumulating viral videos of all-time on the web, world-wide. Up to March 2010, the leading music videos were:

THE MOST WATCHED VIDEOS ON THE WORLD WIDE WEB

1	Crank Dat	Soulja Boy	722,438,268
2	Single Ladies (Put A Ring On It)	Beyoncé	639,966,996
3	Thriller	Michael Jackson	443,535,722
4	Poker Face	Lady Gaga	360,020,327
5	Apologize	Timbaland Presents OneRepublic	355,404,824
6	Touch My Body	Mariah Carey	324,057,568
7	Beat It	Michael Jackson	286,279,009
8	Girlfriend	Avril Lavigne	283,031,356
9	Just Dance	Lady Gaga	272,941,674
10	Bleeding Love	Leona Lewis	264,475,202

YOUTUBE'S TOP MUSIC VIDEOS OF 2009 WORLDWIDE

			Views in Millions
1	I Know You Want Me	Pitbull	82+
2	The Climb	Miley Cyrus	64+
3	Party In The U.S.A.	Miley Cyrus	54+
4	I'm On A Boat	The Lonely Island featuring T-Pain	48+
5	Knock You Down	Keri Hilson	35+

Left: The hugely popular Beyoncé.

THE FIRST DIGITAL DOWNLOAD CHART-TOPPERS IN THE UK

1	Bam Thwok	Pixies	Jun 23, 2004
2	This Love	Maroon 5	Jun 30, 2004
3	Dry Your Eyes	The Streets	Jul 07, 2004
4	Lola's Theme	The Shapeshifters	Aug 11, 2004
5	Flying Without Wings	Westlife	Sep 01, 2004
6	These Words	Natasha Bedingfield	Sept 08, 2004
7	Vertigo	U2	Oct 06, 2004
8	Dogz Don't Kill People (Wabbitz Do)	Mouldie Lookin' Stain	Oct 27, 2004
9	Vertigo	U2	Nov 03, 2004
10	I Believe in You	Kylie Minogue	Dec 01, 2004

THE MOST INTERNET-STREAMED SONGS OF ALL-TIME IN THE US

1	Hips Don't Lie	Shakira featuring Wyclef Jean	85,586,000
2	Because Of You	Kelly Clarkson	43,872,000
3	Run It!	Chris Brown	40,993,000
4	Girlfriend	Avril Lavigne	38,919,000
5	Irreplaceable	Beyoncé	38,192,000
6	Check On It	Beyoncé featuring Slim Thug	37,838,000
7	Buttons	The Pussycat Dolls	36,354,000
8	You're Beautiful	James Blunt	35,178,000
9	My Humps	The Black Eyed Peas	34,642,000
10	Promiscuous	Nelly Furtado featuring Timbaland	34,638,000

This list tallies all results from the inception of documented streaming in 2005 up to the end of 2009.

THE BEST-SELLING DIGITAL SONGS OF ALL-TIME IN THE US

1	Low	Flo Rida featuring T-Pain	5,344,000
2	Just Dance	Lady Gaga featuring Colby O'Donis	4,943,000
3	I'm Yours	Jason Mraz	4,787,000
4	Boom Boom Pow	The Black Eyed Peas	4,762,000
5	Poker Face	Lady Gaga	4,551,000
6	Apologize	Timbaland Presents OneRepublic	4,513,000
7	I Gotta Feeling	The Black Eyed Peas	4,426,000
8	Crank That	Soulja Boy Tell 'Em	4,370,000
9	Viva la Vida	Coldplay	4,261,000
10	Love Story	Taylor Swift	4,254,000

THE BEST-SELLING DIGITAL ARTISTS OF ALL-TIME IN THE US

1	Taylor Swift	24,329,000
2	Rihanna	23,577,000
3	The Black Eyed Peas	22,493,000
4	Kanye West	21,842,000
5	Beyoncé	21,637,000
6	Nickelback	20,366,000
7	Michael Jackson	19,225,000
8	Britney Spears	18,961,000
9	Eminem	17,941,000
10	T.I.	18,153,000

THE BEST-SELLING DIGITAL ALBUMS OF ALL-TIME IN THE US

1	Viva La Vida Or Death And All His Friends	Coldplay	761,000
2	Fearless	Taylor Swift	568,000
3	Twilight (Soundtrack)	Various Artists	564,000
4	Only By The Night	Kings of Leon	533,000
5	Fame	Lady Gaga	511,000
6	Continuum	John Mayer	442,000
7	Daughtry	Daughtry	387,000
8	Back To Black	Amy Winehouse	378,000
9	Sleep Through the Static	Jack Johnson	362,000
10	In Between Dreams	Jack Johnson	358,000

With 2009 being the best-selling year to date for digitally downloaded singles in the UK, five of the top 10 tracks are from that year with Lady Gaga's 'Poker Face' notching up 779,000 sales.

THE BEST-SELLING DOWNLOADS OF ALL-TIME IN THE UK

1	Poker Face	Lady Gaga
2	Sex On Fire	Kings of Leon
3	Just Dance	Lady Gaga
4	Use Somebody	Kings of Leon
5	In For The Kill	La Roux
6	Run	Leona Lewis
7	Hallelujah	Alexandra Burke
8	Bleeding Love	Leona Lewis
9	Chasing Cars	Snow Patrol
10	Rockstar	Nickelback

Below: Soulja Boy Tell 'Em had a hit on phones as well as downloads.

THE TOP RINGTONES OF 2009 IN THE US

1	Kiss Me Thru the Phone	Soulja Boy Tell 'Em	1,289,000
2	Blame It	Jamie Foxx featuring T-Pain	884,000
3	Dead And Gone	T.I. featuring Justin Timberlake	847,000
4	Day 'n' Nite	Kid Cudi	757,000
5	Boom Boom Pow	The Black Eyed Peas	740,000
6	All Summer Long	Kid Rock	672,000
7	Right Round	Flo Rida	671,000
8	Heartless	Kanye West	653,000
9	Birthday Sex	Jeremih	650,000
10	Big Green Tractor	Jason Aldean	611,000

THE BEST-SELLING DOWNLOADS OF ALL-TIME IN JAPAN

1	Kiseki	Greeeen
2	Prisoner of Love	Utada Hikaru
3	Life	Kimaguren
4	Kimi No Subeteni	Spontania featuring JuJu
5	The Birthday: Ti Amo	Exile
6	Sunao Ni Naretara	JuJu featuring Spontania
7	Sobaniirune	Thelma Aoyama featuring SoulJa

The explosion of mobile phone use over the past decade saw the dawn of popular songs being used as ringtones. America was considerably slower on the uptake than Europe.

THE APPLE STORE

The download store forever changed the way people listen to and own music and was launched by Apple in 2003 in the US. By 2009 it was the leading worldwide music retailer, accounting for 70% of online digital music sales. There are more than 10 million tracks available and it sells more than 10 million songs per day.

ITUNES MUSIC STORE MILESTONES

Milestone (number of songs sold)	Date
100 million	July 12, 2004
250 million	March 02, 2005
500 million	July 18, 2005
1 billion	February 23, 2006
2 billion	January 10, 2007
3 billion	July 31, 2007
4 billion	January 15, 2008
5 billion	June 19, 2008
6 billion	January 06, 2009
7 billion	April 28, 2009
8 billion	July 21, 2009
10 billion	February 25, 2010

IPOD MILESTONES

The world's best-selling portable digital music player was launched by Apple as the iPod on October 23, 2001 with a 5GB capacity. The original "classic" iPod has been through six upgrades, available in 2010 as a 160GB media player.

Music Player	Release Date
iPod	Oct 23, 2001
iPod Mini	Jan 06, 2004
iPod U2 Special Edition	Oct 26, 2004
iPod Shuffle	Jan 11, 2005
iPod Nano	Sept 07, 2005
iPod Product Red Nano	Oct 13, 2006
iPod Classic	Sept 05, 2007
iPod Touch	Sept 05, 2007

ITUNES ALL-TIME BEST-SELLING US DOWNLOAD SONGS

Apple issued its all-time iTunes countdown in February 2010 to celebrate its upcoming 10 billionth download. Reflecting sales from April 2003 to February 2010, the only "oldie" on the list is Journey's 1981 rock ballad chestnut, "Don't Stop Believin'" – its popularity revived by its use on the 2009 hit television series, *Glee*.

1	I Gotta Feeling	The Black Eyed Peas
2	Poker Face	Lady Gaga
3	Boom Boom Pow	The Black Eyed Peas
4	I'm Yours	Jason Mraz
5	Viva La Vida	Coldplay
6	Just Dance	Lady Gaga featuring Colby O'Donis
7	Low	Flo Rida featuring T-Pain
8	Love Story	Taylor Swift
9	Bleeding Love	Leona Lewis
10	TiK ToK	Ke$ha
11	Disturbia	Rihanna
12	So What	P!nk
13	I Kissed A Girl	Katy Perry
14	Single Ladies (Put A Ring On It)	Beyoncé
15	Hot N Cold	Katy Perry
16	Stronger	Kanye West
17	Live Your Life	T.I. featuring Rihanna
18	Hey There Delilah	The Plain White T's
19	Right Round	Flo Rida
20	Party In The U.S.A.	Miley Cyrus
21	Don't Stop Believin'	Journey
22	Bad Romance	Lady Gaga
23	Use Somebody	Kings of Leon
24	Fireflies	Owl City
25	How To Save A Life	The Fray

Left: The iPod changed the way we listen, purchase and sort music.

Above: The Black Eyed Peas enjoyed enormous success in 2009 ...

Left: ... as did the typically outrageously dressed Lady Gaga.

THE BEST-SELLING VIDEOS ON ITUNES OF 2009 IN THE UK

1	Thriller	Michael Jackson
2	Poker Face	Lady Gaga
3	Single Ladies (Put A Ring On It)	Beyoncé
4	Love Story	Taylor Swift
5	The Fear	Lily Allen

THE BEST-SELLING SONGS ON ITUNES OF 2009 IN THE UK

1	I Gotta Feeling	The Black Eyed Peas
2	Poker Face	Lady Gaga
3	Just Dance	Lady Gaga featuring Colby O'Donis
4	Boom Boom Pow	The Black Eyed Peas
5	Fight For This Love	Cheryl Cole
6	In For The Kill	La Roux
7	Number 1	Tinchy Stryder
8	Bad Boys	Alexandra Burke featuring Flo Rida
9	The Fear	Lily Allen
10	Use Somebody	Kings of Leon

THE BEST-SELLING ALBUMS ON ITUNES OF 2009 IN THE UK

1	Only By The Night	Kings of Leon
2	It's Not Me It's You	Lily Allen
3	The Fame	Lady Gaga
4	Invaders Must Die	The Prodigy
5	Lungs	Florence + the Machine
6	I Am… Sasha Fierce	Beyoncé
7	West Ryder Pauper Lunatic Asylum	Kasabian
8	Number Ones	Michael Jackson
9	The E.N.D. (The Energy Never Dies)	The Black Eyed Peas
10	The Script	The Script

Left: London's Lily Allen was runner-up to Kings of Leon… but ahead of Lady Gaga.

Below: Kings of Leon bought a harder edge to the US Best-Selling Album chart.

TOP 10 BEST-SELLING ALBUMS ON ITUNES OF 2009 IN THE US

1	Only By The Night	Kings of Leon
2	Twilight (Soundtrack)	Various Artists
3	The Fame	Lady Gaga
4	Fearless	Taylor Swift
5	Big Whiskey And The GrooGrux King	Dave Matthews Band
6	The Essential Michael Jackson	Michael Jackson
7	The Fray	The Fray
8	The Blueprint 3	Jay-Z
9	Relapse	Eminem
10	The E.N.D. (The Energy Never Dies)	The Black Eyed Peas

THE BEST-SELLING SONGS ON ITUNES OF 2009 IN THE US

1	Boom Boom Pow	The Black Eyed Peas
2	Right Round	Flo Rida
3	Poker Face	Lady Gaga
4	I Gotta Feeling	The Black Eyed Peas
5	Gives You Hell	The All-American Rejects
6	Just Dance	Lady Gaga featuring Colby O'Donis
7	Party In The U.S.A.	Miley Cyrus
8	The Climb	Miley Cyrus
9	Dead And Gone	T.I. (featuring Justin Timberlake)
10	Use Somebody	Kings of Leon

MTV MUSIC TELEVISION

GLOBAL BEST-SELLERS

The International Federation of the Phonographic Industry (IFPI) is an organization headquartered in London which represents the interests of national recording industry bodies (for example, the BPI in the UK and the RIAA in the US), record labels and the recording industry as a whole, worldwide. With more than 1,400 members from 72 countries, it is also heavily involved in anti-piracy initiatives. Each year it issues an annual report, including a breakdown of the world's best-selling albums.

Above: Linkin Park had a huge hit with their first album.

THE BEST-SELLING ALBUMS OF 2002 WORLDWIDE

1	The Eminem Show	Eminem
2	Let Go	Avril Lavigne
3	Elvis 30 #1 Hits	Elvis Presley
4	Up!	Shania Twain
5	A New Day Has Come	Céline Dion
6	Nellyville	Nelly
7	Laundry Service	Shakira
8	M!ssundaztood	P!nk
9	8 Mile	Soundtrack
10	By The Way	Red Hot Chili Peppers
11	Come Away With Me	Norah Jones
12	The Best Of 1990–2000	U2
13	Forty Licks	The Rolling Stones
14	Shaman	Santana
15	Home	The Dixie Chicks
16	Escapology	Robbie Williams
17	Ashanti	Ashanti
18	Deep River	Utada Hikaru
19	This Is Me Then	Jennifer Lopez
20	The Rising	Bruce Springsteen

THE BEST-SELLING ALBUMS OF 2001 WORLDWIDE

1	[Hybrid Theory]	Linkin Park
2	No Angel	Dido
3	Survivor	Destiny's Child
4	Hot Shot	Shaggy
5	A Day Without Rain	Enya
6	J Lo	Jennifer Lopez
7	Songs In A Minor	Alicia Keys
8	Break The Cycle	Staind
9	Invincible	Michael Jackson
10	Distance	Utada Hikaru
11	All For You	Janet Jackson
12	GHV2	Madonna
13	Echoes: The Best Of Pink Floyd	Pink Floyd
14	Swing When You're Winning	Robbie Williams
15	8701	Usher
16	O Brother, Where Art Thou?	Soundtrack
17	Escape	Enrique Iglesias
18	Gorillaz	Gorillaz
19	The Scarecrow	Garth Brooks
20	Whoa, Nelly!	Nelly Furtado

[Hybrid Theory] was the first album by California-based, hard-rock quintet Linkin Park. It eventually sold more than 10 million copies in the US alone.

The rapper's fourth album release, The Eminem Show, included a typically bold batch of samples including 'Buffalo Gals' (Malcolm McLaren), 'Dream On' (Aerosmith) and 'We Will Rock You' (Queen).

Left: Eminem had a mega-hit album in 2002.

THE BEST-SELLING ALBUMS OF 2003 WORLDWIDE

1	Come Away With Me	Norah Jones
2	Get Rich Or Die Tryin'	50 Cent
3	Meteora	Linkin Park
4	Life For Rent	Dido
5	Dangerously In Love	Beyoncé
6	A Rush Of Blood To The Head	Coldplay
7	Fallen	Evanescence
8	In The Zone	Britney Spears
9	Let Go	Avril Lavigne
10	One Heart	Céline Dion
11	Speakerboxxx/The Love Below	OutKast
12	200 Km/h In The Wrong Lane	t.A.T.u.
13	Dutty Rock	Sean Paul
14	The Diary Of Alicia Keys	Alicia Keys
15	Greatest Hits	Red Hot Chili Peppers
16	Stripped	Christina Aguilera
17	In Time: The Best Of R.E.M. 1988–2003	R.E.M.
18	St. Anger	Metallica
19	Justified	Justin Timberlake
20	The Eminem Show	Eminem

Above: Lena Katina and Yulia Volkova from t.A.T.u.

Left: Norah Jones' debut album mixed many styles to great acclaim.

With its contemporary jazz stylings and cool folk and blues nuances, Norah Jones' debut album *Come Away With Me* defied easy categorization, but also won four Grammy Awards including Album of the Year.

THE BEST-SELLING ALBUMS OF 2004 WORLDWIDE

1	Confessions	Usher
2	Feels Like Home	Norah Jones
3	Encore	Eminem
4	How To Dismantle An Atomic Bomb	U2
5	Under My Skin	Avril Lavigne
6	Greatest Hits	Robbie Williams
7	Greatest Hits	Shania Twain
8	Destiny Fulfilled	Destiny's Child
9	Greatest Hits	Guns N' Roses
10	Songs About Jane	Maroon 5
11	American Idiot	Green Day
12	Elephunk	The Black Eyed Peas
13	Greatest Hits: My Prerogative	Britney Spears
14	Here For The Party	Gretchen Wilson
15	Anastacia	Anastacia
16	Suit	Nelly
17	Autobiography	Ashlee Simpson
18	D-12 World	D-12
19	Utada Hikaru Single Collection Vol. 1	Utada Hikaru
20	When the Sun Goes Down	Kenny Chesney

Below: Usher's *Confessions* went Diamond in the USA.

This was the year of Usher's career peak, with the R&B star's fourth album, *Confessions*, boosted by the global success of the smash hit, 'Yeah!'

THE BEST-SELLING ALBUMS OF 2005 WORLDWIDE

1	X&Y	Coldplay
2	The Emancipation Of Mimi	Mariah Carey
3	The Massacre	50 Cent
4	Monkey Business	The Black Eyed Peas
5	American Idiot	Green Day
6	Confessions On A Dance Floor	Madonna
7	Breakaway	Kelly Clarkson
8	Curtain Call	Eminem
9	Back To Bedlam	James Blunt
10	Intensive Care	Robbie Williams
11	Demon Days	Gorillaz
12	Love Angel Music Baby	Gwen Stefani
13	It's Time	Michael Bublé
14	Late Registration	Kanye West
15	Amarantine	Enya
16	Il Divo	Il Divo
17	In Between Dreams	Jack Johnson
18	The Documentary	The Game
19	Mezmerize	System of a Down
20	#1's	Destiny's Child

Above: Coldplay's Devon-born singer Chris Martin.

World-conquering Coldplay's third studio album, *X&Y*, sold more than 10 million albums worldwide in 2005.

THE BEST-SELLING ALBUMS OF 2006 WORLDWIDE

1	High School Musical	Soundtrack
2	Stadium Arcadium	Red Hot Chili Peppers
3	Love	The Beatles
4	Back To Bedlam	James Blunt
5	FutureSex/LoveSounds	Justin Timberlake
6	B'Day	Beyoncé
7	U2 18 Singles	U2
8	Me And My Gang	Rascal Flatts
9	Siempre	Il Divo
10	Amore	Andrea Bocelli
11	Eyes Open	Snow Patrol
12	PCD	The Pussycat Dolls
13	Loose	Nelly Furtado
14	The Open Door	Evanescence
15	Back To Basics	Christina Aguilera
16	Some Hearts	Carrie Underwood
17	I'm Not Dead	P!nk
18	Rudebox	Robbie Williams
19	Sam's Town	The Killers
20	A Girl Like Me	Rihanna

Above: Flea and Anthony Kiedis from Red Hot Chili Peppers.

Right: The men of Il Divo: Urs Bühler, Sébastien Izambard, Carlos Marin and David Miller.

A Disney Channel Original Movie, *High School Musical* was a made-for-television film directed by Kenny Ortega, who in 2009 directed *Michael Jackson's This Is It*. 2006 saw physical and digital sales combined for the first time.

THE BEST-SELLING
ALBUMS OF 2007 WORLDWIDE

1	High School Musical 2	Soundtrack
2	Back To Black	Amy Winehouse
3	Nöel	Josh Groban
4	The Best Damn Thing	Avril Lavigne
5	Long Road Out Of Eden	The Eagles
6	Minutes To Midnight	Linkin Park
7	As I Am	Alicia Keys
8	Call Me Irresponsible	Michael Bublé
9	Life In Cartoon Motion	Mika
10	Not Too Late	Norah Jones
11	Hannah Montana 2/ Meet Miley Cyrus	Hannah Montana/Miley Cyrus
12	Good Girl Gone Bad	Rihanna
13	Loose	Nelly Furtado
14	FutureSex/LoveSounds	Justin Timberlake
15	Shock Value	Timbaland
16	It Won't Be Soon Before Long	Maroon 5
17	Graduation	Kanye West
18	All The Lost Souls	James Blunt
19	Taking Chances	Céline Dion
20	The Dutchess	Fergie

Left: The controversial but hugely talented Amy Winehouse.

Teen heartthrob Zac Efron reprised his role for *High School Musical 2* — and was featured singing on five of the soundtrack album's 11 tracks.

THE BEST-SELLING
ALBUMS OF 2008 WORLDWIDE

1	Viva La Vida Or Death And All His Friends	Coldplay
2	Black Ice	AC/DC
3	Mamma Mia!	Soundtrack
4	Rockferry	Duffy
5	Death Magnetic	Metallica
6	Spirit	Leona Lewis
7	Back To Black	Amy Winehouse
8	High School Musical 3: Senior Year	Soundtrack
9	Tha Carter III	Lil Wayne
10	Good Girl Gone Bad	Rihanna
11	Hard Candy	Madonna
12	I Am... Sasha Fierce	Beyoncé
13	Funhouse	P!nk
14	Chinese Democracy	Guns N' Roses
15	Circus	Britney Spears
16	Sleep Through The Static	Jack Johnson
17	The Promise	Il Divo
18	Fearless	Taylor Swift
19	A Little Bit Longer	The Jonas Brothers
20	Camp Rock Soundtrack	Various Artists

Left: Duffy's debut album *Rockferry* went straight to the number one spot in the UK upon release.

Below: Brian Johnson and Angus Young from AC/DC.

Coldplay's *Viva La Vida...* album debuted in pole position in no less than 36 countries around the world.

THE BEST-SELLING SINGLES OF 2009 WORLDWIDE

1	I Gotta Feeling	The Black Eyed Peas
2	Poker Face	Lady Gaga
3	Boom Boom Pow	The Black Eyed Peas
4	Right Round	Flo Rida
5	Sexy Bitch	David Guetta featuring Akon
6	I Know You Want Me (Calle Ocho)	Pitbull
7	Just Dance	Lady Gaga featuring Colby O'Donis
8	Paparazzi	Lady Gaga
9	Down	Jay Sean featuring Lil Wayne
10	When Love Takes Over	David Guetta featuring Kelly Rowland
11	Halo	Beyoncé
12	Use Somebody	Kings of Leon
13	Empire State Of Mind	Jay-Z featuring Alicia Keys
14	Love Story	Taylor Swift
15	Hot N Cold	Katy Perry
16	You Belong With Me	Taylor Swift
17	Meet Me Halfway	The Black Eyed Peas
18	My Life Would Suck Without You	Kelly Clarkson
19	Dead And Gone	T.I. featuring Justin Timberlake
20	Party In The U.S.A.	Miley Cyrus
21	Bad Romance	Lady Gaga
22	Day 'N' Nite	Kid Cudi vs Crookers
23	Evacuate The Dancefloor	Cascada
24	Knock You Down	Keri Hilson featuring Kanye West & Ne-Yo
25	Whatcha Say	Jason DeRülo
26	Run This Town	Jay-Z, Rihanna & Kanye West
27	LoveGame	Lady Gaga
28	Gives You Hell	The All-American Rejects
29	Broken Strings	James Morrison featuring Nelly Furtado
30	Jai Ho! (You Are My Destiny)	A.R. Rahman & The Pussycat Dolls featuring Nicole Scherzinger

THE BEST-SELLING ALBUMS OF 2009 WORLDWIDE

1	I Dreamed A Dream	Susan Boyle
2	The Fame	Lady Gaga
3	The E.N.D. (The Energy Never Dies)	The Black Eyed Peas
4	Fearless	Taylor Swift
5	Only By The Night	Kings of Leon
6	No Line On The Horizon	U2
7	I Am Sasha Fierce	Beyoncé
8	Crazy Love	Michael Bublé
9	Michael Jackson's This Is It	Michael Jackson
10	Hannah Montana: The Movie	Soundtrack
11	Funhouse	P!nk
12	Number Ones	Michael Jackson
13	Relapse	Eminem
14	My Christmas	Andrea Bocelli
15	21st Century Breakdown	Green Day
16	The Essential	Michael Jackson
17	Twilight (Soundtrack)	Various Artists
18	King Of Pop	Michael Jackson
19	Thriller (25th Anniversary Edition)	Michael Jackson
20	Dark Horse	Nickelback
21	The Blueprint 3	Jay-Z
22	Working On A Dream	Bruce Springsteen
23	The Fame	Lady Gaga
24	The Resistance	Muse
25	It's Not Me, It's You	Lily Allen
26	I Look To You	Whitney Houston
27	Time Of Our Lives (EP)	Miley Cyrus
28	Reality Killed The Video Star	Robbie Williams
29	We Sing, We Dance, We Steal Things	Jason Mraz
30	All The Best! 1999–2009	Arashi

Dominating the world's clubs, airwaves and charts during 2009 were two American acts: the glam-pop sex kitten, Lady Gaga, and the ubiquitous hip-hop/pop quartet, The Black Eyed Peas. Lady Gaga was the most successful female artiste of the year. Born Stefani Joanne Angelina Germanotta on March 28, 1986, Gaga studied music at the prestigious Tisch School of the Arts in New York before teaming with Moroccan/Swedish co-writer and producer, Nadir Khayat (aka RedOne).

Right: Scot Susan Boyle was catapulted to success after her appearance on *Britain's Got Talent*.

Left: After working with many stars, David Guetta had his own hit in 2009.

It was a tight race for the top spot in 2009: Lady Gaga had it sewn up until December, but was pipped at the post by *X Factor* and Youtube spinster sensation Susan Boyle, whose debut album sold 5,979,900 copies compared to Gaga's 5,683,000. Most of Boyle's tally came in the lead up to Christmas, traditionally the strongest selling sales period worldwide. The only other album to sail past the 5 million mark was *The E.N.D. (The Energy Never Dies)*.

THE BEST-SELLING ARTISTS OF ALL-TIME WORLDWIDE

1 The Beatles
2 Elvis Presley
3 Michael Jackson
4 Abba
5 Elton John
6 Bee Gees
7 Madonna
8 Queen
9 Céline Dion
10 The Rolling Stones

Definitive data regarding the best-selling artists of all time is impossible to collate for several reasons: first, few countries outside the US or UK had reliable chart-gathering mechanisms in place until the 1980s; second, over the years, record labels and publicists have been respectively reluctant and/or over-exaggerating in their claims.

From available certified gold, platinum and diamond awards, however, the Beatles combined haul of singles and albums is reliably estimated to be more than 230 million units worldwide – although the real number may be more than twice that. *The Guinness Book Of Records* claims that the Beatles have sold more than 1 billion records, though this number has never been audited or verified.

From purely certified awards levels, Elvis Presley's total is approximately 190 million (unverified claims range from 600 million to 1 billion) with Michael Jackson now over 150 million following his death in 2009 (unverified claims range from 300 million to 750 million).

Above: Paul, John and George – three-quarters of The Beatles.

THE BEST-SELLING ALBUMS ALL-TIME WORLDWIDE

1	Thriller	Michael Jackson	1982
2	Back In Black	AC/DC	1980
3	Dark Side Of The Moon	Pink Floyd	1973
4	Bat Out Of Hell	Meat Loaf	1977
5	Their Greatest Hits 1971–75	The Eagles	1976
6	Dirty Dancing	Soundtrack	1987
7	The Bodyguard	Soundtrack	1992
8	Millennium	Backstreet Boys	1999
9	Rumours	Fleetwood Mac	1977
10	Saturday Night Fever	Soundtrack	1977

Although reliable certified statistics for the best-selling albums of all time are unavailable (see earlier note), it is estimated – and widely reported – that Michael Jackson's *Thriller* is the only album to have topped 100 million unit sales worldwide. Each of the remaining titles in the top 10 has estimated global sales of between 40 and 50 million. 50% of the albums on this list were released during the 1970s.

Right: The undisputed King of Pop: Michael Jackson.

GLOBAL ALBUM SALES 2000 TO 2008

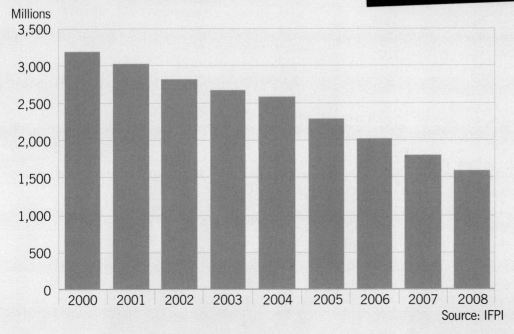

Millions

Source: IFPI

MTV MUSIC TELEVISION

BEST-SELLERS IN THE USA

The United States has been responsible not only for the evolution of rock 'n' roll, but also for creating a considerable number of sub-genres including rhythm & blues, country, rap, grunge, bluegrass, folk and disco. In addition to discovering, recording and supplying the most popular music bought worldwide, the US is also the planet's largest consumer of music, accounting for more than 30% of the global sales market.

THE BEST-SELLING ALBUMS OF ALL TIME IN THE US

29m	Their Greatest Hits 1971–1975	The Eagles	1976
=	Thriller	Michael Jackson	1983
23m	Led Zeppelin IV	Led Zeppelin	1971
22m	Back In Black	AC/DC	1980
20m	Come On Over	Shania Twain	1997
19m	Rumours	Fleetwood Mac	1977
18m	Appetite For Destruction	Guns N' Roses	1988
17m	Boston	Boston	1976
=	No Fences	Garth Brooks	1990
=	The Bodyguard	Soundtrack	1992
16m	Hotel California	The Eagles	1977
=	Cracked Rear View	Hootie & the Blowfish	1995
=	Greatest Hits	Elton John	1974
=	Jagged Little Pill	Alanis Morissette	1995
15m	Greatest Hits	Journey	1989
=	Physical Graffitti	Led Zeppelin	1975
=	Metallica	Metallica	1991
=	Dark Side Of The Moon	Pink Floyd	1973
=	Supernatural	Santana	1999
=	Born in the U.S.A.	Bruce Springsteen	1984
14m	Backstreet Boys	Backstreet Boys	1998
=	Ropin' The Wind	Garth Brooks	1991
=	Bat Out Of Hell	Meat Loaf	1978
=	Simon & Garfunkel's Greatest Hits	Simon & Garfunkel	1972
=	… Baby One More Time	Britney Spears	1999
13m	Millennium	Backstreet Boys	1999
=	Whitney Houston	Whitney Houston	1986
=	Ten	Pearl Jam	1992
=	Purple Rain	Prince	1984

THE BEST-SELLING SINGLES OF ALL-TIME IN THE US

11m	Candle In The Wind 1997/ Something About The Way You Look Tonight	Elton John	1997
8m	We Are The World	USA for Africa	1985
5m	Low	Flo Rida featuring T-Pain	2008
4m	Hey Jude	The Beatles	1968
=	Hound Dog/Don't Be Cruel	Elvis Presley	1956
=	I'm Yours	Jason Mraz	2008
=	I Will Always Love You	Whitney Houston	1982
=	Just Dance	Lady Gaga featuring Colby O'Donis	2008
=	Love Story	Taylor Swift	2008
=	Macarena (Bayside Boys Mix)	Los Del Rio	1995
=	Poker Face	Lady Gaga	2008
=	Whoomp! (There It Is)	Tag Team	1993

The list of the best-selling singles in the US from the 1950s to the present day changed radically in 2008/2009. With the advent of digital downloading in the mid-2000s, individual song sales soared to new heights with no less than five single tracks released in 2008 having sold more than four million digital copies each by the decade's end.

Below: An early Eagles line-up.

Above: Elton John's flamboyant performances have won him fans the world over.

In 1999, the Recording Industry Association of America introduced Diamond Awards, honouring sales of 10 million or more copies. The Eagles' greatest hits collection was the long-time sales leader until the death of Michael Jackson.

THE BEST-SELLING ALBUMS OF THE 2000S IN THE US

#	Album	Artist	Sales
1	1	The Beatles	11,515,000
2	No Strings Attached	*NSync	11,112,000
3	Come Away With Me	Norah Jones	10,557,000
4	The Marshall Mathers LP	Eminem	10,208,000
5	The Eminem Show	Eminem	9,806,000
6	Confessions	Usher	9,719,000
7	[Hybrid Theory]	Linkin Park	9,676,000
8	Human Clay	Creed	9,492,000
9	Oops! … I Did It Again	Britney Spears	9,185,000
10	Country Grammar	Nelly	8,462,000
11	Get Rich Or Die Tryin'	50 Cent	7,906,000
12	O Brother, Where Art Thou?	Soundtrack	7,517,000
13	Fallen	Evanescence	7,318,000
14	All The Right Reasons	Nickelback	7,264,000
15	Supernatural	Santana	6,953,000
16	A Day Without Rain	Enya	6,926,000
17	Some Hearts	Carrie Underwood	6,876,000
18	Hotshot	Shaggy	6,800,000
19	Let Go	Avril Lavigne	6,732,000
20	Chocolate Starfish And The Hot Dog Flavored Water	Limp Bizkit	6,703,000
21	Nellyville	Nelly	6,458,000
22	Weathered	Creed	6,380,000
23	Songs In A Minor	Alicia Keys	6,210,000
24	Breakaway	Kelly Clarkson	6,109,000
25	Greatest Hits	Tim McGraw	6,020,000
26	Home	The Dixie Chicks	6,007,000
27	The Emancipation Of Mimi	Mariah Carey	5,922,000
28	American Idiot	Green Day	5,911,000
29	Closer	Josh Groban	5,792,000
30	Meteora	Linkin Park	5,732,000
31	Speakerboxx/ The Love Below	OutKast	5,674,000
32	Fly	The Dixie Chicks	5,640,000
33	Break The Cycle	Staind	5,593,000
34	The Better Life	3 Doors Down	5,563,000
35	Silver Side Up	Nickelback	5,446,000
36	M!ssundazstood	P!nk	5,441,000
37	Black & Blue	The Backstreet Boys	5,414,000
38	Dr. Dre – 2001	Dr. Dre	5,404,000
39	Up!	Shania Twain	5,396,000
40	The Massacre	50 Cent	5,217,000
41	Encore	Eminem	5,156,000
42	Feels Like Today	Rascal Flatts	5,152,000
43	Breathe	Faith Hill	5,083,000
44	Cocky	Kid Rock	5,072,000
45	Josh Groban	Josh Groban	5,047,000
46	All The Way… A Decade Of Song	Céline Dion	4,997,000
47	Celebrity	*NSync	4,903,000
48	High School Musical	Soundtrack	4,849,000
49	Me And My Gang	Rascal Flatts	4,802,000
50	Now 5	Various Artists	4,789,000

Yet another astonishing feat in the Beatles' record-breaking history: some 40 years after their demise, the Fab Four managed to nab the best-selling album of the most recent decade in the US. Elsewhere 20% of the acts on this list were rappers and 16% were country artists. Of the 50 acts listed, only five are not from North America: the Beatles, Santana, Enya, Shaggy and Céline Dion.

Left: Eminem was a consistent best-seller throughout the whole decade of the 2000s.

Above: Still selling after all these years – The Beatles on top of the charts again.

MTV
MUSIC TELEVISION

THE BEST-SELLING ARTISTS OF THE 2000S IN THE US

1	Eminem	32,241,000		32	Santana	14,975,000
2	The Beatles	30,182,000		33	Destiny's Child	14,878,000
3	Tim McGraw	24,769,000		34	Coldplay	14,604,000
4	Toby Keith	24,469,000		35	Mariah Carey	14,341,000
5	Britney Spears	22,969,000		36	Pink Floyd	14,164,000
6	Kenny Chesney	22,034,000		37	Shania Twain	13,850,000
7	Linkin Park	21,421,000		38	Ludacris	13,442,000
8	Nelly	21,232,000		39	Enya	13,422,000
9	Creed	20,594,000		40	Green Day	13,363,000
10	Jay-Z	20,424,000		41	Andrea Bocelli	13,353,000
11	Nickelback	19,817,000		42	OutKast	13,277,000
12	Rascal Flatts	19,408,000		43	R. Kelly	13,234,000
13	Josh Groban	19,348,000		44	Faith Hill	12,899,000
14	Alan Jackson	18,857,000		45	Mary J. Blige	12,614,000
15	*NSync	18,303,000		46	3 Doors Down	12,551,000
16	The Dixie Chicks	18,178,000		47	Christina Aguilera	12,380,000
17	Johnny Cash	18,143,000		48	Limp Bizkit	12,378,000
18	Kid Rock	17,614,000		49	Bon Jovi	12,378,000
19	Metallica	17,403,000		50	Frank Sinatra	12,221,000
20	Céline Dion	17,363,000				
21	George Strait	17,275,000				
22	Michael Jackson	17,261,000				
23	Norah Jones	17,087,000				
24	U2	16,817,000				
25	Elvis Presley	16,486,000				
26	Usher	16,329,000				
27	Dave Matthews Band	16,025,000				
28	AC/DC	15,935,000				
29	50 Cent	15,868,000				
30	Alicia Keys	15,561,000				
31	Rod Stewart	15,511,000				

At the outset of the 2000s, 54.8% of US record sales were sold through chain stores, but by 2009 that figure had declined to 28.5%, with non-traditional outlets – book shops, independent music stores, etc. – forming the majority for the first time ever (29.8%).

Above: Tim McGraw's huge popularity speaks for itself – #3 on the best-selling artists list.

Kudos to evergreen old-timers like the Beatles, Johnny Cash, Elvis Presley and even Frank Sinatra for making this mighty list amid the flavours of the day. Rap music truly hit its commercial stride during the past decade with five pure hip-hoppers making the cut – led by the irrepressible, rapid-fire talent that is Eminem.

In the general US market, overall album sales in the US decreased by a whopping 45% from their peak in 2000 during their irrevocable ongoing dive throughout the decade. Digital downloads – especially for individual tracks – continued to replace the old retail model though at the end of the 2000s, although CD sales still accounted for 65% of music sold.

Right: *NSync – featuring Justin Timberlake in case you'd forgotten.

Left: Nelly made the top ten, and won two Grammy awards during the 2000s too.

THE BEST-SELLING ARTISTS OF 2009 IN THE US

1	Michael Jackson	8,286,000
2	Taylor Swift	4,643,000
3	The Beatles	3,282,000
4	Susan Boyle	3,104,000
5	Lady Gaga	2,813,000
6	Andrea Bocelli	2,668,000
7	Michael Bublé	2,280,000
8	Eminem	2,166,000
9	Carrie Underwood	1,895,000
10	The Black Eyed Peas	1,881,000

While Country singer-songwriter Taylor Swift sold more than four million copies in consecutive years in the US (2008/2009) – a remarkable achievement – it was Michael Jackson's passing which dominated both the media and the record sales market at the end of the decade. Having not released a new studio album since 2001's *Invincible*, sales of his back catalogue and several compilations – not to mention the *This Is It* documentary film soundtrack – took the King of Pop's 12-month tally to more than eight million.

Below: Miley Cyrus – the face of Hannah Montana.

THE BEST-SELLING ALBUMS OF 2009 IN THE US

1	Fearless	Taylor Swift	3,217,000
2	I Dreamed A Dream	Susan Boyle	3,104,000
3	Number Ones	Michael Jackson	2,355,000
4	Fame	Lady Gaga	2,238,000
5	My Christmas	Andrea Bocelli	2,207,000
6	Hannah Montana: The Movie	Soundtrack	1,823,000
7	The E.N.D. (The Energy Never Dies)	The Black Eyed Peas	1,787,000
8	Relapse	Eminem	1,735,000
9	Blueprint 3	Jay-Z	1,515,000
10	Only By The Night	Kings of Leon	1,398,000

As well as being the year's best-seller, Taylor Swift's sophomore album, *Fearless* was named Album of the Year at the 2010 Grammy Awards. Her 2009 earnings were estimated by *Forbes* magazine to be $18 million. 405,000 copies of Susan Boyle's debut album were bought over the Internet – a record for the year.

THE BEST-SELLING VINYL ALBUMS OF 2009 IN THE US

1	Abbey Road	The Beatles	34,800
2	Thriller	Michael Jackson	29,800
3	Merriweather Post Pavilion	Animal Collective	14,000
4	Wilco	Wilco	13,200
5	Fleet Foxes	Fleet Foxes	12,700
6	Backspacer	Pearl Jam	12,500
7	Veckatimest	Grizzly Bear	11,600
8	Appetite For Destruction	Guns N' Roses	11,500
9	Big Whiskey And The GrooGrux King	Dave Matthews Band	11,500
10	In Rainbows	Radiohead	11,400

THE BEST-SELLING VINYL ARTISTS 2009 IN THE US

1	Radiohead	45,700
2	The Beatles	38,800
3	Michael Jackson	30,400
4	Metallica	30,200
5	Wilco	29,600
6	Bob Dylan	24,500
7	Animal Collective	20,600
8	Pearl Jam	19,900
9	Bon Iver	17,100
10	Iron & Wine	16,600

Below: Radiohead – vinyl chart-toppers in the USA.

The much-beloved long-playing 12" vinyl album (aka the LP) – introduced in 1948 – rapidly went out of fashion with the arrival of the CD in the early 1980s. Almost extinct by 2000, recent years have seen a renewed interest in releasing limited edition vinyl albums for devoted fans of certain genres, mostly electronic dance music (especially for DJs), hardcore punk/metal and indie rock. Although still only a niche market, vinyl LP sales in the US have increased by more than 75% each year since 2006.

THE BEST-SELLING SINGLES BY YEAR IN THE US

The RCA Victor label released the first commercially available 45-rpm vinyl disc "single" in February 1949. It was 7" in diameter and had a maximum playing time of eight minutes. During the 1950s, the single – together with 12" LPs – replaced the shellac 78-rpm disc.

THE 1960S

Year	Title	Artist
1960	It's Now Or Never	Elvis Presley
1961	Runaway	Del Shannon
1962	I Can't Stop Loving You	Ray Charles
1963	Sugar Shack	Jimmy Gilmer & the Fireballs
1964	I Want To Hold Your Hand	The Beatles
1965	Help!	The Beatles
1966	The Ballad Of The Green Berets	Staff Sergeant Barry Sadler
1967	To Sir With Love	Lulu
1968	Hey Jude	The Beatles
1969	Sugar Sugar	The Archies

The lyrics for Scottish singer Lulu's 1967 smash, 'To Sir With Love' were penned by renowned British writer Don Black for the movie of the same name, which starred Sidney Poitier.

THE 1980S

Year	Title	Artist
1980	Another One Bites The Dust	Queen
1981	Physical	Olivia Newton-John
1982	Eye Of The Tiger	Survivor
1983	Islands In The Stream	Kenny Rogers & Dolly Parton
1984	When Doves Cry	Prince
1985	We Are The World	USA for Africa
1986	That's What Friends Are For	Dionne Warwick & Friends
1987	I Wanna Dance With Somebody (Who Loves Me)	Whitney Houston
1988	Kokomo	The Beach Boys
1989	Wild Thing	Tone Loc

Tone Loc's two million-plus selling rap smash "Wild Thing" included an uncredited sample of "Jamie's Cryin'" by Van Halen.

THE 1990S

Year	Title	Artist
1990	Vogue	Madonna
1991	(Everything I Do) I Do It For You	Bryan Adams
1992	I Will Always Love You	Whitney Houston
1993	Whoomp! (There It Is)	Tag Team
1994	I'll Make Love To You	Boyz II Men
1995	Macarena (Bayside Boys Mix)	Los Del Rio
1996	Killing Me Softly	The Fugees
1997	Candle In The Wind 1997/ Something About The Way You Look Tonight	Elton John
1998	The Boy Is Mine	Brandy & Monica
1999	Believe	Cher

Below: The hugely talented actress and singer Barbra Streisand.

Whitney's biggest hit, 1992's "I Will Always Love You" from *The Bodyguard* film soundtrack, was written by Dolly Parton in 1973. It was co-star Kevin Costner who recommended that Whitney sing the song in the movie.

THE 1970S

Year	Title	Artist
1970	I'll Be There	The Jackson 5
1971	Joy To The World	Three Dog Night
1972	The First Time Ever I Saw Your Face	Roberta Flack
1973	Tie A Yellow Ribbon Round The Ole Oak Tree	Dawn featuring Tony Orlando
1974	The Way We Were	Barbra Streisand
1975	Love Will Keep Us Together	The Captain & Tennille
1976	Disco Lady	Johnnie Taylor
1977	You Light Up My Life	Debby Boone
1978	Night Fever	The Bee Gees
1979	I Will Survive	Gloria Gaynor

Robert Flack's haunting ballad 'The First Time Ever I Saw Your Face' was featured in the Clint Eastwood movie *Play Misty For Me*.

THE 2000S

Year	Title	Artist
2000	Maria Maria	Santana featuring the Product G&B
2001	Loverboy	Mariah Carey
2002	Before Your Love/ A Moment Like This	Kelly Clarkson
2003	Bridge Over Troubled Water	Clay Aiken
2004	I Believe	Fantasia
2005	Hollaback Girl	Gwen Stefani
2006	Bad Day	Daniel Powter
2007	Crank That	Soulja Boy Tell 'Em
2008	Bleeding Love	Leona Lewis
2009	Boom Boom Pow	The Black Eyed Peas

No Doubt's lead singer Gwen Stefani's first solo chart-topper, 'Hollaback Girl' in 2005 was written with with co-producer Pharrell Williams, also one-half of the Neptunes.

THE BEST-SELLING ALBUMS BY YEAR IN THE US

The most popular format for albums sales from the 1960s to the mid-1980s was the LP – long player. 12" in diameter, made from vinyl and spinning at 33 $\frac{1}{3}$ revolutions per minute (RPMs), these phonographic records were first introduced by the Columbia label in the US in June 1948.

THE 1960S

1960	The Sound Of Music	Original Cast
1961	Judy At Carnegie Hall	Judy Garland
1962	West Side Story	Soundtrack
1963	John Fitzgerald Kennedy – A Memorial Album	Documentary
1964	Meet The Beatles	The Beatles
1965	Mary Poppins	Soundtrack
1966	Whipped Cream And Other Delights	Herb Alpert & the Tijuana Brass
1967	Sgt. Pepper's Lonely Hearts Club Band	The Beatles
1968	The Beatles	The Beatles
1969	Hair	Original Cast

John Fitzgerald Kennedy – A Memorial Album was taken from a radio documentary broadcast by WMCA in New York.

THE 1970S

1970	Bridge Over Troubled Water	Simon & Garfunkel
1971	Tapestry	Carole King
1972	American Pie	Don McLean
1973	Dark Side Of The Moon	Pink Floyd
1974	John Denver's Greatest Hits	John Denver
1975	Captain Fantastic And The Brown Dirt Cowboy	Elton John
1976	Frampton Comes Alive!	Peter Frampton
1977	Rumours	Fleetwood Mac
1978	Saturday Night Fever	Soundtrack
1979	Breakfast In America	Supertramp

One of only a handful of live albums to reach number one in the US, *Frampton Comes Alive!* is all the more remarkable for being a double album.

THE 1980S

1980	The Wall	Pink Floyd
1981	Hi Infidelity	REO Speedwagon
1982	Asia	Asia
1983	Thriller	Michael Jackson
1984	Purple Rain	Prince
1985	Like A Virgin	Madonna
1986	Whitney Houston	Whitney Houston
1987	Slippery When Wet	Bon Jovi
1988	Faith	George Michael
1989	Girl You Know It's True	Milli Vanilli

George Michael's Faith was his first solo album after Wham! split up, and included four US number one hit singles: 'Faith', 'Father Figure', 'Monkey' and 'One More Try'.

THE 1990S

1990	Please Hammer Don't Hurt 'Em	MC Hammer
1991	Ropin' The Wind	Garth Brooks
1992	Ropin' The Wind	Garth Brooks
1993	The Bodyguard	Soundtrack/ Whitney Houston
1994	The Lion King	Soundtrack
1995	Cracked Rear View	Hootie & the Blowfish
1996	Jagged Little Pill	Alanis Morissette
1997	Spice	Spice Girls
1998	Titanic	Soundtrack
1999	Millennium	The Backstreet Boys

In the 1990s, Garth Brooks became the biggest-selling country artist ever. His *Ropin' the Wind* album included his future wife, Trisha Yearwood, on backing vocals.

Right: The legendary MC Hammer.

THE 2000S

2000	No Strings Attached	*NSync
2001	[Hybrid Theory]	Linkin Park
2002	The Eminem Show	Eminem
2003	Get Rich Or Die Tryin'	50 Cent
2004	Confessions	Usher
2005	The Emancipation Of Mimi	Mariah Carey
2006	High School Musical	Soundtrack
2007	Noël	Josh Groban
2008	Tha Carter III	Lil Wayne
2009	Fearless	Taylor Swift

Dwayne Michael Carter Jr., aka Lil Wayne – who scored the biggest-selling album of 2008 – was a former member of New Orleans-based teen hip-hop troupe, the Hot Boys.

THE CHRISTMAS NUMBER ONES IN THE US

As much as the British tradition of betting on what's going to be the Christmas number one is a national pastime, the US could not care less: only once has a Christmas-themed record topped the chart at Christmas, and that was in 1952 with Jimmy Boyd's 'I Saw Mommy Kissing Santa Claus'.

THE 1950S

Year	Title	Artist
1950	The Tennessee Waltz	Patti Page
1951	Cry	Johnnie Ray & the Four Lads
1952	I Saw Mommy Kissing Santa Claus	Jimmy Boyd
1953	Rags To Riches	Tony Bennett
1954	Mr. Sandman	The Chordettes
1955	Sixteen Tons	"Tennessee" Ernie Ford
1956	Singing The Blues	Guy Mitchell
1957	April Love	Pat Boone
1958	The Chipmunk Song	David Seville & the Chipmunks
1959	Heartaches By The Number	Guy Mitchell

Left: Guy Mitchell, who went to the top of the charts.

Below: Marvin Gaye scored his first number one hit in 1968.

THE 1960S

Year	Title	Artist
1960	Are You Lonesome Tonight?	Elvis Presley
1961	The Lion Sleeps Tonight	The Tokens
1962	Telstar	The Tornadoes
1963	Dominique	The Singing Nun
1964	I Feel Fine	The Beatles
1965	Over And Over	The Dave Clark Five
1966	Good Vibrations	The Beach Boys
1967	Hello Goodbye	The Beatles
1968	I Heard It Through The Grapevine	Marvin Gaye
1969	Someday We'll Be Together	Diana Ross & the Supremes

THE 1970S

Right: Chic freak out in 1978.

Year	Title	Artist
1970	My Sweet Lord	George Harrison
1971	Brand New Key	Melanie
1972	Me And Mrs. Jones	Billy Paul
1973	Time In A Bottle	Jim Croce
1974	Angie Baby	Helen Reddy
1975	Let's Do It Again	The Staple Singers
1976	Tonight's The Night (Gonna Be Alright)	Rod Stewart
1977	How Deep Is Your Love	Bee Gees
1978	Le Freak	Chic
1979	Escape (The Pina Colada Song)	Rupert Holmes

THE 1980S

Year	Song	Artist
1980	(Just Like) Starting Over	John Lennon
1981	Physical	Olivia Newton-John
1982	Maneater	Daryl Hall & John Oates
1983	Say Say Say	Paul McCartney & Michael Jackson
1984	Like A Virgin	Madonna
1985	Say You, Say Me	Lionel Richie
1986	Walk Like An Egyptian	The Bangles
1987	Faith	George Michael
1988	Every Rose Has Its Thorn	Poison
1989	Another Day In Paradise	Phil Collins

THE 1990S

Year	Song	Artist
1990	Because I Love You (The Postman Song)	Stevie B
1991	Black Or White	Michael Jackson
1992	I Will Always Love You	Whitney Houston
1993	Hero	Mariah Carey
1994	Here Comes The Hotstepper	Ini Kamoze
1995	One Sweet Day	Mariah Carey & Boyz II Men
1996	Un-Break My Heart	Toni Braxton
1997	Candle In The Wind 1997/ Something About The Way You Look Tonight	Elton John
1998	I'm Your Angel	R. Kelly & Céline Dion
1999	Smooth	Santana

Above: The Bangles practising what they preached – Walking like an Egyptian.

Left: Toni Braxton's 'Un-Break My Heart' spent 11 weeks on the top spot.

THE 2000S

Year	Song	Artist
2000	Independent Woman Part 1	Destiny's Child
2001	How You Remind Me	Nickelback
2002	Lose Yourself	Eminem
2003	Hey Ya!	OutKast
2004	Drop It Like It's Hot	Snoop Dogg featuring Pharrell
2005	Don't Forget About Us	Mariah Carey
2006	Irreplaceable	Beyoncé
2007	No One	Alicia Keys
2008	Single Ladies (Put A Ring On It)	Beyoncé
2009	Empire State of Mind	Jay Z & Alicia Keys

Right: OutKast crossed all sorts of musical boundaries on their way to the top.

MTV
MUSIC TELEVISION

A FOREIGN AFFAIR: NATIONALITIES TO TOP THE US SINGLES CHART

Artists from 24 countries, other than those from the UK or US, have topped the US singles chart. Here are lists of every artist who got to the top of the American charts – by nationality.

INXS were one of Australia's biggest exports.

AUSTRALIA (10)

Helen Reddy	I Am Woman	Dec 09, 1972
	Delta Dawn	Sep 15, 1973
	Angie Baby	Dec 28, 1974
Air Supply	The One That You Love	Jul 25, 1981
Rick Springfield	Jessie's Girl	Aug 01, 1981
Men at Work	Who Can It Be Now?	Oct 30, 1982
	Down Under	Jan 15, 1983
INXS	Need You Tonight	Jan 30, 1988
Savage Garden	Truly Madly Deeply	Jan 17, 1998
	I Knew I Loved You	Jan 29, 2000

AUSTRIA (1)

Falco	Rock Me Amadeus	Mar 29, 1986

BARBADOS (4)

Rihanna	SOS	May 13, 2006
	Umbrella (featuring Jay-Z)	Jun 09, 2007
	Take A Bow	May 24, 2008
	Disturbia	Aug 23, 2008

BELGIUM (1)

The Singing Nun	Dominique	Dec 07, 1963

CANADA (25)

Paul Anka	Diana	Sep 14, 1957
	Lonely Boy	Jul 18, 1959
Lorne Greene	Ringo	Dec 5, 1964
Neil Young	Heart Of Gold	Mar 18, 1972
Terry Jacks	Seasons In The Sun	Mar 02, 1974
Gordon Lightfoot	Sundown	Jun 29, 1974
Andy Kim	Rock Me Gently	Sep 28, 1974
Bachman-Turner Overdrive	You Ain't Seen Nothing Yet	Nov 09, 1974
Anne Murray	You Needed Me	Nov 04, 1978
Bryan Adams	Heaven	Jun 29, 1985
	(Everything I Do) I Do It For You	Jul 27, 1991
	All For Love (with Rod Stewart & Sting)	Jan 22, 1994
	Have You Ever Really Loved A Woman?	Jun 03, 1995
Sheriff	When I'm With You	Feb 04, 1989
Alannah Myles	Black Velvet	Mar 24, 1990
Snow	Informer	Mar 13, 1993
Céline Dion	The Power Of Love	Feb 12, 1994
	Because You Loved Me	Mar 23, 1996
	My Heart Will Go On	Feb 28, 1998
	I'm Your Angel (with R. Kelly)	Dec 05, 1998
Barenaked Ladies	One Week	Oct 17, 1998
Daniel Powter	Bad Day	Apr 08, 2006
Nelly Furtado	Promiscuous (featuring Timbaland)	Jul 08, 2006
	Say It Right	Feb 24, 2007
Avril Lavigne	Girlfriend	May 05, 2007

Paul Anka, Canada's first US-chart-topping artist.

COLOMBIA (1)

Shakira	Hips Don't Lie (featuring Wyclef Jean)	Jun 17, 2006

CZECHOSLOVAKIA (1)

Jan Hammer	Miami Vice Theme	Nov 09, 1985

CUBA (4)

Perez Prado	Cherry Pink And Apple Blossom White	Apr 30, 1955
	Patricia	Aug 02, 1958
Gloria Estefan & the Miami Sound Machine	Anything For You	May 14, 1988

Left: Gloria Estefan had many hits in the USA but few number 1 singles.

Right: U2 topped the charts twice in four months in 1987.

FRANCE (1)

Paul Mauriat	Love Is Blue	Feb 10, 1968

GERMANY (5)

Bert Kaempfert	Wonderland By Night	Jan 14, 1961
Silver Convention	Fly, Robin, Fly	Nov 29, 1975
Milli Vanilli	Baby Don't Forget My Number	Jul 01, 1989
	Girl I'm Gonna Miss You	Sep 23, 1989
	Blame It On The Rain	Nov 25, 1989

(Milli Vanilli spokesmodels Morvan and Pilatus were French and American/German respectively. Neither of them sang on the records, but the group was the creation of German producer Frank Farian.)

GREECE (1)

Vangelis	Chariots Of Fire	May 08, 1982

HOLLAND (1)

Shocking Blue	Venus	Feb 07, 1970

IRELAND (3)

Gilbert O'Sullivan	Alone Again (Naturally)	Jul 29, 1972
U2	With Or Without You	May 16, 1987
	I Still Haven't Found What I'm Looking For	Aug 08, 1987

ITALY (1)

Domenico Modugno	Nel Blu Dipinto Di Blu (Volare)	Aug 23, 1958

Left: Milli Vanilli were hugely popular in the late 1980s.

JAMAICA (7)

Carl Douglas	Kung Fu Fighting	Dec 07, 1974
Ini Kamoze	Here Comes The Hotstepper	Dec 17, 1994
Shaggy (featuring RikRok)	It Wasn't Me	Feb 03, 2001
	Angel (featuring Rayvon)	Mar 31, 2001
Sean Paul	Get Busy	May 10, 2003
	Temperature	Apr 01, 2006
Sean Kingston	Beautiful Girls	Aug 11, 2007

Above: Sean Paul is one of Jamaica's biggest artists, and has collaborated with many famous acts as well as succeeding with his own solo career.

JAPAN (1)

Kyu Sakamoto	Sukiyaki	Jun 15, 1963

SOUTH AFRICA (1)

Hugh Masekela	Grazing In The Grass	Jul 20, 1968

NORWAY (1)

a-ha	Take on Me	Oct 19, 1985

Left: One of Norway's biggest exports, a-ha.

SPAIN (3)

Los Del Rio	Macarena (Bayside Boys Mix)	Aug 03, 1996
Enrique Iglesias	Bailamos	Sep 04, 1999
	Be With You	Jun 24, 2000

SWEDEN (7)

Blue Swede	Hooked On A Feeling	Apr 06, 1974
Abba	Dancing Queen	Apr 09, 1977
Roxette	The Look	Apr 08, 1989
	Listen To Your Heart	Nov 04, 1989
	It Must Have Been Love	Jun 16, 1990
	Joyride	May 11, 1991
Ace Of Base	The Sign	Mar 12, 1994

PUERTO RICO (1)

Ricky Martin	Livin' La Vida Loca	May 08, 1999

TRINIDAD (2)

Billy Ocean	There'll Be Sad Songs (To Make You Cry)	Jul 05, 1986
	Get Outta My Dreams, Get Into My Car	Apr 09, 1988

SCOTLAND (5)

Lulu	To Sir With Love	Oct 21, 1967
Average White Band	Pick Up The Pieces	Feb 22, 1975
The Bay City Rollers	Saturday Night	Jan 03, 1976
Sheena Easton	Morning Train (Nine To Five)	May 02, 1981
Simple Minds	Don't You (Forget About Me)	May 18, 1985

WALES (1)

Bonnie Tyler	Total Eclipse Of The Heart	Oct 01, 1983

TOTAL NUMBER 1 HITS ON US AND UK SINGLES CHARTS BY ARTISTS WHO ARE NOT ENGLISH OR AMERICAN

THE MEDAL TABLE	US and UK combined				
Ireland	44	Italy	6	Belgium	1
Canada	31	Cuba	5	British Virgin Islands	1
Scotland	27	France	5	Czechoslovakia	1
Australia	25	Denmark	4	Georgia	1
Sweden	22	Austria	3	Guyana	1
Jamaica	21	Colombia	3	Japan	1
Germany	16	New Zealand	3	Palestine	1
Wales	11	Greece	2	Portugal	1
Spain	7	Northern Ireland	2	Romania	1
Barbados	6	Norway	2	Russia	1
Holland	6	Puerto Rico	2	St. Lucia	1
		South Africa	2		
		Trinidad	2		

Left: Briton Brian Johnson, lead singer from rock gods AC/DC.

Above: Gilbert O'Sullivan – a contributor to Ireland's recording successes around the world.

THE BEST-SELLING ARTISTS BY NATIONALITY

Australia	AC/DC	Greece	Nana Mouskouri	Russia	Alla Pugacheva
Brazil	Roberto Carlos	India	A.R. Rahman	Spain	Julio Iglesias
Canada	Céline Dion	Ireland	U2	Sweden	Abba
China	Wei Wei	Italy	Luciano Pavarotti	UK	The Beatles
Colombia	Shakira	Jamaica	Bob Marley	US	Elvis Presley
France	Charles Aznavour	Japan	Michiya Mihashi		
Germany	Boney M	Mexico	Carlos Santana		

Russia's Alla Pugacheva has been performing – originally in the Soviet Union – since 1965 and has recorded more than 20 popular studio albums. The talented mezzo-soprano pop singer was awarded the Order of Merit for the Fatherland by President Dmitry Medvedev on her 60th birthday on April 15, 2009.

Left: An emotional Bob Marley in concert.

Right: Alla Pugacheva.

MTV MUSIC TELEVISION

BEST-SELLERS IN THE UK

With the cultural advantage of supplying the main language of rock 'n' roll – English – Britain provides the second largest repertoire of popular music behind the United States. Influential home-grown genres include skiffle, punk and of course BritPop. The UK is also the world's third largest music consumer market (after the US and Japan) – and British people own more CDs per head of population than any other country. 129 million albums and 153 million singles/tracks were sold in the UK in 2009.

THE BEST-SELLING SINGLES OF ALL-TIME IN THE UK

#	Title	Artist	Year
1	Candle In The Wind 1997/ Something About The Way You Look Tonight	Elton John	1997
2	Do They Know It's Christmas?	Band Aid	1984
3	Bohemian Rhapsody	Queen	1975
4	Mull Of Kintyre/Girls' School	Wings	1977
5	You're The One That I Want	John Travolta & Olivia Newton John	1978
6	Rivers Of Babylon/ Brown Girl In The Ring	Boney M	1978
7	Relax	Frankie Goes To Hollywood	1984
8	She Loves You	The Beatles	1963
9	Unchained Melody/ (There'll Be Bluebirds Over The) White Cliffs Of Dover	Robson Green & Jerome Flynn	1995
10	Mary's Boy Child/Oh My Lord	Boney M	1978
11	Love Is All Around	Wet Wet Wet	1994
12	Anything Is Possible/Evergreen	Will Young	2002
13	I Just Called To Say I Love You	Stevie Wonder	1984
14	I Want To Hold Your Hand	The Beatles	1963
15	Barbie Girl	Aqua	1997
16	Believe	Cher	1998
17	Perfect Day	Various Artists	1997
18	(Everything I Do) I Do It For You	Bryan Adams	1991
19	Tears	Ken Dodd	1965
20	Can't Buy Me Love	The Beatles	1964
21	Summer Nights	John Travolta & Olivia Newton-John	1978
22	Two Tribes	Frankie Goes To Hollywood	1984
23	Imagine	John Lennon	1975
24	... Baby One More Time	Britney Spears	1999
25	Don't You Want Me	Human League	1981
26	Last Christmas/ Everything She Wants	Wham!	1984
27	I Feel Fine	The Beatles	1964
28	I'll Be Missing You	Puff Daddy & Faith Evans with 112	1997
29	Karma Chameleon	Culture Club	1983
30	The Carnival Is Over	The Seekers	1965
31	(We're Gonna) Rock Around The Clock	Bill Haley & His Comets	1955
32	We Can Work It Out/ Day Tripper	The Beatles	1965
33	YMCA	The Village People	1978
34	Careless Whisper	George Michael	1984
35	Release Me	Engelbert Humperdinck	1967
36	I Will Always Love You	Whitney Houston	1992
37	The Power Of Love	Jennifer Rush	1985
38	Unchained Melody	Gareth Gates	2002
39	My Heart Will Go On	Céline Dion	1998
40	Wannabe	Spice Girls	1996
41	Killing Me Softly	The Fugees	1996
42	Never Ever	All Saints	1997
43	Gangsta's Paradise	Coolio featuring LV	1995
44	Diana	Paul Anka	1957
45	Think Twice	Céline Dion	1994
46	It's Now Or Never	Elvis Presley	1960
47	Green Green Grass Of Home	Tom Jones	1966
48	Come On Eileen	Dexy's Midnight Runners	1982
49	It Wasn't Me	Shaggy featuring RikRok	2001
50	Heart Of Glass	Blondie	1979

Elton John's 'Candle In The Wind 1997' is not only the best-selling single of all-time in his home country – but also the top-selling single ever, worldwide. Sir Elton and Bernie Taupin recast their 1973 hit as a lyrically reworked ode to Diana, Princess of Wales, who died in 1997.

Right: Mark Knopfler (centre) and Dire Straits.

As of December 2009, Queen's *Greatest Hits* had sold 5,680,000 copies in its home country — with the Beatles *Sgt. Pepper* opus standing at 4,910,000. The most recent album on the list is Oasis' *(What's the Story) Morning Glory?* Brit-pop classic from 1995.

THE BEST-SELLING ALBUMS OF ALL TIME IN THE UK

#	Album	Artist	Year
1	Greatest Hits	Queen	1981
2	Sgt. Pepper's Lonely Hearts Club Band	The Beatles	1967
3	Gold – Greatest Hits	Abba	1992
4	(What's The Story) Morning Glory?	Oasis	1995
5	Brothers In Arms	Dire Straits	1985
6	The Dark Side Of The Moon	Pink Floyd	1983
7	Thriller	Michael Jackson	1983
8	Greatest Hits II	Queen	1991
9	Bad	Michael Jackson	1987
10	The Immaculate Collection	Madonna	1990
11	Stars	Simply Red	1991
12	Come On Over	Shania Twain	1999
13	Rumours	Fleetwood Mac	1978
14	Back to Bedlam	James Blunt	2005
15	Urban Hymns	Verve	1997
16	No Angel	Dido	2001
17	Bridge Over Troubled Water	Simon & Garfunkel	1970
18	Back To Black	Amy Winehouse	2007
19	Talk On Corners	The Corrs	1998
20	Bat Out Of Hell	Meat Loaf	1981
21	Spice	Spice Girls	1996
22	White Ladder	David Gray	2001
23	Dirty Dancing	Soundtrack	1988
24	Life For Rent	Dido	2003
25	Legend	Bob Marley & the Wailers	1984
26	1	The Beatles	2000
27	Spirit	Leona Lewis	2007
28	The Joshua Tree	U2	1987
29	But Seriously	Phil Collins	1989
30	A Rush Of Blood To The Head	Coldplay	2002
31	Hopes And Fears	Keane	2004
32	Scissor Sisters	Scissor Sisters	2004
33	The Man Who	Travis	1999
34	Tubular Bells	Mike Oldfield	1974
35	Beautiful World	Take That	2006
36	Greatest Hits	Abba	1976
37	Jagged Little Pill	Alanis Morissette	1996
38	I've Been Expecting You	Robbie Williams	1998
39	X&Y	Coldplay	2005
40	Jeff Wayne's Musical Version Of The War Of The Worlds	Various Artists	1978
41	The Sound Of Music	Soundtrack	1965
42	Ladies & Gentlemen – The Best Of George Michael	George Michael	1998
43	Grease	Soundtrack	1978
44	Come Away With Me	Norah Jones	2003
45	Tracy Chapman	Tracy Chapman	1988
46	Robson & Jerome	Robson & Jerome	1995
47	Tango In The Night	Fleetwood Mac	1987
48	Parachutes	Coldplay	2000
49	Automatic For The People	R.E.M.	1992
50	Whitney	Whitney Houston	1987

Best of British: Oasis (left) and Queen (right).

MTV
MUSIC TELEVISION

THE BEST-SELLING SINGLES OF THE 2000S IN THE UK

1	Anything Is Possible/Evergreen	Will Young
2	Unchained Melody	Gareth Gates
3	Is This The Way To Amarillo?	Tony Christie featuring Peter Kay
4	It Wasn't Me	Shaggy featuring RikRok
5	Hallelujah	Alexandra Burke
6	Do They Know It's Christmas?	Band Aid 20
7	Can't Get You Out of My Head	Kylie Minogue
8	That's My Goal	Shayne Ward
9	Pure And Simple	Hear'Say
10	Can We Fix It?	Bob the Builder

Talent shows, talent shows: Will Young won the first *Pop Idol* in 2002 – Gareth Gates was runner-up. Alexandra Burke blew audiences away with her rendition of Leonard Cohen's 'Hallelujah' on the *The X Factor* in 2008. Shayne Ward won the second series of *The X Factor* while Hear'Say triumphed in the *Popstars* talent show in 2001.

Left: Will Young, Britain's first ever *Pop Idol*.

Below: La Roux's Eleanor Jackson.

THE BEST-SELLING SINGLES OF 2009 IN THE UK

1	Poker Face	Lady Gaga
2	I Gotta Feeling	The Black Eyed Peas
3	Just Dance	Lady Gaga featuring Colby O'Donis
4	Fight For This Love	Cheryl Cole
5	The Climb	Joe McElderry
6	In For The Kill	La Roux
7	Boom Boom Pow	The Black Eyed Peas
8	Killing In The Name	Rage Against The Machine
9	Bad Boys	Alexandra Burke & Flo Rida
10	Meet Me Halfway	The Black Eyed Peas
11	Number 1	Tinchy Stryder & N Dubz
12	Sexy Bitch	David Guetta featuring Akon
13	Use Somebody	Kings of Leon
14	The Fear	Lily Allen
15	Bonkers	Dizzee Rascal
16	Beat Again	JLS
17	Bad Romance	Lady Gaga
18	Sex On Fire	Kings of Leon
19	Broken Strings	James Morrison featuring Nelly Furtado
20	When Love Takes Over	David Guetta featuring Kelly Rowland
21	Paparazzi	Lady Gaga
22	Right Round	Flo Rida featuring Ke$ha
23	I'm Not Alone	Calvin Harris
24	Bulletproof	La Roux
25	Halo	Beyoncé
26	Jai Ho! (You Are My Destiny)	A.R. Rahman & the Pussycat Dolls featuring Nicole Scherzinger
27	The Official BBC Children In Need Medley	Peter Kay's Animated All-Star Band
28	You Are Not Alone	*X Factor* Finalists 2009
29	Love Story	Taylor Swift
30	Empire State Of Mind	Jay Z featuring Alicia Keys

SINGLES SALES VOLUME OF THE 2000S IN THE UK

Physical Singles		Digital Singles Sales (began in 2004)	
2000	55,700,000		
2001	51,200,000	2004	5,800,000
2002	43,900,000	2005	26,400,000
2003	30,900,000	2006	53,100,000
2004	26,500,000	2007	78,000,000
2005	21,400,000	2008	110,300,000
2006	13,800,000	2009	149,700,000
2007	8,600,000		
2008	4,900,000		
2009	3,100,000		

Astonishingly, only six British acts in this top 30 are not annexed to a television show: La Roux, Dizzee Rascal, Tinchy Stryder, Lily Allen, James Morrison and Calvin Harris.

THE BEST-SELLING ALBUMS OF THE 2000S IN THE UK

1	Back To Bedlam	James Blunt
2	No Angel	Dido
3	Back To Black	Amy Winehouse
4	Spirit	Leona Lewis
5	White Ladder	David Gray
6	1	The Beatles
7	Life For Rent	Dido
8	A Rush Of Blood To The Head	Coldplay
9	Scissor Sisters	Scissor Sisters
10	Beautiful World	Take That

Apart from America's Scissor Sisters, every act in this UK top 10 of the noughties is British.

Left: Former soldier James Blunt.

Below: David Gray topped the UK charts three times, the first with *White Ladder*.

THE BEST-SELLING ALBUMS 2009 IN THE UK

1	I Dreamed A Dream	Susan Boyle
2	The Fame	Lady Gaga
3	Crazy Love	Michael Bublé
4	The E.N.D. (The Energy Never Dies)	The Black Eyed Peas
5	Only By The Night	Kings of Leon
6	Now That's What I Call Music 74	Various Artists
7	JLS	JLS
8	I Am... Sasha Fierce	Beyoncé
9	Sunny Side Up	Paolo Nutini
10	It's Not Me It's You	Lily Allen

If the compilation album *Now That's What I Call Music 74* was excluded because it's a compilation each of the titles below it would move up one place – with the tenth best-selling album of the year being *Reality Killed the Video Star* by Robbie Williams.

ALBUMS SALES VOLUME OF THE 2000S IN THE UK

Physical Albums		Digital Albums Sales
2000	134,300,000	
2001	144,900,000	Unheard of prior to the noughties, digital album sales began to find a meaningful market in 2006.
2002	149,200,000	
2003	159,300,000	
2004	163,400,000	
2005	159,000,000	2006 2,800,000
2006	151,900,000	2007 6,300,000
2007	131,800,000	2008 10,300,000
2008	123,300,000	2009 16,100,000
2009	112,900,000	

From a mid-decade peak, annual albums sales in Britain have witnessed a dramatic decline, down 24% by 2009. The main culprit of course has been the Internet, which has given rise to widespread piracy, and to the popularity of both digital albums sales and the more popular single digital download. By 2009 digital download albums accounted for 12.5% of the overall market.

Above: The hugely popular singer Paolo Nutini hails from Scotland.

THE BEST-SELLING SINGLES BY YEAR IN THE UK

Prior to the advent of rock 'n' roll – imported by Elvis Presley, Chuck Berry and Bill Haley and copied by the likes of homegrown Cliff Richard, Adam Faith and Billy Fury - the British music scene was largely populated by the top easy listening pop vocal stylists of the day like Frank Sinatra, Frankie Laine and Vera Lynn.

THE 1960S

Year	Title	Artist
1960	It's Now Or Never	Elvis Presley
1961	Are You Lonesome Tonight?	Elvis Presley
1962	I Remember You	Frank Ifield
1963	She Loves You	The Beatles
1964	Can't Buy Me Love	The Beatles
1965	Tears	Ken Dodd
1966	Green Green Grass Of Home	Tom Jones
1967	Release Me	Engelbert Humperdinck
1968	Hey Jude	The Beatles
1969	Sugar Sugar	The Archies

Paul McCartney wrote 1968's 'Hey Jude', originally titled 'Hey Jules', about John Lennon's five-year-old son Julian.

THE 1970S

Year	Title	Artist
1970	The Wonder Of You	Elvis Presley
1971	My Sweet Lord	George Harrison
1972	I'd Like To Teach The World To Sing	The New Seekers
1973	I Love You Love Me Love	Gary Glitter
1974	You Won't Find Another Fool Like Me	The New Seekers
1975	Bohemian Rhapsody	Queen
1976	Save Your Kisses For Me	Brotherhood of Man
1977	Mull Of Kintyre/Girls' School	Wings
1978	Rivers Of Babylon/Brown Girl In The Ring	Boney M
1979	Y.M.C.A.	The Village People

The front men for the Village People's decade-ending dance hit 'Y.M.C.A.' were styled as a Native American, a construction worker, a cowboy, a biker, a police officer and a soldier.

THE 1980S

Year	Title	Artist
1980	Don't Stand So Close To Me	The Police
1981	Tainted Love	Soft Cell
1982	Come On Eileen	Dexy's Midnight Runners
1983	Karma Chameleon	Culture Club
1984	Do They Know It's Christmas?	Band Aid
1985	The Power Of Love	Jennifer Rush
1986	Don't Leave Me This Way	The Communards
1987	Never Gonna Give You Up	Rick Astley
1988	Mistletoe And Wine	Cliff Richard
1989	Ride On Time	Black Box

A huge Italo-House crossover dance hit in 1989, Black Box's 'Ride On Time' featured the powerful vocal chops of uncredited R&B singer Loletta Holloway.

THE 1990S

Year	Title	Artist
1990	Unchained Melody	The Righteous Brothers
1991	(Everything I Do) I Do It For You	Bryan Adams
1992	I Will Always Love You	Whitney Houston
1993	I'd Do Anything For Love (But I Won't Do That)	Meat Loaf
1994	Love Is All Around	Wet Wet Wet
1995	Unchained Melody/ The White Cliffs Of Dover	Robson & Jerome
1996	Killing Me Softly	The Fugees
1997	Candle In The Wind 1997/Something About The Way You Look Tonight	Elton John
1998	Believe	Cher
1999	… Baby One More Time	Britney Spears

Britney Spears' debut single and first UK chart-topper in 1999 was recorded in Sweden under the helm of Swedish pop production maestros Max Martin (who also wrote the song), Denniz PoP and Rami.

Above: Leona Lewis was another talent show winner: X Factor.

THE 2000S

Year	Title	Artist
2000	Can We Fix It	Bob the Builder
2001	It Wasn't Me	Shaggy featuring RikRok
2002	Anything Is Possible/Evergreen	Will Young
2003	Where Is The Love?	The Black Eyed Peas
2004	Do They Know It's Christmas?	Band Aid 20
2005	(Is This The Way To) Amarillo	Tony Christie featuring Peter Kay
2006	Crazy	Gnarls Barkley
2007	Bleeding Love	Leona Lewis
2008	Hallelujah	Alexandra Burke
2009	Poker Face	Lady Gaga

Gnarls Barkley – who scored with the global dance/pop smash 'Crazy' in 2006 – are a musical duo comprising producer/multi-instrumentalist Brian Burton (aka Danger Mouse) and rapper/singer Thomas Callaway (aka Cee-Lo).

THE BEST-SELLING ALBUMS BY YEAR IN THE UK

The cassette album – also known as cassette tape, compact cassette and audiocassette – was a magnetic tape sound-recording format, offering a portable alternative to the LP. Mass-produced for the first time in Germany in 1964, its popularity grew steadily until it peaked with the success of the Sony Walkman.

THE 1960S

Year	Album	Artist
1960	South Pacific	Soundtrack
1961	G.I. Blues	Elvis Presley
1962	West Side Story	Soundtrack
1963	With The Beatles	The Beatles
1964	Beatles For Sale	The Beatles
1965	The Sound Of Music	Soundtrack
1966	The Sound Of Music	Soundtrack
1967	Sgt. Pepper's Lonely Hearts Club Band	The Beatles
1968	The Sound Of Music	Soundtrack
1969	Abbey Road	The Beatles

The Sound of Music: No other album in history has ever topped the best-selling annual lists for three separate years.

THE 1990S

Year	Album	Artist
1990	But Seriously	Phil Collins
1991	Stars	Simply Red
1992	Stars	Simply Red
1993	Bat Out Of Hell II – Back Into Hell	Meat Loaf
1994	Cross Road – The Best Of Bon Jovi	Bon Jovi
1995	Robson & Jerome	Robson Green & Jerome Flynn
1996	Jagged Little Pill	Alanis Morissette
1997	Be Here Now	Oasis
1998	Talk On Corners	The Corrs
1999	Come On Over	Shania Twain

Talk On Corners was the first album from Celtic folk-rock family quartet The Corrs: Andrea, Sharon, Caroline and brother Jim.

THE 1970S

Year	Album	Artist
1970	Bridge Over Troubled Water	Simon & Garfunkel
1971	Bridge Over Troubled Water	Simon & Garfunkel
1972	20 Dynamic Hits	Various Artists
1973	Don't Shoot Me, I'm Only The Piano Player	Elton John
1974	The Singles 1969–1973	The Carpenters
1975	The Best Of The Stylistics	Stylistics
1976	Greatest Hits	Abba
1977	Arrival	Abba
1978	Saturday Night Fever	Soundtrack
1979	Parallel Lines	Blondie

Above: Art Garfunkel and Paul Simon.

Blondie's album *Parallel Lines* was produced by songwriter/producer Mike Chapman who was one half (with Nicky Chinn) of the ChinniChap pop production line which provided dozens of hits for other acts too.

Right: Dido Florian Cloud de Bounevialle O'Malley Armstrong, better known as Dido.

THE 2000S

Year	Album	Artist
2000	1	The Beatles
2001	No Angel	Dido
2002	Escapology	Robbie Williams
2003	Life For Rent	Dido
2004	Scissor Sisters	Scissor Sisters
2005	Back To Bedlam	James Blunt
2006	Eyes Open	Snow Patrol
2007	Back To Black	Amy Winehouse
2008	Rockferry	Duffy
2009	I Dreamed A Dream	Susan Boyle

THE 1980S

Year	Album	Artist
1980	Super Trouper	Abba
1981	Kings Of The Wild Frontier	Adam & the Ants
1982	Love Songs	Barbra Streisand
1983	Thriller	Michael Jackson
1984	Can't Slow Down	Lionel Richie
1985	Brothers In Arms	Dire Straits
1986	True Blue	Madonna
1987	Bad	Michael Jackson
1988	Kylie	Kylie Minogue
1989	Ten Good Reasons	Jason Donovan

Aimée Ann Duffy – better known simply as Duffy – was born in Bangor, Gwynedd in Wales in 1984. Her 2008 blue-eyed soul-drenched debut album stormed the European charts in 2008 and was named Best Pop Vocal at the Grammy Awards the following year.

Kylie Minogue's maiden offering, *Kylie*, was a 35-minute, ten-track collection of pop confection produced and written by hit-making trio Stock, Aitken & Waterman.

THE MILLION-SELLING SINGLES
IN THE UK

Despite their being more than a dozen million-selling 45s in the fifties and sixties, formal sales certification by the British Phonographic Industry (BPI) only began in 1973 for singles and albums. The current award qualification levels for hit singles in the UK are: Silver: 200,000, Gold: 400,000 and Platinum: 600,000.

THE 1950S (3)

(We're Gonna) Rock Around The Clock	Bill Haley & His Comets	1955
Diana	Paul Anka	1957
Mary's Boy Child	Harry Belafonte	1957

THE 1960S (14)

It's Now Or Never	Elvis Presley	1960
Stranger On The Shore	Mr. Acker Bilk	1961
I Remember You	Frank Ifield	1962
The Young Ones	Cliff Richard & the Shadows	1962
She Loves You	The Beatles	1963
I Want To Hold Your Hand	The Beatles	1963
Can't Buy Me Love	The Beatles	1964
I Feel Fine	The Beatles	1964
Tears	Ken Dodd	1965
The Carnival Is Over	The Seekers	1965
We Can Work It Out/ Day Tripper	The Beatles	1965
Green Green Grass Of Home	Tom Jones	1966
Release Me	Engelbert Humperdinck	1967
The Last Waltz	Engelbert Humperdinck	1967

Above: Bill Haley was the original rock and roller.

Below: John Travolta and Olivial Newton-John in *Grease*.

THE 1970S (15)

Eye Level	The Simon Park Orchestra	1972
I Love You Love Me Love	Gary Glitter	1973
Merry Xmas Everybody	Slade	1973
Imagine	John Lennon	1975
Bohemian Rhapsody	Queen	1975
Save Your Kisses For Me	Brotherhood of Man	1976
Don't Give Up On Us	David Soul	1976
Mull Of Kintyre/Girls' School	Wings	1977
Rivers Of Babylon/ Brown Girl In The Ring	Boney M	1978
You're the One That I Want	John Travolta & Olivia Newton-John	1978
Summer Nights	John Travolta & Olivia Newton-John	1978
Y.M.C.A.	The Village People	1978
Mary's Boy Child – Oh My Lord	Boney M	1978
Heart Of Glass	Blondie	1979
Bright Eyes	Art Garfunkel	1979

Left: The eternally popular Engelbert Humperdinck.

Born in India, pop crooner Engelbert Humperdinck's real name is Arnold George Dorsey. He was one of ten children born to Mervyn Dorsey, a British Army Officer.

American pop balladeer David Soul's day job during the seventies was as an actor, notably the role of Detective Kenneth "Hutch" Hutchinson in the TV cop series *Starsky and Hutch*.

THE 1980S (12)

Tainted Love	Soft Cell	1981
Don't You Want Me	Human League	1981
Come on Eileen	Dexy's Midnight Runners	1982
Relax	Frankie Goes To Hollywood	1983
Karma Chameleon	Culture Club	1983
Blue Monday	New Order	1983
I Just Called To Say I Love You	Stevie Wonder	1984
Two Tribes	Frankie Goes To Hollywood	1984
Careless Whisper	George Michael	1984
Last Christmas/ Everything She Wants	Wham!	1984
Do They Know It's Christmas?	Band Aid	1984
The Power Of Love	Jennifer Rush	1985

New Order's indie classic 'Blue Monday' is widely regarded as the biggest-selling 12" single of all-time in the UK, but this was never officially confirmed because its label, the iconic Factory Records, never joined the BPI – and hence could not have any sales certified.

Above: Frankie Goes To Hollywood in 1984.

THE 1990S (26)

(Everything I Do) I Do It For You	Bryan Adams	1991
I Will Always Love You	Whitney Houston	1982
Love Is All Around	Wet Wet Wet	1994
Think Twice	Céline Dion	1994
Saturday Night	Whigfield	1994
Unchained Melody/(There'll Be Bluebirds Over The) White Cliffs Of Dover	Robson Green & Jerome Flynn	1995
Gangsta's Paradise	Coolio featuring LV	1995
I Believe/Up On The Roof	Robson & Jerome	1995
Earth Song	Michael Jackson	1995
Wannabe	Spice Girls	1996
Killing Me Softly	The Fugees	1996
Spaceman	Babylon Zoo	1996
2 Become 1	Spice Girls	1996
Barbie Girl	Aqua	1997
Perfect Day	Various Artists	1997
I'll Be Missing You	Puff Daddy & Faith Evans with 112	1997
Candle In The Wind 1997/ Something About The Way You Look Tonight	Elton John	1997
Never Ever	All Saints	1997
Teletubbies Say "Eh-Oh!"	The Teletubbies	1997
Believe	Cher	1998
My Heart Will Go On	Céline Dion	1998
Heartbeat/Tragedy	Steps	1998
It's Like That	Run-DMC vs Jason Nevins	1998
No Matter What	Boyzone	1998
… Baby One More Time	Britney Spears	1999
Blue (Da Ba Bee)	Eiffel 65	1999

Pop veteran Cher scored the biggest hit of her solo career with the dance anthem 'Believe' in 1998. It was also one of the first hits to use the 'Auto-Tune' pitch sound-effect, which became prevalent over the following decade.

THE 2000S (10)

Can We Fix It?	Bob the Builder	2000
Whole Again	Atomic Kitten	2001
It Wasn't Me	Shaggy featuring RikRok	2001
Pure And Simple	Hear'Say	2001
Can't Get You Out Of My Head	Kylie Minogue	2001
Anything Is Possible/ Evergreen	Will Young	2002
Unchained Melody	Gareth Gates	2002
Do They Know It's Christmas?	Band Aid	2004
Is This The Way To Amarillo?	Tony Christie featuring Peter Kay	2005
That's My Goal	Shayne Ward	2005

TV reality show winners Hear'Say split less than two years after their huge 2001 hit, 'Pure and Simple'.

Girl Power: The Spice Girls (above) and Kylie Minogue (left).

THE CHRISTMAS NUMBER ONES IN THE UK

Although the "What will be the Christmas number one?" discussion is a fun cultural tradition each December in Britain (unmatched in any other country), 2009 saw the least Christmassy song ever reach the top spot: the Facebook-driven success of Rage Against The Machine's 'Killing In The Name'.

THE 1950S

1952	Here In My Heart	Al Martino
1953	Answer Me	Frankie Laine
1954	Let's Have Another Party	Winifred Atwell
1955	Christmas Alphabet	Dickie Valentine
1956	Just Walkin' In The Rain	Johnnie Ray
1957	Mary's Boy Child	Harry Belafonte
1958	It's Only Make Believe	Conway Twitty
1959	What Do You Want To Make Those Eyes At Me For?	Emile Ford & the Checkmates

Left: Johnnie Ray on *The Wheeltappers and Shunters Social Club.*

THE 1960S

Right: Rolf Harris was popular for his TV shows as well as his songs.

Below: Slade make an appearance in the charts every Christmas in the UK.

1960	I Love You	Cliff Richard & the Shadows
1961	Tower Of Strength	Frankie Vaughan
1962	Return To Sender	Elvis Presley
1963	I Want To Hold Your Hand	The Beatles
1964	I Feel Fine	The Beatles
1965	We Can Work It Out/ Day Tripper	The Beatles
1966	Green Green Grass Of Home	Tom Jones
1967	Hello, Goodbye	The Beatles
1968	Lily The Pink	Scaffold
1969	Two Little Boys	Rolf Harris

THE 1970S

1970	I Hear You Knocking	Dave Edmunds
1971	Ernie (The Fastest Milk Man In The West)	Benny Hill
1972	Long Haired Lover From Liverpool	Little Jimmy Osmond
1973	Merry Xmas Everybody	Slade
1974	Lonely This Christmas	Mud
1975	Bohemian Rhapsody	Queen
1976	When A Child Is Born (Soleado)	Johnny Mathis
1977	Mull Of Kintyre/Girls' School	Wings
1978	Mary Boy's Child – Oh My Lord	Boney M
1979	Another Brick In The Wall (Part II)	Pink Floyd

THE 1980S

1980	There's No One Quite Like Grandma	St. Winifred's School Choir
1981	Don't You Want Me	Human League
1982	Save Your Love	Renee & Renato
1983	Only You	The Flying Pickets
1984	Do They Know It's Christmas?	Band Aid
1985	Merry Christmas Everyone	Shakin' Stevens
1986	Reet Petite	Jackie Wilson
1987	Always On My Mind	The Pet Shop Boys
1988	Mistletoe And Wine	Cliff Richard
1989	Do They Know It's Christmas?	Band Aid II

Above: The Human League's 'Don't You Want Me' had no Christmas connection.

Below: The Spice Girls topped the charts three years in a row in the late 1990s.

THE 1990S

1990	Saviour's Day	Cliff Richard
1991	Bohemian Rhapsody/These Are the Days Of Our Lives	Queen
1992	I Will Always Love You	Whitney Houston
1993	Mr. Blobby	Mr. Blobby
1994	Stay Another Day	East 17
1995	Earth Song	Michael Jackson
1996	2 Become 1	Spice Girls
1997	Too Much	Spice Girls
1998	Goodbye	Spice Girls
1999	I Have A Dream/ Seasons In The Sun	Westlife

Below: Rage Against The Machine was the surprise Christmas hit of 2009.

THE 2000S

2000	Can We Fix It?	Bob the Builder
2001	Something Stupid	Robbie Williams & Nicole Kidman
2002	Sound Of The Underground	Girls Aloud
2003	Mad World	Michael Andrews & Gary Jules
2004	Do They Know It's Christmas?	Band Aid 20
2005	That's My Goal	Shayne Ward
2006	A Moment Like This	Leona Lewis
2007	When You Believe	Leon Jackson
2008	Hallelujah	Alexandra Burke
2009	Killing In The Name	Rage Against The Machine

Band Aid's 'Do They Know It's Christmas?' has sold over 3,500,000 copies in the UK alone, while Slade's 'Merry Xmas Everybody' has charted on 13 seasonal occasions, including each of the past four years. Bing Crosby's 'White Christmas', despite having reputedly sold over 30,000,000 copies worldwide since 1942, charted for the first time in the UK as late as 1977, a few weeks after the singer's death.

MTV
MUSIC TELEVISION

A FOREIGN AFFAIR: NATIONALITIES TO TOP THE BRITISH SINGLES CHART

Other than artists from either the UK or the US, music acts from 32 other countries have topped the UK singles chart. Here are lists of every country to do so by nationality.

AUSTRALIA (15)

The Seekers	The Carnival Is Over	Nov 27, 1965
Men At Work	Down Under	Jan 29, 1983
Madison Avenue	Don't Call Me Baby	May 14, 2000
Kylie Minogue	I Should Be So Lucky	Feb 20 1988
	Hand On Your Heart	May 13, 1989
	Spinning Around	Jun 25, 2000
	Tears On My Pillow	Jan 21, 1990
	Can't Get You Out Of	
	My Head	Sep 23, 2001
	Slow	Nov 09, 2003
Kylie Minogue &		
Jason Donovan	Especially For You	Jan 07, 1989
Jason Donovan	Too Many Broken Hearts	Mar 11, 1989
	Sealed With A Kiss	Jun 10, 1989
	Any Dream Will Do	Jun 23, 1991
Baz Luhrmann	Everybody's Free	
	(To Wear Sunscreen)	Jun 06, 1999
Holly Valance	Kiss Kiss	May 05, 2002

AUSTRIA (2)

Falco	Rock Me Amadeus	May 10, 1986
DJ Otzi	Hey Baby	Sep 16, 2001

BARBADOS (2)

Rihanna	Umbrella (featuring Jay-Z)	May 20, 2007
	Take A Bow	May 25, 2008

Left: Barbados-born Rihanna moved to the US aged 16.

BRITISH VIRGIN ISLANDS (1)

CANADA (6)

Paul Anka	Diana	Aug 31, 1957
Terry Jacks	Seasons In The Sun	Apr 06, 1974
J.J. Barrie	No Charge	Jun 05, 1976
Bryan Adams	(Everything I Do)	
	I Do It For You	July 07, 1991
Céline Dion	Think Twice	Jan 29, 1995
	My Heart Will Go On	Feb 15, 1998
Nelly Furtado	Maneater	Jun 11, 2006

COLOMBIA (2)

Shakira	Hips Don't Lie	Jul 30, 2006
	Beautiful Liar (with Beyoncé)	Apr 22, 2007

CUBA (1)

Perez Prado	Cherry Pink And	
	Apple Blossom White	Apr 30, 1955

DENMARK (4)

Whigfield	Saturday Night	Sep 11, 1994
Aqua	Barbie Girl	Oct 26, 1997
	Doctor Jones	Feb 01, 1998
	Turn Back Time	May 10, 1998

Right: Denmark's Sannie Charlotte Carlson, better known as Whigfield.

FRANCE (4)

Charles Aznavour	She	Jun 29 1974
Modjo	Lady	
	(Hear Me Tonight)	Sep 10, 2000
Mr. Oizo	Flat Beat	Mar 28, 1999
David Guetta	Sexy Bitch/Sexy Chick	
	(featuring Akon)	Aug 23, 2009

Left: Electro-pop legends Karftwerk in 1981.

GERMANY (11)

Kraftwerk	The Model/Computer Love	Feb 06, 1982
Goombay Dance Band	Seven Tears	Mar 27, 1982
Nicole	A Little Peace	May 15, 1982
Nena	99 Red Balloons	Mar 03, 1984
Fragma	Toca's Miracle	Apr 16, 2000
Snap!	The Power	Mar 25, 1990
	Rhythm Is A Dancer	Aug 02, 1992
Culture Beat	Mr. Vain	Aug 22, 1993
	9pm (Till I Come)	Jun 27, 1999
Lou Bega	Mambo No. 5 (A Little Bit Of...)	Aug 29, 1999
Tomcraft	Loneliness	May 04, 2003

GEORGIA (1)

Katie Melua	What A Wonderful World (with Eva Cassidy)	Dec 16, 2007

GREECE (1)

Demis Roussos	The Roussos Phenomenon (EP)	Jul 17, 1976

Right: Demis Roussos was originally in the band Aphrodite's Child with Vangelis.

GUYANA (1)

Eddy Grant	I Don't Wanna Dance	Nov 13, 1982

HOLLAND (5)

Pussycat	Mississippi	Oct 16, 1976
Doop	Doop	Mar 13, 1994
Vengaboys	Boom Boom Boom Boom	Jun 20, 1999
	We're Going To Ibiza	Sep 12, 1999
Fedde Le Grand	Put Your Hands Up For Detroit	Nov 05, 2006

IRELAND (41)

Dana	All Kinds Of Everything	Apr 18, 1970
Gilbert O'Sullivan	Clair	Nov 11, 1972
	Get Down	Apr 07, 1973
Johnny Logan	What's Another Year	May 17, 1980
Chris de Burgh	The Lady In Red	Aug 02, 1986
The Corrs	Breathless	Jul 09, 2000
Ronan Keating	When You Say Nothing At All	Aug 01, 1999
	Life Is A Rollercoaster	Jul 16, 2000
	If Tomorrow Never Comes	May 12, 2002
U2	Desire	Oct 08, 1988
	The Fly	Oct 27, 1991
	Discotheque	Feb 09, 1997
	Beautiful Day	Oct 15, 2000
	Vertigo	Nov 14, 2004
	Sometimes You Can't Make It On Your Own	Feb 13, 2005
Enya	Orinoco Flow	Oct 29, 1988
Sinéad O'Connor	Nothing Compares 2 U	Jan 28, 1990
Boyzone	Words	Oct 13, 1996
	A Different Beat	Dec 08, 1996
	All That I Need	Apr 26, 1998
	No Matter What	Aug 09, 1998
	When the Going Gets Tough, The Tough Get Going	Mar 07, 1999
	You Needed Me	May 16, 1999
Westlife	Swear It Again	Apr 25, 1999
	If I Let You Go	Aug 15, 1999
	Flying Without Wings	Oct 24, 1999
	I Have A Dream/ Seasons In The Sun	Dec 19, 1999
	Fool Again	Apr 02, 2000
	My Love	Nov 05, 2000
	Uptown Girl	Mar 11, 2001
	Queen Of My Heart	Nov 11, 2001
	World Of Our Own	Feb 24, 2002
	Unbreakable	Nov 10, 2002
	Mandy	Nov 23, 2003
	You Raise Me Up	Oct 30, 2005
	The Rose	Nov 12, 2006
B*witched	C'est La Vie	May 31, 1998
	Rollercoaster	Sep 27, 1998
	To You I Belong	Dec 13, 1998
	Blame It On The Weatherman	Mar 21, 1999
Brian McFadden	Real To Me	Sep 12, 2004

Left: Ireland's hugely popular Westlife.

ITALY (5)

Mantovani	Moulin Rouge	Aug 15, 1953
Black Box	Ride On Time	Sep 09, 1989
Tamperer featuring Maya	Feel It	May 24, 1998
Black Legend	You See The Trouble With Me	Jun 18, 2000
Eiffel 65	Blue (Da Ba Dee)	Sep 15, 1999

Left: Jeffrey Jey, Maurizio Lobina and Gabry Ponte from Eiffel 65.

JAMAICA (14)

Desmond Dekker & the Aces	The Israelites	Apr 19, 1969
Dave & Ansell Collins	Double Barrel	May 01, 1971
Carl Douglas	Kung Fu Fighting	Sep 21, 1974
Ken Boothe	Everything I Own	Oct 26, 1974
Althia & Donna	Uptown Top Ranking	Feb 04, 1978
Boney M	Rivers Of Babylon	May 13, 1978
	Mary's Boy Child – Oh My Lord	Dec 15, 1978

(two of Boney M were Jamaican, the others Montserratian and Aruban)

Boris Gardiner	I Want To Wake Up With You	Aug 23, 1986
Shaggy	Oh Carolina	Mar 14, 1993
	Boombastic	Sep 17, 1995
	It Wasn't Me	Mar 04, 2001
	Angel	Jun 03, 2001
Chaka Demus & Pliers	Twist And Shout	Jan 02, 1994
Sean Kingston	Beautiful Girls	Sep 02, 2007

Left: Jamaican chart-topper Shaggy.

NORWAY (1)

a-ha	The Sun Always Shines On TV	Jan 25, 1986

PALESTINE (1)

Esther & Abi Ofarim	Cinderella Rockefella	Mar 02, 1968

PORTUGAL (1)

Rui da Silva	Touch Me	Jan 07, 2001

PUERTO RICO (1)

Ricky Martin	Livin' La Vida Loca	Jul 11, 1999

NEW ZEALAND (3)

Daniel Bedingfield	Gotta Get Thru This	Jan 06, 2002
	If You're Not The One	Dec 01, 2002
	Never Gonna Leave Your Side	Jul 27, 2003

NORTHERN IRELAND (2)

Feargal Sharkey	A Good Heart	Nov 16, 1985
D:Ream	Things Can Only Get Better	Jan 16, 1994

ROMANIA (1)

Enigma	Sadeness (Part 1)	Jan 13, 1991

RUSSIA (1)

t.A.T.u.	All The Things She Said	Feb 02, 2003

ST. LUCIA (1)

Emile Ford & the Checkmates	What Do You Want to Make Those Eyes at Me For?	Dec 19, 1959

Left: The tartan-bedecked Bay City Rollers.

SWEDEN (15)

Abba	Waterloo	May 04, 1974
	Mamma Mia	Jan 31, 1976
	Fernando	May 08, 1976
	Dancing Queen	Sep 04, 1976
	Knowing Me, Knowing You	Apr 02, 1977
	The Name Of The Game	Nov 04, 1977
	Take A Chance On Me	Feb 18, 1978
	The Winner Takes It All	Aug 09, 1980
	Super Trouper	Nov 29, 1980
Ace Of Base	All That She Wants	May 16, 1993
Rednex	Cotton Eye Joe	Jan 08, 1995
Eric Prydz	Call On Me	Sep 19, 2004
Crazy Frog	Axel F	May 29, 2005
Robyn with Kleerup	With Every Heartbeat	Aug 12, 2007
Basshunter	Now You're Gone	Jan 13, 2008

SCOTLAND (22)

Middle of the Road	Chirpy Chirpy Cheep Cheep	Jun 19, 1971
Pilot	January	Feb 01, 1975
The Bay City Rollers	Bye Bye Baby	Mar 22, 1975
	Give A Little Love	July 19, 1975
Billy Connolly	D.I.V.O.R.C.E.	Nov 22, 1975
Slik	Forever And Ever	Feb 14, 1976
Lena Martell	One Day At A Time	Oct 27, 1979
Kelly Marie	Feels Like I'm In Love	Sep 13, 1980
Aneka	Japanese Boy	Aug 29, 1981
Jim Diamond	I Should Have Known Better	Dec 01, 1984
Barbara Dickson	I Know Him So Well (duet with Elaine Paige)	Feb 09, 1985
Midge Ure	If I Was	Oct 05, 1985
Fairground Attraction	Perfect	May 14, 1988
Simple Minds	Belfast Child	Feb 25, 1989
The Bluebells	Young At Heart	Mar 28, 1993
Dunblane	Knockin' On Heaven's Door/ Throw These Guns Away	Dec 15, 1996
Darius	Colourblind	Aug 04, 2002
David Sneddon	Stop Living The Lie	Jan 19, 2003
Sandi Thom	I Wish I Was A Punk Rocker (With Flowers In My Hair)	Jun 04, 2006
The Proclaimers featuring Brian Potter & Andy Pipkin	I'm Gonna Be (500 Miles)	Mar 25, 2007
Leon Jackson	When You Believe	Dec 23, 2007
Calvin Harris	I'm Not Alone	Apr 12, 2009

TRINIDAD (2)

Winifred Atwell	Let's Have Another Party	Dec 04, 1954
Billy Ocean	When The Going Gets Tough, The Tough Get Going	Feb 08, 1986

WALES (10)

Dave Edmunds	I Hear You Knockin'	Nov 28, 1970
Shakin' Stevens	This Ole House	Mar 28, 1981
	Green Door	Aug 01, 1981
	Oh Julie	Jan 30, 1982
	Merry Christmas Everyone	Dec 28, 1985
Bonnie Tyler	Total Eclipse Of The Heart	Mar 12, 1983
Manic Street Preachers	If You Tolerate This Your Children Will Be Next	Aug 30, 1998
	The Masses Against The Classes	Jan 16, 2000
Chico	It's Chico Time	Mar 05, 2006
Duffy	Mercy	Feb 17, 2008

SOUTH AFRICA (1)

Danny Williams	Moon River	Dec 30, 1961

SPAIN (4)

Baccara	Yes Sir, I Can Boogie	Oct 29, 1977
Julio Iglesias	Begin The Beguine (Volver A Emprezar)	Dec 05, 1981
Enrique Iglesias	Hero	Jan 27, 2002
Las Ketchup	The Ketchup Song (Aserjé)	Oct 13, 2002

Above: Sean Moore, Nicky Wire and James Dean Bradfield – The Manic Street Preachers.

Although digital downloads increased dramatically as the noughties drew to an end, overall worldwide music sales continued to decline with a 7% fall in 2009 over the previous year. Spain, Japan and Italy saw the sharpest drops, though sales in 13 other countries grew, including those in Australia, Brazil and Sweden. Total worldwide music sales revenues amounted to $17 billion – with American and British acts continuing to dominate airwaves and charts around the globe.

BRAZIL

The Brazilian charts are compiled by Crowley Broadcast Analysis and published in the Brazilian edition of *Billboard*.

THE BEST-SELLING SINGLES OF 2009 IN BRAZIL

1	Circus	Britney Spears
2	Halo	Beyoncé
3	Agenda	Ornella Di Santis & Belo
4	Não Tente Me Impedir	Bruno & Marrone
5	Te Amo	Rihanna
6	Foi Você Quem Trouxe	Edson & Hudson
7	Boom Boom Pow	The Black Eyed Peas
8	Just Dance	Lady Gaga featuring Colby O'Donis
9	Deus E Eu No Sertão	Victor & Leo
10	Fly	Wanessa Camargo & Ja Rule
11	Single Ladies (Put A Ring On It)	Beyoncé
12	Paparazzi	Lady Gaga
13	A Lhe Esperar	Os Paralamas do Sucesso
14	Poker Face	Lady Gaga
15	I Gotta Feeling	The Black Eyed Peas
16	Sutilmente	Skank
17	Me Encontra	Charlie Brown Jr.
18	Hot N Cold	Katy Perry
19	Cadê Dalila	Ivete Sangalo
20	Me Adora	Pitty

THE BEST-SELLING ALBUMS OF ALL TIME IN BRAZIL

1	Músicas para Louvar O Senhor	Padre Marcelo Rossi	1998
2	Xou Da Xuxa 3	Xuxa	1988
3	Leandro & Leonardo	Leandro & Leonardo	1990
4	Só Pra Contrariar	Só Pra Contrariar	1997
5	4º Xou Da Xuxa	Xuxa	1989
6	Xegundo Xou Da Xuxa	Xuxa	1987
7	Um Sonhador	Leandro & Leonardo	1998
8	Xou Da Xuxa	Xuxa	1986
9	Mamonas Assassinas	Mamonas Assassinas	1995
10	Terra Samba Ao Vivo E A Cores	Terra Samba	1998

Brazil's best-selling album was recorded by a Catholic Priest who still preaches to huge congregations at the Santuário do Terço Bizantino in Sao Paulo. His *Músicas para Louvar o Senhor* received a triple Diamond sales award.

Ironically, despite her 'Circus' topping the list, Britney's *The Circus* world tour played just about everywhere in 2009 – except Brazil.

Right: Britney Spears cleaning up at 2008's MTV Video Music Awards.

CANADA

Nielsen SoundScan compiles the Canadian chart. The first-ever Canadian top 30 was broadcast by radio station CHUM in May 1957 and featured Elvis Presley's 'All Shook Up' as its first number one, Paul Anka's 'Diana' was the first home-grown chart-topper.

THE BEST-SELLING SINGLES OF 2009 IN CANADA

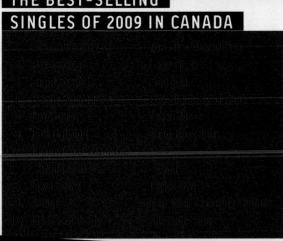

THE BEST-SELLING ALBUMS OF 2009 IN CANADA

1	Dark Horse	Nickelback
2	Fearless	Taylor Swift
3	The Fame	Lady Gaga
4	The E.N.D. (The Energy Never Dies)	The Black Eyed Peas
5	Circus	Britney Spears
6	Fais-Moi La Tendresse	Ginette Reno
7	Only by the Night	Kings of Leon
8	The Promise	Il Divo
9	Relapse	Eminem
10	Hannah Montana – The Movie	Soundtrack

Below: Nickelback's Chad Croeder playing live in Sydney Australia, 2009.

Although the Canadian charts frequently mirror the most popular songs in the US, a standout exception is 'Africa', the hit cover version of the Toto oldie by Lebanese/Canadian singer Karl Wolf featuring Canadian rapper Culture.

Canada's biggest-selling rock export, Nickelback was formed in 1995 in Hanna, Alberta and is now based in Vancouver. The multi-platinum Dark Horse is the band's sixth studio album. The only other Canadian act in the top 10 is veteran singer Ginette Reno.

JAPAN

The Japanese charts are compiled by the Recording Industry Association of Japan (RIAJ), which was originally founded in 1942 as the Japan Phonogram Record Cultural Association.

THE BEST-SELLING SINGLES OF 2009 IN JAPAN

1	Ichibu To Zenbu	B'z
2	Believe	Arashi
3	My SunShine	Rock'a'trench
4	Niji	Kobukuro
5	My Girl	Arashi
6	Himawari	Yusuke
7	Everything	Arashi
8	Ashita No	Kioku
9	Ai No Mamade	Junko Akimoto
10	Someday	Exile

A popular fixture on the Japanese music scene for two decades, B'z is the hard-rock duo of Tak Matsumoto and Koshi Inaba (pictured below).

THE BEST-SELLING SINGLES OF ALL-TIME BY INTERNATIONAL ARTISTS IN JAPAN

1	Beautiful Sunday	Daniel Boone	1976
2	All I Want For Christmas Is You	Mariah Carey	1995
3	To Love You More	Céline Dion	1995
4	I Will Always Love You	Whitney Houston	1992
5	The Sound Of Silence	Simon & Garfunkel	1968
6	Otoko No Sekai (Mando – The Lovers Of The World)	Jerry Wallace	1970
7	Flashdance... What a Feeling	Irene Cara	1983
8	I'm In The Mood For Dancing	The Nolans	1980
9	Ani Holem Al Naomi	Hedva & David	1971
10	Last Christmas	Wham!	1984

Born in Birmingham, England, singer-songwriter Daniel Boone (Peter Charles Green) became a surprise one-hit-wonder around the world with 'Beautiful Sunday'. Having already made US Number 15 and UK Number 21 upon its release in 1972, the song become a smash in Japan four years later, where it has sold more than two million copies.

MTV
MUSIC TELEVISION

Record sales in Australia are collated by the Australian Recording Industry Association (ARIA), a trade group which was established in 1983 by six major record companies. It replaced the earlier Association of Australian Record Manufacturers (AARM).

THE BEST-SELLING
SINGLES OF THE 2000S IN AUSTRALIA

#	Title	Artist	Year
1	Angels Brought Me Here	Guy Sebastian	2003
2	The Prayer	Anthony Callea	2005
3	I Gotta Feeling	The Black Eyed Peas	2009
4	Poker Face	Lady Gaga	2008
5	What About Me	Shannon Noll	2004
6	So What	P!nk	2008
7	Lose Yourself	Eminem	2002
8	Sexy Bitch	David Guetta featuring Akon	2009
9	Sex On Fire	Kings of Leon	2008
10	Love Story	Taylor Swift	2009
11	The Ketchup Song (Aserejé)	Las Ketchup	2002
12	Just Dance	Lady Gaga featuring Colby O'Donis	2008
13	Low	Flo Rida featuring T-Pain	2008
14	Boom Boom Pow	The Black Eyed Peas	2009
15	I'm Yours	Jason Mraz	2008
16	Without Me	Eminem	2002
17	Teenage Dirtbag	Wheatus	2000
18	Right Round	Flo Rida featuring Ke$ha	2009
19	Born To Try	Delta Goodrem	2003
20	Dilemma	Nelly featuring Kelly Rowland	2002

Guy Sebastian was the *Australian Idol* winner in 2003. His ballad, 'Angels Brought Me Here' also topped charts in four Asian countries and New Zealand.

THE BEST-SELLING
SINGLES OF 2009 IN AUSTRALIA

Right: Australia's very own Guy Sebastian – top of the 2009 singles chart.

THE BEST-SELLING ALBUMS OF 2009 IN AUSTRALIA

1	I Dreamed A Dream	Susan Boyle
2	Funhouse	P!nk
3	The E.N.D. (The Energy Never Dies)	The Black Eyed Peas
4	Fearless	Taylor Swift
5	It's Not Me, It's You	Lily Allen
6	Crazy Love	Michael Bublé
7	Only By The Night	Kings of Leon
8	The Essential Michael Jackson	Michael Jackson
9	The Fame	Lady Gaga
10	I Am... Sasha Fierce	Beyoncé
11	Twilight	Soundtrack
12	State Of The Art	Hilltop Hoods
13	Number Ones	Michael Jackson
14	Cradlesong	Rob Thomas
15	Hannah Montana – The Movie	Soundtrack
16	Dark Horse	Nickelback
17	Relapse	Eminem
18	Walking On A Dream	Empire of the Sun
19	21st Century Breakdown	Green Day
20	Been Waiting	Jessica Mauboy

Six of the top 10 are by female artistes, and only three of the top 20 albums (#s 12, 18 and 20) were recorded by home-grown talent.

THE BEST-SELLING ALBUMS OF THE 2000S IN AUSTRALIA

1	Innocent Eyes	Delta Goodrem	2003
2	Funhouse	P!nk	2008
3	I'm Not Dead	P!nk	2006
4	Come Away With Me	Norah Jones	2003
5	The Sound Of White	Missy Higgins	2005
6	Only By The Night	Kings of Leon	2008
7	Get Born	Jet	2004
8	Back To Bedlam	James Blunt	2006
9	Greatest Hits	Robbie Williams	2004
10	The Eminem Show	Eminem	2002
11	Odyssey Number Five	Powderfinger	2000
12	Michael Bublé	Michael Bublé	2004
13	Fever	Kylie Minogue	2001
14	Let Go	Avril Lavigne	2002
15	Fallen	Evanescence	2004
16	Life For Rent	Dido	2003
17	Feeler	Pete Murray	2004
18	I Dreamed A Dream	Susan Boyle	2009
19	A Rush Of Blood To The Head	Coldplay	2003
20	1	The Beatles	2000

THE BEST-SELLING ALBUMS OF ALL-TIME IN AUSTRALIA

1	Whispering Jack	John Farnham	1986
2	Bat Out Of Hell	Meat Loaf	1977
3	Thriller	Michael Jackson	1982
4	Come On Over	Shania Twain	1997
5	Innocent Eyes	Delta Goodrem	2003
6	Jagged Little Pill	Alanis Morissette	1995
7	Greatest Hits	Queen	1981
8	Born In The U.S.A.	Bruce Springsteen	1984
9	Recurring Dream – The Very Best Of Crowded House	Crowded House	1986
10	Rumours	Fleetwood Mac	1977

Although born in England, John Farnham has lived in Australia since the age of ten, where he became a teen pop idol in the 1960s. Graduating to a harder rock/pop sound in the 1980s, the success of his best-selling *Whispering Jack* album was boosted by the anthemic, award-winning Aussie number one hit single, 'You're the Voice' in 1986.

The New Zealand charts are compiled by the Recording Industry Association of New Zealand (RIANZ), a non-profit organization representing artists, producers and distributors.

Left: Smashproof: Tyree, Deach and Young Sid.

1	I Gotta Feeling	The Black Eyed Peas
2	Brother	Smashproof featuring Gin
3	Sexy Bitch	David Guetta featuring Akon
4	TiK ToK	Ke$ha
5	Boom Boom Pow	The Black Eyed Peas
6	I'm Yours	Jason Mraz
7	Right Round	Flo Rida featuring Ke$ha
8	Halo	Beyoncé
9	Sweet Dreams	Beyoncé
10	Knock You Down	Keri Hilson featuring Kanye West

THE BEST-SELLING ALBUMS OF 2009 IN NEW ZEALAND

The top-selling album by an indigenous artist was by Virginia Wigmore, aka Gin – who recorded her debut album, *Holy Smoke*, with members from Ryan Adams' backing band, the Cardinals.

Beyoncé's 'Halo' spent 33 weeks on the New Zealand chart, more than any other single in 2009.

MUSIC TELEVISION

European sales data has been collated by *Billboard* and *Music & Media* magazines since 1984. The singles chart is based on sales from 15 European countries – Austria, Belgium, Denmark, Finland, France, Germany, Hungary, Ireland, Italy, the Netherlands, Norway, Spain, Sweden, Switzerland and the UK.

THE BEST-SELLING SINGLES OF 2009 IN EUROPE

1	Poker Face	Lady Gaga
2	Hot N Cold	Katy Perry
3	Sexy Bitch	David Guetta featuring Akon
4	I Gotta Feeling	The Black Eyed Peas
5	Infinity 2008	The Guru Josh Project
6	When Love Takes Over	David Guetta featuring Kelly Rowland
7	Womanizer	Britney Spears
8	I Know You Want Me (Calle Ocho)	Pitbull
9	Broken Strings	James Morrison featuring Nelly Furtado
10	Ça M'enerve	Helmut Fritz

Not a rock song in sight for the year's Top 10, which is dominated by dancefloor pop.

THE BEST-SELLING ALBUMS OF 2009 IN EUROPE

Acts from the United States monopolize the top four slots for the best-selling albums in Europe.

IRELAND

Irish sales figures are compiled by the Irish Recorded Music Association (IRMA), a non-profit organization established by record companies and comprising 51 members.

THE BEST-SELLING ALBUMS OF 2009 IN IRELAND

With popular Irish stalwarts U2 and Westlife unsurprisingly on the list, it is good to see relative newcomers The Script anchoring the Number 10 position. The Dublin rock/pop trio of Danny O'Donoghue, Mark Sheehan and Glen Power released their self-titled debut album to glowing reviews in August 2008.

THE BEST-SELLING SINGLES OF 2009 IN IRELAND

1	The Climb	Joe McElderry
2	I Gotta Feeling	The Black Eyed Peas
3	Poker Face	Lady Gaga
4	Just Dance	Lady Gaga featuring Colby O'Donis
5	Fight For This Love	Cheryl Cole
6	Meet Me Halfway	The Black Eyed Peas
7	Hallelujah	Alexandra Burke
8	Bad Boys	Alexandra Burke featuring Flo Rida
9	Broken Strings	James Morrison featuring Nelly Furtado
10	Bad Romance	Lady Gaga

English singer Joe McElderry won the sixth series of *X Factor* in the UK performing his version of the Miley Cyrus hit ballad 'The Climb', which subsequently spent four weeks atop the Irish chart.

French sales data is compiled by the Syndicat National de l'Edition Phonographique (SNEP), which has been in existence since 1922 and has 48 member companies.

THE BEST-SELLING SINGLES OF 2009 IN FRANCE

1	Ça M'énerve	Helmut Fritz
2	Même Pas Fatigué!!!	Magic System & Khaled
3	Tatoue-moi	Mikelangelo Loconte
4	Poker Face	Lady Gaga
5	Takin' Back My Love	Enrique Iglesias featuring Ciara
6	J'aimerais Tellement	Jena Lee
7	I Know You Want Me (Calle Ocho)	Pitbull
8	Lady Melody	Tom Frager
9	I Hate This Part	The Pussycat Dolls
10	Like A Hobo	Charlie Winston

Despite his German-sounding name, Helmut Fritz is the performing name of Eric Greff, a Frenchman. The literal translation of his top-selling Ça M'énerve is 'It Gets On My Nerves'.

THE BEST-SELLING SINGLES ALL-TIME IN FRANCE

1	La Danse Des Canards	J.J. Lionel	1981
2	Belle	Patrick Fiori, Garou & Daniel Lavoie	1998
3	Candle In The Wind 1997	Elton John	1997
4	You're The One That I Want	John Travolta & Olivia Newton-John	1978
5	Aserejé (The Ketchup Song)	Las Ketchup	2002
6	Lambada	Kaoma	1989
7	Éthiopie	Chanteurs Sans Frontières	1985
8	Chante	Les Forbans	1982
9	Mambo No. 5	Lou Bega	1999
10	Ces Soirées-là	Yannick	2000
11	Pour Le Plaisir	Herbert Léonard	1981
12	YMCA	Village People	1978
13	La Musique (Angelica)	Star Academy	2001
14	Rockcollection	Laurent Voulzy	1977
15	Alane	Wes	1997
16	La Tribu De Dana	Manau	1998
17	Born To Be Alive	Patrick Hernandez	1978
18	Les Rois Du Monde	Roméo et Juliette	2000
19	La Chenille	La Bande A Basile	1977
20	(Un, Dos, Tres) Maria	Ricky Martin	1996

Translated as 'The Dance of the Ducks', J.J. Lionel's 1981 novelty smash has sold more than 3,500,000 copies in France. Elton John's reversioned 'Candle In The Wind 1997' blew past the two million mark in the year of its release – and is the only song by a British artist to have made it into the French top 20.

THE BEST-SELLING ALBUMS OF 2009 IN FRANCE

1	Les Enfoirés Font Leur Cinéma	Les Enfoirés
2	Soul	Seal
3	Hobo	Charlie Winston
4	Mozart, l'Opéra Rock	Mozart, l'Opéra Rock
5	Toi + Moi	Grégoire
6	The E.N.D. (The Energy Never Dies)	The Black Eyed Peas
7	No Line on the Horizon	U2
8	The Resistance	Muse
9	L'embellie	Calogero
10	One Love	David Guetta

Les Enfoirés is an annual collaboration of musicians and celebrities – never the same lineup – who perform together in concert to raise funds for Les Restos du Coeur charity. Font Leur Cinéma is the organization's 19th album since 1989.

Right: Elton John singing live in concert in 2008.

German charts were introduced in 1953, when *Der Automatenmarkt* ("The Vending Machine Market") published a monthly list based on jukebox plays. In 1977, Media Control GfK International began compiling official sales charts and continues to do so.

THE BEST-SELLING SINGLES OF 2009 IN GERMANY

1	Poker Face	Lady Gaga
2	Jungle Drum	Emilíana Torrini
3	Ayo Technology	Milow
4	Stadt	Cassandra Steen featuring Adel Tawi
5	Dance With Somebody	Mando Diao
6	Wire To Wire	Razorlight
7	Irgendwas Bleibt	Silbermond
8	Heavy Cross	Gossip
9	I Gotta Feeling	The Black Eyed Peas
10	When Love Takes Over	David Guetta featuring Kelly Rowland
11	If A Song Could Get Me You	Marit Larsen
12	Broken Strings	James Morrison featuring Nelly Furtado
13	Hot N Cold	Katy Perry
14	Sexy Bitch	David Guetta featuring Akon
15	Allein Allein	Polarkreis 18
16	Bodies	Robbie Williams
17	Haus Am See	Peter Fox
18	Halo	Beyoncé
19	Anything But Love	Daniel Schuhmacher
20	Mamacita	Mark Medlock

Runner-up Emiliana Torrini is the best-selling Icelandic female singer after Björk. Recording since 1993, she performed the notable end-theme song to the 2002 movie *The Lord of the Rings: The Two Towers*.

THE BEST-SELLING SINGLES OF THE 2000S IN GERMANY

1	Ein Stern (Der Deinen Namen Trägt)	DJ Ötzi & Nik P.
2	The Ketchup Song (Aserejé)	Las Ketchup
3	Poker Face	Lady Gaga
4	Apologize	Timbaland Presents OneRepublic
5	Daylight	No Angels
6	Der Steuersong	Die Gerd-Show
7	Only Time (Remix)	Enya
8	Believe	Bro'Sis
9	Whenever, Wherever	Shakira
10	We Have A Dream	DSDS
11	Schnappi, Das Kleine Krokodil	Schnappi
12	Dragostea Din Tei	The O-Zone
13	All Good Things (Come To An End)	Nelly Furtado
14	From Sarah With Love	Sarah Connor
15	Can't Get You Out Of My Head	Kylie Minogue
16	Das Beste	Silbermond
17	Es Ist Geil, Ein Arschloch Zu Sein	Christian
18	Played-A-Live (The Bongosong)	Safri Duo
19	Spirit Of The Hawk	Rednex
20	La Passion	Gigi D'Agostino

DJ Ötzi is an Austrian-born entertainer who began his career as a karaoke singer in his native Tirol. His 'Ein Stern' smash was also named Single of the Year at the 2008 German *ECHO* Awards.

THE BEST-SELLING ALBUMS OF THE 2000S IN GERMANY

1	Mensch	Herbert Grönemeyer
2	1	The Beatles
3	Swing When You're Winning	Robbie Williams
4	Back To Black	Amy Winehouse
5	Vom Selben Stern	Ich+Ich
6	Greatest Hits	Robbie Williams
7	Escapology	Robbie Williams
8	Loose	Nelly Furtado
9	Die Neue Best Of…	Andrea Berg
10	Intensive Care	Robbie Williams
11	Black Ice	AC/DC
12	Das Große Leben	Rosenstolzo
13	Piece By Piece	Katie Melua
14	Stadtaffe	Peter Fox
15	Telegramm Für X	Xavier Naidoo
16	Come Away With Me	Norah Jones
17	So Weit… Best Of Westernhagen	Westernhagen
18	A Day Without Rain	Enya
19	Freak Of Nature	Anastacia
20	This Is The Life	Amy Macdonald

In addition to being one of his country's best-selling German-language singers, Herbert Grönemeyer is a popular actor who first came to international attention as war correspondent Lieutenant Werner in the 1981 epic, *Das Boot*. Outside of the UK, Germany remains the most successful market for Robbie Williams, who dominates the top 10 with four entries.

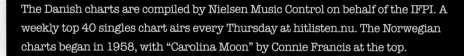

The Danish charts are compiled by Nielsen Music Control on behalf of the IFPI. A weekly top 40 singles chart airs every Thursday at hitlisten.nu. The Norwegian charts began in 1958, with "Carolina Moon" by Connie Francis at the top.

Below: Medina at the 2009 MTV Europe Music awards in Gemany.

THE BEST-SELLING SINGLES OF 2009 IN DENMARK

1	Kun For Mig	Medina
2	Poker Face	Lady Gaga
3	Back To The '80s	Aqua
4	Engel	Rasmus Seebach
5	Taxa	Sanne Salomonsen
6	Ayo Technology	Milow
7	Yo-Yo	Joey Moe
8	When Love Takes Over	David Guetta featuring Kelly Rowland
9	Det Bedste Til Sidst	Linda Andrews
10	Velkommen Til Medina	Medina

THE BEST-SELLING ALBUMS OF 2009 IN DENMARK

THE BEST-SELLING SINGLES ALL-TIME IN NORWAY

1	Love Hurts	Nazareth	1975
2	Ambitions	Donkeyboy	2009
3	I Love You Because	Jim Reeves	1964
4	I Can Help	Billy Swan	1975
5	Daddy Cool	Boney M	1976
6	Yes Sir, I Can Boogie	Baccara	1977
7	Livet Er For Kjipt	Lars Kilevold	1980
8	Living Next Door To Alice	Smokie	1977
9	I Love To Love	Tina Charles	1976
10	Moviestar	Harpo	1976

THE BEST-SELLING ALBUMS ALL-TIME IN NORWAY

1	The Best Of Buck Owens	Buck Owens	1967
2	Du Ar Den Ende	Lill Lindfors	1967
3	Bridge Over Troubled Water	Simon & Garfunkel	1970
4	!!Going Places!!	Herb Alpert & the Tijuana Brass	1967
5	Jesus Christ Superstar	Soundtrack	1971
6	The Sound Of Music	Soundtrack	1967
7	Born In The U.S.A.	Bruce Springsteen	1984
8	Hair	Original Cast	1969
9	Dark Side Of The Moon	Pink Floyd	1973
10	Teaser And The Firecat	Cat Stevens	1971

Right: Nazareth hailed from Scotland but were huge in Norway.

THE BEST-SELLING SINGLES OF 2009 IN SWEDEN

THE BEST-SELLING SINGLES ALL-TIME IN SWEDEN

1	Curly Sue	Takida	2007
2	Halo	Beyoncé	2009
3	Poker Face	Lady Gaga	2008
4	Det Vackraste	Cecilia Vennersten	1995
5	Moviestar	Harpo	1975
6	Everytime We Touch	Cascada	2006
7	När Vi Gräver Guid I USA	Glenmark Eriksson Strömstedt	1994
8	Viva La Vida	Coldplay	2008
9	Candle In The Wind 1997/(Something About the Way) You Look Tonight	Elton John	1997
10	Bring Me To Life	Evanescence	2003

The first Dutch chart was compiled in January 1965, and saw the Beatles' 'I Feel Fine' at the pole position. Radio 538 broadcasts the top 40 on Friday afternoons.

THE BEST-SELLING SINGLES
OF ALL-TIME IN THE NETHERLANDS

1	No One But You	B-Yentl	2008
2	Kabouterdans	Kabouter Plop	2001
3	This Is The Life	Amy Macdonald	2007
4	Rood	Marco Borsato	2006
5	Viva La Vida	Coldplay	2008
6	Que Si Que No	Jody Bernal	2000
7	The Road Ahead	City To City	1999
8	Sweet Goodbyes	Krezip	2009
9	Rosanne	Nick & Simon	2008
10	Het Is Een Nacht	Guus Meeuwis & Vagant	1995

THE BEST-SELLING ALBUMS
OF ALL-TIME IN THE NETHERLANDS

1	Buena Vista Social Club	Buena Vista Social Club	1997
2	Al 15 Jaar Gewoon André	André Hazes	1995
3	Als Geen Ander	Marco Borsato	1995
4	World Of Hurt	Ilse DeLange	1998
5	Romanza	Andrea Bocelli	1997
6	Jagged Little Pill	Alanis Morissette	1995
7	Come Away With Me	Norah Jones	2002
8	19	Adele	2008
9	Back To Black	Amy Winehouse	2006
10	Vandaag	Nick & Simon	2007

The Netherlands has long been a region in which World Music has thrived. The genre's most successful project, *Buena Vista Social Club*, was recorded in Cuba by American guitarist Ry Cooder in 1996.

Left: Amy Macdonald live in Germany in 2009.

Left: Manuel Galban and Barbarito Torres from the Buena Vista Social Club.

The Swiss charts are compiled by Media Control AG. The first-ever chart was published in January 1968, with Roland W.'s 'Monja' at the top, subsequently replaced by John Fred & His Playboy Band's 'Judy in Disguise (With Glasses)'.

THE BEST-SELLING SINGLES
IN SWITZERLAND OF ALL-TIME

The entire top 10 consists of songs released since 2005: the advent of mass digital downloading has rescued declining singles sales worldwide.

1	Gold – Greatest Hits	Abba	1992
2	Back To Black	Amy Winehouse	2007
3	Come Away With Me	Norah Jones	2002
4	Uf U Dervo	Gölä	1998
5	D'eux	Céline Dion	1995
6	Private Dancer	Tina Turner	1984
7	Californication	Red Hot Chili Peppers	1999
8	Piece By Piece	Katie Melua	2005
9	This Is The Life	Amy Macdonald	2008
10	Not That Kind	Anastacia	2000

Gölä – a home-grown rock band named after its monosyllabic front man – is responsible for the most popular German-speaking Swiss album of all time, attaining quintuple platinum award status.

The Italian charts are compiled by Federazione Industria Musicale Italiana (FIMI), which has been doing so since January 2000, with Ronan Keating's "When You Say Nothing at All" taking the honours as the first official number one.

THE BEST-SELLING SINGLES OF 2009 IN ITALY

1	Domani 21.04.2009	Artisti Uniti Per L'Abruzzo
2	Sincerita	Arisa
3	I Gotta Feeling	The Black Eyed Peas
4	Poker Face	Lady Gaga
5	Il Regalo Piu' Grande	Tiziano Ferro
6	L'amore Si Odia	Noemi featuring Fiorella Mannoia
7	She Wolf/Loba	Shakira
8	This Is The Life	Amy Macdonald
9	Meraviglioso	Negramaro
10	Come Foglie	Malika Ayane

Above: Arisa, the hugely popular and talented singer from Italy.

More than 50 Italian musicians came together as Artists United for Abruzzo to record a single to raise money for the reconstruction and restoration of historic buildings damaged or destroyed by earthquake that devastated Abruzzo, Central Italy on April 6, 2009. The result was the top-selling single of the year.

THE BEST-SELLING ALBUMS OF 2009 IN ITALY

Born in Latina, Italian pop singer/pianist Tiziano Ferro – who was named Best Italian Artist at the 2004 MTV Europe Music Awards – also records his albums in Spanish.

The official Spanish charts, compiled by PROMUSICAE (Productores de Musica de Espana), have been in existence since 2005.

THE BEST-SELLING SINGLES OF 2009 IN SPAIN

1	Colgando En Tus Manos	Carlos Baute & Marta Sanchez
2	Infinity 2008	The Guru Josh Project
3	I Know You Want Me (Calle Ocho)	Pitbull
4	Moving	Macaco
5	I Gotta A Feeling	The Black Eyed Peas
6	This Is My Life	Amy Macdonald
7	Loba	Shakira
8	Malu Que Nadie	Manuel Carrasco
9	Halo	Beyoncé
10	Viva La Vida	Coldplay

'Colgando En Tus Manos' by the Venezuelan/Spanish pairing of Carlos Baute and Marta Sanchez spent a record 29 weeks atop the Spanish chart (including its run in December 2008).

THE BEST-SELLING ALBUMS OF 2009 IN SPAIN

1	Vinagre Y Rosas	Joaquin Sabina
2	Antes De Que Cuente Diez	Fito Y Los Fitipaldis
3	Paridiso Express	Alejandro Sanz
4	Sin Mirar Atras	David Bisbal
5	Duermevela	El Barrio
6	Amaia Montero	Amaia Montero
7	No Line On The Horizon	U2
8	Estopa X Anniversarivm	Estopa
9	50 Anos Despues	Raphael
10	El Canto Del Loco	El Canto Del Loco

61-year old Spanish singer-songwriter and poet Joaquin Sabina made a triumphant return to the Spanish music scene with his best-selling 'Vinagre Y Rosas' ("Vinegar and Roses").

I WANT MY MTV

On August 1, 1981 at 12:01 am Eastern Standard Time, MTV was launched with the greeting: "Ladies and Gentleman, rock and roll," spoken by network executive John Lack. The original theme music, composed by John Petersen and Jonathan Elias, was then played over a montage of public domain footage of the Apollo 11 moon landing with an MTV logo flag inserted into the moon's earth, followed by the playing of its first video. Ironically, although a chart-topper in its native UK, Buggles' 'Video Killed the Radio Star' was only a modest success in the US (reaching number 40 in 1979).

THE FIRST MUSIC VIDEOS BROADCAST ON MTV

Video Killed The Radio Star	The Buggles
You Better Run	Pat Benatar
She Won't Dance With Me	Rod Stewart
You Better You Bet	The Who
Little Suzi's On The Up	PhD
We Don't Talk Anymore	Cliff Richard
Brass In Pocket	The Pretenders
Time Heals	Todd Rundgren
Take It On The Run	REO Speedwagon
Rockin' The Paradise	Styx
When Things Go Wrong	Robin Lane & the Chartbusters
History Never Repeats	Split Enz
Hold On Loosely	38 Special
Just Between You And Me	April Wine
Sailing	Rod Stewart
Iron Maiden	Iron Maiden
Keep On Loving You	REO Speedwagon
Message Of Love	The Pretenders
Mr. Briefcase	Lee Ritenour
Double Life	The Cars
In The Air Tonight	Phil Collins
Looking For Clues	Robert Palmer
Too Late	Shoes
Stop Draggin' My Heart Around	Stevie Nicks & Tom Petty & the Heartbreakers
Surface Tension	Rupert Hine
One Step Beyond	Madness
Baker Street	Gerry Rafferty
I'm Gonna Follow You	Pat Benatar
Savannah Nights	Tom Johnston
Lucille	Rockestra

Above: Geoff Downes and Trevor Horn: Buggles.

Below: Eric Clapton goes acoustic in 1992.

THE FIRST ACTS ON MTV UNPLUGGED

Date of performance, all filmed at the National Video Center, New York, NY:

October 31, 1989
Squeeze
Syd Straw
Elliot Easton

December 13, 1989
Smithereens
Graham Parker

10,000 Maniacs
Michael Penn

December 14, 1989
Alarm
Nuclear Valdez
Joe Walsh
Dr. John

THE BEST-SELLING MTV UNPLUGGED ALBUMS IN THE US

1	Unplugged – Eric Clapton	1992
2	MTV Unplugged in New York – Nirvana	1994
3	Unplugged – Shakira	2000
4	MTV Unplugged – Maná	1999
5	Unplugged... and Seated – Rod Stewart	1993
6	MTV Unplugged EP – Mariah Carey	1992
7	MTV Unplugged – Ricky Martin	2006
8	MTV Unplugged – 10,000 Maniacs	1993
9	MTV Unplugged – Alejandro Sanz	2001
10	MTV Unplugged – Tony Bennett	1995

Clapton's acoustic classic – with 10 million in US sales – has sold twice as many as Nirvana's runner-up. The first artist to release an MTV unplugged performance as an album was Paul McCartney: his recording from January 25, 1991 was issued as *Unplugged (The Official Bootleg)* on May 20, 1991.

THE GREATEST POP SONGS, COMPILED BY ROLLING STONE AND MTV IN 2000

#	Song	Artist	Year
1	Yesterday	The Beatles	1965
2	(I Can't Get No) Satisfaction	The Rolling Stones	1965
3	Smells Like Teen Spirit	Nirvana	1992
4	Like a Virgin	Madonna	1985
5	Billie Jean	Michael Jackson	1983
6	I Want To Hold Your Hand	The Beatles	1964
7	Respect	Aretha Franklin	1967
8	With Or Without You	U2	1987
9	I Want You Back	The Jackson 5	1969
10	I Want It That Way	The Backstreet Boys	1999
11	Hotel California	The Eagles	1976
12	Where Did Our Love Go	The Supremes	1964
13	Sweet Child O' Mine	Guns N' Roses	1988
14	Brown Sugar	The Rolling Stones	1971
15	Imagine	John Lennon	1971
16	Nothing Compares 2 U	Sinéad O'Connor	1990
17	Superstition	Stevie Wonder	1972
18	Losing My Religion	R.E.M.	1991
19	Vogue	Madonna	1990
20	Like A Rolling Stone	Bob Dylan	1965
21	Brown Eyed Girl	Van Morrison	1967
22	Beat It	Michael Jackson	1983
23	Oh, Pretty Woman	Roy Orbison	1964
24	What's Goin' On	Marvin Gaye	1971
25	... Baby One More Time	Britney Spears	1999
26	Go Your Own Way	Fleetwood Mac	1976
27	When Doves Cry	Prince	1984
28	Mmm Bop	Hanson	1997
29	Bohemian Rhapsody	Queen	1975
30	Your Song	Elton John	1971
31	Smooth	Santana featuring Rob Thomas	1999
32	(Sittin' On) The Dock Of The Bay	Otis Redding	1968
33	My Generation	The Who	1966
34	Ironic	Alanis Morissette	1996
35	Born To Run	Bruce Springsteen	1975
36	Waterfalls	TLC	1995
37	O.P.P.	Naughty By Nature	1991
38	Changes	David Bowie	1971
39	Iris	The Goo Goo Dolls	1998
40	I Will Always Love You	Whitney Houston	1993
41	Proud Mary	Creedence Clearwater Revival	1969
42	Every Breath You Take	The Police	1983
43	Miss You	The Rolling Stones	1978
44	Dancing Queen	Abba	1976
45	Tears In Heaven	Eric Clapton	1992
46	The Track Of My Tears	Smokey Robinson & the Miracles	1965
47	Jump	Van Halen	1984
48	Jeremy	Pearl Jam	1992
49	Tangled Up In Blue	Bob Dylan	1975
50	Little Red Corvette	Prince	1983

Below: Dire Straits' Mark Knopfler live in '85.

THE FIRST MUSIC VIDEOS BROADCAST ON MTV EUROPE

#	Song	Artist
1	Money For Nothing	Dire Straits
2	Fake	Alexander O'Neal
3	You Got The Look	Prince with Sheena Easton
4	It's A Sin	Pet Shop Boys
5	I Wanna Dance With Somebody	Whitney Houston
6	I Want Your Sex	George Michael
7	Who's That Girl	Madonna
8	I Really Didn't Mean It	Luther Vandross
9	Misfit	Curiosity Killed The Cat
10	Higher And Higher	Jackie Wilson

MTV Europe began its pan-European broadcasting on August 1, 1987 with Dire Straits' 'Money For Nothing' clip featuring the opening lyric, sung by its co-writer, Sting: 'I Want My MTV'. MTV Europe celebrated its fifth anniversary in 1992 with a party at the House of Commons. From August 2007, its editorial headquarters moved from London to Warsaw in Poland, though it still transmits its signal from the UK capital.

MTV EUROPE MOST PLAYED VIDEO SONGS OF 2009

#	Song	Artist
1	Poker Face	Lady Gaga
2	I Gotta Feeling	The Black Eyed Peas
3	Sexy Chick	David Guetta featuring Akon
4	When Love Takes Over	David Guetta featuring Kelly Rowland
5	I Know You Want Me (Calle Ocho)	Pitbull
6	Hot N Cold	Katy Perry
7	Broken Strings	James Morrison featuring Nelly Furtado
8	Live Your Live	T.I. featuring Rihanna
9	Boom Boom Pow	The Black Eyed Peas
10	Jai Ho! (You Are My Destiny)	A.R. Rahman & the Pussycat Dolls featuring Nicole Scherzinger

MTV
MUSIC TELEVISION

MTV VIDEO MUSIC AWARDS

Three years after launching, MTV introduced an annual awards ceremony to celebrate the best music videos of the year. The first ceremony took place at New York's Radio City Music Hall on September 14, 1984 and has been held annually ever since.

THE WINNERS OF THE VIDEO OF THE YEAR AWARD

You Might Think	The Cars	1984
The Boys Of Summer	Don Henley	1985
Money For Nothing	Dire Straits	1986
Sledgehammer	Peter Gabriel	1987
Need You Tonight/Mediate	INXS	1988
This Note's For You	Neil Young	1989
Nothing Compares 2 U	Sinéad O'Connor	1990
Losing My Religion	R.E.M.	1991
Right Now	Van Halen	1992
Jeremy	Pearl Jam	1993
Cryin'	Aerosmith	1994
Waterfalls	TLC	1995
Tonight, Tonight	The Smashing Pumpkins	1996
Virtual Insanity	Jamiroquai	1997
Ray Of Light	Madonna	1998
Doo Wop (That Thing)	Lauryn Hill	1999
The Real Slim Shady	Eminem	2000
Lady Marmalade	Christina Aguilera, Lil' Kim, Mya & P!nk featuring Missy Elliott	2001
Without Me	Eminem	2002
Work It	Missy Elliott	2003
Hey Ya	OutKast	2004
Boulevard of Broken Dreams	Green Day	2005
I Write Sins Not Tragedies	Panic! At The Disco	2006
Umbrella	Rihanna featuring Jay-Z	2007
Piece Of Me	Britney Spears	2008
Single Ladies (Put A Ring On It)	Beyoncé	2009

Below: Rihanna, 2007's MTV VMA Video of the Year award winner: 'Umbrella' (featuring Jay-Z).

Eminem and Missy Elliott (the latter sharing the award as a featured artist in 2001) are the only artists to have lifted MTV's Video of the Year trophy twice.

Right: Madonna flies the flag for the USA.

THE ARTISTS WITH THE MOST MTV AWARDS

Madonna	20
Peter Gabriel	13
R.E.M.	12
Green Day	11
Aerosmith	10
Beyoncé	9
Eminem	9
Jay-Z	9
a-ha	8
Fatboy Slim	8
Janet Jackson	8
En Vogue	7
Michael Jackson	7
Red Hot Chili Peppers	7
Paula Abdul	6
Beck	6
*NSync	6
The Smashing Pumpkins	6
Justin Timberlake	6
Don Henley	5
U2	5

THE WINNERS OF THE VIDEO VANGUARD AWARD

Richard Lester	1984	Julien Temple	1987	R.E.M.	1995
The Beatles	1984	Peter Gabriel	1987	LL Cool J	1997
David Bowie	1984	Michael Jackson	1988	Mark Romanek	1997
Kevin Godley & Lol Creme	1985	George Michael	1989	The Beastie Boys	1998
Russell Mulcahy	1985	Janet Jackson	1990	Red Hot Chili Peppers	2000
David Byrne	1985	Bon Jovi & Wayne Isham	1991	U2	2001
Zbigniew Rybczynski	1986	Guns N' Roses	1992	Duran Duran	2003
Madonna	1986	Tom Petty	1994	Hype Williams	2006

THE WINNERS OF THE MTV VIEWER'S CHOICE AWARD

Thriller	Michael Jackson	1984
We Are The World	USA for Africa	1985
Take On Me	a-ha	1986
With Or Without You	U2	1987
Need You Tonight/Mediate	INXS	1988
Like A Prayer	Madonna	1989
Janie's Got A Gun	Aerosmith	1990
Silent Lucidity	Queensryche	1991
Under The Bridge	Red Hot Chili Peppers	1992
Livin' On The Edge	Aerosmith	1993
Cryin'	Aerosmith	1994
Waterfalls	TLC	1995
Glycerine	Bush	1996
Breathe	Prodigy	1997
It's All About The Benjamins	Puff Daddy & the Family	1998
I Want It That Way	Backstreet Boys	1999
Bye Bye Bye	*NSync	2000
Pop	*NSync	2001
Everywhere	Michelle Branch	2002
Lifestyles Of The Rich and Famous	Good Charlotte	2003
Breaking The Habit	Linkin Park	2004
American Idiot	Green Day	2005
Dance, Dance	Fall Out Boy	2006

THE WINNERS OF THE BEST NEW ARTIST IN A VIDEO AWARD

Sweet Dreams (Are Made of This)	Eurythmics	1984
Voices Carry	'Til Tuesday	1985
Take On Me	a-ha	1986
Don't Dream It's Over	Crowded House	1987
Welcome To The Jungle	Guns N' Roses	1988
Cult Of Personality	Living Colour	1989
No Myth	Michael Penn	1990
Right Here, Right Now	Jesus Jones	1991
Smells Like Teen Spirit	Nirvana	1992
Plush	Stone Temple Pilots	1993
Mr. Jones	Counting Crows	1994
Hold My Hand	Hootie & the Blowfish	1995
Ironic	Alanis Morissette	1996
Sleep To Dream	Fiona Apple	1997
Torn	Natalie Imbruglia	1998
My Name Is	Eminem	1999
I Try	Macy Gray	2000
Fallin	Alicia Keys	2001
Complicated	Avril Lavigne	2002
In Da Club	50 Cent	2003
This Love	Maroon 5	2004
Mr. Brightside	The Killers	2005
Bat Country	Avenged Sevenfold	2006
Gym Class Heroes	Gym Class Heroes	2007
Ready, Set, Go!	Tokio Hotel	2008
Poker Face	Lady Gaga	2009

The category was renamed Best New Artist in 2007.

Left: A scene from Michael Jackson's seminal 'Thriller' video.

Right: The Killers, from Las Vegas.

MTV MUSIC TELEVISION

THE PERFORMERS AT THE
MTV VIDEO MUSIC AWARDS

Since their inauguration in 1984 – when Madonna stole the show with an eye-popping rendition of 'Like A Virgin' – the MTV Video Music Awards have frequently featured provocative and legendary live performances by rock's top acts. Here are annual lists of the performers, and some unforgettable highlights.

1984

Rod Stewart • Madonna • Huey Lewis & the News • David Bowie • Tina Turner • ZZ Top • Ray Parker Jr.

Highlight: Madonna gave a show-stopping performance of 'Like a Virgin' wearing a provocative wedding gown/bustier ensemble.

1985

Eurythmics • David Ruffin, Eddie Kendrick & Daryl Hall & John Oates • Tears For Fears • John 'Cougar' Mellencamp • Pat Benatar • Sting • Eddie Murphy

1986

Robert Palmer • The Hooters • The Monkees • 'Til Tuesday • INXS • Van Halen • Mr. Mister • Simply Red • Whitney Houston • The Pet Shop Boys • Tina Turner • Genesis

Highlight: Whitney Houston wowed the audience with the up-tempo 'How Will I Know' and the timeless ballad 'Greatest Love of All'.

1987

Los Lobos • Bryan Adams • The Bangles • Bon Jovi • Crowded House • Madonna • Whitesnake • Whitney Houston • The Cars • David Bowie • Prince • Cyndi Lauper • Run-DMC & Steven Tyler

1988

Rod Stewart • Jody Watley • Aerosmith • Elton John • Bobby McFerrin • Depeche Mode • Crowded House • Michael Jackson • Cher • Chubby Checker & the Fat Boys • Guns N' Roses • INXS

Highlight: Michael Jackson made his first appearance at these VMAs, performing 'Bad'.

1989

Madonna • Bobby Brown • Def Leppard • Tone Loc • The Cult • Paula Abdul • Jon Bon Jovi & Richie Sambora • The Cure • Cher • The Rolling Stones • Axl Rose & Tom Petty & the Heartbreakers

1990

Janet Jackson • Mötley Crüe • MC Hammer • INXS • Sinead O'Connor • New Edition featuring Bobby Brown • Faith No More • Phil Collins • 2 Live Crew • World Party • Aerosmith • Madonna

1991

Van Halen • C+C Music Factory • Poison • Mariah Carey • EMF • Paula Abdul • Queensryche • LL Cool J • Metallica • Don Henley • Guns N' Roses • Prince & the New Power Generation

1992

The Black Crowes • Bobby Brown • U2 • Def Leppard • Nirvana • Elton John • Pearl Jam • Red Hot Chili Peppers • Michael Jackson • Bryan Adams • En Vogue • Eric Clapton • Guns N' Roses & Elton John

Highlights: Nirvana made their only MTV VMA performance in 1992, performing 'Lithium'. Elton John and Guns N' Roses combined on the latter's rock ballad, 'November Rain'.

1993

Madonna • Lenny Kravitz • Sting • Soul Asylum, Peter Buck & Victoria Williams • Aerosmith • Naughty By Nature • R.E.M. • Spin Doctors • Neil Young & Pearl Jam • The Edge • Janet Jackson

1994

Aerosmith • Boyz II Men • The Smashing Pumpkins • The Rolling Stones • Green Day • Beastie Boys • Alexander Red Army Ensemble & the Leningrad Cowboys • Salt-n-Pepa • Tom Petty & the Heartbreakers • Snoop Dogg • Stone Temple Pilots • Bruce Springsteen

Highlight: David Letterman made a surprise appearance, arm-in-arm with presenter Madonna. His only words: "I'll be out by the car. Watch your language."

1995

Michael Jackson • Live • TLC • R.E.M. • Red Hot Chili Peppers • Bon Jovi • Alanis Morissette • Hootie & the Blowfish • Hole • Green Day • White Zombie

Highlight: repeating their collaboration from the studio recording, Michael Jackson was joined onstage by Guns N' Roses guitarist Slash for a searing performance of 'Black or White'.

1996

The Smashing Pumpkins • The Fugees featuring Nas • Metallica • LL Cool J • Neil Young • Hootie & the Blowfish • Alanis Morissette • Bush • The Cranberries • Oasis • Bone Thugs-N-Harmony • Kiss

1997

Puff Daddy & the Family, 112, Faith Evans & Sting • Jewel • The Prodigy • Bruce Springsteen & the Wallflowers • Angie Martinez, Da Brat, Left Eye, Lil' Kim & Missy Elliott • U2 • Beck • Spice Girls • Jamiroquai • Marilyn Manson

1998

Madonna • Pras featuring Mya, Ol' Dirty Bastard & Wyclef Jean • Hole • Master P • The Backstreet Boys • The Beastie Boys • Brandy & Monica • The Dave Matthews Band • Marilyn Manson • The Brian Setzer Orchestra

1999

Kid Rock featuring Aerosmith & Run-DMC • Lauryn Hill • The Backstreet Boys • Ricky Martin • Nine Inch Nails • TLC • Fatboy Slim • Amil & Jay-Z • *NSync & Britney Spears • Eminem, Dr. Dre & Snoop Dogg

2000

Janet Jackson • Rage Against the Machine • Sisqo • Britney Spears • Eminem • Red Hot Chili Peppers • *NSync • Nelly • Christina Aguilera featuring Fred Durst • blink-182

Highlight: Britney Spears' performance of 'Oops!... I Did It Again' was the evening's showstopper with the pop diva wearing a revealing skin-coloured bodysuit.

2001

Alien Ant Farm • City High featuring Eve • Jennifer Lopez featuring Ja Rule • Linkin Park • Alicia Keys • *NSync & Michael Jackson • Jay-Z • Staind • Missy Elliott featuring Ludacris, Nelly Furtado & Trina • U2 • Britney Spears

Highlight: Michael Jackson made an unannounced appearance toward the finale of *NSync's 'Pop' performance.

2002

Avril Lavigne • Ludacris featuring I-20 & Mystikal • Bruce Springsteen & the E Street Band • P!nk • Ashanti, Ja Rule & Nas • Shakira • Eminem • Busta Rhymes, Ginuwine, P. Diddy, Pharrell & Usher • Sheryl Crow • The Hives • The Vines • Justin Timberlake featuring Clipse • Guns N' Roses

2003

The Black Eyed Peas • Sean Paul • Madonna featuring Britney Spears & Christina Aguilera & Missy Elliott • Good Charlotte • Christina Aguilera featuring Dave Navarro & Redman • 50 Cent featuring Snoop Dogg • Mary J. Blige featuring 50 Cent & Method Man • Coldplay • Beyoncé featuring Jay-Z • Metallica

Highlight: Once again, it was the ladies who provided the evening's most provocative moment with Madonna famously kissing both Britney Spears and Christina Aguilera.

2004

Anthony Hamilton & Jadakiss • Ashlee Simpson • New Found Glory • Usher featuring Lil' Jon & Ludacris • Jet • Yellowcard • Hoobastank • Kanye West featuring Chaka Khan • Eastside Boyz & Lil' Jon • The Ying Yang Twins • Petey Pablo • Terror Squad featuring Fat Joe • Jessica Simpson • Nelly featuring Christina Aguilera • Alicia Keys featuring Lenny Kravitz & Stevie Wonder • Polyphonic Spree • OutKast

Highlight: The awards were held for the first time outside their traditional home cities of Los Angeles or New York – at the American Airlines Arena in Miami.

2005

Green Day • Ludacris featuring Bobby Valentino • MC Hammer • Shakira featuring Alejandro Sanz • R. Kelly • The Killers • Diddy & Snoop Dogg • Don Omar • Tego Calderon • Daddy Yankee • Coldplay • Kanye West featuring Jamie Foxx • Mariah Carey • 50 Cent featuring Mobb Deep & Tony Yayo • My Chemical Romance • Kelly Clarkson

2006

Fergie • My Chemical Romance • The All-American Rejects • Justin Timberlake featuring Timbaland • Shakira featuring Wyclef Jean • Ludacris, Pharrell & the Pussycat Dolls • OK Go • Beyoncé • T.I. • Panic! At the Disco • Christina Aguilera • Tenacious D • The Killers

2007

Britney Spears • Kanye West • Akon & Mark Ronson • Fall Out Boy • Foo Fighters • Maroon 5 & Mark Ronson • T.I. featuring Justin Timberlake • Chris Brown featuring Rihanna • Justice, Mark Ronson & Wale • Foo Fighters featuring Cee-Lo • 50 Cent featuring Justin Timberlake • Linkin Park featuring Timbaland • Foo Fighters featuring Serj Tankian • Rihanna featuring Fall Out Boy • Alicia Keys • Common featuring Kanye West • Gym Class Heroes featuring Patrick Stump (Fall Out Boy) • 50 Cent • Mark Ronson & Daniel Merriweather • Mastodon featuring Josh Homme • Nelly Furtado, Keri Hilson, Timbaland & Justin Timberlake

2008

Rihanna • The Jonas Brothers • Paramore • P!nk • T.I. • Christina Aguilera • Kanye West • Katy Perry • Kid Rock • The Ting Tings • LL Cool J • Lupe Fiasco

2009

Janet Jackson • Katy Perry & Joe Perry • Taylor Swift • Lady Gaga • Green Day • Beyoncé • Muse • P!nk • Jay-Z (featuring Alicia Keys) • 3OH!3 • The All-American Rejects • Daniel Merriweather • Pitbull • Kid Cudi • Solange

Hosted by British comedian/actor Russell Brand, the show opened with a spoken tribute to Michael Jackson by Madonna and included a Janet Jackson tribute to her late brother, including 'Thriller', 'Bad', 'Smooth Criminal' and 'Scream'. Kanye West later controversially hijacked Taylor Swift's Best Female Video acceptance speech.

THE MTV EUROPE MUSIC AWARDS

The MTV Europe Music Awards were established in 1994 by MTV Networks Europe to honour the most popular music videos of the year in Europe. Unlike the MTV Awards in the US, most are voted for by the public. The first ceremony was staged in front of the Brandenburg Gate in Berlin, Germany in 1994.

1994

Best Song	Youssou N'Dour & Neneh Cherry – '7 Seconds'
Best Video	Whale – 'Hobo Humpin' Slobo Babe'
Best Female	Mariah Carey
Best Male	Bryan Adams
Best Group	Take That
Best New Act	Crash Test Dummies
Best Dance	The Prodigy
Best Rock	Aerosmith
Best Cover Song	Gun – 'Word Up!'
Free Your Mind	Amnesty International

Highlights: Prince dived into the crowd while playing 'Preach'; Bono collected the first Free Your Mind Award on behalf of Amnesty International.

1995

Best Song	The Cranberries – 'Zombie'
Best Video	Massive Attack – 'Protection'
Best Female	Björk
Best Male	Michael Jackson
Best Group	U2
Best New Act	Dog Eat Dog
Best Dance	East 17
Best Rock	Bon Jovi
Best Live Act	Take That
Free Your Mind	Greenpeace

Below: The Cranberries show off their Best Song Award in 1995.

1996

Best Song	Oasis – 'Wonderwall'
Best Female	Alanis Morissette
Best Male	George Michael
Best Group	Oasis
Best New Act	Garbage
Best Dance	The Prodigy
Best Rock	The Smashing Pumpkins
MTV Amour	The Fugees
MTV Select	Backstreet Boys – 'Get Down (You're The One For Me)'
Free Your Mind	The Buddies & Carers of Europe

Highlights: Held in London. Robbie Williams was MC and George Michael performed 'Star People'.

1997

Best Song	Hanson – 'MMMBop'
Best Video	The Prodigy – 'Breathe'
Best Female	Janet Jackson
Best Male	Jon Bon Jovi
Best Group	Spice Girls
Best New Act	Hanson
Best Dance	The Prodigy
Best Rock	Oasis
Best Alternative	The Prodigy
Best R&B	Blackstreet
Best Hip–Hop	Will Smith
Best Live Act	U2
MTV Select	Backstreet Boys – 'As Long As You Love Me'
Free Your Mind	The Landmine Survivors Network

1998

Best Song	Natalie Imbruglia – 'Torn'
Best Video	Massive Attack – 'Teardrop'
Best Album	Madonna – Ray Of Light
Best Female	Madonna
Best Male	Robbie Williams
Best Group	Spice Girls
Best New Act	All Saints
Best Pop	Spice Girls
Best Dance	The Prodigy
Best Rock	Aerosmith
Best Hip–Hop	The Beastie Boys
Free Your Mind	B92

1999

Best Song	Britney Spears – '... Baby One More Time'
Best Video	Blur – 'Coffee & TV'
Best Album	Boyzone – By Request
Best Female	Britney Spears
Best Male	Will Smith
Best Group	Backstreet Boys
Best New Act	Britney Spears
Best Pop	Britney Spears
Best Dance	Fatboy Slim
Best Rock	The Offspring
Best R&B	Whitney Houston
Best Hip Hop	Eminem
Free Your Mind	Bono

Highlights: Boyzone's Ronan Keating became the first person to host the Awards twice (also in 1997); punk veteran Iggy Pop powered through a typically energetic seven-minute version of 'Lust For Life'.

2000

Best Song	Robbie Williams – 'Rock DJ'
Best Video	Moby – 'Natural Blues'
Best Album	Eminem – *The Marshall Mathers LP*
Best Female	Madonna
Best Male	Ricky Martin
Best Group	Backstreet Boys
Best New Act	Blink-182
Best Pop	All Saints
Best Dance	Madonna
Best Rock	Red Hot Chili Peppers
Best R&B	Jennifer Lopez
Best Hip Hop	Eminem
Free Your Mind	Otpor

Highlights: Kylie Minogue and Robbie Williams teamed on 'Kids'; guest presenters included 'Mr. Madonna' Guy Ritchie, and über-model Heidi Klum.

2001

Best Song	Gorillaz – 'Clint Eastwood'
Best Video	The Avalanches – 'Since I Left You'
Best Album	Limp Bizkit – *Chocolate Starfish And The Hot Dog Flavored Water*
Best Female	Jennifer Lopez
Best Male	Robbie Williams
Best Group	Limp Bizkit
Best New Act	Dido
Best Pop	Anastacia
Best Dance	Gorillaz
Best Rock	Blink-182
Best R&B	Craig David
Best Hip Hop	Eminem
Web Award	Limp Bizkit www.limpbizkit.com
Free Your Mind	The Treatment Action Campaign (TAC)

2002

Best Song	P!nk – 'Get the Party Started'
Best Video	Röyksopp – 'Remind Me'
Best Album	Eminem – *The Eminem Show*
Best Female	Jennifer Lopez
Best Male	Eminem
Best Group	Linkin Park
Best New Act	The Calling
Best Pop	Kylie Minogue
Best Dance	Kylie Minogue
Best Rock	Red Hot Chili Peppers
Best Hard Rock	Linkin Park
Best R&B	Alicia Keys
Best Hip Hop	Eminem
Best Live Act	Red Hot Chili Peppers
Web Award	Moby www.moby.com
Free Your Mind	Football Against Racism in Europe (FARE)

Highlights: Hosted by P. Diddy, this year's event attracted the largest live audience to date with 15,000 attendees crowding into the Palau Sant Jordi in Barcelona.

2003

Best Song	Beyoncé (featuring Jay-Z) – 'Crazy in Love'
Best Video	Sigur Rós – 'Untitled #1'
Best Album	Justin Timberlake – *Justified*
Best Female	Christina Aguilera
Best Male	Justin Timberlake
Best Group	Coldplay
Best New Act	Sean Paul
Best Pop	Justin Timberlake
Best Dance	Panjabi MC
Best Rock	The White Stripes
Best R&B	Beyoncé
Best Hip Hop	Eminem
Web Award	Goldfrapp www.goldfrapp.co.uk
Free Your Mind	Aung San Suu Kyi

2004

Best Song	OutKast – 'Hey Ya!'
Best Video	OutKast – 'Hey Ya!'
Best Album	Usher – *Confessions*
Best Female	Britney Spears
Best Male	Usher
Best Group	OutKast
Best New Act	Maroon 5
Best Pop	The Black Eyed Peas
Best Rock	Linkin Park
Best Alternative	Muse
Best R&B	Alicia Keys
Best Hip Hop	D12
Free Your Mind	La Strada

Above: OutKast scooped an MTV Award double in 2004.

Highlights: Held in Rome. Eminem got things underway with 'Like Toy Soldiers'; Gwen Stefani performed 'What You Waiting For?' hanging from a huge clock.

2005

Best Song	Coldplay – 'Speed Of Sound'
Best Video	The Chemical Brothers – 'Believe'
Best Album	Green Day – *American Idiot*
Best Female	Shakira
Best Male	Robbie Williams
Best Group	Gorillaz
Best New Act	James Blunt
Best Pop	The Black Eyed Peas
Best Rock	Green Day
Best Alternative	System Of A Down
Best R&B	Alicia Keys
Best Hip-Hop	Snoop Dogg
Free Your Mind	Bob Geldof

Highlights: Sacha Baron Cohen returned in his second hosting role, this time as Borat – taking aim at all and sundry, especially Madonna; Band Aid co-founder Bob Geldof received the Free Your Mind honour.

2006

Best Song	Gnarls Barkley – 'Crazy'
Best Video	Justice vs Simian – 'We Are Your Friends'
Best Album	Red Hot Chili Peppers – *Stadium Arcadium*
Best Female	Christina Aguilera
Best Male	Justin Timberlake
Best Group	Depeche Mode
Future Sounds	Gnarls Barkley
Best Pop	Justin Timberlake
Best Rock	The Killers
Best Alternative	Muse
Best R&B	Rihanna
Best Hip-Hop	Kanye West

Highlights: Host Justin Timberlake also performed during the evening, including his global smash 'SexyBack'. Kanye West hijacked the Best Category presentation from victors Justice vs Simon, complaining that his effort was a more deserving winner.

Above: Kanye West with his Best Hip-Hop Award in 2006.

2007

Best Song	Avril Lavigne – 'Girlfriend'
Best Video	Justice Vs. Simon – 'D.A.N.C.E'
Best Album	Nelly Furtado – *Loose*
Best Solo	Avril Lavigne
Best Group	Linkin Park
New Sounds of Europe	The Bedwetters
Best Rock	30 Seconds To Mars
Best Urban	Rihanna
Best Headliner	Muse
Best International Act	Tokio Hotel
Artist's Choice	Amy Winehouse
Free Your Mind	Anton Abele

Highlights: Although the Munich-staged Awards were hosted by a laid-back Snoop Dogg, Foo Fighters' front man Dave Grohl had the mike in the VIP Glamour Pit, interviewing attending stars.

2009

Best Song	Beyoncé – 'Halo'
Best Video	Beyoncé – 'Single Ladies (Put A Ring On It)'
Best Female	Beyoncé
Best Male	Eminem
Best Group	Tokio Hotel
Best New Act	Lady Gaga
Best Rock	Green Day
Best Alternative	Placebo
Best Urban	Jay-Z
Best Live Act	U2
Best Push Act	Pixie Lott
Best World Stage Performance	Linkin Park
Best European Act	maNga

2008

Highlights: Held in Liverpool. Sir Paul McCartney was fittingly honoured with the Ultimate Legend award; of the eleven live acts, seven were female, including hot newcomers Duffy and Katy Perry – who also hosted.

Highlights: The Awards returned to the site of its inaugural event at the Brandenburg Gate in Berlin, hosted for the second year running by Katy Perry. U2 was joined by Jay Z for the memorable closing performance of 'Sunday Bloody Sunday' in front of the Gate.

Left: Katy Perry in one of her ten costume changes at the 2008 Awards.

Middle: Beyoncé Knowles with her Awards in 2009.

Above: Bono of U2 and Jay-Z take the stage together.

MOST WINS

Eminem	9	Red Hot Chili Peppers	4	Oasis	3
Britney Spears	7	Robbie Williams	4	OutKast	3
The Prodigy	6	Gorillaz	3	Spice Girls	3
Beyoncé	5	Green Day	3	30 Seconds To Mars	3
Linkin Park	5	Alicia Keys	3	Tokio Hotel	3
Justin Timberlake	5	Limp Bizkit	3	U2	3
Backstreet Boys	4	Jennifer Lopez	3		
Madonna	4	Muse	3		

BEST SONG

7 Seconds	Youssou N'Dour & Neneh Cherry	1994
Zombie	The Cranberries	1995
Wonderwall	Oasis	1996
MMMBop	Hanson	1997
Torn	Natalie Imbruglia	1998
... Baby One More Time	Britney Spears	1999
Rock DJ	Robbie Williams	2000
Clint Eastwood	Gorillaz	2001
Get The Party Started	P!nk	2002
Crazy In Love	Beyoncé (featuring Jay-Z)	2003
Hey Ya!	OutKast	2004
Speed Of Sound	Coldplay	2005
Crazy	Gnarls Barkley	2006
Girlfriend	Avril Lavigne	2007
So What	P!nk	2008
Halo	Beyoncé	2009

BEST NEW ACT

Crash Test Dummies	1994
Dog Eat Dog	1995
Garbage	1996
Hanson	1997
All Saints	1998
Britney Spears	1999
Blink-182	2000
Dido	2001
The Calling	2002
Sean Paul	2003
Maroon 5	2004
James Blunt	2005
Katy Perry	2008
Lady Gaga	2009

The first winner of the Best New Act category, Canadian combo Crash Test Dummies smashed onto the music scene in 1993 with their un-vowelled hit 'Mmm Mmm Mmm Mmm' – highlighted by lead singer Brad Roberts' deep, mesmerising bass-baritone vocal chops.

BEST GROUP

Below: Tokio Hotel won the Best Group Award in 2009.

Take That	1994
U2	1995
Oasis	1996
Spice Girls	1997
Spice Girls	1998
Backstreet Boys	1999
Backstreet Boys	2000
Limp Bizkit	2001
Linkin Park	2002
Coldplay	2003
OutKast	2004
Gorillaz	2005
Depeche Mode	2006
Linkin Park	2007
Tokio Hotel	2009

In winning the last Best Group award of the noughties, Tokio Hotel became the first such act not to come from either the US or the UK. The German rock quartet formed in 2001 and released its first English-speaking album, *Scream*, in 2007.

BEST ALBUM

Ray Of Light	Madonna	1998
By Request	Boyzone	1999
The Marshall Mathers LP	Eminem	2000
Chocolate Starfish And The Hot Dog Flavored Water	Limp Bizkit	2001
The Eminem Show	Eminem	2002
Justified	Justin Timberlake	2003
Confessions	Usher	2004
American Idiot	Green Day	2005
Stadium Arcadium	Red Hot Chili Peppers	2006
Loose	Nelly Furtado	2007
Blackout	Britney Spears	2008

With no Best Album trophy handed out from 1994-1997 or in 2009, a British act has yet to win one of the Awards' most prominent categories.

ROCK ON THE SMALL SCREEN

Music and television have been enduring and important dance partners since *American Bandstand* began broadcasting in the US in 1952. Preceding this legendary series by four years, the first music tv variety show was *Arthur Godfrey's Talent Scouts* (an old school *American Idol*) which bowed in 1948 and featured upcoming vocal acts including Pat Boone, the Chordettes and Connie Francis. Both Elvis and Buddy Holly auditioned for the series but were rejected.

IT'S NUMBER ONE, IT'S TOP OF THE POPS

Songs and artists featured on the inaugural show were:

I Wanna Be Your Man	The Rolling Stones
I Only Want To Be With You	Dusty Springfield
24 Hours From Tulsa	Gene Pitney
Glad All Over	The Dave Clark Five
Don't Talk To Him	Cliff Richard & the Shadows
Stay	The Hollies
She Loves You	The Beatles
Hippy Hippy Shake	The Swinging Blue Jeans
You Were Made For Me	Freddie & the Dreamers
I Want To Hold Your Hand	The Beatles

The first-ever *Top of the Pops* was broadcast on New Year's Day in 1964 from a BBC studio in Rusholme, Manchester, and was presented by Jimmy Savile. It aired weekly before finally running out of gas on July 30, 2006.

The Rolling Stones, Dusty Springfield, The Dave Clark Five, The Hollies and The Swinging Blue Jeans performed in the studio lip-synching, the remaining acts appeared by film clips and/or dance sequences.

Above: The Rolling Stones started their first US tour in June 1964.

OH BOY

The artists who appeared on the first show:

Marty Wilde
The Dallas Boys
The John Barry Seven
Lord Rockingham's XI
Cherry Wainer with Red Price
Neville Taylor & the Cutters
The Vernons Girls
Bernice Reading
Dudley Heslop
Kerry Martin

The Jack Good-produced *Oh Boy* was the first entirely rock 'n' roll oriented show broadcast on British television and set the standard for all that followed. It was broadcast live from the stage of the Hackney Empire in London every Saturday in the 6pm ITV slot and ran from June 15, 1958 until the end of May the following year. The influential series was largely responsible for making Cliff Richard – who first appeared during its third week, and in 19 shows thereafter – into a national star.

READY STEADY GO!

The acts on the inaugural broadcast were:

Chris Barber
Pat Boone
Billy Fury
Brian Poole & the Tremeloes
Burl Ives
Joe Loss
Mitch Murray

Above: Billy Fury recorded the live album *We Want Billy!* in 1963.

First broadcast on August 9, 1963 on ITV in the UK and hosted by Keith Fordyce, *Ready Steady Go!* aired on Friday evenings, with the catchphrase "The weekend starts here". The opening music theme for this first show was the Surfaris' 'Wipe Out', but it subsequently switched to Manfred Mann's '5-4-3-2-1'.

DON KIRSHNER'S ROCK CONCERT

On the debut show:

The Doobie Brothers	('China Grove', 'Long Train Runnin'', 'Clear As The Driven Snow', 'Without Love')
Earth, Wind and Fire	('Head To The Sky', 'Evil')
Cross Country	('In The Midnight Hour', 'City Lights', 'Tastes So Good To Me', 'Cross Country')
The Rolling Stones	('Angie', 'Silver Train', 'Dancing With Mr. D.')

The successful stepson of ABC-TV's late-night *In Concert* rock series, which debuted in 1972 in the US, the more popular *Don Kirshner's Rock Concert* first aired on September 28, 1973. Producer/host Kirshner was known as "The Man With The Golden Ear" having previously managed the Monkees and been a producer/promoter for dozens of top artists including Neil Diamond, Carole King and Bobby Darin. Among the guests on the opening night, the Rolling Stones – performing on tape from London – made their first US TV appearance in four years. The influential series endured for eight years.

THE OLD GREY WHISTLE TEST

The first acts on the show:

Tom Paxton	Bill Haley & His Comets
America	Clyde McPhatter
Lesley Duncan	Jimi Hendrix
Alice Cooper	Bob Dylan
Alice Stuart	

Conceived as Britain's first "serious" rock music series, the barebones *Old Grey Whistle Test* was created by BBC producer, Rowan Ayers and initially hosted by *Melody Maker* scribe Richard Williams. Bowing on September 21, 1971 – and initially filmed live in the tiny "Pres B" studio at Television Centre – the influential show lasted for more than 16 years on BBC2. Its most genial host was the modestly quiet "Whispering" Bob Harris, who carried the series from 1972 to 1978.

Harris claimed the show's name was taken "from a Tin Pan Alley phrase from years ago. When they got the first pressing of a record they would play it to people they called the old greys (New York doormen who wore grey suits). The ones they could remember and could whistle having heard it just once or twice had passed the Old Grey Whistle Test."

SOUL TRAIN

The first musical performers were:

Gladys Knight & the Pips
Eddie Kendricks
The Honey Cone
Bobby Hutton

America's iconic R&B music series *Soul Train* first aired on October 2, 1971. Created by producer Don Cornelius, who also hosted the weekly show from its inception until 1993. Although production of original weekly episodes came to an end on March 26, 2006, *Soul Train* remains the longest-running syndicated series in US television history.

Above: Gladys Knight and the Pips took the 'Midnight Train To Georgia' in 1973.

Above: Gerry Beckley and Dewey Bunnell, two thirds of folk rock group America.

Below: Art Garfunkel and Paul Simon perform on *Saturday Night Live* in 1975.

THE FIRST MUSICIANS TO HOST SATURDAY NIGHT LIVE

Here are the first ten artists to host the show:

Host	Date	Musical guest(s)
Paul Simon	Oct 18, 1975	Randy Newman, Phoebe Snow & Art Garfunkel
Kris Kristofferson	Jul 31, 1976	Rita Coolidge
Paul Simon	Nov 20, 1976	George Harrison
Ray Charles	Nov 12, 1977	Ray Charles
Art Garfunkel	Mar 11, 1978	Stephen Bishop
The Rolling Stones	Oct 07, 1978	The Rolling Stones
Frank Zappa	Oct 21, 1978	Frank Zappa
Rick Nelson	Feb 17, 1979	Judy Collins
Debbie Harry	Feb 14, 1981	Funky Four Plus One
Johnny Cash	Apr 17, 1982	Elton John

In addition to featuring a musical guest every week since its launch in 1975, NBC's long-running *Saturday Night Live* comedy sketch series has regularly invited musicians to host its shows and participate in its comedy shorts.

THE LONGEST-RUNNING UK MUSIC TV SERIES

Six-Five Special	1957 – 58
Oh Boy!	1958 – 59
Juke Box Jury	1959 – 67
Thank Your Lucky Stars	1961 – 66
Ready, Steady, Go!	1963 – 66
Top of the Pops	1964 – 2006
The Old Grey Whistle Test/ Whistle Test	1971 – 87
The Oxford Road Show	1981 – 85
The Tube	1982 – 87
Rapido	1988 – 92
The Word	1990 – 95
Later With Jools Holland	1992 – present
Top of the Pops 2	1994 – present
Popworld	2001 – 07
The Album Chart Show	2006 – present
Live From Abbey Road	2007 – present

AMERICAN BANDSTAND'S GREATEST ALL-STAR ROCK BAND OF ALL TIME

Above: Legendary guitarist Bo Diddley.

Bo Diddley (guitar)	Charlie Daniels (fiddle)
Duane Eddy (guitar)	Doug Kershaw (fiddle)
Al Jardine (guitar)	Mick Fleetwood (drums)
Ray Parker Jr. (guitar)	Nigel Olsson (drums)
Lee Ritenour (guitar)	George Duke (clavichord)
Johnny Rivers (guitar)	Mickey Gilley (piano)
George Thorogood (guitar)	Billy Preston (organ)
Stanley Clarke (bass)	Frankie Avalon (trumpet)
Larry Graham (bass)	Donald Byrd (trumpet)
James William Guercio (bass)	Boots Randolph (sax)
	Tom Scott (sax)
Dash Crofts (mandolin)	Jr. Walker (sax)

Hosted by the legendary Dick Clark from 1957 until 1989 (though the series began in 1952), *American Bandstand* remains a cornerstone of popular American culture. As part of the series' 30th birthday celebrations, Clark assembled an all-star band of invited guests to play together on the seminal rock hit, 'Rock Around The Clock'.

ARTISTS WITH THEIR OWN MUSIC TELEVISION SERIES

The Beatles animated series yielded 39 episodes from September 25, 1965 until October 21, 1967, all broadcast on ABC-TV in the US. Only two actors were used for the four Liverpudlians: Paul Frees and Lance Percival.

The irreverent Jools Holland has fronted his own late-night music series on BBC2 in the UK since October 8, 1992, when his first guests were the Neville Brothers, The Christians, Nu Colours and D-Influence. An in-demand session pianist and solo artist in his own right, Holland was also a co-founder of Squeeze, the popular British New Wave band.

Right: Blackheath's boogie-woogie man, Jools Holland OBE.

Michael Jackson's appearance in the first episode in Season 3 was credited as John Jay Smith. Green Day appeared (as themselves) in the 2007 release, *The Simpsons Movie*.

A chronological and comprehensive look at all the musicians who have guested on the landmark animated series which was launched on FOX TV in the US on December 17, 1989 – and hasn't skipped a beat since. All of these artists portrayed themselves on the show, except where noted:

Ringo Starr	Brush With Greatness
Michael Jackson	Stark Raving Dad (Leon Kompwsky)
Aerosmith	Flaming Moe's
Sting	Radio Bart
Tom Jones	Marge Gets a Job
Linda Ronstadt	Mr. Plow
Barry White	Whacking Day
David Crosby	Homer's Barbershop Quartet
Bette Midler	Krusty Gets Kancelled
Red Hot Chili Peppers	Krusty Gets Kancelled
George Harrison	Homer's Barbershop Quartet
The Ramones	Rosebud
James Brown	Bart's Inner Child
James Taylor	Deep Space Homer
Paul McCartney	Lisa the Vegetarian
Linda McCartney	Lisa the Vegetarian
Paul Anka	Treehouse of Horror VI
Cypress Hill	Homerpalooza
Peter Frampton	Homerpalooza
The Smashing Pumpkins	Homerpalooza
Sonic Youth	Homerpalooza
Johnny Cash	The Mysterious Voyage of Homer (Coyote)
Hank Williams Jr.	The Last Temptation of Krust
U2	Trash of the Titans
The Moody Blues	Viva Ned Flanders
Cyndi Lauper	Wild Barts Can't Be Broken
Dolly Parton	Sunday, Cruddy Sunday
Elton John	I'm With Cupid
NRBQ	The Old Man and the C Student
The B-52s	E-I-E-I (Annoyed Grunt)
Clarence Clemons	Grift of the Magi (narrator)

Britney Spears	The Mansion Family
Randy Bachman	Saddlesore Galactica
Shawn Colvin	Alone Again, Natura-Diddily (Rachel Jordan)
Kid Rock	Kill the Alligator and Run
Willie Nelson	Behind the Laughter
The Who	A Tale of Two Springfields
*NSync	New Kids on the Blecch
R.E.M.	Homer the Moe
Phish	Weekend at Burnsie's
Elvis Costello	How I Spent My Strummer Vacation
Mick Jagger	How I Spent My Strummer Vacation
Lenny Kravitz	How I Spent My Strummer Vacation
Tom Petty	How I Spent My Strummer Vacation
Keith Richards	How I Spent My Strummer Vacation
Brian Setzer	How I Spent My Strummer Vacation
Little Richard	Special Edna
Blink 182	Barting Over
David Byrne	Dude, Where's My Ranch
Jackson Browne	Brake My Wife, Please
Simon Cowell	Smart and Smarter (Henry)
50 Cent	Pranksta Rap
Los Lobos	Thank God it's Doomsday
Metallica	The Mook, the Chef, the Wife and Her Homer
The White Stripes	Jazzy and the Pussycats
Sir Mix-a-lot	Treehouse of Horror VXII
Ludacris	You Kent Always Say What You Want
Lionel Richie	He Loves to Fly and He D'ohs
Ted Nugent	I Don't Wanna Know Why the Caged Bird Sings
Dixie Chicks	Papa Don't Leech
Fall Out Boy	Lisa the Drama Queen
Eartha Kitt	Once Upon a Time in Springfield

ANIMATED MUSIC GROUPS

Alvin & the Chipmunks (TV)
The Archies (TV)
The Beatles (TV)
The California Raisins (TV commercial, TV)
Gorillaz (TV)
Gorillaz (virtual)
The Jackson 5 (TV)
KISS (TV)
Josie & the Pussycats (TV)
New Kids On The Block (TV)
The Osmonds (TV)

Conceived solely as an animated cartoon series band, The Archies comprised Archie Andrews (lead guitar), Reggie (rhythm/bass guitar), Jughead (drums), Betty (tambourine, percussion), Veronica (organ/keyboard) and Hot Dog (mascot). The real lead singer for the "group" was Ron Dante (born Carmine Granito), who also sang lead on the Cufflinks' one-hit wonder 'Tracy'. He is perhaps best known as being a one-time producer of Barry Manilow. The Archies' 1969 global smash, 'Sugar, Sugar' defined the short-lived bubblegum pop era.

Above: The Archies, artificial as saccharin but still sugar sweet.

Right: Being a virtual band doesn't stop Gorillaz appearing in concert.

IDOL WORSHIP

The *Pop Idol* music talent show debuted on Thames Television in the UK on October 5, 2001. Although it only lasted for two seasons it spawned an *Idol* franchise with 42-spin-off series worldwide. A one-off *World Idol* competition was held in 2003: the winner was Kurt Nilsen from Norway.

POP IDOL
FINALISTS – IN ORDER
OF ELIMINATION

Series 1 (2001/2002):

Will Young	Winner
Gareth Gates	Feb 09, 2002
Darius Danesh	Feb 02, 2002
Zoë Birkett	Jan 26, 2002
Hayley Evetts	Jan 19, 2002
Rosie Ribbons	Jan 12, 2002
Laura Doherty	Jan 05, 2002
Aaron Bayley	Dec 29, 2001
Jessica Garlick	Dec 22, 2001
Chris "Korben" Niblett/ Rik Waller	Dec 15, 2001

Series 2 (2003)

Michelle McManus	Winner
Mark Rhodes	Dec 20, 2003
Sam Nixon	Dec 13, 2003
Chris Hide	Dec 06, 2003
Susanne Manning	Nov 29, 2003
Roxanne Cooper	Nov 22, 2003
Andy Scott-Lee	Nov 15, 2003
Kim Gee	Nov 08, 2003
Marc Dillon/ Brian Ormond	Nov 01, 2003
Kirsty Crawford/ Leon McPherson	Oct 26, 2003

AMERICAN IDOL WINNERS

Kelly Clarkson	2002
Ruben Studdard	2003
Fantasia Barrino	2004
Carrie Underwood	2005
Taylor Hicks	2006
Jordin Sparks	2007
David Cook	2008
Kris Allen	2009
Lee DeWyze	2010

With US audience ratings frequently topping 30m at the height of its popularity, *American Idol's* viewership averaged around 20m in 2010. Its ninth season was the last with Simon Cowell.

Above: Kelly Clarkson, the only American Idol to have a UK Number 1.

THE BEST-SELLING AMERICAN IDOL CONTESTANTS

			US sales
1	Carrie Underwood	(Season 4, Winner)	11,248,000
2	Kelly Clarkson	(Season 1, Winner)	10,462,000
3	Chris Daughtry	(Season 5, 4th Place)	5,542,000
4	Clay Aiken	(Season 2, Runner-Up)	4,853,000
5	Ruben Studdard	(Season 2, Winner)	2,553,000
6	Fantasia Barrino	(Season 3, Winner)	2,289,000
7	David Cook	(Season 7, Winner)	1,279,000
8	Kellie Pickler	(Season 5, 6th Place)	1,226,000
9	Jordin Sparks	(Season 6, Winner)	1,184,000
10	David Archuleta	(Season 7, Runner-Up)	962,000
11	Jennifer Hudson	(Season 3, 7th Place)	786,000
12	Josh Gracin	(Season 2, 4th Place)	779,000
13	Taylor Hicks	(Season 5, Winner)	753,400
14	Bo Bice	(Season 4, Runner-Up)	734,000
15	Elliott Yamin	(Season 5, 3rd Place)	681,000

Above: Will Young, the original Pop Idol.

Right: Grammy Award-winning country music star Carrie Underwood.

THE X FACTOR WINNERS

Steve Brookstein	Series 1	Sep 04 – Dec 11, 2004
Shayne Ward	Series 2	Aug 20 – Dec 17, 2005
Leona Lewis	Series 3	Aug 19 – Dec 16, 2006
Leon Jackson	Series 4	Aug 18 – Dec 15, 2007
Alexandra Burke	Series 5	Aug 16 – Dec 13, 2008
Joe McElderry	Series 6	Aug 22 – Dec 13, 2009

The X Factor was launched as a UK replacement for *Pop Idol* in 2004. There are now *X Factor* series in Australia, Belgium, Bulgaria, Colombia, the Czech Republic, Denmark, Finland, France, Greece, Iceland, India, Italy, Kazakhstan, Morocco, the Netherlands, Norway, Portugal, Russia, Spain, Sweden, Turkey and the Middle East – with the American franchise scheduled to air in 2010.

Left: Simon Cowell, one of the most important men in showbusiness.

SIMON SAYS

Between them, fellow Brits Simon Fuller and Simon Cowell have separately created and produced the most popular television talent shows of the modern era.

SIMON COWELL TELEVISION SHOWS

The X Factor (UK)	2004
X Factor franchise (in 22 other countries)	
America's Got Talent (USA)	2006
Britain's Got Talent (UK)	2007
Got Talent franchise (in 31 other countries)	
American Inventor (USA)	2006
Celebrity Duets (USA)	2006
Grease is the Word (UK)	2007
The X Factor (USA)	2010

In addition to his role as a judge on the original (British) *Pop Idol* and subsequent *American Idol* series (which he neither created nor produced), Cowell is the executive producer (and judge/mentor on the UK *X Factor*) of the above television series via his own SYCOtv company.

SIMON FULLER – TV SHOWS

S Club 7 (UK)	1999
Pop Idol (UK)	2001
American Idol (USA)	2002
Idol franchise (44 countries)	
World Idol	2003
So You Think You Can Dance (USA)	2005
Little Britain USA (USA)	2008
If I Can Dream (USA)	2010
Boy Band (2010)	

Music/entertainment impresario Simon Fuller began creating/producing music television series in 1999 when he auditioned more than 10,000 people to become members of his manufactured S Club 7 group.

Above: There was no party like an S Club 7 party in 1999.

Below: Simon Fuller, a man who makes stars shine.

19 ENTERTAINMENT

In addition to partnering with Fremantle Media on the immensely popular Idol franchise, Fuller – through his 19 Entertainment/CKX company – remains one of the most successful managers in history. He named his original 19 management company after the hit by his client Paul Hardcastle, who scored a global smash with his 1985 Vietnam War-themed single '19'. Fuller currently oversees the careers of:

Kris Allen	Gareth Gates	Orianthi
David Beckham	Geri Halliwell	Samantha Ronson
The David Beckham Academy	Allison Iraheta	Sam & Mark
	Adam Lambert	Jordin Sparks
Victoria Beckham	Annie Lennox	Spice Girls
Emma Bunton	Mini Viva	Carrie Underwood
David Cook	Roland Mouret	Will Young
Daughtry	Muhammad Ali	
Cathy Dennis	Andy Murray	

MTV MUSIC TELEVISION

Since the 1920s, music's most popular and natural home has been on radio. In cars, at home and in offices around the world, radio still provides the musical backdrop to our daily lives. Becoming the most efficient and consistent medium for artists and labels to deliver their music, radio was increasingly formatted into different genres following the widespread introduction of FM in the 1970s. Despite the increasing popularity of music delivery and discovery via the Internet, radio remains a vital cornerstone of popular culture.

THE 10 MOST-PLAYED SONGS OF 2009 IN THE US

Nielsen/Soundscan collated all the Most-Played lists from the US.

			US radio plays
1	You Belong To Me	Taylor Swift	465,100
2	Love Story	Taylor Swift	413,100
3	You Found Me	The Fray	412,900
4	Use Somebody	Kings of Leon	383,500
5	Boom Boom Pow	The Black Eyed Peas	379,400
6	Blame It	Jamie Foxx featuring T-Pain	376,100
7	I Gotta Feeling	The Black Eyed Peas	375,100
8	Second Chance	Shinedown	374,600
9	Knock You Down	Keri Hilson featuring Kanye West & Ne-Yo	372,300
10	Poker Face	Lady Gaga	370,900

Including the airing of album tracks not featured on this list, Taylor Swift's music was played more than 1,000,000 times on US radio during 2009.

THE MOST-PLAYED SONGS OF THE 2000s IN THE US

1	How You Remind Me	Nickelback	1,218,000
2	Drops of Jupiter (Tell Me)	Train	1,141,000
3	Hanging by a Moment	Lifehouse	1,104,000
4	Breathe	Faith Hill	1,080,000
5	Kryptonite	3 Doors Down	1,062,000
6	The Way You Love Me	Faith Hill	1,046,000
7	I Hope You Dance	Lee Ann Womack	1,030,000
8	Wherever You Will Go	The Calling	996,000
9	Smooth	Santana featuring Rob Thomas	985,000
10	The Reason	Hoobastank	982,000

Right: Nickelback rock the Canadian Juno Awards in 2009.

Below: Taylor Swift was the first country music artist to win an MTV Video Music Award.

THE 10 MOST-PLAYED ARTISTS OF 2009 IN THE US

Country radio remains a formidable format in the States – the artists at number 1, 4, 8 (to some degree), 9 and 10 dominate the most popular radio artists list for the year.

THE MOST-PLAYED ARTISTS OF THE 2000S IN THE US

1	Tim McGraw	7,965,000
2	Toby Keith	7,862,000
3	George Strait	7,638,000
4	Alan Jackson	6,885,000
5	Nickelback	6,877,000
6	Kenny Chesney	6,492,000
7	Rascal Flatts	5,658,000
8	Brooks & Dunn	5,567,000
9	Garth Brooks	5,519,000
10	Green Day	5,435,000

Once again, country radio rules the airwaves – all but Nickelback and Green Day being non-twangers.

TOP RADIO MARKETS OF 2009 IN THE US

		Radio audience reach			
1	New York	15,669,500	12	Miami-Fort Lauderdale-Hollywood	3,580,000
2	Los Angeles	10,999,100	13	Seattle-Tacoma	3,390,900
3	Chicago	7,862,200	14	Puerto Rico	3,344,200
4	San Francisco	6,145,800	15	Phoenix	3,300,300
5	Dallas-Fort Worth	5,216,100	16	Minneapolis-St. Paul	2,712,500
6	Houston-Galveston	4,815,700	17	San Diego	2,578,900
7	Atlanta	4,413,800	18	Nassau-Suffolk (Long Island)	2,439,800
8	Philadelphia	4,357,600			
9	Washington, DC	4,279,900	19	Tampa-St. Petersburg-Clearwater	2,379,300
10	Boston	3,977,400			
11	Detroit	3,831,100	20	Denver-Boulder	2,336,100

According to Arbitron, the leading radio audience research company in the US, New York is the most-listened to city in the country, with WLTW-FM 106.7 – aka Lite FM – its most popular radio station.

BMI'S ALL-TIME MOST PERFORMED SONGS

12 Million Performances

You've Lost That Lovin' Feelin' — Barry Mann, Phil Spector & Cynthia Weil

10 Million Performances

Stand By Me — Ben E. King, Jerry Leiber & Mike Stoller
Baby, I Need Your Loving — Lamont Dozier, Brian Holland & Eddie Holland
Take It Easy — Glenn Frey & Jackson Browne
Every Breath You Take — Sting

9 Million Performances

I Heard It Through The Grapevine — Barrett Strong & Norman Whitfield
When A Man Loves A Woman — Calvin Lewis & Andrew J. Wright
Oh Pretty Woman — Bill Dees & Roy Orbison
(Sittin' On) The Dock Of The Bay — Steve Cropper & Otis Redding
Never My Love — Donald Addrisi & Richard Addrisi
Can't Take My Eyes Off You — Bob Crewe & Bob Gaudio
Brown Eyed Girl — Van Morrison
Mrs. Robinson — Paul Simon
Proud Mary — John Fogerty
You Can't Hurry Love — Lamont Dozier, Brian Holland & Eddie Holland
Rhythm of the Rain — John Gummoe

8 Million Performances

Yesterday — John Lennon & Paul McCartney
How Sweet It Is (To Be Loved By You) — Lamont Dozier, Brian Holland & Eddie Holland
I Will Always Love You — Dolly Parton
Suspicious Minds — Mark James
Sounds of Silence — Paul Simon
Cherish — Terry Kirkman
On Broadway — Jerry Leiber, Barry Mann, Mike Stoller & Cynthia Weil
Your Song — Elton John & Bernie Taupin
Everlasting Love — Buzz Cason & Mac Gayden
Georgia on My Mind — Hoagy Carmichael & Stuart Gorrell

7 Million Performances

(What A) Wonderful World — Lou Adler, Herb Alpert & Sam Cooke
Margaritaville — Jimmy Buffett
Oh Girl — Eugene Record
Angel Of The Morning — Chip Taylor
Happy Together — Garry Bonner & Alan Gordon
Lean On Me — Bill Withers
Layla — Eric Clapton & Jim Gordon
Killing Me Softly With His Song — Charles Fox & Norman Gimbel
If You Don't Know Me By Now — Kenneth Gamble & Leon Huff
Mony Mony — Bobby Bloom, Ritchie Cordell, Bo Gentry & Tommy James
(Your Love Has Lifted Me) Higher and Higher — Gary Jackson, Raynard Miner & Carl William Smith
(I Can't Get No) Satisfaction — Mick Jagger & Keith Richards
Listen to the Music — Tom Johnston
More — Marcello Ciorciolini, Norman Newell, Nino Oliviero & Riz Ortolani
My Maria — Daniel Moore & B.W. Stevenson
Hooked On A Feeling — Mark James
Everybody's Talkin' — Fred Neil
Wind Beneath My Wings — Larry Henley & Jeff Silbar
Goin' Out of My Head — Teddy Randazzo & Bobby Weinstein
The Letter — Wayne Carson
Sunny — Bobby Hebb
Dreams — Stevie Nicks
Save The Last Dance For Me — Doc Pomus & Mort Shuman
Daydream Believer — John Stewart

One of three performing rights organization in the US (along with ASCAP and SESAC), Broadcast Music Inc (BMI) collects performance license fees from all media for royalty distribution to its songwriter and music publisher members. Founded in 1939, above are its most popular songs from combined radio, television, concert venue, restaurants, clubs and digital media performance research.

BRITISH RADIO MILESTONES

UK RADIO STATIONS WITH THE MOST LISTENERS

1	BBC Radio 2	13.6m
2	BBC Radio 1	11.1m
3	BBC Radio 4	10.2m
4	Heart	7.4m
5	BBC Radio 5 live	6.5m
6	Classic FM	5.4m
7	Galaxy	3.8m
8	Magic	3.6m
9	Kiss	3.5m
10	Smooth	2.8m

RAJAR (Radio Joint Audience Research Limited) the official body in charge of measuring radio audiences revealed that the most popular radio station in the UK is BBC Radio 2, which plays mostly Adult Contemporary music, its success underpinned by legendary DJ personalities including Steve Wright, Bob Harris, Paul Gambaccini, Chris Evans and Sir Terry Wogan (who made his final *Breakfast Show* broadcast on December 18, 2009).

Left: Guglielmo Marconi, inventor of the radio telegraph system.

Below: 'Poptastic' DJ Tony Blackburn.

Year	Station	Song	Artist
1964	Radio Caroline	Not Fade Away	The Rolling Stones
1967	BBC Radio 1	Flowers In The Rain	The Move
1969	University Radio York (the John Peel re-launch)	Let There Be More Light	Pink Floyd
1970	UBN – United Biscuits Network	Reach Out I'll Be There	The Four Tops
1973	Capital Radio	Bridge Over Troubled Water	Simon & Garfunkel
1973	Radio Clyde	The Song Of The Clyde	Kenneth McKellar
1974	Piccadilly Radio	Good Vibrations	The Beach Boys
1974	194 Radio City	You Are The Sunshine Of My Life	Stevie Wonder
1974	Radio Hallam	I've Got The Music In Me	Kiki Dee (which jumped)
1974	Swansea Sound	Love Is The Message	MFSB
1975	Pennine Radio	I Can't Let Maggie Go	Honeybus
1975	Radio Trent	July July July	Billy Paul
1975	Radio Forth	January	Pilot
1975	Radio Victory	Everything That Touches You	The Association
1976	Downtown Radio	Concrete And Clay	Randy Edelman
1976	Radio 210	We've Only Just Begun	The Carpenters
1976	Beacon Radio	Sunrise	Eric Carmen
1980	CBC Cardiff	I Hear You Now	Jon & Vangelis
1980	Mercia Sound	This Is It	Dan Hartman
1980	Hereward Radio	Let Your Love Flow	The Bellamy Brothers
1980	Radio Tay	The Road And The Miles To Dundee	Andy Stewart
1980	Severn Sound	Arrival	Mike Oldfield
1980	Devon Air	Here Comes The Sun	The Beatles
1980	2CR	Arrival	Mike Oldfield
1980	BBC Radio Norfolk	Modern Girl	Sheena Easton
1981	Essex Radio	Wired For Sound	Cliff Richard
1981	Centre Radio	Wired For Sound	Cliff Richard
1981	Chiltern Radio	I Can Hear Music	The Beach Boys
1981	Radio West	Ain't No Stopping Us Now	McFadden & Whitehead
1981	West Sound	Arrival	Abba
1982	Radio Wyvern	Daydream Believer	The Monkees
1982	Wiltshire Radio	H.A.P.P.Y Radio	Edwin Starr
1982	Red Rose Radio	Evergreen (Love Theme from 'A Star is Born')	Barbra Streisand
1987	BBC Radio 1 FM	FM (No Static At All)	Steely Dan
1988	BBC GLR	Born To Run	Bruce Springsteen
1988	Power FM	New Sensation	INXS
1993	Virgin Radio	Born To Be Wild	INXS
1994	Mix 96	Dancing Queen	Abba
1995	Virgin 105.8 (Lon)	Born To Be Wild	INXS
1995	Heart 106.2	Something Got Me Started	Simply Red
1996	Spirit FM	Spirit In The Sky	Norman Greenbaum
1997	XFM	Kick Out The Jams	The MC5s
2000	Kick FM	Alive And Kicking	Simple Minds
2000	The Groove	ABC	The Jackson 5
2002	BBC 6Music	Burn Baby Burn	Ash
2002	BBC 1Xtra	Dangerous	Rodney P & Skitz
2004	Virgin Radio Classic Rock	Born To Be Wild	Steppenwolf
2004	Kerrang! 105.2	All My Life	The Foo Fighters
2004	Source FM	Without Me	Eminem
2006	Source Radio	Talk	Coldplay
2006	Atlantic FM	Beautiful Day	U2
2007	XFM South Wales	A Design For Life	The Manic Street Preachers
2009	BFBS Radio	The Boys Are Back In Town	Thin Lizzy

UK RADIO GROUPS WITH THE MOST LISTENERS

The Absolute Radio station – with its "no-repeat guarantee" playlist policy – was formerly Virgin Radio until its rebranding by new owner the Absolute Radio Group in September 2008.

HIT RECORDS BANNED BY THE BBC

Let's Spend The Night Together	The Rolling Stones	1967
Lucy In The Sky With Diamonds	The Beatles	1967
Light My Fire	Jose Feliciano	1968
Je T'Aime... Moi Non Plus	Jane Birkin & Serge Gainsbourg	1969
Give Ireland Back To The Irish	Wings	1972
Hi, Hi, Hi	Wings	1972
Love To Love You Baby	Donna Summer	1975
God Save the Queen	The Sex Pistols	1977
Glad To Be Gay	The Tom Robinson Band	1978
Killing An Arab	The Cure	1979
Invisible Sun	The Police	1981
Relax	Frankie Goes To Hollywood	1984
Fairytale Of New York	The Pogues	1987
Ebeneezer Goode	The Shamen	1992

As a government-owned public service, the BBC long felt obliged to ban – temporarily or permanently – records it found distasteful or too controversial. This usually involved explicit sexual content, overt political posturing or foul language. The above songs became UK hits despite the censorship.

Above: The ever-controversial Frankie Goes to Hollywood. Their single 'Relax' hit the Number 1 spot despite being banned by the BBC.

THE MOST PLAYED SONGS
OF THE LAST DECADE (2000–2009)

The London-based Phonographic Performance Limited (PPL) is a non-profit music licensing organization which issues licenses to public broadcasters (including radio stations, television networks, concert venues and digital media companies) giving them the right to perform/broadcast recorded music.

Left: Take That successfully reformed in 2005, minus Robbie Williams.

Below: Snow Patrol's Gary Lightbody.

Calling it his "purest love song", Snow Patrol front man Gary Lightbody wrote 'Chasing Cars' in the back garden of a friend's cottage after downing several glasses of wine. It peaked at number 6 in the UK – and proved a career-changing breakthrough hit in the US where it reached number 5 following its use in a season-ending episode of the *Grey's Anatomy* TV drama.

BBC RADIO – MOST POPULAR NATIONAL STATIONS

		Weekly audience reach
1	BBC Radio 2	13.47 million
2	BBC Radio 1	10.76 million
3	BBC Radio 4	9.84 million
4	BBC Radio 5 Live	6.19 million
5	BBC Radio 3	1.87 million
6	BBC World Service	1.23 million
7	BBC Radio 7	0.93 million
8	BBC 6 Music (digital)	0.69 million
9	BBC 1Xtra	0.53 million
10	BBC Asian Network	0.36 million

Not unexpectedly, RAJAR's research revealed that BBC Radio 2 is the most listened to radio station in the UK, its flagship *Breakfast Show* averaging 8.1 million listeners during its final three months on the air in 2009. Classic FM is Britain's most popular commercial radio station.

BBC RADIO 1
BREAKFAST SHOW PRESENTERS

Tony Blackburn	Sep 1967 – Jun 1973	5 years, 8 months
Noel Edmonds	Jun 1973 – Apr 1978	4 years, 10 months
Dave Lee Travis	May 1978 – Dec 1980	2 years, 7 months
Mike Read	Jan 1981 – Apr 1986	5 years, 3 months
Mike Smith	May 1986 – May 1988	2 years
Simon Mayo	May 1988 – Sep 1993	5 years, 4 months
Mark Goodier	Oct 1993 – Dec 1993	2 months
Steve Wright	Jan 1994 – Apr 1995	1 year, 3 months
Chris Evans	Apr 1995 – Jan 1997	1 year, 9 months
Mark & Lard	Feb 1997 – Oct 1997	8 months
Kevin Greening & Zoë Ball	Oct 1997 – Sep 1998	11 months
Zoë Ball	Sep 1998 – Mar 2000	1 year, 6 months
Sara Cox	Mar 2000 – Dec 2003	3 years, 8 months
Chris Moyles	Jan 2004 – Present	

Above: The self-styled "Saviour of Early-Morning Radio" Chris Moyles.

Right: Moody post-punk band Joy Division were a favourite of DJ John Peel.

Based in London, BBC Radio 1 began broadcasting on September 30, 1967. Hosting its *Breakfast Show* programme became the most prestigious job in British radio, with 14 DJs having occupied the peak-time morning slot.

JOHN PEEL'S FESTIVE MILLENNIUM CHART

1	Atmosphere	Joy Division
2	Teenage Kicks	The Undertones
3	Love Will Tear Us Apart	Joy Division
4	Anarchy In The UK	The Sex Pistols
5	White Man In Hammersmith Palais	The Clash
6	Blue Monday	New Order
7	How Soon Is Now?	The Smiths
8	Smells Like Teen Spirit	Nirvana
9	There Is A Light That Never Goes Out	The Smiths
10	Song To The Siren	This Mortal Coil
11	Shipbuilding	Robert Wyatt
12	Common People	Pulp
13	Big Eyed Beans From Venus	Captain Beefheart & His Magic Band
14	Holiday In Cambodia	The Dead Kennedys
15	New Dawn Fades	Joy Division
16	Soon	My Bloody Valentine
17	Ceremony	New Order
18	Another Girl, Another Planet	The Only Ones
19	Temptation	New Order
20	She's Lost Control	Joy Division
21	Brassneck	The Wedding Present
22	This Charming Man	The Smiths
23	Birthday	The Sugarcubes
24	How I Wrote 'Elastic Man'	The Fall
25	My Favourite Dress	The Wedding Present
26	Pull The Wires From The Wall	The Delgados
27	Feed Me With Your Kiss	My Bloody Valentine
28	Transmission	Joy Division
29	Pretty Vacant	The Sex Pistols
30	Debaser	Pixies
31	True Faith	New Order
32	Complete Control	The Clash
33	Totally Wired	The Fall
34	Going Underground	The Jam
35	French Disco	Stereolab
36	All Along The Watchtower	Jimi Hendrix
37	The Classical	The Fall
38	New Rose	The Damned
39	Song To The Siren	Tim Buckley
40	God Only Knows	The Beach Boys
41	Heroin	Velvet Underground
42	Northern Sky	Nick Drake
43	Visions Of Johanna	Bob Dylan
44	I Am The Walrus	The Beatles
45	Good Vibrations	The Beach Boys
46	Can't Be Sure	The Sundays
47	Lion Rock	Culture
48	Shee-La-Na-Gig	PJ Harvey
49	Crystal Lake	Grandaddy
50	Here	Pavement

Iconic British DJ John Peel began broadcasting for BBC Radio 1 in September 1967 and developed a reputation for playing obscure music from outside the mainstream. From 1976 Peel compiled a countdown of his listeners' favourite tracks of the year and broadcast it as "The Festive Fifty". In 2000 he assembled an all-time "millennium" ranking, which is reproduced above.

MTV
MUSIC TELEVISION

SONGS FOR ALL SEASONS

PRS For Music is the British performance royalties collection agency for songwriters, composers and music publishers. Extracting data from its database, the non-profit organisation occasionally compiles UK lists of the most performed songs (radio, television, any media/environment where music in played) on different topics.

THE MOST POPULAR SONGS TO BE TAKEN TO A DESERT ISLAND

1	Bohemian Rhapsody	Queen
2	Angels	Robbie Williams
3	Don't Stop Me Now	Queen
4	Hallelujah	Jeff Buckley
5	Dancing Queen	Abba
6	Billie Jean	Michael Jackson
7	Suspicious Minds	Elvis Presley
8	(What A) Wonderful World	Louis Armstrong
9	Sweet Child O' Mine	Guns N' Roses
10	Poker Face	Lady Gaga

Left: The late Jeff Buckley at Glastonbury in 1995.

No sign of the Animals' 'We've Gotta Get Out of This Place' here – nor anything that conjures up sand and sunshine.

THE MOST POPULAR CHEESY SUMMER ANTHEMS IN THE UK

1	Mysterious Girl	Peter Andre
2	Agadoo	Black Lace
3	Itsy Bitsy Teenie Weenie Yellow Polka Dot Bikini	Brian Hyland
4	The Birdie Song	The Tweets
5	Barbie Girl	Aqua
6	We're Going To Ibiza	Vengaboys
7	Blue (Da Ba De)	Eiffel 65
8	Cheeky Song	Cheeky Girls
9	The Ketchup Song (Aserejé)	Las Ketchup
10	I'm Too Sexy	Right Said Fred

THE MOST ELVIS VALENTINE SONGS IN THE UK

1	Bleeding Love	Leona Lewis
2	I Will Always Love You	Whitney Houston
3	My Heart Will Go On	Céline Dion
4	Without You	Mariah Carey
5	Can't Take My Eyes Off You	Andy Williams
6	Can't Help Falling In Love With You	Elvis Presley
7	Beautiful	Christina Aguilera
8	Unchained Melody	The Righteous Brothers
9	Everything I Do (I Do It For You)	Bryan Adams
10	I'm Yours	Jason Mraz

Leona Lewis, winner of The X Factor, had the best-selling single of 2007 in Britain with the yearning pop anthem 'Bleeding Love' – it went on to top charts in 33 other countries too.

THE MOST POPULAR SONGS TO MAKE LOVE TO IN THE UK

Left: Peter Andre makes his bid for stardom.

The British charts have never shied away from cheesy hit singles. Bare-chested singer Peter Andre's reggae-pop nugget, 'Mysterious Girl', failed to make a big impression in the UK when first issued in 1995; it needed a re-release nine years later to finally make it.

Although reliable statistics are unavailable, R&B/soul heavyweights Marvin Gaye and Barry White are probably responsible for more births in the UK than any other artists.

THE MOST POPULAR HALLOWEEN PARTY SONGS IN THE UK

1	Thriller	Michael Jackson
2	Somebody's Watching Me	Rockwell
3	Bat Out Of Hell	Meat Loaf
4	Ghost Town	The Specials
5	Devil Woman	Cliff Richard
6	There's A Ghost In My House	R. Dean Taylor/ The Fall
7	Ghostbusters	Ray Parker Jr.
8	Monster Mash	Bobby Pickett & the Crypt Kickers
9	Witchy Woman	The Eagles
10	The Addams Family	Vic Mizzy

Although unsurprisingly topping this list of horror-themed hits with 'Thriller', Michael Jackson is also the featured backing vocalist on the runner-up, 'Somebody's Watching Me'.

Above: The Specials in 1980's Coventry - the inspiration for their hit single 'Ghost Town'.

Left: Dizzee Rascal got everyone in the 'Holiday' mood in 2009.

THE MOST POPULAR SONGS USED BY [...] IN THE UK

1	Beat Again	JLS
2	Sweet Dreams	Beyoncé
3	Holiday	Dizzee Rascal
4	When Love Takes Over	David Guetta featuring Kelly Rowland
5	I Know You Want Me (Calle Ocho)	Pitbull

THE MOST POPULAR MUSIC GENRE IN THE FASHION WORLD IN THE UK

THE MOST POPULAR SONGS FOR SINGLES IN THE UK

1	Hot N Cold	Katy Perry
2	I'm A Survivor	Destiny's Child
3	With Or Without You	U2
4	I Will Survive	Gloria Gaynor
5	Irreplaceable	Beyoncé
6	Cry Me A River	Justin Timberlake
7	Nothing Compares 2 U	Sinéad O'Connor
8	Girls Just Wanna Have Fun	Cyndi Lauper
9	It's My Life	Bon Jovi
10	Goodbye My Lover	James Blunt

Left: Cyndi Lauper started fun-loving girl power back in 1984.

THE MOST POPULAR MUSICAL INSTRUMENT AS A HOBBY IN THE UK

1	Piano	34%
2	Trumpet	14%
3	Electric Guitar	13%
4	Saxophone	11%
5	Acoustic Guitar	11%
6	Drums	7%
7	Keyboard	3%
8	Violin	3%
9	Cello	2%
10	Flute	1%

MTV
MUSIC TELEVISION

THE MOST PLAYED
TALENT SHOW WINNERS IN THE UK

1	A Moment Like This	Leona Lewis	X Factor	2006
2	Sound Of The Underground	Girls Aloud	Popstars – The Rivals	2002
3	That's My Goal	Shayne Ward	X Factor	2005
4	All This Time	Michelle McManus	Pop Idol	2003
5	Stop Living The Lie	David Sneddon	Fame Academy	2002
6	Against All Odds (Take A Look At Me Now)	Steve Brookstein	X Factor	2004
7	Evergreen	Will Young	Pop Idol	2002
8	Pure And Simple	Hear'Say	Popstars	2001
9	Maybe That's What It Takes	Alex Parks	Fame Academy	2003
10	When You Believe	Leon Jackson	X Factor	2007

1	EastEnders	37%
2	National Anthem	36%
3	Match of the Day	14%
4	Coronation Street	12%

Left: Girls Aloud, the UK's most successful TV talent show pop group.

THE MOST POPULAR
CLASSICAL TUNES IN THE UK

1	Adagio For Strings	Samuel Barber
2	Toccata In D Minor	Johann Sebastian Bach
3	Canon In D Major	Johann Pachelbel
4	Prelude A L'Apres-Midi D'un Faune	Claude Debussy
5	The Swan From The Carnival Of The Animals	Camille Saint-Saens
6	Clair De Lune	Claude Debussy
7	Thais – Meditation	Jules Massenet
8	Adagio Of Spartacus And Phrygia	Aram Khachaturian
9	Rhapsody On A Theme Of Paganini Opus 43	Sergei Rachmaninov
10	Cavalleria Rusticana – Intermezzo	Pietro Mascagni

Above: Samuel Barber was twice awarded the Pulitzer Prize for music.

Right: 'Bad Boys' Andrew Ridgeley and George Michael (Wham!) in 1983.

1	Die Another Day	Madonna
2	Live And Let Die	Paul McCartney & Wings
3	The World Is Not Enough	Garbage
4	Nobody Does It Better	Carly Simon
5	A View To A Kill	Duran Duran
6	GoldenEye	Tina Turner
7	Goldfinger	Shirley Bassey
8	Licence To Kill	Gladys Knight
9	For Your Eyes Only	Sheena Easton
10	Octopussy	Rita Coolidge

With 007 ever the ladies' man, eight of these ten hits were sung by women – including Garbage's lead vocalist, Shirley Manson.

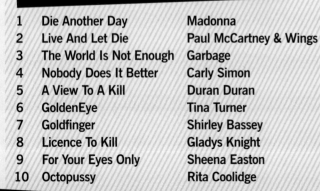

THE MOST PLAYED
CHRISTMAS SONGS IN THE UK

Wham! donated all the royalties from 'Last Christmas'/ 'Everything She Wants' (it was released a double-A side) to the Ethiopian famine appeal.

THE MOST PERFORMED
KARAOKE TUNES IN THE UK

Left: Gloria Gaynor
did more than just
survive in 1979.

The Karaoke machine was invented by Daisuke Inoue in Japan, in the early 1970s. Finland holds the record for the largest number of people singing karaoke at one time, when 80,000 people sang 'Hard Rock Hallelujah' on May 26, 2006 in Helsinki following Lordi's historic win at the Eurovision Song Contest.

THE MOST POPULAR HEAVY METAL SONGS IN THE UK

1	One	Metallica
2	Welcome To The Jungle	Guns N' Roses
3	Before I Forget	Slip Knot
4	Back In Black	AC/DC
5	Paranoid	Black Sabbath
6	Ace Of Spades	Motorhead
7	Smoke On The Water	Deep Purple
8	The Number Of The Beast	Iron Maiden
9	Twisted Transistor	Korn
10	When Love And Hate Collide	Def Leppard
11	Iron Man	Black Sabbath
12	Master Of Puppets	Metallica
13	Angel Of Death	Slayer
14	The Beautiful People	Marilyn Manson
15	Girls Girls Girls	Mötley Crüe
16	Cemetery Gates	Pantera
17	Painkiller	Judas Priest
18	Holy Wars... The Punishment Due	Megadeth
19	Love Gun	Kiss
20	Cowboys From Hell	Pantera

THE MOST POPULAR
DRIVING SONGS IN THE UK

1	Bat Out Of Hell	Meatloaf
2	Bohemian Rhapsody	Queen
3	Don't Stop Me Now	Queen
4	Mr. Brightside	The Killers
5	Dancing Queen	Abba
6	Sex On Fire	Kings of Leon
7	I Want To Break Free	Queen
8	Thriller	Michael Jackson
9	Sweet Child O' Mine	Guns N' Roses
10	Freebird	Lynryd Skynrd

Not making the cut: Chris Rea's 1989 hit 'The Road to Hell' written about the frustration of driving around England's notoriously jammed M25 motorway.

Left: Guns N' Roses
released two albums at
the same time in 1990.
Both went straight to the
top of the charts.

TWELVE MUSICAL GUESTS ON DESERT ISLAND DISCS

First broadcast by the BBC on January 29, 1942, *Desert Island Discs* is the longest-running radio series in the world. Guests are invited to choose eight music selections, one book and one luxury item, which they would take with them if stranded on a desert island.

BRIAN MAY (SEP 15, 2002)

DAVID GILMOUR (APR 06, 2003)

1	Waterloo Sunset	The Kinks
2	Ballad In Plain D	Bob Dylan
3	I'm Still Here	Tom Waits
4	Dancing In The Street	Martha & the Vandellas
5	Anthem	Leonard Cohen
6	A Man Needs A Maid	Neil Young
7	For Free	Joni Mitchell
8	Rudi With A Flashlight	Lemonheads

Book: An English translation of The Koran
Luxury: An acoustic Martin D35 guitar

SUGGS (MAY 19, 2002)

1	Cry Me A River	Julie London
2	Sex & Drugs & Rock & Roll	Ian Dury
3	London's Burning	The Clash
4	On A Portrait Of A Deaf Man	John Betjeman accompanied by Jim Parker
5	Al Capone	Prince Buster
6	Is That All There Is?	Peggy Lee
7	The Village Green Preservation Society	The Kinks
8	Cleaning Windows	Van Morrison

EMMYLOU HARRIS (DEC 21, 2003)

1	Dreaming My Dreams With You	Waylon Jennings
2	Uncloudy Day	The Staple Singers
3	Up On Cripple Creek	The Band
4	(Talk To Me Of) Mendocino	Kate & Anna McGarrigle
5	The Emperor Of Wyoming	Neil Young
6	Mansion Of The Hill	Bruce Springsteen
7	The Maker	Daniel Lanois
8	Polegnala E Todora (Theodora Is Dozing)	Ensemble of the Bulgarian Republic conducted by Philip Koutev

Book: Blank book
Luxury: Library

GENE PITNEY (MAR 02, 2003)

1	The Last Song	Elton John
2	C C Rider	Chuck Willis
3	Roll Over Beethoven	Chuck Berry
4	Tear My Stillhouse Down	Gillian Welch
5	Over The Rainbow	Israil Kamakaiwoole
6	Nightingale	Norah Jones
7	Queda Te Aqui	The Gipsy Kings
8	Con Te Partiro – Time To Say Goodbye	Andrea Bocelli & Sarah Brightman

Book: *The Giant Book of Mensa Puzzles* by Robert Allen
Luxury: Case of Opus One wine

JARVIS COCKER (APR 24, 2005)

[redacted]

1	Why Can't The English? (from *My Fair Lady*)	Rex Harrison
2	She Loves You	The Beatles
3	Vaughan Williams' Fantasia on a theme by Thomas Tallis	Sinfonia of London conducted by Sir John Barbirolli
4	Changes	David Bowie
5	Give Me Tonight	Shannon
6	Good Morning Heartache	Billie Holiday
7	I Don't Want To Hear It Anymore	Dusty Springfield
8	The 1st Movement of Shostakovich's Symphony No. 5 in D Minor	New York Philharmonic conducted by Leonard Bernstein

Book: *The Human Comedy* by Honore De Balzac
Luxury: DVD projector and DVDs

RANDY NEWMAN (OCT 19, 2008)

[redacted]

GEORGE MICHAEL (SEP 30, 2007)

1	Love Is A Losing Game	Amy Winehouse
2	Do The Strand	Roxy Music
3	Crazy	Gnarls Barkley
4	Smells Like Teen Spirit	Nirvana
5	Being Boring	Pet Shop Boys
6	Paper Bag	Goldfrapp
7	Gold Digger	Kanye West
8	Going To Town	Rufus Wainwright

Book: Any book of short stories by Doris Lessing
Luxury: Aston Martin DB9 car

BARRY MANILOW (OCT 02, 2009)

1	One For My Baby	Frank Sinatra
2	Over The Rainbow	Judy Garland
3	What Is There to Say?	The Gerry Mulligan Quartet
4	Candide	Original Broadway Cast
5	Emmie	Laura Nyro
6	Third Movement of Brahms' Symphony No. 3	The London Symphony Orchestra
7	Fragile	Sting
8	Don't Give Up	Peter Gabriel & Kate Bush

[redacted]

1	Wichita Lineman	Glen Campbell
2	Penny Lane	The Beatles
3	Debussy's Syrinx	James Galway
4	Hole In My Shoe	Traffic
5	I Say A Little Prayer	Aretha Franklin
6	A Walk Across The Rooftops	The Blue Nile
7	The 1st Movement of Winter from Vivaldi's Four Seasons	Michel Schwalbe & Berliner Philharmoniker
8	(Sittin on) The Dock Of The Bay	Otis Redding

Book: *Power of Now* by Eckhart Tolle
Luxury: Suncream

SIMON COWELL (AUG 13, 2006)

1	Mack The Knife	Bobby Darin
2	This Guy's In Love With You	Herb Alpert
3	She	Charles Aznavour
4	Unchained Melody	The Righteous Brothers
5	Danke Schoen	Wayne Newton
6	If You're Not The One	Daniel Bedingfield
7	Summer Wind	Frank Sinatra
8	Mr. Bojangles	Sammy Davis Jr.

EUROVISION

The first Eurovision Song Contest – an annual pop song contest between various European countries – took place in Lugano, Switzerland in May 1956. Seven nations took part, with two entries each. Each jury member had two votes, but only the winner was announced. In all, 47 countries have taken part. Germany have made the most appearances – 53; the only year they failed to enter was in 1996.

EUROVISION ENTRIES

Germany	54	Bosnia &	
France	53	Herzegovina	16
United Kingdom	53	Russia	14
Spain	50	Romania	12
Sweden	50	Estonia	11
Norway	48	Poland	11
Belgium	47	Slovenia	11
Switzerland	47	Latvia	9
Netherlands	46	FYR Macedonia	8
Finland	42	Lithuania	8
Austria	41	Ukraine	8
Ireland	41	Hungary	6
Portugal	40	Albania	5
Luxembourg	37	Armenia	5
Denmark	37	Moldova	5
Italy	36	Slovakia	4
Turkey	32	Azerbaijan	3
Greece	31	Georgia	3
Israel	30	Serbia	3
Yugoslavia	27	Serbia &	
Cyprus	24	Montenegro	2
Monaco	21	Belarus	2
Malta	21	Bulgaria	2
Iceland	20	Morocco	1
Croatia	17		

The 2010 competition saw some regulars and not-so-regulars fail to enter or qualify for the competition: Austria, Luxembourg, Italy, Monaco, Hungary, Serbia & Montenegro, Morocco and Yugoslavia were those that did not compete in the Norwegian capital, Oslo in May 2010.

EUROVISION WINS

Ireland (1970, 1980, 1987, 1992, 1993, 1994, 1996)	7
France (1958, 1960, 1962, 1969, 1977)	5
Luxembourg (1961, 1965, 1972, 1973, 1983)	5
United Kingdom (1967, 1969, 1976, 1981, 1997)	5
Netherlands (1957, 1959, 1969, 1975)	4
Sweden (1974, 1984, 1991, 1999)	4
Israel (1978, 1979, 1998)	3
Norway (1985, 1995, 2009)	3
Germany (1982, 2010)	2
Spain (1968, 1969)	2
Switzerland (1956, 1988)	2
Italy (1964, 1990)	2
Denmark (1963, 2000)	2
Austria (1966)	1
Monaco (1971)	1
Belgium (1986)	1
Yugoslavia (1989)	1
Estonia (2001)	1
Latvia (2002)	1
Turkey (2003)	1
Ukraine (2004)	1
Greece (2005)	1
Finland (2006)	1
Serbia (2007)	1
Russia (2008)	1

The competition's most successful country, Ireland, is also the only one to have won in three consecutive years.

Right: Ireland's 1992 Eurovision winner, Linda Martin, with composer Johnny Logan.

Below: Lys Assia, the first Eurovision winner in 1956.

Right: Monsters of rock, Lordi stormed to victory in the 2006 contest.

WINNERS

Year	Country	Artist	Song
1956	Switzerland	Lys Assia	Refrain
1957	Netherlands	Corry Brokken	Net Als Toen
1958	France	André Claveau	Dors, Mon Amour
1959	Netherlands	Teddy Scholten	Een Beetje
1960	France	Jacqueline Boyer	Tom Pillibi
1961	Luxembourg	Jean-Claude Pascal	Nous Les Amoureux
1962	France	Isabelle Aubret	Un Premier Amour
1963	Denmark	Grethe & Jørgen Ingmann	Dansevise
1964	Italy	Gigliola Cinquetti	Non Ho L'età
1965	Luxembourg	France Gall	Poupée De Cire, Poupée De Don
1966	Austria	Udo Jürgens	Merci Chérie
1967	United Kingdom	Sandie Shaw	Puppet On A String
1968	Spain	Massiel	La, La, La
1969	Spain	Salomé	Vivo Cantando
1969	United Kingdom	Lulu	Boom Bang-A-Bang
1969	Netherlands	Lennie Kuhr	De Troubadour
1969	France	Frida Boccara	Un Jour, Un Enfant
1970	Ireland	Dana	All Kinds Of Everything
1971	Monaco	Severine	Un Banc, Un Arbre, Une Rue
1972	Luxembourg	Vicky Leandros	Aprés Toi
1973	Luxembourg	Anne-Marie David	Tu Te Reconnaîtras
1974	Sweden	Abba	Waterloo
1975	Netherlands	Teach-In	Ding-A-Dong
1976	United Kingdom	Brotherhood of Man	Save Your Kisses For Me
1977	France	Marie Myriam	L'oiseau Et L'enfant
1978	Israel	Izhar Cohen & Alphabeta	A-Ba-Ni-Bi
1979	Israel	Gali Atari & Milk and Honey	Hallelujah
1980	Ireland	Johnny Logan	What's Another Year?
1981	United Kingdom	Bucks Fizz	Making Your Mind Up
1982	Germany	Nicole	Ein Bißchen Frieden
1983	Luxembourg	Corinne Hermés	Si La Vie Est Cadeau
1984	Sweden	The Herreys	Diggi-Loo Diggi-Ley
1985	Norway	Bobbysocks	La Det Swinge
1986	Belgium	Sandra Kim	J'aime La Vie
1987	Ireland	Johnny Logan	Hold Me Now
1988	Switzerland	Céline Dion	Ne Partez Pas Sans Moi
1989	Yugoslavia	Riva	Rock Me
1990	Italy	Toto Cutugno	Insieme 1992
1991	Sweden	Carola	Fångad Av En Stormvind
1992	Ireland	Linda Martin	Why Me?
1993	Ireland	Niamh Kavanagh	In Your Eyes
1994	Ireland	Paul Harrington & Charlie McGettigan	Rock 'N' Roll Kids
1995	Norway	Secret Garden	Nocturne
1996	Ireland	Eimear Quinn	The Voice
1997	United Kingdom	Katrina & the Waves	Love Shine A Light
1998	Israel	Dana International	Diva
1999	Sweden	Charlotte Nilsson	Take Me To Your Heaven
2000	Denmark	Olsen Brothers	Fly On the Wings Of Love
2001	Estonia	Tanel Padar, Dave Benton & 2XL	Everybody
2002	Latvia	Marie N	I Wanna
2003	Turkey	Sertab Erener	Everyway That I Can
2004	Ukraine	Ruslana	Wild Dances
2005	Greece	Helena Paparizou	My Number One
2006	Finland	Lordi	Hard Rock Hallelujah
2007	Serbia	Marija Serifovic	Molitva
2008	Russia	Dima Bilan	Believe
2009	Norway	Alexander Rybak	Fairytale
2010	Germany	Lena	Satellite

Of all the artists who have won the Eurovision Song Contest, Abba and Céline Dion remain by far its most enduring popular contestants. The 2009 winner, Alexander Rybak, scored the highest winning score in the competition's history with 387 points.

MTV MUSIC TELEVISION

NIL POINTS

Austria	3	Germany	2	Lithuania	1
Finland	3	Netherlands	2	Luxembourg	1
Norway	3	Portugal	2	Monaco	1
Spain	3	Turkey	2	Sweden	1
Switzerland	3	Iceland	1	United Kingdom	1
Belgium	2	Italy	1	Yugoslavia	1

The most ignominious moment dreaded by all participants at the Eurovision Song Contest – which is broadcast live around the world to hundreds of millions of viewers – is receiving zero votes.

Below: Italian singer-songwriter Domenico Modugno.

THE 50TH ANNIVERSARY CELEBRATIONS

Waterloo	Abba	1974
Nel Blu, Di Pinto Di Blu (Volare)	Domenico Modugno	1958
Hold Me Now	Johnny Logan	1987
My Number One	Helena Paparizou	2005
Save Your Kisses For Me	Brotherhood of Man	1976

On October 22, 2005, viewers in 31 countries across Europe watched a special show in Copenhagen, Denmark, to celebrate Eurovision's 50th birthday. The following songs were voted the all-time Top 5. Domenico Modugno's 1958 entry was the only one not to have been a Eurovision winner.

RUNNERS-UP

United Kingdom	15
France	4
Germany	4
Ireland	4
Spain	4
Switzerland	3
Belgium	2
Iceland	2
Israel	2
Malta	2
Russia	2
Ukraine	2
Denmark	1
Italy	1
Monaco	1
Norway	1
Poland	1
Serbia & Montenegro	1
Sweden	1
Turkey	1

Although a four-time contest winner, the United Kingdom has accumulated an astonishing 15 second-places – the same as 11 other countries combined.

Left: Abba went from Eurovision success to international pop stardom.

THE LANGUAGES

English   24
United Kingdom (1967, 1969, 1976, 1981, 1997)
Ireland (1970, 1980, 1987, 1992, 1993, 1994, 1996)
Sweden (1974, 1999)
Netherlands (1975)
Denmark (2000)
Estonia (2001)
Latvia (2002)
Turkey (2003)
Ukraine (2004)
Greece (2005)
Finland (2006)
Russia (2008)
Norway (2009)

French   14
Belgium (1986)
France (1958, 1960, 1962, 1969, 1977)
Luxembourg (1961, 1965, 1972, 1973, 1983)
Monaco (1971)
Switzerland (1956, 1988)

Dutch   3
Netherlands (1957, 1959, 1969)

German   3
Austria (1966), Germany (1982, 2010)

Hebrew   3
Israel (1978, 1979, 1998)

Norwegian   2
Norway (1985, 1995)

Swedish   2
Sweden (1984, 1991)

Italian   2
Italy (1964, 1990)

Spanish   2
Spain (1968, 1969)

Danish   1
Denmark (1963)

Croatian   1
Yugoslavia (1989)

Ukrainian   1
Ukraine (2004)

Serbian   1
Serbia (2007)

Although English remains by far the language of choice for most winning songs, the one song which included the highest number of languages within its lyrics is Romania's 2007 entry, Todomondo's 'Liubi, Liubi, I Love You', which included words in English, French, Romanian, Russian, Spanish and Italian.

Above: Marija Serifovic performs her winning song 'Molitva' in 2007.

Below: Lena was Germany's 2010 Eurovision winner.

Bottom Right: Norway's high-scoring Alexander Rybak.

THE BIGGEST WINNING MARGINS

All entries have won by a margin of 25 or more points.

2009	Norway (Alexander Rybak)	169
2010	Germany (Lena)	76
1997	United Kingdom (Katrina and the Waves)	70
1982	Germany (Nicole)	61
1994	Ireland (Paul Harrington & Charlie McGettigan)	60
1996	Ireland (Eimear Quinn)	48
2006	Finland (Lordi)	44
2008	Russia (Dima Bilan)	42
2000	Denmark (Olsen Brothers)	40
2005	Greece (Helena Paparizou)	38
1986	Belgium (Sandra Kim)	36
2007	Serbia (Marija Serifovic)	33
1978	Israel (Izhar Cohen & Alphabeta)	32
1964	Italy (Gigliola Cinquetti)	32
1987	Ireland (Johnny Logan)	31
1995	Norway (Secret Garden)	29

HIGHEST POINTS TALLY

2009	Norway (Alexander Rybak)	387
2006	Finland (Lordi)	292
2004	Ukraine (Ruslana)	280
2008	Russia (Dima Bilan)	272
2007	Serbia (Marija Serifovic)	268
2010	Germany (Lena)	246
2005	Greece (Helena Paparizou)	230
1997	United Kingdom (Katrina and the Waves)	227
1994	Ireland (Paul Harrington & Charlie McGettigan)	226
2001	Estonia (Tanel Padar, Dave Benton & 2XL)	198
2000	Denmark (Olsen Brothers)	195
1993	Ireland (Niamh Kavanagh)	187
1986	Belgium (Sandra Kim)	176
2002	Latvia (Marie N)	176
1987	Ireland (Johnny Logan)	172
1998	Israel (Dana International)	172
2003	Turkey (Sertab Erener)	167
1976	United Kingdom (Brotherhood of Man)	164
1999	Sweden (Charlotte Nilsson)	163
1996	Ireland (Eimear Quinn)	162
1982	Germany (Nicole)	161
1978	Israel (Izhar Cohen & Alphabeta)	157
1992	Ireland (Linda Martin)	155

These figures are somewhat misleading in that over the years the scoring system has frequently changed. In 1957 – the first year that points were announced for each entry – the Netherlands came first with 31 points out of a possible maximum 100 points.

MUSIC AND FILM

Music and film have always been close entertainment cousins, the former playing a critical, emotion-stirring role in nearly all motion pictures. In the contemporary music arena many musicians have tried their hand at acting, while actors have proved more reluctant musicians. A few stars seem adept at both, successfully juggling parallel careers. One of the earliest examples in the rock 'n' roll era of the powerful synchronicity of celluloid and music was 1955's *Blackboard Jungle*, a social commentary movie set in an inner-city school, and featuring the culture-changing performance of *Rock Around the Clock* – which set off teen riots on both sides of the Atlantic.

NOTABLE ROCK BIO MOVIES

The Buddy Holly Story	Buddy Holly	1978
Elvis	Elvis Presley	1979
Coal Miner's Daughter	Loretta Lynn	1980
Sweet Dreams	Patsy Cline	1985
Sid And Nancy	Sid Vicious	1986
Crossroads	Robert Johnson	1986
La Bamba	Ritchie Valens	1987
Great Balls Of Fire	Jerry Lee Lewis	1989
The Five Heartbeats	The Temptations	1991
The Doors	The Doors	1991
What's Love Got to Do With It	Tina Turner	1993
Selena	Selena	1997
Why Do Fools Fall In Love	Frankie Lymon	1998
8 Mile	Eminem	2002
24 Hour Party People	Tony Wilson/ Factory Records	2002
Ray	Ray Charles	2004
Beyond The Sea	Bobby Darin	2004
Walk The Line	Johnny Cash	2005
Last Days	Kurt Cobain	2005
Stoned	Brian Jones	2005
Get Rich Or Die Tryin'	50 Cent	2005
Dreamgirls	Supremes	2006
I'm Not There	Bob Dylan	2007
Control	Ian Curtis/Joy Division	2007
Cadillac Records	Chess Record label	2008
Notorious	The Notorious B.I.G.	2009
Sex & Drugs & Rock & Roll	Ian Dury	2010
The Runaways	The Runaways	2010

TOP BOX-OFFICE GROSSING MUSICIAN/ACTORS

1	Will Smith	$2,542,908,988
2	Queen Latifah	$1,627,969,551
3	Bette Midler	$1,046,150,514
4	Jamie Foxx	$862,142,693
5	Barbra Streisand	$833,737,567
6	Kris Kristofferson	$828,455,532
7	Ice Cube	$816,096,429
8	Jennifer Lopez	$809,264,709
9	LL Cool J	$709,548,938
10	Madonna	$544,521,982
11	Beyoncé	$506,077,242
12	Common	$452,802,847
13	Snoop Dogg	$439,951,211
14	Willie Nelson	$431,829,506
15	Meat Loaf	$401,473,717

Although far busier and more successful as an actor, Will Smith has enjoyed a successful parallel music career as one half of the hip-hop/pop teen duo DJ Jazzy Jeff & The Fresh Prince and subsequently as a popular R&B/pop artist in his own right.

I'm Not There may count as the most unusual of all rock biography movies with no fewer than six actors separately portraying Bob Dylan: Christian Bale, Marcus Carl Franklin, Ben Wishaw, Richard Gere, Heath Ledger... and Cate Blanchett, whose gender-altering performance nabbed a Best Supporting Actress Oscar nomination.

Right: The 'Fresh Prince' – Will Smith back in the '90s.

ROCK MOVIES OF THE 1950S

The Big Beat	1957
Bop Girl	1957
Calypso Heat	1957
Carnival Rock	1957
Disc Jockey Jamboree	1957
Don't Knock The Rock	1956
The Duke Wore Jeans	1958
Expresso Bongo	1959
The Girl Can't Help It	1956
The Ghost Of Dragstrip Hollow	1959
Go Johnny Go!	1959
The Golden Disc	1958
Hey Boy, Hey Girl	1959
High School Confidential	1958
Hot Rod Gang	1958
Jamboree!	1957
Juke Box Rhythm	1959
Let's Rock	1958
Mister Rock And Roll	1957
Rock All Night	1957
Rock, Baby, Rock It!	1957
Rock, Rock, Rock	1956
Rock You Sinners	1957
Rockin' The Blues	1957
Shake, Rattle And Rock	1956
Sing Boy Sing	1958
The Tommy Steely Story	1957
Untamed Youth	1957

Below: English rock movie *The Duke Wore Jeans* at the Dominion Theatre.

THE TOP-GROSSING MUSIC MOVIES OF ALL-TIME GLOBALLY

1	Mamma Mia!	$602,600,000
2	The Bodyguard	$410,900,000
3	Grease	$387,209,000
4	Saturday Night Fever	$282,400,000
5	Michael Jackson's This Is It	$251,844,000

Above: *Mamma Mia!* Another huge commercial success from Abba's musical legacy.

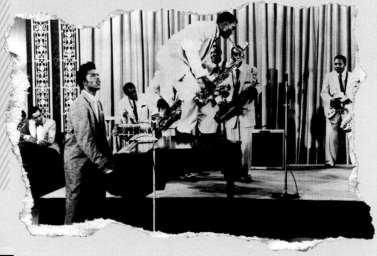

Left: Little Richard hits the keys in the 1956 movie *Don't Knock The Rock.*

MICK JAGGER AT THE MOVIES

Performance	1968
Invocation Of My Demon Brother	1969
Ned Kelly	1970
Umano Non Umano	1972
Fitzcarraldo	1981
Running Out Of Luck	1987
Freejack	1992
Bent	1997
My Best Fiend	1999
Enigma	2001
The Man From Elysian Fields	2001
The Bank Job	2008

Does not include documentaries.

Left: Jagger took the title role in the 1970's movie *Ned Kelly.*

Jagger most recently appeared on celluloid, uncredited, as a bank employee in the 2008 Jason Statham-starring hit, *The Bank Job.*

THE OSCAR-WINNING SONGS

The Academy Award for Best Original Song – first presented at the seventh Oscars ceremony in 1934 – is given to the songwriter(s) who compose the winning song. The first winner was Con Conrad and Herb Magidson's 'The Continental' from *The Gay Divorcee*.

THE 1950S

1950	Mona Lisa	Captain Carey
1951	In the Cool, Cool of the Evening	Here Comes The Groom
1952	High Noon	High Noon
1953	Secret Love	Calamity Jane
1954	Three Coins in the Fountain	Three Coins In The Fountain
1955	Love is a Many-Splendored Thing	Love Is A Many-Splendored Thing
1956	Whatever Will Be, Will Be	The Man Who Knew Too Much
1957	All the Way	The Joker Is Wild
1958	Gigi	Gigi
1959	High Hopes	A Hole In The Head

As unrivalled achievement, legendary lyricist/songwriter Sammy Cahn co-wrote the winners from 1954, 1957 and 1959. He was also nominated in 1950, 1951, 1952, 1955, 1956, and 1958 – but failed to win.

THE 1960S

1960	Never On A Sunday	Never On A Sunday
1961	Moon River	Breakfast At Tiffany's
1962	Days Of Wine And Roses	Days Of Wine And Roses
1963	Call Me Irresponsible	Papa's Delicate Condition
1964	Chim Chim Cheree	Mary Poppins
1965	The Shadow Of Your Smile	The Sandpiper
1966	Born Free	Born Free
1967	Talk To The Animals	Dr. Doolittle
1968	The Windmills Of Your Mind	The Thomas Crown Affair
1969	Raindrops Keep Falling On My Head	Butch Cassidy And The Sundance Kid

THE 1970S

1970	For All We Know	Lovers And Other Strangers
1971	Theme From Shaft	Shaft
1972	The Morning After	The Poseidon Adventure
1973	The Way We Were	The Way We Were
1974	We May Never Love Like This Again	The Towering Inferno
1975	I'm Easy	Nashville
1976	Evergreen (Love Theme from A Star Is Born)	A Star Is Born
1977	You Light Up My Life	You Light Up My Life
1978	Last Dance	Thank God it's Friday
1979	It Goes Like It Goes	Norma Rae

With lyrics by Alan and Marilyn Bergman and music by Marvin Hamlisch, the ballad 'The Way We Were' was the title theme to the film of the same name starring Barbra Streisand and Robert Redford. Streisand's hit song topped the US chart with Gladys Knight reviving it for a US number 11 success in 1975.

THE 1980S

1980	Fame	Fame
1981	Arthur's Theme (Best That You Can Do)	Arthur
1982	Up Where We Belong	An Officer And A Gentleman
1983	Flashdance... What a Feeling	Flashdance
1984	I Just Called to Say I Love You	The Woman in Red
1985	Say You, Say Me	White Nights
1986	Take My Breath Away	Top Gun
1987	(I've Had) the Time of My Life	Dirty Dancing
1988	Let the River Run	Working Girl
1989	Under the Sea	The Little Mermaid

B. J. Thomas' 'Raindrops Keep Falling on My Head' hit the US Top 10, while French crooner Sacha Distel's cover version of the 1969 Oscar-winner charted no less than five times in the UK, all in 1970.

Above: Burt Bacharach (pictured with then-wife Angie Dickinson) received two Academy Awards for music in *Butch Cassidy And The Sundance Kid*.

Right: Jennifer Warnes.

Recorded by ex-Righteous Brother Bill Medley and Jennifer Warnes (the latter also sang the 1979 Oscar-winning song, 'Norma Rae'), '(I've Had) The Time Of My Life' was written as the main theme for the Patrick Swayze-starring romantic dance movie, *Dirty Dancing* by Franke Previte, John DeNicola and Donald Markowitz.

THE 1990S

1990	Sooner Or Later (I Always Get My Man)	Dick Tracy
1991	Beauty And The Beast	Beauty And The Beast
1992	A Whole New World	Aladdin
1993	Streets Of Philadelphia	Philadelphia
1994	Can You Feel The Love Tonight?	The Lion King
1995	Colors Of The Wind	Pocahontas
1996	You Must Love Me	Evita
1997	My Heart Will Go On	Titanic
1998	When You Believe	The Prince Of Egypt
1999	You'll Be in My Heart	Tarzan

One of the Academy Awards' most nominated composers, Alan Menken became the king of animated feature length film music during the 1990s, picking up awards for the winning songs in 1991, 1992 and 1995. His lyricist co-writer on 'A Whole New World' – Tim Rice – managed three victories during the decade, also winning in 1994 and 1996.

Right: Randy Newman finally gets his Academy Award in 2001.

THE 2000S

2000	Things Have Changed	Wonder Boys
2001	If I Didn't Have You	Monsters, Inc.
2002	Lose Yourself	8 Mile
2003	Into The West	The Lord Of The Rings – The Return Of The King
2004	Al Otro Lado del Río	The Motorcycle Diaries
2005	It's Hard Out Here For A Pimp	Hustle & Flow
2006	I Need To Wake Up	An Inconvenient Truth
2007	Falling Slowly	Once
2008	Jai Ho!	Slumdog Millionaire
2009	The Weary Kind	Crazy Heart

Singer-songwriter and film composer Randy Newman finally nixed a 15-nomination losing streak (chalked up in both the Best Original Song and Best Original Score categories) in 2001 with 'If I Didn't Have You'.

SONGWRITERS WITH MOST WINS

Sammy Cahn, Johnny Mercer, Jimmy Van Heusen and Alan Menken lead the pack with four wins each. Cahn has 26 nominations – by far the most – followed by Mercer (18), Paul Francis Webster (16), Alan and Marilyn Bergman (15), Van Heusen (14) and Menken (13).

FEMALE WINNERS

Dorothy Fields was the first female to win an Oscar for Best Song in 1936. Thirty-two years went by before another woman did the same, when Marilyn Bergman won for 'The Windmills of Your Mind'. Since then a further nine women have been so honoured.

Left: Multi-award winning songwriter Sammy Cahn.

Right: Marilyn Bergman with husband and fellow songwriter, Alan.

AMERICAN FILM INSTITUTE

Founded in 1967 as a national arts organization to train filmmakers and preserve America's film heritage, the American Film Institute (AFI) compiles *AFI 100 Years...* lists as an ongoing celebration of the first century of cinema, subsequently revealed on a CBS television special.

AFI'S 100 YEARS OF FILM SCORES

#	Film	Composer	Year
1	Star Wars	John Williams	1977
2	Gone With The Wind	Max Steiner	1939
3	Lawrence Of Arabia	Maurice Jarre	1962
4	Psycho	Bernard Herrmann	1960
5	The Godfather	Nino Rota	1972
6	Jaws	John Williams	1975
7	Laura	David Raksin	1944
8	The Magnificent Seven	Elmer Bernstein	1960
9	Chinatown	Jerry Goldsmith	1974
10	High Noon	Dimitri Tiomkin	1952
11	The Adventures Of Robin Hood	Erich Wolfgang Korngold	1938
12	Vertigo	Bernard Herrmann	1958
13	King Kong	Max Steiner	1933
14	E.T. The Extra-Terrestrial	John Williams	1982
15	Out Of Africa	John Barry	1985
16	Sunset Blvd.	Franz Waxman	1950
17	To Kill A Mockingbird	Elmer Bernstein	1962
18	Planet Of The Apes	Jerry Goldsmith	1968
19	A Streetcar Named Desire	Alex North	1951
20	The Pink Panther	Henry Mancini	1964
21	Ben-Hur	Miklos Rozsa	1959
22	On The Waterfront	Leonard Bernstein	1954
23	The Mission	Ennio Morricone	1986
24	On Golden Pond	Dave Grusin	1981
25	How The West Was Won	Alfred Newman	1962

Abovet: Gene Kelly was *Singin' In The Rain* in 1952.

Left: Nicole Kidman and Ewan McGregor duet in *Moulin Rouge!*.

AFI'S THE GREATEST MOVIE MUSICALS

#	Film	Year
1	Singin' In The Rain	1952
2	West Side Story	1961
3	The Wizard Of Oz	1939
4	The Sound Of Music	1965
5	Cabaret	1972
6	Mary Poppins	1964
7	A Star Is Born	1954
8	My Fair Lady	1964
9	An American In Paris	1951
10	Meet Me In St. Louis	1944
11	The King And I	1956
12	Chicago	2002
13	42nd Street	1933
14	All That Jazz	1979
15	Top Hat	1935
16	Funny Girl	1968
17	The Band Wagon	1953
18	Yankee Doodle Dandy	1942
19	On The Town	1949
20	Grease	1978
21	Seven Brides For Seven Brothers	1954
22	Beauty And The Beast	1991
23	Guys And Dolls	1955
24	Show Boat	1936
25	Moulin Rouge!	2001

The criteria considered by the AFI judging panel of music and film critics, artists, directors, producers and historians, for the music-related lists above are:

Feature-Length Fiction Film: The film must be in narrative format, typically more than 60 minutes in length.

Song: Music and lyrics featured in an American film that set a tone or mood, define character, advance plot and/or express the film's themes in a manner that elevates the moving image art form. Songs may have been written and/or recorded specifically for the film or previously written and/or recorded and selected by the filmmaker to achieve the above goals.

American Film: The film must be in the English language with significant creative and/or financial production elements from the United States.

Cultural Impact: Songs that have captured the nation's heart, echoed beyond the walls of a movie theatre, and ultimately stand in our collective memory of the film itself.

Legacy: Songs that resonate across the century, enriching America's film heritage and captivating artists and audiences today."

#	Song	Film	Year
1	Over The Rainbow	The Wizard Of Oz	1939
2	As Time Goes By	Casablanca	1942
3	Singin' In The Rain	Singin' In The Rain	1952
4	Moon River	Breakfast At Tiffany's	1961
5	White Christmas	Holiday Inn	1942
6	Mrs. Robinson	The Graduate	1967
7	When You Wish Upon A Star	Pinocchio	1940
8	The Way We Were	The Way We Were	1973
9	Stayin' Alive	Saturday Night Fever	1977
10	The Sound Of Music	The Sound Of Music	1965
11	The Man That Got Away	A Star Is Born	1954
12	Diamonds Are A Girl's Best Friend	Gentlemen Prefer Blondes	1953
13	People	Funny Girl	1968
14	My Heart Will Go On	Titanic	1997
15	Cheek To Cheek	Top Hat	1935
16	Evergreen (Love Theme from A Star Is Born)	A Star Is Born	1976
17	I Could Have Danced All Night	My Fair Lady	1964
18	Cabaret	Cabaret	1972
19	Some Day My Prince Will Come	Snow White And The Seven Dwarfs	1937
20	Somewhere	West Side Story	1961
21	Jailhouse Rock	Jailhouse Rock	1957
22	Everybody's Talkin'	Midnight Cowboy	1969
23	Raindrops Keep Fallin' On My Head	Butch Cassidy And The Sundance Kid	1969
24	Ol' Man River	Show Boat	1936
25	High Noon (Do Not Forsake Me, Oh My Darlin')	High Noon	1952
26	The Trolley Song	Meet Me In St. Louis	1944
27	Unchained Melody	Ghost	1990
28	Some Enchanted Evening	South Pacific	1958
29	Born To Be Wild	Easy Rider	1969
30	Stormy Weather	Stormy Weather	1943
31	Theme From New York, New York	New York, New York	1977
32	I Got Rhythm	An American In Paris	1951
33	Aquarius	Hair	1979
34	Let's Call The Whole Thing Off	Shall We Dance	1937
35	America	West Side Story	1961
36	Supercalifragilistic expialidocious	Mary Poppins	1964
37	Swinging On A Star	Going My Way	1944
38	Theme From Shaft	Shaft	1971
39	Days Of Wine And Roses	Days Of Wine And Roses	1963
40	Fight The Power	Do The Right Thing	1989
41	New York, New York	On The Town	1949
42	Luck Be A Lady	Guys And Dolls	1955
43	The Way You Look Tonight	Swing Time	1936
44	Wind Beneath My Wings	Beaches	1988
45	That's Entertainment	The Band Wagon	1953
46	Don't Rain On My Parade	Funny Girl	1968
47	Zip-A-Dee-Doo-Dah	Song Of The South	1947
48	Whatever Will Be, Will Be (Que Sera, Sera)	The Man Who Knew Too Much	1956
49	Make 'Em Laugh	Singin' In The Rain	1952
50	Rock Around The Clock	Blackboard Jungle	1955
51	Fame	Fame	1980
52	Summertime	Porgy and Bess	1959
53	Goldfinger	Goldfinger	1964
54	Shall We Dance	The King and I	1956
55	Flashdance ... What A Feeling	Flashdance	1983
56	Thank Heaven For Little Girls	Gigi	1958
57	The Windmills Of Your Mind	The Thomas Crown Affair	1968
58	Gonna Fly Now	Rocky	1976
59	Tonight	West Side Story	1961
60	It Had To Be You	When Harry Met Sally	1989
61	Get Happy	Summer Stock	1950
62	Beauty and the Beast	Beauty And The Beast	1991
63	Thanks For The Memory	The Big Broadcast Of 1938	1938
64	My Favourite Things	The Sound of Music	1965
65	I Will Always Love You	The Bodyguard	1992
66	Suicide Is Painless	M*A*S*H	1970
67	Nobody Does It Better	The Spy Who Loved Me	1977
68	Streets Of Philadelphia	Philadelphia	1993
69	On The Good Ship Lollipop	Bright Eyes	1934
70	Summer Nights	Grease	1978
71	The Yankee Doodle Boy	Yankee Doodle Dandy	1942
72	Good Morning	Singin' in the Rain	1952
73	Isn't It Romantic?	Love Me Tonight	1932
74	Rainbow Connection	The Muppet Movie	1979
75	Up Where We Belong	An Officer And A Gentleman	1982
76	Have Yourself a Merry Little Christmas	Meet Me In St. Louis	1944
77	The Shadow of Your Smile	The Sandpiper	1965
78	9 To 5	9 To 5	1980
79	Arthur's Theme (Best That You Can Do)	Arthur	1981
80	Springtime For Hitler	The Producers	1968
81	I'm Easy	Nashville	1975
82	Ding Dong The Witch is Dead	The Wizard Of Oz	1939
83	The Rose	The Rose	1979
84	Put The Blame On Mame	Gilda	1946
85	Come What May	Moulin Rouge!	2001
86	(I've Had) The Time Of My Life	Dirty Dancing	1987
87	Buttons And Bows	The Paleface	1948
88	Do Re Mi	The Sound Of Music	1965
89	Puttin' On The Ritz	Young Frankenstein	1974
90	Seems Like Old Times	Annie Hall	1977
91	Let The River Run	Working Girl	1988
92	Long Ago And Far Away	Cover Girl	1944
93	Lose Yourself	8 Mile	2002
94	Ain't Too Proud To Beg	The Big Chill	1983
95	(We're Off On The) Road To Morocco	Road To Morocco	1942
96	Footloose	Footloose	1984
97	42nd Street	42nd Street	1933
98	All That Jazz	Chicago	2002
99	Hakuna Matata	The Lion King	1994
100	Old Time Rock And Roll	Risky Business	1983

Left: "Follow the Yellow Brick Road". *The Wizard of Oz* 1939.

Right: Maurice, Barry and Robin Gibb aka The Bee Gees.

MUSIC TELEVISION

The most successful music act in history, the Fab Four have sold more than 600 million records worldwide and continue to rack up new chart records some 40 years after they dissolved. Remarkably Lennon, McCartney, Harrison and Starr were only together for nine years and stopped performing live in 1966. During their relatively brief time together The Beatles redefined rock music, recording 12 studio albums, which became the soundtrack to the sixties and inspired each new generation of musicians.

THEIR BEST-SELLING UK SINGLES

1	She Loves You	16	A Hard Day's Night
2	I Want To Hold Your Hand	17	Penny Lane/
3	Can't Buy Me Love		Strawberry Fields Forever
4	I Feel Fine	18	Lady Madonna
5	We Can Work It Out/	19	Love Me Do
	Day Tripper	20	Please Please Me
6	Hey Jude	21	The Ballad Of John and
7	From Me To You		Yoko
8	Help!	22	Let It Be
9	Hello Goodbye	23	Free As A Bird
10	Get Back	24	Something/Come Together
11	Paperback Writer	25	Beatles Movie Medley
12	All You Need Is Love	26	Yesterday
13	Yellow Submarine/	27	Real Love
	Eleanor Rigby	28	Baby It's You
14	Ticket To Ride	29	Back In The U.S.S.R.
15	Magical Mystery Tour (EP)	30	Strawberry Fields Forever

Left: 1968 saw the release of the group's psychedelic movie, *Yellow Submarine*.

THE DAY JOHN LENNON MET PAUL MCCARTNEY

On July 6, 1957, John Lennon and Paul McCartney met for the first time when Lennon's Quarry Men Skiffle Group played at the St. Peter's Parish Church Garden Fête in Woolton, Liverpool and he met McCartney backstage after the band had played.

THE FIRST HIT

The Beatles' first British hit was 'Love Me Do'. It entered the chart on October 13, 1962 at number 49, one place below Little Richard's 'He Got What He Wanted'. The Tornados were at number one with 'Telstar' and Elvis and Cliff stood at numbers five and six respectively. 'Love Me Do' took eight weeks to reach its peak of number 17 in Christmas week, no doubt helped by their manager Brian Epstein ensuring copies were bought at stores to inflate its chart position. In the NME chart, it spent a solitary week at number 27.

THEIR NUMBER ONES BY COUNTRY

Australia	26	Germany	18	Switzerland	8
Canada	22	United Kingdom	17	Zimbabwe	8
Sweden	22	Hong Kong	16	Austria	6
Holland	21	New Zealand	15	Belgium	6
Norway	21	Ireland	13	Finland	5
United States	20	Malaysia	13	Italy	4
Denmark	18	Spain	9	Ethiopia	2

The Beatles' She Loves You	(I Want To Hold Your Hand)
The Beatles' Can't Buy Me Love	(She Loves You)
Louis Armstrong's Hello, Dolly!	(Can't Buy Me Love)
The Dixie Cups' Chapel Of Love	(Love Me Do)
Dean Martin's Everybody Loves Somebody	(A Hard Day's Night)
The Supremes' Come See About Me	(I Feel Fine)
The Supremes' Stop! In The Name Of Love	(Eight Days A Week)
The Beach Boys' Help Me Rhonda	(Ticket To Ride)
Barry McGuire's Eve Of Destruction	(Help!)
The Rolling Stones' Get Off Of My Cloud	(Yesterday)
Petula Clark's My Love	(We Can Work It Out)
Frank Sinatra's Strangers In The Night	(Paperback Writer)
The Turtles' Happy Together	(Penny Lane)
Bobbie Gentry's Ode To Billie Joe	(All You Need Is Love)
John Fred & His Playboy Band's Judy In Disguise (With Glasses)	(Hello Goodbye)
Diana Ross & the Supremes' Love Child	(Hey Jude)
Henry Mancini & His Orchestra's Love Theme from *Romeo and Juliet*	(Get Back)
Steam's Na Na Hey Hey Kiss Him Goodbye	(Come Together/Something)
Jackson 5's ABC	(Let It Be)
Jackson 5's The Love You Save	(The Long And Winding Road/ For You Blue)

THEIR NUMBER ONE HIT SINGLES IN THE UK

Until the publication of the first *Guinness Hit Singles* book, 'Please Please Me' was seen as the group's first number 1, but because that book sourced data from *Record Retailer*, where it peaked at number 2, it isn't classified as a number 1 – even though it topped many other charts.

THE BESTSELLERS

Over the past two decades, the Beatles have never sold less than 1 million CDs in a year in the United States. The group has scored 15 number one albums in the UK, the most of any act, and 17 UK chart-topping singles – another record.

THE BIGGEST EVER CROWD

In August 1965, the Beatles played to the largest crowd ever when 55,600 fans saw the band in concert at the Shea Stadium baseball stadium in New York. Their record stood for nearly eight years, when Led Zeppelin were seen by 56,800 fans at Tamps Stadium in Florida.

Left: The band opened their 1965 North American tour at New York's Shea Stadium.

DON'T SHOOT ME, I'M ONLY THE HARMONIUM PLAYER

In December 1965, the Beatles starred in the TV show *The Music of Lennon-McCartney*. Performing 'We Can Work It Out', John Lennon played the harmonium used by Ena Sharples at the Glad Tidings Mission in TV soap opera *Coronation Street*.

Right: In 1962 the band had their first recording session at Abbey Road Studios.

THEIR ALBUMS

Please Please Me	1963
With The Beatles	1963
A Hard Day's Night	1964
Beatles For Sale	1964
Help!	1965
Rubber Soul	1965
Revolver	1966
Sgt. Pepper's Lonely Hearts Club Band	1967
The Beatles	1968
Yellow Submarine	1969
Abbey Road	1969
Let It Be	1970

The Beatles' entire studio recording legacy was created in just eight short years between 1963 and 1970. In the time it takes Sade to record one album, the group recorded 12 (not including the 1967 double-EP, *Magical Mystery Tour*) and each one was a seminal musical classic.

THE ED SULLIVAN SHOW

On February 9, 1964 – with screaming, hysterical teenage girls in the studio audience – an estimated 73 million viewers watched the Beatles' American television debut on *The Ed Sullivan Show*. (The crime rate in US cities was reported to have dropped dramatically during the show's broadcast time.) Also appearing on the programme were Georgia Brown and the children's chorus from the hit Broadway show *Oliver!* (including future Monkee Davy Jones), Welsh actress/singer Tessie O'Shea and impressionist Frank Gorshin.

THE LEGENDARY TOP 5

On April 4, 1964, the Beatles had the numbers one to five on the American singles chart with 'Can't Buy Me Love' (number 1), 'Twist and Shout' (number two), 'She Loves You' (number three), 'I Want To Hold Your Hand' (number four) and 'Please Please Me' (number five.) In addition, 'I Saw Her Standing There' was at number 31, 'From Me To You' at number 41, 'Do You Want To Know A Secret?' at number 46, 'All My Loving' at number 58, 'You Can't Do That' at number 65, 'Roll Over Beethoven' at number 68 and 'Thank You Girl' at number 79. The following week two more records entered the chart, giving the Beatles 14 in total.

Left: Lennon and McCartney at the start of Beatlemania in 1963.

JUKE BOX JURY

On December 7, 1963, all four Beatles appeared on BBC-TV's weekly pop panel programme *Juke Box Jury*. This is how they rated the ten records, together with each disc's subsequent UK chart performance:

1 The Chants – 'I Could Write A Book'
The Fab Four raved over this choral vocal disc from a fellow Liverpool group. They all voted it a hit, with host David Jacobs asking rhetorically, "Are they being too generous?" (A MISS)

2 Elvis Presley – 'Kiss Me Quick'
The overall review was that Elvis' voice was great but his material was scrappy in comparison with his earlier records. Nevertheless, all four voted it a hit. (REACHED NO. 14)

3 The Swinging Blue Jeans – 'Hippy Hippy Shake'
Ringo didn't like it as much as the Chan Romero original, but George said it was a popular number around Liverpool already and the Beatles used to cover it themselves. All four voted it a hit. (REACHED NO. 2)

4 Paul Anka – 'Did You Have A Happy Birthday?'
George said he did, but that hearing this would put him off. His cohorts all disliked the song or the treatment, or both. Each voted it a miss. (A MISS)

5 Shirley Ellis – 'The Nitty Gritty'
With this 45 already shooting up the US charts, all four said that they liked this style of record a lot, but that it wouldn't be a UK hit with George saying "We haven't got around to that sort of thing yet." All four voted it a miss. David Jacobs thought it stood a good chance, however, and asked the second jury (three audience members) how they would vote on it. They rated it a miss too. (A MISS)

6 Steve Lawrence & Eydie Gorme – 'I Can't Stop Talking About You'
Paul and Ringo liked it, George admired the relaxed feel. John said it sounded relaxed because "they're getting on a bit – I don't like it." Verdict: a hit by 3 to 1. (A MISS)

7 Billy Fury – 'Do You Really Love Me Too'
John and George reservedly approved, Ringo said "not for me" and Paul "quite liked it". They all recognized Fury's hit-making status, however, and all four voted it a hit. (REACHED NO. 13)

8 Bobby Vinton – 'There I've Said It Again'
America's fastest-rising hit at the time, George thought it okay but not commercial, while John and Paul mused about the desirability of reviving old ballads. Ringo liked the smoothness: "Especially if you're sitting in one night and not alone," to which David Jacobs replied "Thank you, Don Juan Starr." All four voted it a miss. It turned out to be the record the Beatles knocked off the top of the American chart in February 1964 when they had their first US number one single with 'I Want to Hold Your Hand'. (REACHED NO. 34)

9 The Orchids – 'Love Hit Me'
John thought it was a straight poach of the Spector sound, though Paul thought that quality made it sound quite good for a British release. Ringo couldn't see it selling many, while George thought he'd rather have British groups borrow from the Crystals. It was voted a miss by 3 to 1.
The Orchids (three schoolgirls) were then introduced, having been secretly present. John thought it was a dirty trick. (A MISS)

10 The Merseybeats – 'I Think Of You'
With time running short, there was no chance for discussion of this single by another fellow Liverpudlian group. Asked for a quick verdict without comments, all four voted it a hit. (REACHED NO. 5)

Their revered compositions have been covered by thousands of artists over the years, and provided career-changing material for a host of acts during their own decade. Written by McCartney in 1965 (though credited to Lennon/McCartney as were all of their Beatles songs) 'Yesterday' remains the most covered song of all time with more than 3,000 different versions recorded.

Left: Paul and John:
Two men with a lot
to smile about.

ELVIS PRESLEY

Although several other artists from the 1950s can lay claim to being pioneers of the different threads which formed the rock 'n' roll fabric (notably Louis Jordan, Little Richard, Chuck Berry, Ray Charles), Presley was unique in distilling all the necessary musical ingredients that cooked the rock 'n' roll stew. His music combined influences from gospel, rhythm & blues, country, bluegrass and swing. Toss in some blessed vocal chops, lean good looks and a daring, hip-swivelling performance style and the poor white kid from Tupelo, Mississippi was on his way to unmatched global superstardom.

HIS UK NUMBER ONE ALBUMS

Elvis Is Back!	Jul 30, 1960
G.I. Blues	Jan 14, 1961
Blue Hawaii	Jan 06, 1962
Pot Luck With Elvis	July 28, 1962
From Elvis In Memphis	Aug 30, 1969
Elvis' 40 Greatest	Sep 10, 1977
Elv1s - 30 #1 Hits	Oct 05, 2002
The King	Aug 25, 2007

Above: Elvis in the movie *Jailhouse Rock* in 1957.

Elvis has accumulated more UK chart-toppers than any other artist, with 22 in total – despite a 25-year gap from 1977 to 2002.

ELVIS ON SCREEN

Love Me Tender	Clint Reno	1956
Loving You	Jimmy Tomkins/	
	Deke Rivers	1957
Jailhouse Rock	Vince Everett	1957
King Creole	Danny Fisher	1958
GI Blues	Tulsa McLean	1960
Flaming Star	Pacer Burton	1960
Wild In The Country	Glenn Tyler	1961
Blue Hawaii	Chad Gates	1961
Follow That Dream	Toby Kwimper	1962
Kid Galahad	Walter Gulick	1962
Girls! Girls! Girls!	Ross Carpenter	1962
It Happened At The		
World's Fair	Mike Edwards	1963
Fun In Acapulco	Mike Windgren	1963
Kissin' Cousins	Josh Morgan/Jodie Traum	1964
Viva Las Vegas	Lucky Jackson	1964
Roustabout	Charlie Rogers	1964
Girl Happy	Rusty Wells	1964
Tickle Me	Lonnie Beale/Panhandle Kid	1965
Harum Scarum	Johnny Tyrone	1965
Frankie And Johnny	Johnny	1966
Paradise, Hawaiian Style	Rick Richards	1966
Spinout	Mike McCoy	1966
Easy Come, Easy Go	Lt. Ted Jackson	1967
Double Trouble	Guy Lambert	1967
Clambake	Scott Hayward/Tom Wilson	1967
Stay Away Joe	Joe Lightcloud	1968
Speedway	Steve Grayson	1968
Live A Little, Love A Little	Greg Nolan	1968
Charro!	Jess Wade	1969
The Trouble With Girls	Walter Hale	1969
Change Of Habit	Dr. John Carpenter	1969

Elvis made 31 feature movies (not including concert films such as 1970's *Elvis: That's the Way it is* and 1972's *Elvis On Tour*) over a 13-year period. He played characters with the first name "Mike" in three films (Mike Edwards in *It Happened at the World's Fair*, Mike Windgren in *Fun in Acapulco* and Mike McCoy in *Spinout*).

ELVIS AT THE GRAMMYS

Elvis was nominated 14 times for a Grammy, but only came away a winner three times – all for his gospel recordings.

Best Sacred Performance for 'How Great Thou Art'	1967
Best Inspirational Performance for 'He Touched Me'	1972
Best Inspirational Performance (Non-Classical) for 'How Great Thou Art'	1974

Four of his recordings have been inducted into the NARAS Hall of Fame.

'Hound Dog' (1956)	1988
'Heartbreak Hotel' (1956)	1995
'That's All Right' (1954)	1998
'Suspicious Minds' (1969)	1999

ELVIS' MOST SUCCESSFUL SONGWRITERS

Jerry Leiber & Mike Stoller	9
Ben Weisman	7
Doc Pomus & Mort Shuman	6
Otis Blackwell	6
Fred Wise	6
Mac Davis	5
Aaron Schroeder	5
Mark James	4
Don Robertson	4
Winfield Scott	4
Sid Wayne	4

Most of his hits were co-written credits, for example Ben Weisman's songs were either written with Fred Wise or Sid Wayne & Dolores Fuller. Leiber & Stoller's first Elvis hit, 'Hound Dog' in 1956 was originally written for R&B singer, Big Mama Thornton in 1952.

Left: The King in 1976

HIS FIRST TV APPEARANCE

On January 28, 1956, Presley made his first television appearance. It was on *Stage Show*, produced by Jackie Gleason Enterprises and hosted by Tommy and Jimmy Dorsey, which aired live from CBS Studio 50 in New York. Introduced by Bill Randle, Elvis sang 'Shake Rattle And Roll' with 'Flip, Flop And Fly' and 'I Got a Woman'. Gleason stated after the show: "He can't last. I tell you flatly, he can't last." Presley was paid $1,250 for the appearance.

ELVIS SETS FOOT IN THE UK

On March 2, 1960, on his way home for demobilization from Frankfurt, the plane in which Presley was flying made a refuelling stop at Prestwick Airport in Scotland and while on the ground he talked to fans through a fence. This is the only occasion on which he set foot on British soil. The main reason that Elvis never played abroad was because his manager, Colonel Parker, was living as an illegal alien (from Holland) in the US and would not risk having to re-enter the country.

ELVIS SIGNS ON THE DOTTED LINE

Presley signed a formal management contract with Colonel Tom Parker on August 15, 1955. Parker immediately spread word that Presley's contract with Sun Records might be up for grabs. Decca Records' bid of $5,000 was turned down by Sun owner Sam Phillips, as was Dot Records' offer of $7,500. Parker heard that Mercury Records was considering a $10,000 bid and alerted CBS/Columbia's Mitch Miller, who said he was willing to increase their interest to $15,000. Parker hinted that RCA was considering $20,000, at which point Miller claimed "no singer is worth that much". Ahmet Ertegun at Atlantic Records disagreed and was willing to risk $25,000, but Parker insisted nearly twice as much as that was, in his words, "more realistic". Eventually RCA won the bidding war – and Elvis would remain with them throughout his career. Sun boss Phillips took his windfall and invested in the fledgling Holiday Inn hotel chain.

Above: *Loving You* (1957) was Elvis' second movie.

Above: The legendary
'68 Comeback Special.

HIS FIRST 10 US SINGLES

That's All Right Mama/		
Blue Moon Of Kentucky	Sun 209	Jul 19, 1954
Good Rockin' Tonight/		
I Don't Care If The Sun Don't Shine	Sun 210	Sep 25, 1954
Milkcow Blues Boogie/		
You're A Heartbreaker	Sun 215	Dec 28, 1954
Baby Let's Play House/		
I'm Left, You're Right, She's Gone	Sun 217	Apr 10, 1955
I Forgot To Remember To Forget/		
Mystery Train	Sun 223	Aug 06, 1955
Heartbreak Hotel/I Was The One	RCA 6420	Feb 1956
I Want You, I Need You, I Love You/		
My Baby Left Me	RCA 6420	May 1956
Hound Dog/Don't Be Cruel	RCA 6604	Jul 1954
Love Me Tender/		
Any Way You Want Me	RCA 6643	Jan 1957
Too Much/Playing For Keeps	RCA 6800	Jan 1957

HIS BIGGEST-SELLING SINGLES IN THE UK

1	It's Now Or Never	1960
2	Jailhouse Rock	1958
3	Are You Lonesome Tonight?	1961
4	Wooden Heart	1961
5	Return To Sender	1962
6	Can't Help Falling In Love/Rock-A-Hula-Baby	1962
7	The Wonder Of You	1970
8	Surrender	1961
9	Way Down	1977
10	All Shook Up	1957

This list reflects half of Elvis Presley's chart-topping British hits: 'It's Now Or Never', at number one for nine weeks at the end of 1960, was easily his biggest UK success – and his only UK million-seller.

Sun Records was a small independent label in Memphis, Tennessee where Presley's recording career was born. The first of the Sun releases to find national success was 'I Forgot To Remember To Forget', which made the top 10 in the Country & Western charts.

Above: Elvis rocked on into the mid '70s, despite his deteriorating health.

THE ELVIS-DOMINATED UK SINGLES CHARTS

The *New Musical Express* singles chart of November 2, 1957 featured six Elvis singles, comprising 20 per cent of the survey: 'Party' (No. 4), 'Teddy Bear' (No. 12), 'All Shook Up' (No. 16), 'Trying to Get to You' (No. 20), 'Got A Lot O' Livin' To Do' (No. 21), 'Loving You' (No. 24) and 'Paralysed' (No. 26).

Following his death in August 1977, the September 3 UK chart featured the following Elvis singles: 'Way Down' (No. 1), 'It's Now Or Never' (No. 39), 'Crying In The Chapel' (No. 43), 'Jailhouse Rock' (No. 44), 'Are You Lonesome Tonight?' (No. 46), 'The Wonder Of You' (No. 48) and 'Return To Sender' (No. 50).

ELVIS COLLECTIBLES

The Collectibles Today website sells hundreds of different pieces of Elvis memorabilia. Here are some of the offerings:

Commemorative Baby Doll Collection – Baby Let's Rock!	$179.99
The Ultimate Elvis Presley Antique-Style Telephone	$149.95
Elvis Presley Express HO-Scale Train Collection – King of Rock 'n' Roll	$69.95
Elvis Presley Stained-Glass Wall Décor Art – Graceland by Thomas Kinkade	$149.95
Elvis Presley Collectible Cuckoo Clock – Elvis For All Time	$179.99
Love Me Tender Elvis Fan Pajama Set	$69.95
Elvis Rock and Roll Christmas Village Collection	$59.95
Elvis Presley Figurine Collection with Mirror Display – Reflections of Elvis	$39.95
Elvis Presley Tribute M&M's Characters Figurine – A Little M Conversation	$19.99
Elvis Presley Velour Sweat Suit Loungewear Set – The King of Rock 'n' Roll	$99.95
Elvis Presley Reversible Earrings Featuring "Aloha From Hawaii" Portrait	$99.00
Elvis Presley Heirloom Porcelain Turtle Music Box Collection – L'il Elvis Tribute	$49.99
Elvis Presley Light–Up Porcelain Tabletop Christmas Tree – Blue Christmas	$135.00
Mickey's Magical Tribute to the King Collectible Mickey and Elvis Collection	$19.95
Elvis Presley Chopper Figurine Collection	$59.95
Elvis Presley Merry Christmas Flag – Elvis Home Décor	$19.95
Elvis Presley 68 Comeback Special Collectible Tabletop Lamp	$129.96
Elvis Presley Happy Halloween Flag	$19.95

HIS FUNERAL

Following his death on August 16, 1977, Presley's funeral service, arranged by singer J.D. Sumner and conducted by the Reverend C.W. Bradley, was held two days later at his Graceland home in Memphis with 150 people attending, and 75,000 more outside the gates. His body was moved by hearse in a 19-Cadillac cortège to Forest Hill cemetery, for entombment at 4.30pm in a mausoleum alongside his mother. With two prayers, one poem and 150 mourners, the legend was laid to rest in a grey marble crypt, 9' long, 27" high, surrounded by thousands of floral tributes which required over 100 vans to take them from Graceland to the burial site. The King was buried wearing his TCB ("Taking Care of Business") ring. Teenagers Alice Hovatar and Juanita Johnson were killed during an all-night vigil at Graceland after a car ploughed into the assembled crowd.

Above: 'Aloha from Hawaii' – the concert in 1973.

Below: The King's hearse passes through the gates of Graceland.

RETURN TO SENDER

When the Presley postage stamp, designed by Mark Stutzman and issued after years of campaigning by Pat Geiger, went on sale on January 8, 1993, many fans deliberately addressed letters to false destinations so that they would be returned stamped "Return To Sender".

HIS FAVOURITE MEAL

On what would have been Presley's 56th birthday on January 8, 1991, the Hard Rock Café in Orlando, Florida, served what they claimed was his favourite meal:

6lb beef roast
Creamed potatoes with butter
Mixed vegetables with butter
Peas with salt pork
Cornbread

And for dessert... banana pudding.

ELVIS HAS LEFT THE BUILDING

Bio Science Laboratories revealed that at the time of his death, Presley's body contained the following drugs:

Butabarbital
Codeine
Morphine
Pentobarbital
Placidyl
Quaalude
Valium
Valmid

ELVIS HAS NOT LEFT THE BUILDING

ACRSK is an acronym for the Agency for Confirmations and Registration of Sightings of the King. Their website lists just four confirmed sightings:

Moon S. Duepre at an abandoned schoolhouse in Midlothian, Virginia	Sep 09, 1988
Paul B. Doe at the Deutscheplatz in Berlin	Jul 11, 1991
Oscar J. Peterson in the men's room at Fuddrucker's in Coconut Grove	Sep 07, 1996
Baleva Sacessfa at a sidewalk café in San Clemente	Mar 13, 2001

ELVIS HAS NOT ARRIVED AT THE BUILDING

When he was head coach with the Houston Oilers and Atlanta Falcons American Football teams, Jerry Glanville always used to leave tickets for Elvis (long after his death) at home games.

CLIFF RICHARD

Cliff Richard served a musical apprenticeship with the Dick Teague Skiffle Group and as front man for his own Quintones vocal group at the age of 17 before forming Cliff Richard & The Drifters in 1958. Following a successful demo session at Abbey Road studios where they cut 'Schoolboy Crush' and 'Move It', Richard was quickly snapped up by EMI's Columbia imprint, quitting his job as a credit control clerk at Atlas Lamps in Enfield, Middlesex. He was initially marketed as Britain's answer to Elvis Presley with his first hit reaching number 2 on the UK chart before the end of the year.

HIS BEST-SELLING ALBUMS

1	Private Collection, 1977–88	1988
2	From a Distance – The Event	1990
3	Love Songs	1981
4	Always Guaranteed	1987
5	The Young Ones	1961
6	Summer Holiday	1963
7	40 Golden Greats	1977
8	Stronger	1989
9	Wired For Sound	1981
10	Rock 'n' Roll Juvenile	1979

Among performers who first found success in the 1950s, Cliff Richard stands alone in still maintaining a high-selling contemporary profile in the twenty-first century. His 2009 album, *Reunited* – which saw the 69-year old pop legend reworking his earlier hits with The Shadows – the group he first paired with 50 years earlier, peaked at UK No. 4.

HIS NUMBER ONE HIT SINGLES IN THE UK

Living Doll	Aug 01, 1959
Travellin' Light	Oct 31, 1959
Please Don't Tease	Jul 30, 1960
I Love You	Dec 31, 1960
The Young Ones	Jan 13, 1962
The Next Time	Jan 05, 1963
Bachelor Boy/The Next Time	Jan 12, 1963
Summer Holiday	Mar 16, 1963
The Minute You're Gone	Apr 17, 1965
Congratulations	Apr 13, 1968
We Don't Talk Anymore	Aug 25, 1979
Living Doll (with the Young Ones featuring Hank Marvin)	Mar 29, 1986
Mistletoe And Wine	Dec 10, 1988
Saviour's Day	Dec 29, 1990
The Millennium Prayer	Dec 04, 1999

Above: Cliff was definitely one of 'The Young Ones' in 1962.

Cliff Richard is the only act to have notched up UK No. 1 singles in five decades, from the 1950s to the 1990s. 'Daddy's Home', despite selling 500,000+ copies, only reached No. 2 in 1981 behind the Human League's million-selling 'Don't You Want Me'.

CLIFF AT THE MOVIES

Serious Charge	Curley Thompson	1959
Expresso Bongo	Bert Rudge/ Bongo Herbert	1959
The Young Ones	Nicky	1961
Summer Holiday	Don	1963
Wonderful Life	Johnnie	1964
Finders Keepers	Cliff	1966
Two A Penny	Jamie Hopkins	1967
Take Me High	Tim Matthews	1973

He also made an uncredited vocal appearance as Cliff Richard Jr. in the 1966 movie *Thunderbirds Are Go*. Perhaps his most popular film, *The Young Ones* was released in the US as *Wonderful to Be Young*.

CLIFF ONSTAGE

Aladdin	London Palladium	1964
Cinderella	London Palladium	1966
Five Finger Exercise	New Theatre, Bromley	1970
The Potting Shed	Sadlers Wells Theatre	1971
Time	Dominion Theatre	1986
Heathcliff	National Arena, Birmingham (and then on tour)	1996

HIS TOP
SINGLES WORLDWIDE

1	We Don't Talk Anymore	1979
2	The Young Ones	1962
3	Devil Woman	1976
4	Congratulations	1968
5	Living Doll	1959
6	The Next Time/Bachelor Boy	1962
7	Summer Holiday	1963
8	Lucky Lips	1963
9	Please Don't Tease	1960
10	Travellin' Light	1959

Above: 'Bachelor Boy.'
Cliff in the '60s.

The first five hits each sold over 2,000,000 apiece. Cliff's best-selling singles on a global basis differ substantially from his UK thhop 10 – with the million-selling 'Mistletoe and Wine' not an international success, and 'Lucky Lips' his most successful single ever in Germany.

HIS TOP DUET SINGLES IN THE UK

1	Living Doll	The Young Ones
2	All I Ask Of You	Sarah Brightman
3	Throw Down A Line	Hank Marvin
4	She Means Nothing To Me	Phil Everly
5	Suddenly	Olivia Newton-John
6	Whenever God Shines His Light	Van Morrison
7	Joy Of Living	Hank Marvin
8	Slow Rivers	Elton John
9	Drifting	Sheila Walsh
10	Two To The Power of Love	Janet Jackson

The top six of these all reached the UK top 20; all the others – apart from Cliff's 1984 duet with Janet Jackson – made the top 75. That single, together with numbers four, five, six, eight and nine, all credit Cliff after the main credited artist.

CLIFF'S TV DEBUT

Cliff made his small screen debut on September 13, 1958, on Jack Good's seminal *Oh Boy*, singing 'Move it'.

Below: Sir Cliff receiving his knighthood in 1995.

CLIFF AT EUROVISION

Cliff (who was born in India to Anglo/Indian parents) has represented the United Kingdom twice in the Eurovision Song Contest – the first time in 1968 when 'Congratulations' was pipped by un point by 'La, La, La', performed by Massiel from Spain. A 2008 television documentary claimed that General Franco's fascist regime in Spain rigged the contest to ensure a Spanish win. In 1973, Cliff's 'Power To All Our Friends' came third.

CLIFF NOTES

According to Cliff's official website, he has released 149 singles, 44 EPs, 84 albums and 11 compilations. His total UK record sales over a 50-plus year career are estimated at 21 million.

Above: Cliff represented the UK at the 1968 Eurovision Song Contest.

CLIFF'S AWARDS

Nordoff Robbins' Silver Clef for Outstanding Services to the Music Industry	1974
Best British Male Solo Artist – Britannia Awards	1977
Gold Badge Award – Songwriters' Guild of Great Britain	1978
Order of the British Empire – the Queen's New Year's Honours List	1980
Best British Male Solo Artist – BRIT Awards	1982
Outstanding Contribution to British Music – BRIT Awards	1989
Lifetime Achievement Award – Ivor Novello Awards	1990
Knighthood	1995
Silver Accolade – Nordoff Robbins' Music Therapy	1998

He has also received awards from the *TV Times*, *The Sun*, *Disc & Music Echo*, *Melody Maker*, *New Musical Express*, *Record Mirror*, UK Music Hall of Fame and the Lawn Tennis Association among many others.

BOB DYLAN

Widely regarded as the foremost songwriter of his generation, Robert Allen Zimmerman was born on May 24, 1941 in Duluth, Minnesota and played in several high school bands while attending Hibbing High School. Following a brief stint as a pianist in Bobby's Vee's backing band in 1959, Dylan reverted to the acoustic guitar learned while growing up, to play solo gigs while studying at the University of Minnesota. He then relocated to Greenwich village in New York where he became a popular fixture on the burgeoning Greenwich coffee-house folk scene. Dylan signed to Columbia Records in October 1961.

HIS BEST-SELLING ALBUMS

1	Bob Dylan's Greatest Hits	1967
2	Bob Dylan's Greatest Hits Volume II	1971
3	Desire	1976
4	Blood On The Tracks	1975
5	Blonde On Blonde	1966
6	The Essential Bob Dylan	2000
7	Slow Train Coming	1979
8	John Wesley Harding	1967
9	Bringing It All Back Home	1965
10	Nashville Skyline	1969
11	Highway 61 Revisited	1965
12	The Freewheelin' Bob Dylan	1963
13	Time Out Of Mind	1997
14	Modern Times	2006
15	Before The Flood	1974

Below: Dylan with his trademark harmonica and guitar.

HIS MOST POPULAR SINGLES IN THE UK

1	Like A Rolling Stone	1965
2	Lay Lady Lay	1969
3	Positively 4th Street	1965
4	Rainy Day Women, Nos. 12 & 35	1966
5	The Times They Are A-Changin'	1965
6	Subterranean Homesick Blues	1965
7	Baby Stop Crying	1978
8	Knockin' On Heaven's Door	1973
9	I Want You	1966
10	Watching The River Flow	1971

More successful as an album-selling act, Dylan's greatest UK singles chart successes came in 1965, the year he made a perceived transition from folk to rock. 'Like A Rolling Stone' is his only 45 to exceed 250,000 UK sales. 'Knockin' On Heaven's Door' was recorded for the movie, *Pat Garrett and Billy the Kid*, in which Dylan had an acting role.

HIS MOST POPULAR SINGLES IN THE US

1	Like A Rolling Stone	1965
2	Rainy Day Women, Nos. 12 & 35	1966
3	Positively 4th Street	1965
4	Lay Lady Lay	1969
5	Knockin' On Heaven's Door	1973
6	I Want You	1966
7	Just Like A Woman	1966
8	Gotta Serve Somebody	1979
9	Hurricane	1976
10	Subterranean Homesick Blues	1965

Right: After dropping out of college, he moved to New York in 1961.

SONGWRITERS HALL OF FAME

Upon being inducted into the Songwriters Hall of Fame on March 15, 1982 at the New York's Hilton Hotel , Dylan commented: "I think this is pretty amazing because I can't read or write a note of music. Thank you."

THE TOP UK HITS
COMPOSED BY BOB DYLAN

1	Knockin' On Heaven's Door	Eric Clapton, Bob Dylan, Guns N' Roses
2	Mr. Tambourine Man	The Byrds
3	Mighty Quinn (Quinn The Eskimo)	Manfred Mann
4	If You Gotta Go, Go Now *	Manfred Mann
5	All I Really Want To Do	The Byrds, Cher
6	All Along The Watchtower	Jimi Hendrix Experience
7	Like A Rolling Stone	Bob Dylan
8	Blowin' In The Wind	Peter, Paul & Mary, Stevie Wonder
9	Lay Lady Lay	Bob Dylan
10	I'll Be Your Baby Tonight	Robert Palmer & UB40

* Fairport Convention had a hit in 1969 with a French version of 'If You Gotta Go, Go Now', titled 'Si Tu Dois Partir'.

Dylan's compositional strength is demonstrated by the wide variety of acts that have succeeded with cover versions from his prodigious catalogue. Other UK artists just outside the Top 10 who have relied on Robert Zimmerman's songwriting chops include Brian Auger, Bryan Ferry and Siouxsie & the Banshees.

THE TOP US HITS
COMPOSED BY BOB DYLAN

1	Blowin' In The Wind	Peter, Paul & Mary, Stevie Wonder
2	Mr. Tambourine Man	The Byrds
3	Lay Lady Lay	Bob Dylan, Ferrante & Teicher, The Isley Brothers
4	Like A Rolling Stone	Bob Dylan
5	Rainy Day Women #12 and #35	Bob Dylan
6	Don't Think Twice	Peter, Paul & Mary, Wonder Who?
7	It Ain't Me Babe	Johnny Cash, Turtles
8	Mighty Quinn (Quinn The Eskimo)	Manfred Mann
9	Knockin' On Heaven's Door	Bob Dylan
10	All I Really Want To Do	Byrds, Cher

With hundreds of his titles recorded by other artists, Dylan's material has also proved immensely successful for the likes of Jimi Hendrix ('All Along The Watchtower'), Rod Stewart ('Forever Young'), Billy Joel and Garth Brooks (both of whom covered 'Make You Feel My Love'.)

AT THE MOVIES

The Madhouse On Castle Street (TV play)	1963
Pat Garrett And Billy The Kid	1973
Renaldo And Clara	1978
Hearts Of Fire	1987
Catch Fire (TV film)	1990
Paradise Cove	1999
Masked And Anonymous	2003

Below: He co-starred in and wrote the score for *Pat Garrett and Billy The Kid* (1973).

In typically incongruous fashion, Dylan also appeared in a television commercial for Victoria's Secret lingerie in 2004, and in Cadillac Escalade commercials three years later.

AT THE GRAMMYS

Best Rock Vocal Performance, Male for 'Gotta Serve Somebody'	1979
Best Traditional Folk Album for *World Gone Wrong*	1994
Best Contemporary Folk Album for *Time Out of Mind*	1997
Best Male Rock Vocal Performance for 'Cold Irons Bound'	1997
Album of the Year for *Time Out of Mind*	1997
Best Contemporary Folk Album for *Love and Theft*	2001
Best Contemporary Folk/Americana Album for *Modern Times*	2006
Best Solo Rock Vocal Performance for 'Someday Baby'	2006

Dylan was also among the artists honoured for Album of the Year for *The Concert For Bangladesh* in 1972 and as a member of the Traveling Wilburys for their Best Rock Performance by a Duo or Group with Vocal win for *Traveling Wilburys Volume One* in 1989.

Below: Performing at Wembley Stadium in 1985.

GRAMMY HALL OF FAME HONOURS

Blowin' In The Wind	1994
Like A Rolling Stone	1998
Blonde On Blonde	1999
Mr. Tambourine Man	2002
Highway 61 Revisited	2002
Bringing It All Back Home	2006

KNOCKIN' ON HEAVEN'S DOOR

After being released from hospital on June 2, 1977, where he had been treated for histoplasmosis pericarditis – a fungal infection of the lung – Dylan said, "I'm just glad to be feeling better. I really thought I'd be seeing Elvis soon." Later that year, Dylan performed in front of Pope John Paul II at the World Eucharistic Conference in Bologna, Italy.

Arguably his most revered single recording, the 6:09 minute 'Like A Rolling Stone' was recorded on June 15, 1965, and features an iconic keyboard contribution by 21-year old multi-instrumentalist, Al Kooper.

THE ROLLING STONES

The first incarnation of the world's oldest working rock group played its debut concert as the Rollin' Stones on July 12, 1962 at the Marquee Jazz club in London with Mick Jagger, Keith Richard and Brian Jones augmented by Dick Taylor and Ian Stewart. With Taylor leaving and bassist Bill Wyman joining on bass in December 1962, the following month Charlie Watts became the band's permanent drummer. Their commercial breakthrough came after their first television appearance, performing a cover of Chuck Berry's 'Come On' on ITV's *Thank Your Lucky Stars* on July 7, 1963.

THEIR BEST-SELLING ALBUMS

1	Hot Rocks 1964–1971	1972
2	Some Girls	1978
3	Forty Licks	2002
4	Tattoo You	1981
5	Goat's Head Soup	1973
6	Sticky Fingers	1971
7	Let It Bleed	1969
8	Emotional Rescue	1980
9	Steel Wheels	1989
10	Big Hits (High Tide and Green Grass)	1966

THEIR NUMBER ONE HIT SINGLES IN THE UK

It's All Over Now	Jul 18, 1964
Little Red Rooster	Dec 05, 1964
The Last Time	Mar 20, 1965
(I Can't Get No) Satisfaction	Sep 11, 1965
Get Off Of My Cloud	Nov 06, 1965
Paint It Black	May 28, 1966
Jumping Jack Flash	Jun 22, 1968
Honky Tonk Women	Jul 26, 1969

Above: Mick Jagger and Mick Taylor on stage.

Bottom Left: The band donate a guitar to Oxfam.

Bottom Right: 1965 was a good year for the Stones.

UNDERCOVER

Although Jagger/Richards are among the most accomplished of songwriting teams, the Rolling Stones' first five UK singles were all cover versions – Chuck Berry's 'Come On', the Beatles' 'I Wanna Be Your Man', Buddy Holly's 'Not Fade Away', Bobby Womack's 'It's All Over Now' and Willie Dixon's 'Little Red Rooster'. Their sixth was their own composition, 'The Last Time', which topped the charts in March 1965.

WAITING ON A FRIEND

On October 25, 1960 Jagger – a student at the London School of Economics and Richards – who was attending Sidcup Art School – renewed their acquaintance, accidentally meeting on a train. They first met in February 1951, while both were at Maypole County Primary School in Wilmington, Kent, but had subsequently lost contact.

THEIR NUMBER ONE HIT SINGLES IN THE US

(I Can't Get No) Satisfaction	Jul 10, 1965
Get Off Of My Cloud	Nov 06, 1965
Paint It Black	Jun 11, 1966
Ruby Tuesday	Mar 04, 1967
Honky Tonk Women	Aug 23, 1969
Brown Sugar	May 29, 1971
Angie	Oct 20, 1973
Miss You	Aug 05, 1978

THE FIRST TV APPEARANCE

The Rolling Stones made their first television appearance on the weekly pop show *Thank Your Lucky Stars* on July 7, 1963, singing 'Come On'. Over the next three years, they made a further 12 appearances on the series. The following month, on August 23, they made their first of 19 appearances on *Ready, Steady, Go!* – bottom of a bill featuring Gerry & the Pacemakers, Freddie & the Dreamers, Kathy Kirby and Kenny Lynch.

KEITH SAVES THE DAY

In October 1998, Keith Richards donated £30,000 to save the village hall in West Wittering in Sussex, England, which was in need of renovation and a new roof. Built in 1922 in honour of the local First World War dead, the building was being used by the West Wittering Players and was the Welcome Club for the over-60s, among others.

THE FIRST INTERNET GIG

On November 18, 1994, the Rolling Stones became the first major band to have a segment of a concert broadcast live on the Internet. At 10.30pm ET – with the URL http://www.stones.com, 20 minutes of their show at the Cotton Bowl, Fair Park in Dallas was made available by multimedia company Thinking Pictures.

HYDE PARK 1969

The Rolling Stones gave a free concert at London's Hyde Park on July 5, 1969, two days after the death of former guitarist Brian Jones. Their support acts were:

The Third Ear Band • King Crimson • Screw • Alexis Korner's New Church • Family • The Battered Ornaments

The Stones performed 14 songs:

I'm Yours, She's Mine	Love In Vain
Jumpin' Jack Flash	Lovin' Cup
Mercy Mercy	Honky Tonk Women
Stray Cat Blues	Midnight Rambler
No Expectations	(I Can't Get No) Satisfaction
I'm Free	Street Fighting Man
Down Home Girl	Sympathy For The Devil

THEIR US GOLD ALBUMS

Out Of Our Heads	Oct 12, 1965	Love You Live	Oct 04, 1977
December's Children	Jan 15, 1966	Some Girls	Jun 12, 1978
Big Hits		Emotional Rescue	Sep 10, 1980
(High Tide and Green Grass)	Apr 27, 1966	Sucking In The Seventies	Jun 03, 1981
Aftermath	Aug 09, 1966	Tattoo You	Oct 30, 1981
Got Live if You Want It	Jan 19, 1967	Still Life	Jan 18, 1983
Between The Buttons	Feb 24, 1967	Undercover	Jan 04, 1984
Flowers	Aug 16, 1967	Dirty Work	Jun 10, 1986
Their Satanic Majesties		12 x 5	Oct 20, 1989
Request	Dec 06, 1967	The Rolling Stones	Oct 20, 1989
Beggars Banquet	Dec 23, 1968	The Rolling Stones Now	Oct 20, 1989
Through The Past Darkly	Sep 09, 1969	Steel Wheels	Oct 27, 1989
Let It Bleed	Nov 24, 1969	Singles Collection –	
Get Yer Ya-Ya's Out!	Nov 02, 1970	The London Years	Feb 09, 1990
Sticky Fingers	May 11, 1971	Flashpoint	May 28, 1991
Hot Rocks 1964-1971	Jan 20, 1972	Voodoo Lounge	Sep 12, 1994
Exile On Main Street	May 30, 1972	Stripped	Feb 06, 1996
More Hot Rocks		Bridges To Babylon	Nov 11, 1997
(Big Hits and Fazed Cookies)	Jan 17, 1973	Rewind	May 31, 2000
Goat's Head Soup	Sep 25, 1973	Forty Licks	Nov 14, 2002
It's Only Rock 'n' Roll	Oct 31, 1974	Jump Back – The Best of	
Made In The Shade	Aug 07, 1975	the Rolling Stones	Mar 10, 2005
Black And Blue	Apr 26, 1976	A Bigger Bang	Oct 11, 2005

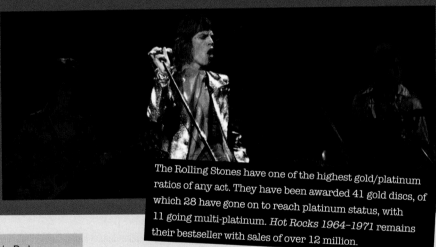

The Rolling Stones have one of the highest gold/platinum ratios of any act. They have been awarded 41 gold discs, of which 28 have gone on to reach platinum status, with 11 going multi-platinum. *Hot Rocks 1964–1971* remains their bestseller with sales of over 12 million.

Below: 1969 free Hyde Park concert in memory of Stones' founding member Brian Jones.

Above: Mick Taylor, Mick Jagger and Charlie Watts.

LED ZEPPELIN

Rising from the ashes of legendary English rock band the Yardbirds in 1968, guitarist Jimmy Page recruited bassist John Paul Jones, lead vocalist Robert Plant and drummer John Bonham to form a new quartet. They made their live debut as Led Zeppelin in October 1968. A near-perfect rock fusion erupted in the form of Led Zeppelin, quickly becoming one of the world's most popular acts. Endlessly creative in blending blues, folk and exotic world music into their heavy rock stew, Led Zeppelin was forged around the dazzling, layered riffs of Page's guitar and the primal, soulful grit of Plant's vocals.

THEIR BEST-SELLING ALBUMS

1	Led Zeppelin IV	1971
2	Physical Graffiti	1975
3	Led Zeppelin II	1969
4	Led Zeppelin	1969
5	Houses Of The Holy	1973
6	In Through The Out Door	1979
7	Led Zeppelin III	1970
8	The Song Remains The Same	1976
9	Presence	1976
10	Led Zeppelin (Boxed Set)	1990

Eventually clocking up seven US No. 1 and seven UK No. 1 chart albums, Led Zeppelin became the biggest-selling albums band of the 1970s. Uniquely, the emphasis was on the long-player format: while a few singles trickled out in Australia and Canada, the group didn't issue 45s in their home country, and of those released in the United States (more than any other territory) only the iconic early rocker, 'Whole Lotta Love' reached the top 10.

JIMMY PAGE'S NOTABLE SESSION WORK

Diamonds	Jet Harris & Tony Meehan
Here Comes The Night	Them
Shout	Lulu & the Luvvers
As Tears Go By	Marianne Faithfull
The Crying Game	Dave Berry
Is It True?	Brenda Lee

Guitarist Page had been a prolific and much in-demand session player in the mid-sixties, also contributing to songs by the Who, the Rolling Stones, the Kinks, the Nashville Teens, Al Stewart and Joe Cocker among others.

THEIR HIT SINGLES IN THE US

Good Times Bad Times	80	(Apr 19, 1969)
Whole Lotta Love	4	(Jan 31, 1970)
Living Loving Maid (She's Just A Woman)	65	(Apr 04, 1970)
Immigrant Song	16	(Jan 30, 1971)
Black Dog	15	(Feb 12, 1972)
Rock And Roll	47	(Apr 15, 1972)
Over The Hills And Far Away	51	(Jul 28, 1973)
D'yer Mak'er	20	(Dec 29, 1973)
Trampled Underfoot	38	(May 17, 1975)
Fool In the Rain	21	(Feb 16, 1980)

Right: Robert Plant, Led Zeppelin's lead vocalist.

Below: Legendary guitarist Jimmy Page.

THE GRAMMYS

Led Zeppelin never won a Grammy, but Jimmy Page and Robert Plant nabbed Best Hard Rock Performance for 'Most High' in 1998, and Plant won a slew of awards with bluegrass singer Alison Krauss in 2007, including Best Pop Collaboration with Vocals for 'Gone Gone Gone (Done Moved On)', Best Contemporary Folk/Americana Album and Album Of The Year for *Raising Sand*, Best Country Collaboration with Vocals for 'Killing The Blues', Best Pop Collaboration with Vocals for 'Rich Woman' and Record of the Year for 'Please Read The Letter'.

Despite being Grammy-less as a group, the band was presented with their Lifetime Achievement Award in 2005.

ON TOUR

Here are the number of gigs the band played around the world:

United States	134
United Kingdom	82
Germany	16
Canada	11
Sweden	11
Denmark	9
France	6
Australia	5
Holland	5
Japan	5
Switzerland	4
Austria	2
Ireland	2
Belgium	1
Finland	1
Iceland	1
Italy	1
New Zealand	1

Led Zeppelin performed live 297 times during their 12 year career, beginning with a concert on September 7, 1968 as the New Yardbirds in Gladsaxe, Denmark, culminating with a performance at the Eissporthalle in Berlin, Germany on July 7, 1980. A further North American tour had been announced for October 1980, but was cancelled following the death of drummer John Bonham.

STAIRWAY TO HEAVEN

One of the most revered rock songs of all-time, Led Zeppelin's signature 'Stairway to Heaven' opus has received many awards and regularly shows up in various Best Of Lists:

Grammy Hall of Fame Award	2003
The Rock and Roll Hall of Fame's 500 Songs that Shaped Rock 'n' Roll	1994
RIAA's Songs of the Century (No. 53)	2001
VH1's The 100 Greatest Rock Songs of All Time (No. 3)	1999
Rolling Stone's The 500 Greatest Songs of All Time (No. 31)	2003
Rolling Stone's 100 Greatest Guitar Songs of All Time (No. 8)	2008
Classic Rock's Ten of the Best Songs Ever (No. 1)	1999
Q's 100 Songs That Changed The World (No. 47)	2003
Q's 100 Greatest Songs of All Time (No. 8)	2006
Guitar World's 100 Greatest Guitar Solos (No. 1)	2006

Below: (back row) John Bonham, Robert Plant, (front row) Jimmy Page and John Paul Jones.

THEIR US CHART DOMINANCE

Physical Graffiti	No. 1
Led Zeppelin	No. 83
Houses of the Holy	No. 92
Led Zeppelin II	No. 104
Led Zeppelin IV	No. 116
Led Zeppelin III	No. 124

On the US chart for March 29, 1975, Led Zeppelin became the first band in history to simultaneously chart six albums.

WHOLE LOTTA LOVE

On June 3, 2007 The Hard Rock Park officially opened in Myrtle Beach, South Carolina. One of the featured attractions was Led Zeppelin – The Ride, synchronized to the tune of 'Whole Lotta Love', blasting from a 1,200-watt sound system, reaching speeds of 65mph and falling from a height of 155 feet.

THEIR FIRST TV APPEARANCE

Led Zeppelin made their television debut performing 'Communication Breakdown' on BBC1's *How Late It Is* on March 21, 1969 at the broadcaster's Lime Grove Studios in London. They were a last-minute replacement for the Flying Burrito Brothers.

Above: In concert at the Royal Albert Hall 1970.

THE REUNION PERFORMANCE

On December 10, 2007 the band reunited – with John Bonham's son Jason on drums – for a tribute concert to Atlantic Records' co-founder, Ahmet Ertegun,h at The O2 Arena in London. This was their set list:

Good Times, Bad Times
Ramble On
Black Dog
In My Time Of Dying
For Your Life
Trampled Underfoot
Nobody's Fault But Mine
No Quarter
Since I've Been Loving You
Dazed And Confused
Stairway To Heaven
The Song Remains The Same
Misty Mountain Hop
Kashmir
Whole Lotta Love
Rock And Roll

MTV
MUSIC TELEVISION

PINK FLOYD

Despite suffering the fractious departure of two of the group's prime movers and songwriters – first Syd Barrett in 1968 and subsequently Roger Waters in 1984 – Pink Floyd evolved from its modest roots as a mid-sixties blues-rock act, through the psychedelic rock underground of the late sixties to become one of the most popular, experimental and progressive rock acts of the past three decades. Following the death of original member Rick Wright in 2008, the only founding member who made it through all of Floyd's trials and tribulations from start to finish was the band's drummer, Nick Mason.

THEIR BEST-SELLING ALBUMS

1	Dark Side Of The Moon	1973
2	The Wall	1979
3	Wish You Were Here	1975
4	Echoes	2001
5	The Division Bell	1994
6	A Momentary Lapse Of Reason	1987
7	Animals	1977
8	Delicate Sound Of Thunder	1988
9	The Final Cut	1983
10	Meddle	1971

One of the most enduring recordings of all-time, *Dark Side of the Moon* is the third best-selling album worldwide, ever. During its recording at Abbey Road Studios between June 1972 and January 1973, the working title for this 42:59 minute project was *Eclipse* – also the name of the album's short closing track.

THEIR HIT SINGLES IN THE UK

Arnold Layne	20	(Apr 22, 1967)
See Emily Play	6	(Jul 29, 1967)
Another Brick In The Wall (Part II)	1	(Dec 15, 1979)
When The Tigers Broke Free	39	(Aug 14, 1982)
Not Now John	30	(May 14, 1983)
On The Turning Away	55	(Dec 26, 1987)
One Slip	50	(Jul 02, 1988)
High Hopes/Keep Talking	26	(Oct 29, 1994)
Take It Back	23	(Jun 04, 1994)

As with Led Zeppelin, Floyd were mostly an albums-orientated band with only one single ever topping both the UK and US charts: 'Another Brick In The Wall (Part II)'.

Above: Singer-songwriter and guitarist, David Gilmour joined the band in 1968.

THEIR HIT SINGLES IN THE US

Above: Roger Waters, Nick Mason, David Gilmour and Rick Wright in 1970.

DOWN THE YELLOW BRICK ROAD

On June 28, 1997 – in its 1,056th week on the survey – *Dark Side of the Moon* returned to the top of *Billboard's* Top Pop Catalog Albums chart, spurred by recent media reports linking the album to the classic film, *The Wizard of Oz*. The Internet became rife with speculation regarding a number of bizarre and striking synchronicities occurring when the classic Floyd album was played simultaneously with the running of the movie, specifically when the music is cued to begin with the third roar of the MGM lion symbol at the start.

PIGS CAN FLY

On December 3, 1976, a film shoot for the sleeve of the band's *Animals* album went disastrously wrong, when a 40 ft tall inflatable pig, designed by German firm Ballon Fabrik, broke free from its mooring above Battersea Power Station. The Civil Aviation Authority issued a warning to all pilots in London airspace that a pig was on the loose. It was last sighted at 18,000 ft over Chatham, Kent.

BANNED IN THE USA

On July 21, 1987, the Sixth Circuit of the United States Court of Appeals rejected an appeal by former Lincoln, Kentucky schoolteacher Jacqueline Fowler, who had been fired for showing the *Pink Floyd – The Wall* to students in grades nine through eleven. The R-rated movie was shown at the request of students on the last day of school in 1984, while she was completing grade cards. The Court ruled that in this case it was not a constitutionally protected educational activity, and that by introducing a "controversial and sexually explicit movie into a classroom of adolescents without preview, preparation, or discussion, the teacher abdicated her function as an educator and demonstrated a blatant lack of judgment."

Above: Roger Waters performing in Hyde Park 1968.

Below: David Gilmour in 1971.

BANNED IN SOUTH AFRICA

'Another Brick In The Wall (Part II)' was banned in South Africa on the grounds that it was "prejudicial to the safety of the state". Black schoolchildren had adopted the song to protest their inferior standard of education in early 1980. Those caught in possession of the record could be fined or jailed, and all unsold copies had to be destroyed.
Police in Durban, armed with batons, broke up a demonstration by black students over the ruling and around 1,000 Cape Town teachers refused to conduct classes in sympathy with the students.

SOLO HIT ALBUMS

Roger Waters

The Pros And Cons Of Hitchhiking	UK 13	(May 12, 1984)
Radio K.A.O.S.	UK 25	(Jun 27, 1987)
The Wall – Live In Berlin	UK 27	(Sep 29, 1990)
Amused to Death	UK 8	(Sep 19, 1992)
The Pros And Cons Of Hitchhiking	US 31	(Jun 09, 1984)
Radio K.A.O.S.	US 50	(Jul 25, 1987)
The Wall – Live in Berlin	US 56	(Sep 29, 1990)
Amused to Death	US 21	(Sep 19, 1992)
In the Flesh – Live	US 136	(Dec 23, 2000)

David Gilmour

David Gilmour	UK 17	(Jun 17, 1978)
About Face	UK 21	(Mar 17, 1984)
On an Island	UK 1	(Mar 18, 2006)
Live in Gdansk	UK 10	(Oct 04, 2008)
David Gilmour	US 29	(Aug 26, 1978)
About Face	US 32	(Jun 09, 1984)
On an Island	US 6	(Mar 25, 2006)
Live in Gdansk	US 26	(Oct 11, 2008)

Rick Wright

Broken China	UK 61	(Oct 19, 1996)

Nick Mason

Nick Mason's Fictitious Sports	US 170	(Jul 11, 1981)
Profiles (with Rick Fenn)	US 154	(Sep 14, 1985)

Syd Barrett

The Madcap Laughs	UK 40	(Feb 07, 1970)

On July 21, 1990 an estimated 200,000 people attended Roger Waters' most ambitious solo project to date, a complete performance of *The Wall* at the site of the Berlin Wall and the former location of the bunker in which Hitler committed suicide in Potzdamer Platz, Berlin, West Germany. Highlighted by the destruction of an artificial wall during the concert, the lineup featured:

Bryan Adams • The Band • James Galway • The Hooters • Cyndi Lauper • Ute Lemper • Joni Mitchell • Van Morrison • Sinéad O'Connor • The Scorpions • Marianne Faithfull • Tim Curry • Albert Finney • Snowy White

The event was broadcast live throughout the world and raised money for the Leonard Cheshire-established Memorial Fund for Disaster Relief. (Waters' father had been a pilot killed during World War II before he was born.) *Variety* reported that 320,000 people paid $5 million in ticket sales, and that the cost of the show, which featured fireworks, parachutes, helicopters, the Red Army band and gold coloured rain, was 7.5 million marks.

Right: *The Wall* concert, Berlin 1990.

JOHN LENNON

John Winston Lennon was born on October 9, 1940 in Woolton, Liverpool, the only child of Fred and Julia. A bored student at the local Quarry Bank High School, Lennon was more interested in music and art and became a proficient guitarist, forming a skiffle group at the age of 16 with school chum, Pete Shotton. Naming themselves the Quarry Men they played at local parties and amateur contests around Liverpool, including a gig at St. Peter's Church Rose Queen garden fête on July 6, 1957, where he was first introduced to Paul McCartney.

HIS BEST-SELLING ALBUMS

1.	The John Lennon Collection	1982
2.	Double Fantasy	1980
3.	Imagine	1971
4.	Lennon Legend – The Very Best John Lennon	1998
5.	Shaved Fish	1975
6.	Walls And Bridges	1974
7.	Mind Games	1973
8.	John Lennon And The Plastic Ono Band	1971
9.	Rock 'n' Roll	1975
10.	Milk And Honey	1984

Not including live albums and compilations (of which there have been many), Lennon recorded ten original studio albums between his 1968 debut *Unfinished Music No. 1: Two Virgins* (with Yoko Ono) and *Double Fantasy* (also with Yoko) in 1980. An 11th studio album, *Milk And Honey*, made just prior to his murder in 1980, emerged in 1984 and included the track, 'Borrowed Time'.

HIS HIT SINGLES IN THE US

Give Peace A Chance	14	(Sep 06, 1969)
Cold Turkey	30	(Jan 17, 1970)
Instant Karma (We All Shine On)	3	(Mar 28, 1970)
Imagine	3	(Nov 13, 1971)
Mother	43	(Jan 30, 1971)
Power To The People	11	(May 01, 1971)
Mind Games	18	(Dec 29, 1973)
#9 Dream	9	(Feb 22, 1975)
Whatever Gets You Thru The Night	1	(Nov 16, 1974)
Stand By Me	20	(Apr 26, 1975)
Starting Over	1	(Dec 27, 1980)
Watching The Wheels	10	(May 23, 1981)
Woman	2	(Mar 21, 1981)
I'm Steppin' Out	55	(Apr 21, 1984)
Nobody Told Me	5	(Mar 03, 1984)
Jealous Guy	80	(Oct 22, 1988)

HIS HIT SINGLES IN THE UK

Give Peace A Chance	2	(Jul 26, 1969)
Cold Turkey	14	(Nov 15, 1969)
Instant Karma	5	(Feb 28, 1970)
Power To The People	7	(Apr 03, 1971)
Mind Games	26	(Dec 08, 1973)
Whatever Gets You Thru' The Night	36	(Nov 02, 1974)
#9 Dream	23	(Mar 08, 1975)
Stand By Me	30	(May 24, 1975)
(Just Like) Starting Over	1	(Dec 20, 1980)
Imagine	1	(Jan 10, 1981)
Happy Xmas (War Is Over)	2	(Jan 10, 1981)
Woman	1	(Feb 07, 1981)
I Saw Her Standing There	40	(Mar 28, 1981)
Watching The Wheels	30	(Apr 18, 1981)
Love	41	(Dec 04, 1982)
Nobody Told Me	6	(Jan 28, 1984)
Borrowed Time	32	(Apr 07, 1984)
Jealous Guy	65	(Nov 30, 1985)
Imagine/Jealous Guy/ Happy Xmas (War Is Over)	45	(Dec 17, 1988)
Imagine	3	(Dec 25, 1999)

Below: 'Instant Karma' 1970.

Ten of Lennon's hits were achieved before his death ('Imagine' and 'Happy Xmas War is Over' had both been hits in the 1970s, but peaked following his passing) and eight followed it.

NOTABLE AWARDS

Outstanding Contribution to British Music, Ivor Novello Awards	1981
Outstanding Contribution to Music, BRIT Awards	1982
Songwriters Hall of Fame	1987
Star on the Hollywood Walk of Fame	1988
Inducted into the Rock and Roll Hall of Fame (as a Beatle)	1989
Inducted into the Rock and Roll Hall of Fame	1994
Nordoff-Robbins Music Therapy Center Silver Clef Award	1997
No. 8 Greatest Briton, BBC Television	2002
No. 38 The Immortal – The Fifty Greatest Artists of All Time, Rolling Stone	2004
No. 5 100 Greatest Singers of All Time, Rolling Stone	2008

HOSTING THE MIKE DOUGLAS SHOW

Between February 15 and 18, 1972 – while based in New York and battling deportation efforts brought by the Nixon administration – John Lennon and Yoko Ono co-hosted the syndicated nightly chat series, *The Mike Douglas Show*. This is the list of their guests:

FEBRUARY 15
Dr. Jesse Steinfeld • Jerry Rubin • Barbara Loden • Yellow Pearl

FEBRUARY 16
Chuck Berry • Joseph Blatchford • Hilary Redleaf • David Rosenboom

FEBRUARY 17
Vivian Reed • Ace Trucking Company • Bobby Seale • Marsha Martin • Donald Williams

FEBRUARY 18
George Carlin • Dr. Gary E. Schwartz • Rena Uviller

THE FIRST SOLO BEATLE TV APPEARANCE

Lennon became the first ex-Beatle to appear on BBC1-TV's *Top of the Pops* as a solo artist, performing his new single, 'Instant Karma! (We All Shine On)' on February 19, 1970. The video was earlier aired on the programme on February 5.

Above: Performing on *The Mike Douglas Show* in 1972.

THE TORONTO ROCK 'N' REVIVAL SHOW

Invited by promoter John Brower to attend the *Toronto Rock 'N' Revival Show* held on September 13, 1969 at Toronto University's Varsity Stadium in Canada, with the offer of first-class airline tickets, Lennon agreed, provided he could perform. Quickly assembling the ad-hoc Plastic Ono Band, he corralled Eric Clapton, Klaus Voormann and Alan White to join him. Rehearsing on the flight over, they performed six numbers, including 'Give Peace A Chance', 'Blue Suede Shoes', 'Dizzy Miss Lizzy' and 'Cold Turkey' – performed live for the first time.

Above: It's all at peace with Eric Clapton.

Below: John and Yoko.

THE PLASTIC ONO BAND'S UK DEBUT

The Plastic Ono Band made its live UK debut on December 15, 1969, headlining the UNICEF Peace For Christmas benefit concert at London's Lyceum Ballroom. Put together at 48 hours' notice, the band comprised:

John Lennon • Yoko Ono • Eric Clapton • Klaus Voormann • Alan White • George Harrison • Bobby Keyes • Billy Preston • Keith Moon • Jim Gordon • Delaney & Bonnie

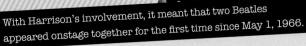
With Harrison's involvement, it meant that two Beatles appeared onstage together for the first time since May 1, 1966.

MTV MUSIC TELEVISION

PAUL McCARTNEY

With a first name James – though always known by his middle name, Paul – McCartney was raised by his mother Mary (a nurse) and father Jim (a pianist and trumpet player for Jim Mac's Jazz Band) in the Liverpool suburbs of Speke and Allerton. As a teenager McCartney learned to play both of his father's instruments (by ear), before writing his first-ever song, 'I Lost My Little Girl' on his Framus Zenith acoustic guitar at the age of 14. He performed publicly for the first time at 15, singing Little Richard's 'Long Tall Sally' at a Butlin's holiday camp.

HIS PLATINUM, GOLD & SILVER SINGLES IN THE UK

Platinum

Mull Of Kintyre	1977

Gold

Band On The Run	1974
Ebony And Ivory (with Stevie Wonder)	1982
We All Stand Together (with the Frog Chorus)	1984

Silver

Silly Love Songs	1976
Let 'Em In	1976
With A Little Luck	1978
Goodnight Tonight	1979
Coming Up	1980
Wonderful Christmastime	1980
Say Say Say (with Michael Jackson)	1983
Pipes Of Peace	1983
No More Lonely Nights	1983

HIS BEST-SELLING ALBUMS

1	Band On The Run	1973
2	All The Best!	1987
3	McCartney	1970
4	Venus And Mars	1975
5	Pipes Of Peace	1984
6	Wings' Greatest	1978
7	Wings At The Speed Of Sound	1976
8	London Town	1978
9	Back To The Egg	1979
10	Tug Of War	1982
11	Ram	1971
12	Wingspan – Hits And History	2001
13	Back In The US – Live 2002	2003
14	Wings Over America	1976
15	Flowers In The Dirt	1989

Above: Paul founded Wings with his late wife Linda (pictured) and Denny Laine.

HIS UK NUMBER ONE HIT SINGLES

Mull Of Kintyre/Girls' School	Dec 03, 1977
Ebony And Ivory	Apr 24, 1982
(with additional vocals by Stevie Wonder)	
Pipes Of Peace	Jan 14, 1984
Ferry 'Cross The Mersey	May 20, 1989
(credited to the Christians, Holly Johnson, Paul McCartney, Gerry Marsden & Stock, Aitken & Waterman)	

McCartney has been – by some distance – the most commercially successful former Beatle on record, with well over 60 post-Fabs UK chart successes. 'Mull of Kintyre' was co-written with Wings band mate, Denny Laine, and went on to sell more than two million copies in the UK. It only reached No. 33 in the US.

McCartney has had more number two-peaking solo hits in the UK than chart-toppers: six, the last being 1984's 'No More Lonely Nights'.

Left: Paul in 1982.

HIS NUMBER ONE HIT SINGLES IN THE US

Say Say Say (with Michael Jackson)	Dec 10, 1983
Coming Up	Jun 28, 1980
Ebony and Ivory (with Stevie Wonder)	May 15, 1982
Band On The Run (credited to Paul McCartney & Wings)	Jun 08, 1974
My Love (credited to Paul McCartney & Wings)	Jun 02, 1973
Listen To What The Man Said (credited to Paul McCartney & Wings)	Jul 19, 1975
Uncle Albert/Admiral Halsey (credited to Paul & Linda McCartney)	Sep 04, 1971
Silly Love Songs (credited to Wings)	May 22, 1976
With A Little Luck (credited to Wings)	Mar 20, 1978

CELEBRITIES FEATURED ON THE COVER OF THE *BAND ON THE RUN* SLEEVE

Paul McCartney • Linda McCartney • Denny Laine • Kenny Lynch • Christopher Lee • James Coburn • Michael Parkinson Clement Freud • John Conteh

The famous cover to McCartney's best-selling album was photographed on October 28, 1973 and featured three singer/ musicians, one wife, two actors, one TV chat show host, one Liberal Member of Parliament and one former pro boxer.

HIS DESERT ISLAND DISCS

When he guested on the long-running BBC Radio programme *Desert Island Discs* on January 30, 1982, McCartney chose the following eight records:

Elvis Presley's 'Heartbreak Hotel'
Chuck Berry's 'Sweet Little Sixteen'
Gene Vincent's 'Be Bop A Lula'
John Lennon's 'Beautiful Boy'
The Coasters' 'Searchin''
Little Richard's 'Tutti Frutti'
The Country Hams' 'Walking In The Park With Eloise'
Julian Bream's 'Courtly Dances' from Benjamin Britten's *Gloriana*

Left: A young McCartney ready to rock in the Big Apple.

Right: A slightly older Macca back in New York on the *David Letterman Show*.

THE GUINNESS RECORD HOLDER

On October 24, 1979, McCartney received a medallion cast in rhodium from the UK Arts Minister at a *Guinness Book of Records* reception at Les Ambassadeurs Club, London, after being declared the most successful composer of all time. From 1962 to 1978, he wrote or co-wrote 43 songs that sold over one million copies each and had sold over 100 million singles and 100 million albums up to that point.

HIS SONG-WRITING CATALOGUE

When Michael Jackson bought the ATV music-publishing catalogue – including a large portion of the invaluable Lennon-McCartney composition songbook – it meant that Jackson began earning more from the song 'Yesterday' than its composer.

MTV UNPLUGGED

McCartney was the first artist to release his performance from the popular *MTV Unplugged* series as an album. His 17-track *Unplugged (The Official Bootleg)* – released in 1991 – included the first song he wrote: the 1:45 minute, 'I Lost My Little Girl', which Macca composed at the age of 14.

HI, HI, HI

On November 13, 2005, McCartney provided the wake-up call for the international space station crew – comprising NASA astronaut Bill McArthur and Russian cosmonaut Valery Tokarev – performing 'Good Day Sunshine' and 'English Tea'. The performance was beamed from the West Coast to the space station crew 220 miles above Earth on its 44th day in orbit and broadcast on NASA television.

THE DAVID LETTERMAN SHOW

On July 15, 2009, McCartney performed live on the marquee above the entrance to the Ed Sullivan Theater in New York – the scene of the Beatles triumphant conquering of the US in February 1964 – for an appearance on the *David Letterman Show*. The set list was:

Get Back
Band On the Run
Let Me Roll It
Coming Up
Sing The Changes
Helter Skelter
Back In The USSR

THE BEE GEES

The Brothers Gibb were all born in the Isle of Man in the 1940s (Maurice and Robin were twins), moved with their family to Manchester in the early fifties, then emigrated to Australia in 1958. While still young kids, they formed vocal harmony group, the Rattlesnakes, before performing as the Bee Gees on Australian television variety shows and at holiday spots around the Queensland coast. Talented and synchronous songwriters from an early age, they signed their first record deal in 1963, releasing their debut Australian album, *The Bee Gees Sing and Play 14 Barry Gibb Songs* in 1965.

THEIR BEST-SELLING ALBUMS

1	Saturday Night Fever	1999
2	Bee Gees' Greatest	1979
3	One Night Only	2001
4	Spirits Having Flown	1979
5	Their Greatest Hits – The Record	2002
6	Here At Last… Bee Gees… Live	1977
7	Still Waters	1997
8	Children Of The World	1976
9	Staying Alive	1983
10	Main Course	1975
11	Number Ones	2005
12	Best of the Bee Gees	1969
13	Bee Gees Gold. Volume 1	1978
14	E.S.P.	1987
15	The Very Best of the Bee Gees	1990

Above: Barry (far right) waits for the band to grow.

THEIR NUMBER ONE HIT SINGLES IN THE US

How Can You Mend A Broken Heart?	Aug 07, 1971
Jive Talkin'	Aug 09, 1975
You Should Be Dancing	Sep 04, 1976
How Deep Is Your Love	Dec 24, 1977
Stayin' Alive	Feb 04, 1978
Night Fever	Mar 18, 1978
Too Much Heaven	Jan 06, 1979
Tragedy	Mar 24, 1979
Love You Inside Out	Jun 09, 1979

Left: The Bee Gees' iconic 1970s disco look.

Top Right: Maurice, Robin and Barry in the 1960s.

THEIR NUMBER ONE HIT SINGLES IN THE UK

Massachusetts	Oct 14, 1967
I've Gotta Get A Message To You	Sep 07, 1968
Night Fever	Apr 29, 1978
Tragedy	Mar 03, 1979
You Win Again	Oct 17, 1987

THE BEE GEES-DOMINATED US TOP 10

On March 18, 1978, the Bee Gees – in assorted capacities – secured a stranglehold at the top of the American singles chart which almost matched the Beatles' occupation of the entire top five, 14 years earlier. The group was at Nos. 1 and 2 with 'Night Fever' and 'Stayin' Alive' respectively, were the writers and producers of Samantha Sang's 'Emotion' at No. 3, while younger brother Andy Gibb was at No. 5 with '(Love Is) Thicker Than Water'. In addition, Yvonne Elliman's version of their composition, 'If I Can't Have You' was at No. 14, their own 'How Deep Is Your Love', on its way down from the top, was at No. 35 and the Tavares resided at No. 60 with 'More Than A Woman'.

Right: A new look and a
new sound in the 1990s.

Left: Barry and
Robin in 2007.

IT'S ONLY WORDS

One of the most successful songwriting teams of all time, the Brothers Gibb (Barry, Maurice and Robin) have lent their songs to more than 2,500 artists over the past four decades – with more than 400 different versions of 'How Deep is Your Love' having been recorded. It is estimated that, at any given time, a song composed by the Bee Gees is being played on a radio somewhere around the world. In more recent years, their music has often been sampled by the likes of Snoop Dogg and Pras Michel.

Of the four Gibb brothers (including solo artist Andy) only Maurice never released a solo album – though he did write the score to the 1984 film *A Breed Apart*.

THE BATLEY VARIETY CLUB

During the lowest ebb of the band's career – which saw RSO label boss Robert Stigwood reject their album, *A Kick in the Pants is Worth Eight in the Head* – the Bee Gees performed at the Batley Variety Club in West Yorkshire, England in 1974 – although it did prove to be a memorable evening. Maurice Gibb (previously married to Lulu) met his future wife, Yvonne Spenceley.

AT THE GRAMMYS

Despite being honoured with the Grammy Lifetime Achievement Award in 2000, the Legend Award in 2003 and the Hall of Fame Award for *Saturday Night Fever* in 2004, the Bee Gees have only received four Grammy Awards. They are:

Best Pop Vocal Performance by a Group for 'How Deep Is Your Love'	1977
Best Pop Vocal Performance by a Duo or Group for *Saturday Night Fever*	1978
Producer of the Year	1978
Album of the Year for *Saturday Night Fever*	1978

BRUSH WITH DEATH

On November 5, 1967, Robin Gibb was returning home from a weekend in Hastings, Sussex, with his girlfriend Molly Hullis, when the train on which he was travelling crashed just outside Hither Green station in South-East London, killing 49 and injuring 78. Gibb suffered shock.

Above: Performing in Sydney 2001.

MTV
MUSIC TELEVISION

Named in 1970 by flamboyant co-founder and lead singer Freddie Mercury, Queen's permanent lineup was completed a year later with the arrival of bassist John Deacon. Following domestic success with its first two albums, the British rock quartet burst onto the international scene with *Sheer Heart Attack* and *A Night at the Opera* in the mid-seventies – the latter containing the career-defining global smash, 'Bohemian Rhapsody'. The group was inducted into the Rock and Roll Hall of Fame in 2001.

THEIR BEST-SELLING ALBUMS

1	Greatest Hits	1981
2	News Of The World	1977
3	The Game	1980
4	A Night At The Opera	1975
5	Classic Queen	1992
6	Greatest Hits Volume II	1991
7	Live Killers	1979
8	Made In Heaven	1995
9	A Kind Of Magic	1986
10	Greatest Hits I, II & III – The Platinum Collection	2002

With Freddie at the helm, Queen recorded 13 albums from 1973's *Queen* to *Innuendo* in 1991, the year of his death.

THEIR NUMBER ONE HIT SINGLES IN THE UK

Bohemian Rhapsody	Nov 29, 1975
Under Pressure (with David Bowie)	Nov 21, 1981
Innuendo	Jan 26, 1991
Bohemian Rhapsody/These Are The Days Of Our Lives	Dec 21, 1991
Five Live (EP) (with George Michael)	May 01, 1993
We Will Rock You (with 5ive)	Jul 29, 2000

Coming in at almost six minutes, the operatic rock classic 'Bohemian Rhapsody' was written by Freddie Mercury and recorded by the band over a three-week period beginning on August 24, 1975 at the Rockfield Studios in Wales. Its accompanying video – directed by Bruce Gowers – is widely acknowledged as a landmark work in the progression of music video making.

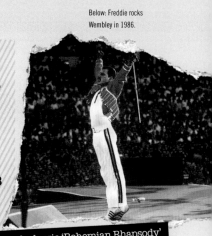
Below: Freddie rocks Wembley in 1986.

Left: Brian May and Liza Minnelli at the Freddie Mercury tribute concert.

"A CONCERT FOR LIFE" FREDDIE MERCURY TRIBUTE

On April 20, 1992 May, Deacon and Taylor staged *A Concert For Life* before a crowd of 70,000 at Wembley Stadium as a tribute to the late Mercury and a fundraiser for AIDS Awareness. Broadcast to 70 countries worldwide, the event featured a plea from Elizabeth Taylor and performances by Metallica, Extreme, Bob Geldof, Spinal Tap, Def Leppard, Guns N' Roses and U2 (via satellite from Sacramento, California), a first-ever live concert link with South Africa and versions of Queen-backed songs by: George Michael ('Year Of 39', 'These Are The Days Of Our Lives' with Lisa Stansfield, and 'Somebody To Love' with the London Community Gospel Choir), David Bowie ('Under Pressure' with Annie Lennox) and Elton John, performing 'Bohemian Rhapsody' with help from Axl Rose and 'The Show Must Go On', a Mercury song which Queen never played live. Liza Minnelli led the all-star choral finale of 'We Are The Champions'. May closed an emotional night, providing the guitar part to 'God Save The Queen' with vocals supplied by the audience. Spinal Tap introduced their performance, resplendent in regal outfits, declaring they would cut short their set by 35 songs "because we know Freddie would have wanted it this way".

WHO WROTE THE HITS?

All four members of Queen have individually been responsible for the success of the band as songwriters. Here is the breakdown by group member:

FREDDIE MERCURY	UK Peak	US Peak	Year
Seven Seas Of Rhye	10		1974
Killer Queen	2	12	1974
Bohemian Rhapsody	1	9	1975
Somebody To Love	2	13	1976
We Are The Champions	2	4	1977
Bicycle Race	11	25	1978
Don't Stop Me Now	9	86	1979
Love Of My Life	63		1979
Crazy Little Thing Called Love	2	1	1979
Play the Game	14	42	1980
Body Language	25	11	1982
It's A Hard Life	6	72	1984
Friends Will Be Friends	14		1986
(written with John Deacon)			
Bohemian Rhapsody	1	2	1991

BRIAN MAY	UK Peak	US Peak	Year
Now I'm Here	11		1975
Tie Your Mother Down	31	49	1977
It's Late		74	1978
Fat Bottomed Girls	11	25	1978
Save Me	11		1980
Flash	10	42	1981
Las Palabras De Amor	17		1982
Hammer To Fall	13		1984
Thank God It's Christmas	21		1984
(written with Roger Taylor)			
Who Wants to Live Forever	24		1986
No-One But You	13		1998
We Will Rock You	1		2000

JOHN DEACON	UK Peak	US Peak	Year
You're My Best Friend	7	16	1976
Spread Your Wings	34		1978
Another One Bites The Dust	7	1	1980
Need Your Loving Tonight		44	1980
Back Chat	40		1982
I Want To Break Free	3	45	1984
Friends Will Be Friends	14		1986
(written with Freddie Mercury)			

ROGER TAYLOR	UK Peak	US Peak	Year
Calling All Girls		60	1982
Radio Ga-Ga	2	16	1984
A Kind Of Magic	3	42	1986
Heaven For Everyone	2		1995
Thank God It's Christmas	21		1984
(written with Brian May)			
C-lebrity	33		2008
(written with Paul Rodgers)			

And those credited to the group	UK Peak	US Peak	Year
Queen's First E.P.	17		1977
One Vision	7	61	1985
Under Pressure	1	29	1989
(written with David Bowie)			
I Want It All	3	50	1989
Breakthru	7		1989
The Invisible Man	12		1989
Scandal	25		1989
The Miracle	21		1989
The Show Must Go On	16		1991
These Are the Days of Our Lives	1		1991

Left: Queen in the 1970s.

Below: Roger Taylor, Freddie Mercury, Brian May and John Deacon.

DECEMBER 1, 1976

The band pulled out of an appearance on the ITV show *Today*, opening the way for the Sex Pistols to make a lewd and legendary appearance, rocketing the punk pioneers to front-page news.

BRAINS OF BRITAIN

At the time of their formation in 1971, all four members of Queen had or were pursuing degrees in higher education.

Freddie Mercury	Graphic Art & Design diploma at the Ealing College of Art
Brian May	Astrophysics at Imperial College (He completed his degree in 2002 and became chancellor of Liverpool John Moores University)
John Deacon	First class Honours degree in Electronics from Chelsea College of Science & Technology
Roger Taylor	Reading for a Biology degree at Imperial College

BRUCE SPRINGSTEEN

With global sales exceeding 120 million, "The Boss" is among the best-selling singer-songwriters ever. Growing up in a working-class area of New Jersey and buying his first guitar for $18 at the age of 13, Springsteen served his musical apprenticeship in bars and clubs around his home state before signing with Columbia Records in 1972. Over the coming decades – and backed by his sturdy E Street Band – he became one of the top live draws in music, his 2007 – 08 *Magic Tour* racking up $221,500,000 in ticket sales.

HIS BEST-SELLING ALBUMS

1	Born In The U.S.A.	1984
2	Born To Run	1975
3	The River	1980
4	Greatest Hits	1995
5	Bruce Springsteen & the E. Street Band (boxed set)	1986
6	Tunnel Of Love	1987
7	Darkness On The Edge Of Town	1978
8	The Rising	2002
9	Greetings From Asbury Park	1975
10	The Wild, the Innocent And The E Street Shuffle	1975

HIS US CHART SINGLES

Born To Run	23	(Nov 01, 1975)
Tenth Avenue Freeze-Out	83	(Feb 07, 1976)
Badlands	42	(Sep 23, 1978)
Prove It All Night	33	(Jul 22, 1978)
Hungry Heart	5	(Dec 27, 1980)
Fade Away	20	(Mar 14, 1981)
Cover Me	7	(Oct 20, 1984)
Dancing In The Dark	2	(Jun 30, 1984)
Born In The U.S.A.	9	(Jan 19, 1985)
Glory Days	5	(Aug 03, 1985)
I'm Goin' Down	9	(Oct 26, 1985)
I'm On Fire	6	(Apr 13, 1985)
My Hometown	6	(Jan 25, 1986)
War	8	(Dec 27, 1986)
Fire	46	(Feb 28, 1987)
Brilliant Disguise	5	(Nov 21, 1987)
Tunnel Of Love	9	(Feb 06, 1988)
One Step Up	13	(Apr 23, 1988)
57 Channels (And Nothin' On)	68	(Jun 27, 1992)
Human Touch/Better Days	16	(Apr 11, 1992)
Streets Of Philadelphia (from *Philadelphia*)	9	(Apr 23, 1994)
Secret Garden	19	(May 24, 1997)
The Rising	52	(Aug 03, 2002)
Devils & Dust	72	(Apr 16, 2005)
Girls In Their Summer Clothes	95	(Feb 02, 2008)
Working On A Dream	33	(Oct 31, 2009)

Above: 'Born in the USA', 1985.

Born In the U.S.A. – the title track of which has become a perennial blue-collar classic – has sold more than 30 million copies worldwide, with half of those bought in the US alone. It spawned no less than seven US top 10 singles – the same as Michael Jackson's *Thriller* – including the chart-topping 'Dancing In The Dark'.

Top Left: Hyde Park 1982.

Above: Robert DeNiro, The Boss and The President.

THE BOSS

On December 6, 2009 Springsteen was bestowed with the prestigious Kennedy Center Honor in Washington, DC – an award celebrated by performances of his songs by the likes of Sting, Eddie Vedder and Melissa Etheridge. President Obama remarked in his tribute speech: "On days like today, we are reminded that, while I am President, he is The Boss."

UK HITS PENNED BY BRUCE SPRINGSTEEN, BUT PERFORMED BY OTHERS

Song	Artist	Position	Year
Blinded By The Light	Manfred Mann's Earth Band	No. 6	1976
Because The Night	The Patti Smith Group	No. 5	1978
Fire	The Pointer Sisters	No. 34	1979
This Little Girl	Gary U.S. Bonds	No. 43	1981
Dancing In The Dark (EP)	Big Daddy	No. 21	1985
Pink Cadillac	Natalie Cole	No. 5	1988
Because The Night	C. Ro featuring Tarlisa	No. 61	1992
Because The Night	10,000 Maniacs	No. 65	1993
Because The Night	Jan Wayne	No. 14	2002
Because The Night	Cascada	No. 28	2008

US HITS PENNED BY BRUCE SPRINGSTEEN, BUT PERFORMED BY OTHERS

Song	Artist	Position	Year
Sandy	The Hollies	No. 85	1975
Blinded By The Light	Manfred Mann's Earth Band	No. 1	1976
Spirit In The Heart	Manfred Mann's Earth Band	No. 97	1976
Spirit In The Night	Manfred Mann's Earth Band	No. 40	1977
Fire	The Pointer Sisters	No. 2	1978
Because The Night	The Patti Smith Group	No. 13	1978
This Little Girl	Gary U.S. Bonds	No. 11	1981
Out Of Work	Gary U.S. Bonds	No. 21	1982
Born In East LA	Cheech & Chong	No. 48	1985
Light Of Day	The Barbusters (Joan Jett & the Blackhearts)	No. 33	1987
Pink Cadillac	Natalie Cole	No. 5	1988
Banned In The USA	Luke featuring The 2 Live Crew	No. 20	1990
Because The Night	10,000 Maniacs	No. 11	1993

WE'RE GOING TO GRACELAND

On April 29, 1976 at 3.00am, after a gig in Memphis, Tennessee, Springsteen, guitarist Stevie Van Zandt and publicist Glen Brunman asked a Memphis cab driver to take them to Elvis Presley's Graceland home. Springsteen climbed over the wall, but a security guard assumed he was just another crank fan and apprehended him.

Below: Rocking Santa Barbara in 1976.

HIS GRAMMY AWARDS

Award	Year
Best Rock Vocal Performance, Male for 'Dancing In The Dark'	1984
Best Rock Vocal Performance, Solo for 'Tunnel Of Love'	1987
Best Song Written Specifically for a Motion Picture or for Television for 'Streets Of Philadelphia'	1994
Best Rock Song for 'Streets Of Philadelphia'	1994
Best Male Rock Vocal Performance for 'Streets Of Philadelphia'	1994
Song of the Year for 'Streets Of Philadelphia'	1994
Best Contemporary Folk Album for The Ghost Of Tom Joad	2002
Best Rock Song for 'The Rising'	2002
Best Male Rock Vocal Performance for 'The Rising'	2002
Best Rock Performance by a Duo or Group with Vocal for 'Disorder In The House'	2003
Best Solo Rock Vocal Performance for 'Code Of Silence'	2004
Best Solo Rock Vocal Performance for 'Devils & Dust'	2005
Best Long Form Music Video for Wings For Wheels – The Making of Born To Run	2006
Best Traditional Folk Album for We Shall Overcome – The Seeger Sessions (also featuring other artists)	2006
Best Rock Song for 'Radio Nowhere'	2007
Best Rock Instrumental Performance for 'Once Up A Time In The West'	2007
Best Rock Song for 'Girls in Their Summer Clothes'	2008
Best Solo Rock Vocal Performance for 'Working On A Dream'	2009

Among many other awards, Springsteen has twice won a Golden Globe in the Best Original Song category: 'Streets Of Philadelphia' (1994 – also won an Oscar) and 2009's 'The Wrestler'.

ROCK AND ROLL HALL OF FAME PRESENTER EXTRAORDINAIRE

Inducted himself in 1999, Springsteen has inducted more artists into the Rock and Roll Hall of Fame than anyone else.

Roy Orbison	1987
Bob Dylan	1988
Creedence Clearwater Revival	1993
Jackson Browne	2004
U2	2005

Left: Welcoming U2 into the Rock & Roll Hall of Fame.

Nicknamed "Little Noni" as a child, Madonna Louise Ciccone was born on August 16, 1958 in Bay City, Michigan. Initially set on a career in contemporary dance, she served vocal apprenticeships in two pop groups, Emmy and Breakfast Club, before signing as a solo artiste to Sire Records in 1981. Over the next three decades, the often controversial and chameleonic singer-songwriter became the most successful female performer of all time with combined estimated global record sales of more than 200 million.

THE BEST SELLING ALBUMS

1	The Immaculate Collection	1990
2	Like a Virgin	1984
3	True Blue	1986
4	Madonna	1983
5	Ray Of Light	1998
6	Like A Prayer	1989
7	Something To Remember	1995
8	Bedtime Stories	1994
9	Erotica	1992
10	Music	2000

HER NUMBER ONE HIT SINGLES IN THE US

Like A Virgin	Dec 22, 1984
Crazy For You	May 11, 1985
Live To Tell	Jun 07, 1986
Papa Don't Preach	Aug 16, 1986
Open Your Heart	Feb 07, 1987
Who's That Girl	Aug 22, 1987
Like A Prayer	Apr 22, 1989
Vogue	May 19, 1990
Justify My Love	Jan 05, 1991
This Used To Be My Playground	Aug 08, 1992
Take A Bow	Feb 25, 1995
Music	Sep 16, 2000

Left: 'Like A Virgin' back in 1984.

HER NUMBER ONE HIT SINGLES IN THE UK

SEX

Unmatched throughout her career in her efforts to tease and shock, Madonna's Sex party – staged to promote her forthcoming album and book (also called *Sex*, a metal-covered collection of provocative photographs featuring herself) – was held at Manhattan's Industria Superstudio for 800 invited guests on October 15, 1992. Ever the media chameleon, Madonna arrived carrying a toy lamb and dressed as Little Bo Peep. The book reportedly sold 500,000 copies in its first week.

Left: Miss 'American Pie' topped the charts in 2000.   Top: 'Like A Prayer' 1989.

AT THE MOVIES

A Certain Sacrifice	1985
Vision Quest	1985
Desperately Seeking Susan	1985
Shanghai Surprise	1986
Who's That Girl	1987
Bloodhounds Of Broadway	1989
Dick Tracy	1990
Shadows And Fog	1991
A League Of Their Own	1992
Body Of Evidence	1993
Dangerous Game	1993
Blue In The Face	1995
Four Rooms	1995
Girl 6	1996
Evita	1996
The Next Best Thing	2000
Swept Away	2002
Die Another Day	2002
Arthur & the Invisibles (voice)	2006

Frequently panned by film critics for her celluloid work, Madonna scooped a Golden Globe Award for Best Actress in a Comedy or Musical for her 1996 portrayal of Eva Perón, the First Lady of Argentina, in *Evita*.

AT THE GRAMMYS

Best Music Video, Long Form for Madonna Blonde Ambition World Tour Live	1991
Best Short Form Music Video for Ray Of Light	1998
Best Pop Album for *Ray Of Light*	1998
Best Dance Recording for *Ray Of Light*	1998
Best Song Written for a Motion Picture, Television or Other Visual Media for 'Beautiful Stranger'	1999
Best Electronic/Dance Album for *Confessions on a Dance Floor*	2006
Best Long Form Music Video for The Confessions Tour	2007

Above: Concert in Hyde Park 2005.

HER MTV AWARDS

Madonna has been nominated for 68 MTV Awards and has collected 20 trophies. These are her winning nods:

Video Vanguard Award	1986
Best Female Video for Papa Don't Preach	1987
Best Direction for Express Yourself	1989
Best Art Direction for Express Yourself	1989
Best Cinematography for Express Yourself	1989
Viewer's Choice for Like A Prayer	1989
Best Direction for Vogue	1990
Best Editing for Vogue	1990
Best Cinematography for Vogue	1990
Best Long Form Video for *The Immaculate Collection*	1991
Best Art Direction for Rain	1993
Best Cinematography for Rain	1993
Best Female Video for Take A Bow	1995
Video of the Year for Ray Of Light	1998
Best Female Video for Ray Of Light	1998
Best Direction for Ray Of Light	1998
Best Choreography for Ray Of Light	1998
Best Special Effects for Frozen	1998
Best Editing for Ray Of Light	1998
Best Video from a Film for Beautiful Stranger	1999

Above: At the 2009 MTV Music Video Awards.

IN DEFENCE OF EMINEM

In a letter written to the *Los Angeles Times* dated February 28, 2001, Madonna wrote: "What is the big problem about Eminem? Since when is offensive language a reason for being unpopular? I find the language of George W. Bush much more offensive. I like the fact that Eminem is brash and angry and politically incorrect." She signs the letter: "Mrs. Ritchie".

ON TOUR

Right: The *Sticky and Sweet* tour, Berlin 2008.

Total amount of dates for each tour is in brackets. Her last four global treks have brought in an estimated combined $802 million in ticket sales.

MICHAEL JACKSON

The most successful all-round singer, songwriter, dancer, entertainer of all time, Michael Jackson changed popular culture forever. From his dazzling debut as the youngest member and lead singer of the Jackson 5 sibling troupe in 1964 through his solo career peak with *Thriller*, to his bizarre and much-scrutinized private life, Jackson remained a mesmerizing talent until his untimely death in 2009, age 50. His glittering and controversial career yielded only ten original solo studio albums in the 37 years which followed his 1972 debut, *Got To Be There*.

HIS WORLDWIDE SALES

United States	89.3 million
United Kingdom	18 million
Germany	10.9 million
France	10.1 million
Australia	5.4 million
Canada	4.5 million
Mexico	3.3 million
Holland	1.9 million
Austria	1 million
Switzerland	900,000
Spain	720,000
Sweden	660,000
Finland	340,000

HIS BEST-SELLING ALBUMS

1	Thriller	1982
2	Bad	1987
3	Dangerous	1991
4	HIStory – Past, Present And Future, Book 1	1995
5	Off The Wall	1979
6	Number Ones	2003
7	The Essential Michael Jackson	2005
8	Michael Jackson's This Is It	2009
9	Invincible	2001
10	Blood on the Dancefloor – History in the Mix	1997

Thriller spent 37 weeks atop the US Album chart, more than any other (non-soundtrack) album in history, and sold more copies in two successive years (1983 and 1984) than any other release. It is the biggest-selling album of all time, worldwide with estimated global sales now over 100 million.

THE UK'S FAVOURITE MICHAEL JACKSON SONGS

1 Thriller
2 Billie Jean
3 Beat It
4 You Rock My World
5 Man In The Mirror
6 The Way You Make Me Feel
7 Smooth Criminal
8 Bad
9 Black Or White
10 Don't Stop Till You Get Enough

Above: Rocking with Slash at Madison Square Garden, 2001.

Top: The award-winning *Thriller* video, 1984.

Left: The King of Pop in Rotterdam 1988.

Following his death, Britain's performing rights society, PRS for Music revealed that 'Thriller' is the UK's most-played Michael Jackson song. The chart was compiled with PRS for Music's unique performance database, which is used to make accurate royalty payments to songwriters, composers and music publishers.

MTV – WEDNESDAY, SEPTEMBER 7, 1988

Having single-handedly pioneered the art of music video making, Jackson collected the prestigious Video Vanguard trophy at the fifth annual MTV Video Music Awards, held at the Universal Amphitheatre in Los Angeles, an honour subsequently renamed the Michael Jackson Video Vanguard Award.

GONE TOO SOON

Shortly after midday, on June 25, 2009, at a mansion the star was renting at North Carolwood Drive in the Holby Hills area of Los Angeles, Jackson entered a state of cardiac arrest. His physician, Dr. Conrad Murray, tried unsuccessfully to revive him. The Los Angeles Fire Department received a 911 call from an unnamed male at 12.21pm local time, with paramedics arriving nine minutes later. CPR was administered, with more efforts at resuscitation attempted en route to the Ronald Reagan UCLA Medical Center, and for a further 60 minutes at the hospital. He was officially pronounced dead, at 2.26 pm.

FILMOGRAPHY

In addition to his groundbreaking video creations – in themselves, mini-films – Jackson appeared in seven movies: *The Wiz* (1978), *Captain EO* (1986), *Moonwalker* (1988), *Ghosts* (1997), *Men in Black II* (2002), *Miss Cast Away and the Island Girls* (2004) and *Michael Jackson's This Is It* (2009).

THE JULY 5, 2009 UK SINGLES CHART

The week after Jackson's death, the UK top 75 featured 27 tracks by Jackson and the Jackson 5 (*):

Man In The Mirror	2	Ben	46
Billie Jean	10	*ABC	50
Thriller	12	Rock With You	54
Smooth Criminal	13	*Blame It On The Boogie	55
Beat It	19	Wanna Be Startin' Somethin'	57
Black Or White	25	Can You Feel It	59
Dirty Diana	26	You Rock My World	60
They Don't Care About Us	32	Heal The World	63
Earth Song	33	*I'll Be There	65
The Way You Make Me Feel	34	Leave Me Alone	66
You Are Not Alone	35	Scream (with Janet Jackson)	70
Don't Stop 'Til You Get Enough	38	Off The Wall	73
Bad	40	Give In To Me	74
*I Want You Back	43		

Above: Michael announces a series of comeback concerts at the O2 Arena, March 2009.

Right: Jackson with his first wife, Lisa Marie Presley, in 1995.

HIS NUMBER ONE HIT SINGLES IN THE UK

One Day In Your Life	Jun 27, 1981
Billie Jean	Mar 05, 1983
I Just Can't Stop Loving You	Aug 15, 1987
Black Or White	Nov 23, 1991
You Are Not Alone	Sep 09, 1995
Earth Song	Dec 09, 1995
Blood On The Dance Floor	May 03, 1997

HIS NUMBER ONE HIT SINGLES IN THE US

Ben	Oct 14, 1972
Don't Stop Till You Get Enough	Oct 13, 1979
Rock With You	Jan 19, 1980
Billie Jean	Mar 05, 1983
Beat It	Apr 30, 1983
Say Say Say	Dec 10, 1983
I Just Can't Stop Loving You	Sep 19, 1987
Bad	Oct 24, 1987
The Way You Make Me Feel	Jan 23, 1988
The Man In The Mirror	Mar 26, 1988
Dirty Diana	Jul 02, 1988
Black Or White	Dec 07, 1991
You Are Not Alone	Sep 02, 1995

Above: Michael, aged 14.

HIS GRAMMY SWEEP

On February 28, 1984, the day after the Pepsi-Cola commercial premiered on MTV and a week after he won trophies for Best British Album (*Thriller*) and Best International Solo Artist at the third annual BRIT Awards in London, Jackson walked away with an unprecedented eight Grammys at the 26th annual ceremonies:

Album of the Year (*Thriller*)
Best Engineered Recording (Non-Classical) (*Thriller*)
Record of the Year ('Beat It')
Best Rock Vocal Performance, Male ('Beat It')
Best New Rhythm & Blues Song ('Billie Jean')
Best R&B Vocal Performance, Male (*Thriller*)
Producer of the Year
Best Recording For Children (*E.T. The Extra-Terrestrial*)

THE DANGEROUS TOUR

Jackson's *Dangerous* world tour opened in Munich, West Germany, at the Olympic Stadium on June 27, 1992 and closed in Mexico City, Mexico on November 11, 1993 (three months earlier than planned due to illness). Sponsored by Pepsi-Cola, Jackson performed to some 3,900,000 fans at 89 concerts on four continents. Two Boeing 747 jet aircrafts were used to transport more than 100 tons of stage equipment to each city. (500,000 cassette copies of the single 'Someone Put Your Hand Out', previously unavailable anywhere, were released in Europe through a Pepsi deal made possible by returning tokens printed on Pepsi packaging.)

THE CATALOGUE

In March 2010, Sony Corp, Jackson's longtime record company, signed the most expensive deal in music history – with the Michael Jackson Estate. The ten-album agreement over seven years combined new collections of previously unreleased songs and new compilations (including the 2009 This Is It soundtrack) for a reported $250 million payment to the Estate. Since his death, nine months earlier, Sony had already sold some 31 million Michael Jackson albums.

Left: Pasadena, California 2002.

THE MADISON SQUARE GARDEN CONCERTS – SEPTEMBER 2001

The all-star lineup comprised the following:

The Jacksons • Whitney Houston • Britney Spears • Monica • Al Jarreau • Gladys Knight • Usher • Luther Vandross • Dionne Warwick • Liza Minnelli • Marc Anthony • *NSync • Shaggy • Slash • Billy Gilman

Left: Jermaine Jackson at his brother's memorial service in Los Angeles.

Above: Michael performs with his brothers in Madison Square Garden, 2001.

THE MICHAEL JACKSON PUBLIC MEMORIAL SERVICE – JULY 07, 2009

The following artists offered tributes:

Mariah Carey with Trey Lorenz	I'll Be There
Lionel Richie	Jesus Is Love
Stevie Wonder	Never Dreamed You'd Leave In Summer
Jennifer Hudson	Will You Be There
John Mayer	Human Nature
Jermaine Jackson	Smile
Usher	Gone Too Soon
Shaheen Jafargholi	Who's Lovin' You
Andre Crouch Choir	Soon And Very Soon

And celebrity renditions of 'We Are The World' and 'Heal The World'.

After 12 days of unrelenting media coverage following his death, the Michael Jackson Public Memorial Service took place at the Staples Center in Los Angeles immediately following a private memorial at Forest Lawn cemetery attended by family members and 100 invited guests.

Above: Usher performing at Jackson's memorial service.

MTV MUSIC TELEVISION™

U2

After playing a handful of shows in the Dublin area as The Hype, U2 won a talent contest sponsored by the *Evening Press* and Harp Lager at the Limerick Civic Week on March 17, 1978. Still in their final year at school and increasingly playing their own material, the group won £500 and the chance to audition for CBS Ireland at the local Keystone Studios. U2 played for the first time on British television more than two years later, performing 'I Will Follow' on ITV's *Get It Together* show. Less than a month later they played for the first time in the USA.

THEIR BEST-SELLING ALBUMS

1	The Joshua Tree	1987
2	Achtung Baby	1991
3	Rattle And Hum	1988
4	All That You Can Leave Behind	2000
5	War	1983
6	How To Dismantle A Bomb	2004
7	Under A Blood Red Sky	1983
8	The Unforgettable Fire	1984
9	The Best of 1980 – 90	1998
10	Zooropa	1993
11	The Best of 1980 – 90/The B Sides	1998
12	The Best of 1990 – 2000	2002
13	No Line On The Horizon	2009
14	October	1981
15	Pop	1997
16	Boy	1980

Recorded in four different studios around Dublin during 1986, *The Joshua Tree* yielded three huge hit singles and elevated the fortunes of the band to global superstardom, eventually selling more than 25 million copies worldwide.

THEIR NUMBER ONE HIT SINGLES IN THE UK

Desire	Oct 08, 1988
The Fly	Nov 02, 1991
Discotheque	Feb 15, 1997
Beautiful Day	Oct 21, 2000
Take Me To The Clouds Above	Feb 07, 2004
Vertigo	Nov 20, 2004
Sometimes You Can't Make It On Your Own	Feb 19, 2005

Left: Bono, Larry Mullen Jnr, Adam Clayton and The Edge in 1984.

Above: The band in 1985.

THEIR NUMBER ONE HIT SINGLES IN THE US

With Or Without You	May 16, 1987
I Still Haven't Found What I'm Looking For	Aug 08, 1987

The band played live in the US for the first time at the Ritz in New York on December 6, 1980.

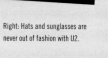

Right: Hats and sunglasses are never out of fashion with U2.

Above: Bono on the *Elevation Tour*, Chicago 2001.

Below: U2 at the Giants Stadium, New York in 2009.

THEIR BRIT AWARDS

These are their winning awards:

Best International Group	1988
Best International Group	1989
Best International Group	1990
Best Live Act	1993
Best International Group	1998
Best International Group	2001

U2 has been nominated 16 times and won 6 at the BRIT Awards, as well as being the recipients of the 2001 Outstanding Contribution honour.

Above: A delighted Bono at the BRIT Awards in 1993.

THEIR TOURS

Boy (157 shows)	Sep 06, 1980–Jun 09, 1981
October (102 shows)	Aug 16, 1981–Aug 07, 1982
War (109 shows)	Dec 01, 1982–Nov 30, 1983
Unforgettable Fire (113 shows)	Aug 29, 1984–Aug 25, 1985
Conspiracy of Hope (6 shows)	Jun 04, 1986–Jun 15, 1986
Joshua Tree (109 shows)	Apr 02, 1987–Dec 20, 1987
Lovetown (47 shows)	Sep 21, 1989–Jan 10, 1990
ZOO TV (158 shows)	Feb 29, 1992–Dec 10, 1993
PopMart (94 shows)	Apr 25, 1997–Mar 21, 1998
Elevation (113 shows)	Mar 24, 2001–Dec 02, 2001
Vertigo (132 shows)	Mar 26, 2005–Dec 09, 2006
360 (82 shows)	Jun 29, 2009–Oct 08, 2010

WHERE THE STREETS HAVE TRAFFIC JAMS

Among U2's many ad-hoc performances on rooftops, in streets and even in a K-Mart store, one of the more memorable occasions brought chaos to the San Francisco business district on November 13, 1987, when they played a "Save the Yuppies" concert at the city's Justine Hermine Plaza. 20,000 fans turned up after a local radio station announced the show one hour earlier. Just two weeks after a crash on the stock market, Bono announced: "The business community is a bit short this week. That's why I'm wearing this hat, we'll be passing it round later."

I'LL GO CRAZY IF I DON'T HAVE PIZZA TONIGHT

At the group's concert at the Palace of Auburn Hills in Auburn Hills, Michigan on March 27, 1992, Bono ordered 10,000 pizzas to go from Speedy Pizza. An hour later, 100 pepperoni pizzas arrived with three deliverymen, who each received a $50 tip.

THEIR MTV AWARDS

Viewer's Choice Award for With Or Without You	1987
Best Video from a Film for When Love Comes To Town	1989
Best Group Video for Even Better Than The Real Thing	1992
Viewer's Choice Award for Hold Me, Thrill Me, Kiss Me, Kill Me	1995
Video Vanguard Award	2001

Left: More success at the the MTV Video Music Awards in 2001.

ELTON JOHN

Reginald Kenneth Dwight began playing the piano at the age of three at his family home in Pinner, Middlesex. Given formal piano lessons from the age of seven, the talented kid won a junior scholarship to the Royal Academy of Music at 11, attending classes every Saturday morning while studying at Pinner County Grammar School during the week – and performing as the weekend pianist at the Northwood Hills Hotel from the age of 15. Unsurprisingly, he left school at 17 before taking his A Levels to pursue a musical career.

HIS BEST-SELLING ALBUMS

1	Greatest Hits	1974
2	Goodbye Yellow Brick Road	1973
3	Elton John's Greatest Hits, Volume II	1977
4	Elton John's Greatest Hits 1970-2002	2002
5	Love Songs	1996
6	Captain Fantastic And The Brown Dirt Cowboy	1975
7	Don't Shoot Me I'm Only The Piano Player	1973
8	The Very Best of Elton John	1990
	Greatest Hits III, 1979 – 87	1987
9	Decade – Elton John's Greatest Hits 1976 – 86	1992
10	Caribou	1974
11	Madman Across The Water	1972
12	The One	1992
13	Sleeping With The Past	1989
14	The Big Picture	1997
15	Duets	1993

Since making his chart debut in 1970, Elton had at least one album on the UK and US album charts every year through 2007.

HIS NUMBER ONE HIT SINGLES IN THE UK

Don't Go Breaking My Heart (with Kiki Dee)	Jul 24, 1976
Sacrifice/Healing Hands	Jun 23, 1990
Something About The Way You Look Tonight/Candle In The Wind 1997	Sep 20, 1997
Sorry Seems To Be The Hardest Word (Blue featuring Elton John)	Dec 21, 2002
Are You Ready For Love?	Sep 06, 2003
Ghetto Gospel (2Pac featuring Elton John)	Jul 02, 2005

Above: Elton enjoys a quieter moment.

HIS NUMBER ONE HIT SINGLES IN THE US

Crocodile Rock	Feb 03, 1973
Bennie And The Jets	Apr 13, 1974
Lucy In The Sky With Diamonds	Jan 04, 1975
Philadelphia Freedom (credited to the Elton John Band)	Apr 12, 1975
Island Girl	Nov 01, 1975
Don't Go Breaking My Heart (with Kiki Dee)	Aug 07, 1976
Candle In The Wind 1997/Something About The Way You Look Tonight	Oct 11, 1997

In over four decades, Elton John has amassed worldwide estimated combined record sales over 250 million – with 'Candle in the Wind 1997/Something About the Way You Look Tonight' acknowledged as the best-selling global single of all time.

Left: Elton was famed for his flamboyant glasses – as well as brilliant songs and performances.

Right: Performing at the Hammersmith Odeon in 1973.

HIS
SONGWRITING PARTNERS

Bernie Taupin	74
Davey Johnstone	4
Gary Osborne	4
Tim Rice	4
Lee Hall	1
Patrick Leonard	1
Tom Robinson	1

Above: The total amount of hits written with his respective lyricists.

FILM AND THEATRE

In addition to his immensely successful contributions to *The Lion King* musical, which included the hits 'Can You Feel the Love Tonight' and 'Circle of Life', Elton has composed three movie soundtracks: *Friends* (1971), the often-overlooked *The Muse* (1999) and *The Road to Eldorado* for the 2000-released animated film of the same name. His stage musical works are *Elton John and Tim Rice's Aida* (1999), *Billy Elliot The Musical* (2005) and *Lestat: The Musical* (2006). John has also co-written five songs for the planned 2010 Disney film, *Gnomeo and Juliet*.

SATURDAY NIGHT'S ALRIGHT FOR FOOTBALL

John has been a lifelong devotee of football, including spells as chairman of Watford Football Club. In 1984, in the midst of a European tour, he flew from Denmark to see the team play in their first-ever FA Cup Final, losing 2–0 to Everton. His cousin Roy Dwight scored a goal and broke his leg in Nottingham Forest's 2–1 win over Luton Town in the 1959 FA Cup Final.

Below: Sir Elton John in 2009.

HIS HIT UK SINGLES AS DUETS

Artist	Song	Pos	Date
Dr. Winston O'Boogie & His Reggae Guitars (John Lennon)	Lucy In The Sky With Diamonds	10	(Dec 14, 1974)
Kiki Dee	Don't Go Breaking My Heart	1	(Jul 24, 1976)
Kiki Dee	Bite Your Lip (Get Up And Dance) /Chicago	28	(Jun 25, 1977)
John Lennon	I Saw Her Standing There	40	(Mar 28, 1981)
Millie Jackson	Act of War	32	(Jun 22, 1985)
Dionne Warwick, Gladys Knight & Stevie Wonder	That's What Friends Are For	16	(Nov 30, 1985)
Cliff Richard	Slow Rivers	44	(Dec 27, 1986)
Jennifer Rush	Flames Of Paradise	59	(Jun 27, 1987)
Aretha Franklin	Through The Storm	41	(May 13, 1989)
Eric Clapton	Runaway Train	31	(Aug 08, 1992)
Kiki Dee	True Love	2	(Nov 27, 1993)
RuPaul	Don't Go Breaking My Heart	7	(Mar 05, 1994)
Marcella Detroit	Ain't Nothing Like The Real Thing	24	(May 21, 1994)
Luciano Pavarotti	Live Like Horses	9	(Dec 14, 1996)
LeAnn Rimes	Written In The Stars	10	(Mar 06, 1999)
Alessandro Safina	Your Song	4	(Jul 27, 2002)
Blue	Sorry Seems To Be The Hardest Word	1	(Dec 21, 2002)
2Pac	Ghetto Gospel	1	(Jul 02, 2005)

AT THE GRAMMYS

Best Pop Performance by a Duo or Group with Vocals for That's What Friends Are For, with Dionne Warwick, Gladys Knight & Stevie Wonder	1986
Best Instrumental Composition for Basque	1991
Best Male Pop Vocal Performance for Can You Feel the Love Tonight	1994
Best Male Pop Vocal Performance for Candle In The Wind 1997	1997
Best Musical Show Album for Elton John & Tim Rice's *Aida*	2000

Among the many honours bestowed on him – including his 1998 knighthood – Sir Elton John is one of a select number of entertainers to have won an Academy Award (1994), a Golden Globe (1994), a Tony Award (2000) and a Grammy. He was also inducted into the Rock and Roll Hall of Fame in 1994.

HIS IVOR NOVELLO AWARDS

John has won 12 Ivor Novello Awards spanning the years 1973 to 2006.

Category	Song	Year
Best Song Musically & Lyrically	Daniel	1973
Best Pop Song	Don't Go Breaking My Heart	1976
Best Instrumental or Popular Orchestral Work	Song For Guy	1978
Best Song Musically & Lyrically	Nikita	1985
Outstanding Contribution to British Music		1986
Best Selling "A" Side	Sacrifice/Healing Hands	1990
Best Song Musically & Lyrically	Sacrifice	1990
Best Song Included in a Film	Circle of Life	1994
Best Selling UK Single	Candle In The Wind 1997	1997
International Hit of the Year	Candle In The Wind 1997	1997
International Achievement in Musical Theatre		1999
PRS Most Performed Work	I Don't Feel Like Dancin'	2006

DAVID BOWIE

Initially performing as Davie Jones and Davy Jones, David Robert Jones finally settled on David Bowie as his performing moniker in 1966. His eponymous debut album, released on the Decca Records imprint, Deram, in 1967, was an entirely self-penned collection of mostly whimsical and theatrical pop vocal cuts. It wa produced by Mike Vernon, and its 14 tracks featured Bowie on vocals, saxophone and guitar. The Thin White Duke was inducted into the Rock and Roll Hall of Fame in 1996.

HIS BEST-SELLING ALBUMS

1	Let's Dance	1983
2	Best Of Bowie	2002
3	Changesbowie	1990
4	Changesonebowie	1976
5	Tonight	1984
6	Ziggy Stardust – The Motion Picture	1982
7	The Rise And Fall Of Ziggy Stardust And The Spiders From Mars	1972
8	Scary Monsters And Super Creeps	1980
9	Hunky Dory	1972
10	The Very Best Otf David Bowie	1981

HIS NUMBER ONE HITS IN THE UK

Ashes To Ashes	Aug 23, 1980
Under Pressure (with Queen)	Nov 21, 1981
Let's Dance	Apr 09, 1983
Dancing In The Street (with Mick Jagger)	Sep 07, 1985

Despite racking up 27 Hot 100 hits in the US, Bowie has only managed two chart-toppers – 'Fame' (September 20, 1975), which peaked no higher then Number 17 in the UK, and 'Let's Dance' (May 21, 1983).

Above: Bowie in the late 80s.

Right: Aladdin Sane, Bowie's glam-rock persona in 1973.

ON TOUR

Ziggy Stardust (182)	Jan 29, 1972 – Jul 03, 1973
Diamond Dogs (73)	Jun 14, 1974 – Dec 02, 1974
Isolar (64)	Feb 02, 1976 – May 18, 1976
Isolar II (77)	Mar 29, 1978 – Dec 12, 1978
Serious Moonlight (96)	May 18, 1983 – Dec 08, 1983
Glass Spider (86)	May 30, 1987 – Nov 28, 1987
Sound+Vision (108)	Mar 04, 1990 – Sep 29, 1990
Outside (68)	Sep 14, 1995 – Feb 20, 1996
Outside Summer Festivals (27)	Jun 04, 1996 – Jul 21, 1996
Earthling (83)	Jun 07, 1997 – Nov 07, 1997
The Hours… (8)	Oct 09, 1999 – Dec 07, 1999
Heathen (36)	Jun 11, 2002 – Oct 23, 2002
A Reality (113)	Oct 07, 2003 – Jul 02, 2004

Total amount of dates for each tour is in brackets.

EYE ODDITY

A master of image and style changes throughout his illustrious career, one notable physical oddity which was not planned is one of Bowie's eyes. Following a fight with a school friend when he was 15, he was punched in the eye, resulting in its pupil being constantly open with a brown tone around it. The injury also left the Thin White Duke with compromised depth perception.

FEATURING DAVID BOWIE

Among many notable guest appearances throughout his career, the seventies proved especially creative and productive. In addition to writing, producing and providing vocals to Mott The Hoople's 1972 glam-rock smash, 'All the Young Dudes', Bowie can be heard on Lou Reed's seminal *Transformer* album from the same year, and on the Iggy & the Stooges album, *The Idiot*, in 1977 – which he also produced. More recently Bowie can be heard on backing vocals on two tracks on actress Scarlett Johansson's 2008 release, *Anywhere I Lay My Head*.

BANDS HE HAS PLAYED IN

The Konrads	1962–63
The Hooker Brothers	1963
Davy Jones & the King Bees	1964
The Manish Boys	1964–65
The Lower Third	1965–66
The Buzz	1966
Pierrot in Turquoise	1967–68
Turquoise	1968
Feathers	1968
Hype	1970
Tin Machine	1988–92

AT THE MOVIES

The Image (short film)	1967
The Virgin Soldiers	1969
The Man Who Fell to Earth	1976
Just a Gigolo	1979
Christiane F.	1981
The Snowman (voice, animated short film)	1982
The Hunger	1983
Merry Christmas, Mr. Lawrence	1983
Yellowbeard	1983
Into the Night	1985
Absolute Beginners	1986
Labyrinth	1986
The Last Temptation of Christ	1988
The Linguini Incident	1991
Twin Peaks – Fire Walk with Me	1992
Basquiat	1996
Il Mio West	1998
Everybody Loves Sunshine	1999
Mr. Rice's Secret	2000
Zoolander	2001
The Prestige	2006
Arthur and the Invisibles	2007
August	2008
Bandslam	2009

Among Bowie's more memorable television appearances is a notable cameo, playing himself, in Ricky Gervais' BBC television comedy series *Extras* in 2006. As a film producer, Bowie was also one of the movers behind the 2006 documentary, *Scott Walker: 30th Century Man*.

SPACE ODDITY

David Bowie was presented with a Special Award for Originality at the 1969 Ivor Novello Awards.

SPONGEBOB SQUAREPANTS

Bowie provided the voice of Lord Royal Highness in an episode of *Spongebob Squarepants* called "Atlantis SquarePantis" on November 12, 2007.

Left: Ziggy Stardust, 1973.

Below: Performing at the Isle of Wight Festival in 2004.

UK GOLD

Bowie has amassed 20 gold albums and singles in the UK.

Pin Ups	Nov 01, 1973
Stage	Jan 01, 1978
Lodger	Jun 08, 1979
Scary Monsters And Super Creeps*	Sep 17, 1980
The Very Best Of David Bowie*	Jan 16, 1981
Changestwobowie	Jan 12, 1982
Hunky Dory*	Jan 25, 1982
Ziggy Stardust – The Motion Picture*	Jan 25, 1982
Let's Dance (single)	Apr 01, 1983
Let's Dance*	Apr 18, 1983
Tonight	Oct 18, 1984
Dancing In The Street	Sep 01, 1985
Never Let Me Down	May 12, 1987
Changesbowie (Sound and Vision)*	Mar 01, 1990
Black Tie White Noise	Apr 01, 1993
The Ultimate Singles Collection*	Dec 01, 1993
David Bowie 1969/1974	Dec 12, 1997
Heathen	Jul 26, 2002
The Best Of Bowie*	Nov 08, 2002
Reality	Sep 26, 2003

Works marked with an asterisk have gone on to achieve Platinum sales.

US PLATINUM

Bowie has achieved 7 million sellers in the US.

Changesonebowie	Sep 15, 1981
Let's Dance	Jun 27, 1983
Tonight	Nov 21, 1984
Changesbowie	Mar 29, 1991
Best Of Bowie	Oct 24, 2006

Two of his videos have been awarded Platinum sales: *Best of Bowie* (May 9, 2003) and *Reality Tour* (January 14, 2005).

ABBA

Formed in Sweden 1972, Abba were catapulted to global fame after winning the Eurovision Song Contest in 1974 with the pop confection, 'Waterloo'. It was actually the group's second attempt to win the competition: their 'Ring Ring' offering failed to become the Swedish entry in 1973, voted into third place in the preliminary round in Sweden. Abba played their first non-Swedish dates on a mini-tour of Austria, Denmark and West Germany in 1974, and scored their second UK chart-topper (following 'Waterloo') in 1975 with the immortal 'Mamma Mia'.

THEIR BEST-SELLING ALBUMS

1	Abba Gold – Greatest Hits	1992
2	Greatest Hits	1976
3	Arrival	1976
4	The Album	1978
5	Super Trouper	1980
6	Voulez-Vous	1979
7	Greatest Hits	1976
8	The Visitors	1981
9	Greatest Hits Volume 2	1979
10	Abba	1975
11	More Abba Gold – More Abba Hits	1993
12	The Singles – The First Ten Years	1982

THEIR NUMBER ONE HIT SINGLES IN THE UK

Waterloo	May 04, 1974
Mamma Mia	Jan 31, 1976
Dancing Queen	Sep 04, 1976
Fernando	May 08, 1976
Knowing Me, Knowing You	Apr 02, 1977
The Name Of The Game	Nov 05, 1977
Take a Chance On Me	Feb 18, 1978
The Winner Takes It All	Aug 09, 1980
Super Trouper	Nov 29, 1980

Abba never replicated its UK success in the US, accruing just one chart-topper – 'Dancing Queen' in April 1977.

THEIR SINGLES BY COUNTRY

Tally of top 10 singles by country, with chart-toppers in brackets

Belgium (14)	22
Switzerland (9)	22
Netherlands (8)	22
West Germany (9)	21
United Kingdom (10)	20
Ireland (12)	18
Austria (3)	18
Norway (2)	17
South Africa (8)	14
Australia (6)	13
France (2)	13
Zimbabwe (2)	13
Mexico (7)	11
Finland (5)	11
Sweden (3)	11
Spain (1)	10
New Zealand (6)	9
Canada	7
United States (1)	4
Italy	3
Argentina	1

Above: Anni-Frid and Agnetha in 1979.

Top Right: The band were on the road to superstardom in 1976.

Right: Winning the Eurovision Song Contest with 'Waterloo' in 1974.

THANK YOU FOR THE MUSIC

After a ten-year ride of phenomenal success, Agnetha, Frida, Benny and Björn performed together for the last time as Abba on December 11, 1982 in Stockholm, transmitted live to BBC1 TV's *The Late, Late Breakfast Show* hosted by Noel Edmonds.

MAMMA MIA!

Based around the songs of Abba and created as musical by British playwright Catherine Johnson, the original production premiered at the Prince Edward Theatre in London's West End on April 6, 1999. It currently stands as the 10th longest-running musical on Broadway. Winning numerous Tony and Olivier Awards *Mamma Mia!* has played in more than 50 countries and in eleven languages, and was adapted into the equally popular *Mamma Mia!* movie in 2008. Costing $52 million to produce, the film has grossed more than $600 million worldwide – both Benny Andersson and Björn Ulvaeus made cameo appearances.

THEIR ALBUMS BY COUNTRY

Tally of Top 10 albums by country, with chart-toppers in brackets

Sweden (9)	11
Belgium (8)	11
Zimbabwe (6)	11
Germany (5)	11
New Zealand (3)	10
United Kingdom (9)	9
Norway (8)	9
Netherlands (4)	9
Finland (2)	9
Switzerland (5)	8
Australia (3)	8
Canada (1)	7
Mexico (5)	6
France (1)	6
Japan (1)	6
Spain (1)	6
Argentina)1)	3
South Africa (1)	2
Italy (0)	2
India (0)	1
Korea (0)	1

ABBA GOLD

Of the group's 25 UK chart hits, ten have achieved gold status.

Fernando	May 1, 1976
Dancing Queen	Sep 1, 1976
Money Money Money	Feb 1, 1977
Knowing Me Knowing You	Apr 1, 1977
The Name of the Game	Nov 1, 1977
Take a Chance on Me	Feb 1, 1978
Chiquitita	Feb 1, 1979
I Have a Dream	Dec 1, 1979
Super Trouper	Nov 1, 1980
One of Us	Dec 1, 1981

Above: Benny, Björn, Anni-Frid and Agnetha in 1977.

Above: The opening night of their first North American tour in 1979.

ABBA LIVE

The band made its live debut in November 1970 at the Festfolk cabaret in Trågår'n, Göteborg. This is a list of all their subsequent concerts.

Swedish Folkpark Tour	Jun 15, 1973 – Sep 09, 1973
European Tour	Nov 17, 1974 – Jan 22, 1975
Swedish Folkpark Tour	Jun 21, 1975 – Jul 09, 1975
European Tour	Jan 28, 1977 – Feb 14, 1977
Australian Tour	Mar 03, 1977 – Mar 12, 1977
North American Tour	Sep 13, 1977 – Oct 07, 1977
European Tour	Oct 19, 1979 – Nov 15, 1979
Japanese Tour	Mar 12, 1980 – Mar 27, 1980

PERFORMANCES BY COUNTRY

Sweden	78
West Germany	17
UK	13
US	13
Japan	11
Australia	8
Denmark	5
Austria	4
Canada	4
Norway	3
Belgium	2
Netherlands	2
Finland	1
France	1
Switzerland	1
Ireland	1

Singer, songwriter, keyboardist and producer, Stevie Wonder is one of few artists to have remained on the same label throughout his entire career. A child prodigy, "Little" Stevie Wonder was signed to Motown's embryonic Tamla label by Berry Gordy in 1961 at the age of 11 – and has remained with the legendary R&B company for nearly 50 years. His breakthrough hit was 'Fingertips (Pt. 2)' taken from the 1963 album, *Recorded Live: The 12-Year-Old Genius*. Wonder was inducted into the Rock and Roll Hall of Fame in 1989 and received the Grammy Lifetime Achievement Award in 1996.

Left: Stevie Wonder's career has lasted decades…

Below: … and his 'look' has changed with the era.

HIS NUMBER ONE
HIT SINGLES IN THE US

Fingertips (Part II)	Aug 10, 1963
Superstition	Jan 27, 1973
You Are The Sunshine Of My Life	May 19, 1973
You Haven't Done Nothin'	Nov 02, 1974
I Wish	Jan 22, 1977
Sir Duke	May 21, 1977
Ebony And Ivory (with Paul McCartney)	May 15, 1982
I Just Called To Say I Love You	Oct 13, 1984
Part-Time Lover	Nov 02, 1985

Below: Stevie puts in some serious studio time.

Only two on Wonder's hit singles have topped the chart in both the US and the UK – 'I Just Called To Say I Love You' and the Paul McCartney duet, 'Ebony And Ivory'. Written by McCartney, produced by George Martin and recorded live in the studio, it also featured Isaac Hayes on backing vocals.

THE BEST-SELLING ALBUMS

1	Songs In The Key Of Life	1976
2	Talking Book	1974
3	Innervisions	1973
4	Fulfillingness' First Finale	1974
5	The Definitive Collection	2005
6	In Square Circle	1985
7	Hotter Than July	1981
8	The Woman In Red	1984
9	Characters	1988
10	Stevie Wonder's Original Musiquarium	1982
11	A Time 2 Love	2005
12	Conversation Peace	1995

Hotter Than July spawned four top 10 UK hits, including the Bob Marley tribute, 'Masterblaster (Jammin')'.

HIGHER GROUND

Ever self-deprecating about his blindness, Wonder made a comedic cameo in a 2010 US television Volkswagen commercial. Titled "PunchDub" the spot features various people playfully punching someone next to them when seeing a Volkswagen car drive by. At the end of the commercial, Wonder jabs actor Tracy Morgan in the arm after "seeing" a red VW pass by, with Morgan immediately asking, "How do you do that?" Born six weeks premature, Wonder has been blind since birth.

MARTIN LUTHER KING

In February 1987, Wonder announced a boycott of the state of Arizona for not recognizing Martin Luther King Day, first observed as a national holiday in 1986.

WONDER-PENNED TOP 50 HITS FOR OTHERS IN THE US

AT THE GRAMMYS

Best Rhythm & Blues Song for 'Superstition'	1973
Best Rhythm & Blues Vocal Performance, Male, for 'Superstition'	1973
Best Pop Vocal Performance, Male, for 'You Are the Sunshine Of My Life'	1973
Album of the Year for *Innervisions*	1973
Best Producer	1973
Best Rhythm & Blues Song for 'Living For The City'	1974
Best Rhythm & Blues Vocal Performance, Male, for 'Boogie On Reggae Woman'	1974
Best Pop Vocal Performance, Male, for 'Fulfillingness' First Finale'	1974
Album of the Year for *Fulfillingness' First Finale*	1974
Best Producer	1974
Best Rhythm & Blues Vocal Performance, Male, for 'I Wish'	1976
Best Pop Vocal Performance, Male, for 'Songs In The Key Of Life'	1976
Best Producer of the Year	1976
Album of the Year for *Songs In The Key of Life*	1976
Best Rhythm & Blues Vocal Performance, Male, for 'In Square Circle'	1985
Best Pop Performance by a Duo or Group with Vocal for 'That's What Friends Are For'	1986
Best Rhythm & Blues Song for 'For Your Love'	1995
Best Male Rhythm & Blues Vocal Performance for 'For Your Love'	1995
Best Instrumental Arrangement Accompanying Vocal(s) for 'St. Louis Blues'	1998
Best Male Rhythm & Blues Vocal Performance for 'St. Louis Blues'	1998
Best Rhythm & Blues Performance by a Duo or Group with Vocal for 'Love's In Need Of Love Today'	2002
Best Rhythm & Blues Performance by a Duo or Group with Vocal for 'So Amazing'	2005
Best Male Pop Vocal Performance for 'From The Bottom Of My Heart'	2005
Best Pop Collaboration with Vocals for 'For Once In My Life'	2006

With 24 awards, Wonder has won more Grammys than any other solo artist. He was also honoured with the Lifetime Achievement Award in 1996.

Left: Wonder with blues guitarist B.B. King.

Above: Performing at Le Zénith, Paris in 2010.

In addition to his songwriting catalogue being a consistently rich goldmine for hit covers by other artists, Wonder's music has also been frequently sampled by hip-hop artists including 50 Cent ('Love's In Need Of Love Today' in 'Ryder Music'), Coolio ('Pastime Paradise' in 'Gangsta's Paradise'), Warren G ('Village Ghetto Land' in 'Ghetto Village') and Will Smith ('I Wish' in the title theme to the film *Wild Wild West*).

ROD STEWART

Son of a Scottish father and English mother, Roderick David Stewart was raised as the youngest of five children in Highgate, London. Mad about football from a young age, Stewart became centre-half for Middlesex Schoolboys before becoming an apprentice with Brentford FC, a third-division professional soccer club. A fan of folk music, mod, rock and rhythm & blues, he got his first gig as a professional musician in October 1963, playing harmonica and providing vocals for R&B combo, the Dimensions.

HIS BEST-SELLING ALBUMS

1	Unplugged… and Sealed	1995
2	Greatest Hits	1980
3	Blondes Have More Fun	1978
4	Foot Loose and Fancy Free	1977
5	It Had To Be You – The Great American Songbook	2002
6	As Time Goes By – The Great American Songbook Vol. 2	2003
7	A Night On The Town	1976
8	Out of Order	1988
9	Downtown Train – Selections From The Storyteller Anthology	1990
10	Every Picture Tells a Story	1771
11	Vagabond Heart	1991
12	Stardust – The Great American Songbook, Vol. 3	2004
13	If We Fall In Love Tonight	1997
14	Thanks For the Memory – The Great American Songbook, Vol. 4	2005
15	Foolish Behaviour	1981
16	The Story So Far – The Very Best of Rod Stewart	2001
17	Storyteller – The Complete Anthology: 1964 – 90	1990
18	The Best of Rod Stewart	1977
19	Atlantic Crossing	1975
20	Still the Same – Great Rock Classics of Our Time	2006

HIS NUMBER ONE HIT SINGLES IN THE UK

Maggie May/Reason to Believe	Oct 09, 1971
You Wear It Well	Sep 02, 1972
Sailing	Sep 06, 1975
I Don't Want To Talk About It/ First Cut Is The Deepest	May 21, 1977
Da' Ya' Think I'm Sexy?	Dec 02, 1978
Baby Jane	Jul 02, 1983

BBC Radio DJ John Peel performed as part of Rod Stewart's backing band on *Top of the Pops* in October 1971, pretending to play the mandolin on Stewart's breakthrough solo hit, 'Maggie May'. Stewart has only had two US Number Ones – 'Maggie May'/'Reason To Believe' (October 2, 1971) and 'Tonight's The Night (Gonna Be Alright)' (November 13, 1976).

Left: Proudly displaying his Scottish heritage in 1978.

Right: Performing at the Rainbow Theatre, London in 1973.

THE LARGEST-EVER CROWD

Stewart holds the record for performing in front of the largest crowd ever, when 3.5 million fans attended his New Year's Eve concert at the Copacabana Beach in Rio de Janeiro, Brazil in 1994.

AWARDS

In a career spanning 46 years – and despite being nominated more than a dozen times – Stewart has only won one Grammy award: Best Traditional Pop Vocal Album for *Stardust – The Great American Songbook Volume III* in 2004. His only other awards of distinction are for Outstanding Contribution at the BRIT Awards in 1993 and International Artist Award at the American Music Awards in 1993.

HIS BEST-SELLING SINGLES IN THE UK

1	Sailing	1975/1976
2	Maggie May	1971
3	Da Ya Think I'm Sexy?	1978
4	Baby Jane	1983
5	You Wear It Well	1972
6	I Don't Want To Talk About It/ First Cut Is The Deepest	1977
7	You're In My Heart	1977
8	The Killing Of Georgie	1976
9	Every Beat Of My Heart	1986
10	Angel/What Made Milwaukee Famous	1972

Written by Gavin Sutherland of the Sutherland Brothers, 'Sailing' was a hit twice, reaching number 1 on its initial outing, and then returning to number 3 a year later when the song was used as the theme for the popular television series *Sailor*. Stewart recorded the anthemic ballad at the legendary Muscle Shoals Sound Studio in Muscle Shoals, Alabama.

Above: Tartan on display: Rod in the 1970s.

Left: In concert in Germany, 2007.

Below: Stewart as a member of The Faces.

SONGS PENNED BY OTHERS

Although the bulk of Stewart's hit singles have been self-penned alone or with band members, he has also called on an impressive group of songwriters. Here is a partial list:

Paul Carrack • Gerry Goffin & Carole King • Tim Hardin • Jimi Hendrix • Holland-Dozier-Holland • Mick Jagger & Keith Richard • Jimmy Jam & Terry Lewis • Elton John & Bernie Taupin • John Lennon & Paul McCartney • Curtis Mayfield • Van Morrison • Robbie Robertson • Tom Waits • Diane Warren

SOME GUYS HAVE ALL THE LUCK

Stewart is the father of seven children by five different women. Here is a list of paramours he is known to have had a relationship with:

Susannah Boffey	1963–64
Dee Harrington	1971–75
Britt Ekland	1977–77
Alana Hamilton	1979–84
Kelly Emberg	1983–90
Rachel Hunter	1990–2006
Penny Lancaster	2007–present

PRINCE

Born on June 7, 1958, Prince Michael Rogers grew up in Minneapolis where he attended a James Brown concert as a ten-year-old – a seminal musical experience which would later permeate his work. Playing in school groups at Minneapolis Central High (including Grand Central and Champagne), Prince recorded his first demo tape at the age of 16 and, two years later, was snapped up by Warner Bros. Records. A gifted singer-songwriter and multi-instrumentalist, he played 23 different instruments on his 1978 debut album, *For You*.

HIS BEST-SELLING ALBUMS

1	Music From Purple Rain	1984
2	1999	1983
3	Diamonds And Pearls	1991
4	Batman	1989
5	Musicology	2004
6	Emancipation	1996
7	Sign "☮" The Times	1987
8	Around The World In A Day	1985
9	⚥	1992
10	Parade – Music From The Motion Picture	1986

Including his 2009 release, *LOtUSFLOW3R*, the prolific artist has released a staggering 32 original albums in 31 years.

Above: *Purple Rain* poster 1984.

HIS NUMBER ONE HIT SINGLES IN THE US

When Doves Cry	Jul 07, 1984
Let's Go Crazy (with the Revolution)	Sep 29, 1984
Kiss (with the Revolution)	Apr 19, 1986
Batdance (from *Batman*)	Aug 05, 1989

Above: In concert, 1984.

Taken from his film, *Purple Rain*, Prince's biggest hit single, 'When Doves Cry' spent five weeks at number one in the US – and has been much covered by the likes of Patti Smith, the Flying Pickets, Damien Rice and Razorlight.

PRINCE SONGS FOR OTHERS IN THE US

When You Were Mine	Mitch Ryder	No. 87	1983
Sex Shooter	Apollonia	No. 84	1984
I Feel For You	Chaka Khan	No. 3	1984
Sugar Walls	Sheena Easton	No. 9	1985
The Borderlines	Jeffrey Osborne	No. 38	1985
A Love Bizarre	Sheila E.	No. 11	1986
Manic Monday	The Bangles	No. 2	1986
Do Me Baby	Meli'sa Morgan	No. 46	1986
Kiss	Art of Noise featuring Tom Jones	No. 31	1989
Nothing Compares 2 U	Sinéad O'Connor	No. 1	1990
Pray	MC Hammer	No. 2	1990
Round And Round	Tevin Campbell	No. 12	1991
Oooh This I Need	Elisa Fiorillo	No. 90	1991
Martika's Kitchen	Martika	No. 93	1992
Get it Up	TLC	No. 41	1993
How Come You Don't Call Me	Alicia Keys	No. 59	2002
'03 Bonnie and Clyde	Jay-Z featuring Beyonce Knowles	No. 4	2002

His most popular cover version, 'Nothing Compares 2U' was originally written by Prince for his sideband, The Family's self-titled 1985 album. Soulfully recorded by Irish singer, Sinéad O'Connor four years later, it became her career-defining hit.

AT THE GRAMMYS

Best Album of Original Score Written for a Motion Picture or a Television Special for *Purple Rain*	1984
Best Rhythm & Blues Song for 'I Feel For You'	1984
Best Rock Performance by a Duo or Group with Vocal for *Purple Rain – Music From The Motion Picture*	1984
Best Rhythm & Blues Performance by a Duo or Group with Vocal for 'Kiss'	1986
Best Traditional Rhythm & Vocal Performance for 'Musicology'	2004
Best Male Rhythm & Blues Vocal Performance for 'Call My Name'	2004
Best Male Rhythm & Blues Performance for 'Future Baby Mama'	2007

SLAVE TO THE RHYTHM

A largely reclusive figure, frequently at odds with the corporate nature of the music business, Prince has often used pseudonyms for his work, including Joey Coco, Christopher, Alexander Nevermind, Jamie Starr and Paisley Park (also the name of his production/recording studios). His most confounding *nom du jour*, came in 1993, where the "artist formerly known as Prince" credited himself as ♀ – an unpronounceable insignia he would use for seven years. This move came about over a dispute with his record label. He would take to appearing in public with the word "Slave" emblazoned on his cheek and issued the following statement: "The first step I have taken towards the ultimate goal of emancipation from the chains that bind me to Warner Bros. was to change my name from Prince to the Love Symbol. Prince is the name that my mother gave me at birth. Warner Bros. took the name, trademarked it, and used it as the main marketing tool to promote all of the music that I wrote. The company owns the name Prince and all related music marketed under Prince. I became merely a pawn used to produce more money for Warner Bros.... I was born Prince and did not want to adopt another conventional name. The only acceptable replacement for my name, and my identity, was the Love Symbol, a symbol with no pronunciation, that is a representation of me and what my music is about. This symbol is present in my work over the years; it is a concept that has evolved from my frustration; it is who I am. It is my name."

HIS US PLATINUM AWARDS

1999	4 times Platinum
Around the World in a Day	2 times Platinum
Batman (Soundtrack)	2 times Platinum
Controversy	
Diamonds and Pearls	2 times Platinum
Emancipation	2 times Platinum
The Hits I	
The Hits II	
The Hits/The B-Sides	
Musicology	2 times Platinum
Prince	
Purple Rain (Soundtrack)	13 times Platinum
Sign "☮" the Times	2 times Platinum
♀ The Very Best Of Prince	

Two of his singles ('Batdance' and 'When Doves Cry') have also been certified platinum.

Above: With his iconic guitar in 1995.

PRINCE SONGS FOR OTHERS IN THE UK

I Feel For You	Chaka Khan	No. 1	1984
Manic Monday	The Bangles	No. 2	1986
Kiss	Age of Chance	No. 50	1987
Wouldn't You Love To Love Me?	Taja Sevelle	No. 59	1988
Kiss	Art of Noise featuring Tom Jones	No. 5	1988
I Feel For You (Remix)	Chaka Khan	No. 45	1989
Sign O' The Times (from the Amsterdam EP)	Simple Minds	No. 18	1989
Nothing Compares 2 U	Sinead O'Connor	No. 1	1990
The Sex Of It	Kid Creole & the Coconuts	No. 29	1990
Nothing Compares 2 U	MXM	No. 68	1990
Get Yourself Together	The Young Disciples	No. 68	1990
Pray	MC Hammer	No. 8	1991
If I Love U 2 Nite	Mica Paris	No. 43	1991
Love... Thy Will Be Done	Martika	No. 9	1991
Martika's Kitchen	Martika	No. 17	1991
Wanna Be Your Lover	Gayle & Gillian	No. 62	1994
Adore	Joe Roberts	No. 45	1994
He's Mine	Mokenstef	No. 70	1995
I Want U	Rosie Gaines	No. 70	1995
When Doves Cry	Ginuwine	No. 10	1997
'03 Bonnie and Clyde	Jay-Z featuring Beyoncé Knowles	No. 2	2003

Above: Playing to the home crowd, Minnesota 1985.

Below: The Purple Rain tour, 1985.

ON TOUR

Prince	1979 – 80	Diamonds and Pearls	1992
Dirty Mind	1980 – 81	Act I	1993
Controversy	1981 – 82	Act II	1993
1999	1982 – 83	Ultimate Live/Gold Experience	1995
Purple Rain	1984 – 85	Emancipation/Love 4 One Another	1996
Hit N Run	1986	Jam of the Year	1997 – 98
Parade (European tour)	1986	Hit N Run	2000 – 01
Sign "☮" the Times (European tour)	1987	One Night Alone	2002
Lovesexy	1988 – 89	Musicology	2004
Nude (European and Japanese tour)	1990	The Earth	2007

MTV
MUSIC TELEVISION

Growing up in the London suburbs of Finchley, Burnt Oak and Radlett, Georgios Kyriacos Panayiotou – aka George Michael – met his future music partner Andrew Ridgeley at Bushey Meads Comprehensive School in 1975. Forming their first band, the Executive, in 1979, they became the fabulously successful Wham! in 1981. The duo co-wrote the global hit ballad, 'Careless Whisper' when they were both just 18. At the height of Wham!'s popularity in 1986, the pair agreed to an amicable split, with George undertaking an even more successful solo career beginning with 'Faith' in 1987.

HIS BEST-SELLING SOLO ALBUMS

1	Faith	1988
2	Ladies & Gentlemen – The Best of George Michael	1998
3	Listen Without Prejudice Vol. 1	1990
4	Older	1996
5	Patience	2004
6	Twentyfive	2008
7	Songs From the Last Century	2000
8	Five Live (with Queen)	1993

HIS SOLO NUMBER ONE SINGLES IN THE UK

Careless Whisper	Aug 18, 1984
A Different Corner	Apr 19, 1986
I Knew You Were Waiting (For Me) (with Aretha Franklin)	Feb 07, 1987
Don't Let the Sun Go Down on Me (with Elton John)	Dec 07, 1991
Five Live (EP) (with Queen)	May 01, 1993
Fastlove	May 04, 1996
Jesus To A Child	Jan 20, 1996

On December 28, 1985, Michael featured on four Top 20 records in the UK Christmas chart: Wham!'s 'I'm Your Man', Wham!'s re-entered 'Last Christmas', Band Aid's re-entered 'Do They Know It's Christmas?' and as backing vocalist on Elton John's still charting 'Nikita'.

Above: George Michael in 1988.

Below: With Elton John at the Ivor Novello Awards.

HIS SOLO NUMBER ONE HIT SINGLES IN THE US

Careless Whisper (credited to Wham! featuring George Michael)	Feb 16, 1985
I Knew You Were Waiting (For Me) (with Aretha Franklin)	Apr 18, 1987
Faith	Dec 12, 1987
One More Try	May 28, 1988
Father Figure	Feb 27, 1988
Monkey	Aug 27, 1988

Including hits with Wham!, 'Monkey' was Michael's eighth US chart-topper of the 1980s, a record beaten only by Michael Jackson with nine.

Left: Performing at the Freddie Mercury Tribute Concert in 1992.

LADIES AND GENTLEMAN – MR. ELTON JOHN

Originally co-written and recorded by Elton John in 1974, Michael revived 'Don't Let the Sun Go Down on Me' with John in a live duet recorded on March 25, 1991 at London's Wembley Arena – topping the charts on both sides of the Atlantic.

WHO WANTS TO BE A MILLIONAIRE?

In December 2003, Michael teamed up with Ronan Keating to take part in a celebrity edition of *Who Wants to Be a Millionaire?* sharing £64,000 after falling at the £125,000 hurdle. After correctly answering "Which of these horse races was run at Arlington Park in 2002?" (C: Breeder's Cup Classic) for £64,000, they got the 12th question wrong – when asked "Which of these is a variety of chili pepper?" they wrongly answered French beret instead of Scotch bonnet.

GEORGE MICHAEL VS SONY

In November 1992, at the start of a lengthy and expensive court process to gain his release from Sony Records, Michael made the following statement: "Since Sony Corporation bought my contract, along with everything and everyone else at CBS, I have seen the great American company that I proudly signed to as a teenager become a small part of the production line for a giant electronics corporation which, quite frankly, has no understanding of the creative process. Sony appears to see artists as little more than software."

THE TOP UK HITS COMPOSED BY GEORGE MICHAEL

1. Last Christmas
2. Everything She Wants   Wham! (three times Platinum)
3. Careless Whisper   George Michael
4. Freedom   Wham!
5. A Different Corner   George Michael
6. I Knew You Were Waiting   Aretha Franklin &
                                 George Michael
7. Young Guns (Go For It)   Wham!
8. Wake Me Up Before You Go-Go   Wham!
9. Outside   George Michael
10. Bad Boys   Wham!
11. Jesus To A Child   George Michael
12. Freedom   Robbie Williams
13. I'm Your Man   Wham!
14. The Edge Of Heaven   Wham!
15. Spinning The Wheel   George Michael

Above: George announced his retirement from touring on his 25 Live Tour in 2008.

Right: George Michael during a photo shoot.

Below: Concert in Stuttgart, Germany, 2006.

HIS US PLATINUM AWARDS

Faith	9 times Platinum
Faith (video)	
George Michael (video)	
'I Want Your Sex' (single)	
Ladies And Gentlemen – The Best of George Michael	2 times Platinum
Listen Without Prejudice	2 times Platinum
Older	

ON TOUR

Faith World Tour (137)	Feb 19, 1988 – Jul 06, 1989
Cover to Cover Tour (30)	Jan 15, 1991 – Oct 31, 1991
25Live Tour (First leg) (44)	Sep 23, 2006 – Dec 15, 2006
25Live Tour (Second leg) (32)	May 12, 2007 – Aug 04, 2007
25Live Tour (Third leg) (25)	Jun 17, 2008 – Aug 30, 2008
Live in Australia (3)	Feb 20, 2010 – Mar 03, 2010

Michael earned a reported £1.5 million for a New Year's Eve concert for Russian billionaire Vladimir Potanin on December 31, 2006.

HIS IVOR NOVELLO AWARDS

Most Performed Work	1984
Songwriter of the Year	1984
International Hit of the Year	1988
Songwriter of the Year	1988
PRS Most Performed Work	1996
Songwriter of the Year	1996

Born on August 9, 1963 and raised in New Jersey, Whitney Elizabeth Houston's musical roots were steeped in faith. Educated at the Mount Saint Dominic Academy, she became a featured soloist in the junior gospel choir at the age of 11 at the New Hope Baptist Church in Newark. Her first performance was 'Guide Me, O Thou Great Jehovah'.. Joining her mother, Cissy Houston on nightclub tours as a teenager, Whitney's first recording was as a backing vocalist at the age of 14 on 'Life's A Party' for R&B combo, the Michael Zager Band.

HER BEST-SELLING ALBUMS

1	The Bodyguard	1992
2	Whitney Houston	1986
3	Whitney	1987
4	I'm Your Baby Tonight	1990
5	My Love Is Your Love	1998
6	Whitney – The Greatest Hits	2000
7	The Preacher's Wife	1997
8	I Look To You	2009
9	Just Whitney…	2002
10	VH1 Divas Live	1999
	(with Cher, Tina Turner & Brandy)	

HER BEST-SELLING SINGLES IN THE UK

1	I Will Always Love You	1992
2	Saving All My Love For You	1985
3	I Wanna Dance With Somebody (Who Loves Me)	1987
4	It's Not Right But It's Okay	1999
5	One Moment In Time	1988
6	How Will I Know	1986
7	Step By Step	1997
8	When You Believe (with Mariah Carey)	1998
9	My Love Is Your Love	1999
10	So Emotional	1987

Prior to focusing solely on music, Houston pursued a career as a model, featuring in US magazine *Glamour* and on the front cover of *Seventeen*, ' and, as an actress, appearing in television shows including *Silver Spoons* and *Gimme a Break*.

WHITNEY HOUSTON'S NUMBER ONE HIT SINGLES IN THE US

Saving All My Love For You	Oct 26, 1985
How Will I Know	Feb 15, 1986
Greatest Love of All	May 17, 1986
I Wanna Dance With Somebody (Who Loves Me)	Jun 27, 1987
Didn't We Almost Have It All	Sep 26, 1987
So Emotional	Jan 09, 1988
Where Do Broken Hearts Go	Apr 23, 1988
I'm Your Baby Tonight	Dec 01, 1990
All The Man That I Need	Feb 23, 1991
I Will Always Love You (from *The Bodyguard*)	Nov 28, 1992
Exhale (Shoop Shoop) (from *Waiting To Exhale*)	Nov 25, 1995

Above: Two visions of Whitney, both from her 'classic' 1980s era.

Propelling her career to new heights and becoming her signature hit, 'I Will Always Love You' was featured in the Houston/Kevin Costner film *The Bodyguard*. The project's producers had originally tried to get the movie made with Steve McQueen and Diana Ross.

GOOD GENES

Three of Whitney's relatives were established singers: her mother, gospel singer Cissy Houston, and cousins Dionne Warwick and Dee Dee Warwick. And Whitney's godmother? Aretha Franklin.

BLUE MOON

On November 29, 1997 Houston pulled out of a scheduled 45-minute $1 million performance at RFK Stadium, in Washington for the World Culture & Sports Festival with a "sudden flu-like illness" after discovering that the festival was a mass wedding for 2,500 Moonie couples.

ON TOUR

Greatest Love Tour	Jul 26, 1986 – Dec 01, 1986
Moment Of Truth Tour (North American leg)	Jul 04, 1987 – Dec 08, 1987
Moment Of Truth Tour (European leg)	Apr 19, 1988 – Jun 26, 1988
Moment Of Truth Tour (Far East/Australian leg)	Sep 21, 1988 – Nov 20, 1988
Feels So Right (Japanese tour)	Jan 01, 1990 – Jan 24, 1990
I'm Your Baby Tonight Tour	Mar 14, 1991 – Oct 02, 1991
The Bodyguard Tour	Jul 05, 1993 – Nov 19, 1994
The Pacific Rim	May 05, 1997 – May 29, 1997
The European Tour	Jun 20, 1998 – Jul 11, 1998
My Love Is Your Love World Tour	Jun 22, 1999 – Nov 08, 1999
Nothing But Love World Tour	Feb 06, 2010 – Jun 10, 2010

Above left: Performing in London 1988.

Right: The Nothing But Love tour, Rome 2010.

HER AMERICAN MUSIC AWARDS

Favorite Soul/R&B Single – 'You Give Good Love'	1986
Favorite Soul/R&B Video Single – 'Saving All My Love For You'	1986
Favorite Pop/Rock Female Artist	1987
Favorite Pop/Rock Album – *Whitney Houston*	1987
Favorite Soul/R&B Female Artist	1987
Favorite Soul/R&B Album – *Whitney Houston*	1987
Favorite Soul/R&B Video Single – 'Greatest Love Of All'	1987
Favorite Pop/Rock Female Artist	1987
Favorite Pop/Rock Single – 'I Wanna Dance With Somebody (Who Loves Me)'	1987
Favorite Pop/Rock Female Artist	1989
Favorite Soul/R&B Female Artist	1989
Favorite Pop/Rock Female Artist	1994
Favorite Pop/Rock Single – 'I Will Always Love You'	1994
Favorite Pop/Rock Album – *The Bodyguard*	1994
Favorite Soul/R&B Female Artist	1994
Favorite Soul/R&B Single – 'I Will Always Love You'	1994
Favorite Soul/R&B Album – *The Bodyguard*	1994
Favorite Adult Contemporary Album – *The Bodyguard*	1994
Award of Merit	1994
Favorite Adult Contemporary Artist	1997
Favorite Soundtrack Album – *Waiting to Exhale*	1997
International Artist Award	2009

Houston has won an astonishing 22 American Music Awards, twice picking up seven at a single ceremony.

AT THE GRAMMYS

Best Pop Vocal Performance, Female, for 'Saving All My Love For You'	1985
Best Pop Vocal Performance, Female, for 'I Wanna Dance With Somebody (Who Loves Me)'	1987
Best Pop Vocal Performance, Female, for 'I Will Always Love You'	1993
Album of the Year for *The Bodyguard*	1993
Record of the Year for 'I Will Always Love You'	1993
Best Female R&B Vocal Performance for 'It's Not Right But it's Okay'	1999

Above: Whitney at the 21st American Music Awards in 1994.

THE MOST BEAUTIFUL BLACK WOMEN IN HISTORY

In its March 2010 issue, *Essence* magazine announced its 25 Most Beautiful Black Women In History.

1 Dorothy Dandridge
2 Michelle Obama
3 Sade
4 Pam Grier
5 Whitney Houston
6 Halle Berry
7 Diana Ross
8 Iman
9 Lauryn Hill
10 Lena Horne

STING

Having grown up in the Newcastle suburb of Wallsend, Sting (Gordon Matthew Sumner) juggled an early career as a teacher – at St. Paul's First School, Cramlington in Tyne & Wear – with his first love, music. Prior to forming the Police, Sting played bass in a number of bands, including the Ronnie Pierson Trio on board Princess Cruises liners; semi-professional jazz-rock combos, Earthrise, Phoenix Jazz Band and the River City Jazz Band; the Newcastle Big Band and Last Exit, who released a single, 'Whispering Voices'.

HIS BEST-SELLING ALBUMS

1	Brand New Day	2000
2	Ten Summoner's Tales	1993
3	The Dream Of The Blue Turtles	1985
4	Fields Of Gold – The Best Of Sting 1984–94	1994
5	… Nothing Like The Sun	1987
6	Mercury Falling	1996
7	The Soul Cages	1991
8	Sacred Love	2003
9	Songs Of Love	2003
10	The Very Best Of Sting & Police	1997
11	All This Time	2001
12	If On A Winter's Night …	2009
13	Songs From The Labyrinth	2006
14	Demolition Man	1993
15	Bring On The Night	1986

Performed only in Portuguese and Spanish, Sting has released one EP, 1988's *Nada como el Sol*, a five-track affair reprising cuts from his earlier album *… Nothing Like The Sun*. It includes the haunting 'Ellas Danzan Solas (Cueca Solas) (They Dance Alone)' written about the widows of the men killed by the regime of Chilean dictator, Augusto Pinochet.

AT THE MOVIES

Quadrophenia	Ace Face	1979
Radio On	Just Like Eddie	1980
Brimstone And Treacle	Martin Taylor	1982
Dune	Feyd Rautha	1984
The Bride	Frankenstein	1985
Plenty	Mick	1985
Giulia e Giulia	Daniel Osler	1987
Stormy Monday	Finney	1988
The Adventures Of Baron Munchausen	Heroic Officer	1988
The Grotesque	Fledge	1995
Lock, Stock And Two Smoking Barrels	JD	1998
Bee Movie	Sting (voice)	2007

In his movie debut, aged 27, spikey blond-haired Sting played Ace Face, a Mod bellboy at a Brighton hotel in the film adaptation of Pete Townshend's rock opera, *Tommy*.

Above: In the 1978 cult classic *Quadrophenia*.

Left: Performing on *Tonight at the London Palladium* in 2000.

NUMBER ONE UK HITS WRITTEN BY STING

Message In A Bottle	Police	Sep 29, 1979
Walking On The Moon	Police	Dec 08, 1979
Don't Stand So Close To Me	Police	Sep 27, 1980
Every Little Thing She Does Is Magic	Police	Nov 14, 1981
Every Breath You Take	Police	Jun 04, 1983
I'll Be Missing You	Puff Daddy & Faith Evans	Jun 28, 1997

Left: Performing with The Police in 1979.

HIS IVOR NOVELLO AWARDS

Songwriter of the Year	1980
Best Pop Song	1981
Best Song Musically & Lyrically	1983
Most Performed Work	1983
Best Song Musically & Lyrically	1988
Best Song Musically & Lyrically	1993
PRS Most Performed Work	1997
International Achievement	2002

PLATINUM & GOLD AWARDS IN THE US

The Dream Of The Blue Turtles	3 times Platinum	May 24, 1994
Nothing Like The Sun	2 times Platinum	Oct 24, 1991
The Soul Cages	Platinum	Apr 08, 1991
Ten Summoner's Tales	3 times Platinum	Apr 29, 1994
Fields Of Gold	2 times Platinum	Apr 02, 1996
Mercury Falling	Platinum	Aug 14, 1996
Brand New Day	3 times Platinum	Jan 30, 2001
… All This Time	Gold	Jan 23, 2002
Sacred Love	Platinum	Jan 09, 2004
Songs Of Love	Platinum	Feb 10, 2004
The Very Best Of Sting And The Police	Gold	Aug 22, 2005
If On A Winter's Night	Gold	Dec 03, 2009

THE RAINFOREST BENEFITS

Among his many philanthropic and social causes, Sting – together with his wife Trudi Styler, Brazilian Kayapó Indian leader Raoni Metuktire and Belgian filmmaker, Jean-Pierre Dutilleux – formed the Rainforest Foundation in 1989 to help protect both rainforests and the indigenous people who live there. For the past 20 years Sting has organized an annual benefit to raise funds and awareness for the Foundation. Sting, Elton John and James Taylor are regular performers, but an eclectic group of performers has taken part over the past two decades.

Antonio Carlos Jobim, Caetano Veloso	1991
Don Henley, Natalie Cole & Whoopi Goldberg	1992
Herb Alpert, Tina Turner, Tom Jones, George Michael & Bryan Adams	1993
Larry Adler, Tammy Wynette, Whitney Houston, Antonio Carlos Jobim, Aaron Neville, Luciano Pavarotti & Branford Marsalis	1994
Jon Bon Jovi, Jessye Norman, Geoffrey Pryema, Bruce Springsteen, Paul Simon & Billy Joel	1995
Andrea Griminelli, Don Henley, Katia & Mariella Labeque, Paco Peña, Diana Ross, Mstislav Rostropovich & Robin Williams	1996
Lyle Lovett, Bonnie Raitt, Stevie Wonder, Bobby McFerrin & Zucchero	1997
Billy Joel, Joe Cocker, Herbie Hancock, Roberta Flack, Emmylou Harris & Madonna	1998
Charles Aznavour, Tony Bennett, Don Henley, Billy Joel & Ricky Martin	1999
Billy Joel, Tom Jones, Gladys Knight, Martha Reeves, Percy Sledge & the Impressions	2000
Jeff Beck, Wynonna Judd, Patti LaBelle, Lulu, Smokey Robinson & Ravi Shankar	2002
India Arie, Bette Midler & Antonio Banderas	2004
Sheryl Crow, Billy Joel, Lenny Kravitz	2006
Billy Joel, Brian Wilson, Chris Botti, Feist & Roberto Alagna	2008
Lady Gaga, Shirley Bassey	2010

AT THE GRAMMYS

Best Rock Instrumental Performance	*Brimstone and Treacle*	1983
Song of the Year	'Every Breath You Take'	1983
Best Music Video, Long Form	Bring on the Night	1986
Best Pop Vocal Performance, Male	Bring on the Night	1987
Best Rock Song	'The Soul Cages'	1991
Best Music Video, Long Form	Ten Summoner's Tale	1993
Best Pop Vocal Performance, Male	'If I Ever Lose My Faith in You'	1993
Best Pop Album	*Brand New Day*	1999
Best Male Pop Vocal Performance	'Brand New Day'	1999
Best Male Pop Vocal Performance	'She Walks This Earth (*Soberana Rose*)'	2000
Best Pop Collaboration with Vocals	'Whenever I Say Your Name' (with Mary J. Blige)	2003

Right: The Grammy Awards in 2000.

Left: An acoustic performance in 2009.

THE BEACH BOYS

Brian, Dennis and Carl Wilson shared a bedroom together while growing up in Hawthorne, California. Influenced by R&B and folk, but entranced by the vocal stylings of fifties' doo-wop groups and close harmony acts – especially the Four Freshmen – Brian began writing simple pop tunes, performed by the siblings with their cousin Mike Love and school friend Al Jardine, briefly known as Carl & the Passions, then the Pendletones and finally, in December '61, The Beach Boys.

THEIR PLATINUM-SELLING ALBUMS IN THE US

1. Endless Summer
2. 20 Good Vibrations – The Greatest Hits
3. Best Of The Beach Boys Volume 2
4. Best Of The Beach Boys
5. Sounds Of Summer – The Very Best Of The Beach Boys
6. Made In The U.S.A.
7. Little Deuce Coupe
8. Pet Sounds
9. Still Cruisin'
10. 20 Golden Greats
11. Summer Dreams – 28 Classic Tracks
12. The Very Best Of The Beach Boys

GRAMMY HALL OF FAME

Four Beach Boys songs have been inducted into the Grammy Hall of Fame:

Song	Year
Good Vibrations (1966)	1994
Pet Sounds (1966)	1998
In My Room (1963)	1999
California Girls (1965)	2010

Astonishingly, the group has never won a Grammy Award, although Brian Wilson managed to win Best Rock Instrumental Performance for the solo 'Mrs. O'Leary's Cow' in 2004.

DENNIS WILSON'S DEATH

Dennis Wilson – ironically the only member of the group which popularised the Surf music craze of the early sixties who could actually surf – died on December 28, 1983, age 39. With a history of alcohol abuse, he drowned at Marina Del Rey following a day of heavy drinking. He was buried at sea, off his beloved California coast, on January 4, 1984.

SANS BRIAN

When Brian Wilson quit touring with the band in 1965, his initial substitute was country/pop vocalist Glen Campbell – though his long-term replacement was singer-songwriter Bruce Johnston: the future composer behind the Barry Manilow hit, 'I Write The Songs'.

SURF AND TURF

On August 5, 1993 Capitol Records honoured the band at its famous offices on the corner of Hollywood and Vine by laying the parking lot with tons of sand to turn it into a beach.

THEIR NUMBER ONE HIT SINGLES IN THE US & THE UK

The Beach Boys have only topped the US and UK singles half-a-dozen times in their career:

US

I Get Around	Jul 04, 1964
Help Me Rhonda	May 29, 1965
Good Vibrations	Dec 10, 1966
Kokomo (From the Cocktail Soundtrack)	Nov 05, 1988

UK

Good Vibrations	Nov 19, 1966
Do It Again	Aug 31, 1968

Above: In 1967 The Beach Boys released their psychedelic *Smiley Smile* album.

Musically conceived and produced by Brian Wilson, the epic 'Good Vibrations' took eight months to record with its meticulous creator painstakingly constructing multiple versions, mixes and layered vocal tracks.

Right: The distinctive striped shirts were the band's touring 'uniform' until 1966.

THE WHO

While both were still attending London's Acton County Grammar School, guitarist Pete Townshend and bassist John Entwistle first played together in 1959 as members of the Confederates. It was not until three years later, however, that they reunited in another band, the Detours, led by Roger Daltrey. Serving their apprenticeship as a rhythm & blues combo on the London pub circuit with semi-professional drummer Doug Sandom, the group changed its name to The Who in 1964, recruiting Keith Moon as its permanent tub-thumper.

THEIR BEST-SELLING ALBUMS

1	Who's Next	1971
2	Tommy	1969
3	Live At Leeds	1970
4	Who Are You	1978
5	The Who's Greatest Hits	1983
6	Quadrophenia	1973
7	The Who By Numbers	1975
8	Face Dances	1981
9	The Kids Are Alright	1979
10	Meaty, Beaty Big & Bouncy	1972
11	The Ultimate Collection	2002
12	20th Century	2003

Their most successful album, *Who's Next* was recorded between March and May, 1971 at the Olympic Studios in London and was co-produced by the band with Glyn Johns. The nine-track album contained elements of a previous project Townshend was working on called *Lifehouse*, which was subsequently scrapped.

MOONING AROUND

On September 17, 1967, when the Who appeared on *The Smothers Brothers Comedy Hour*, Keith Moon set a flash powder explosion in his drum kit, not realising the technical crew had already done so. The resultant explosion left Pete Townshend with singed hair and damaged ears while Moon had a cut on his leg caused by a broken cymbal. Fellow guests Bette Davis and Mickey Rooney looked on, bemused.

THEIR TOP 10 UK HITS

	Peak position	
Anyway, Anyhow, Anywhere	10	(Jul 03, 1965)
I Can't Explain	8	(Apr 17, 1965)
My Generation	2	(Nov 27, 1965)
I'm A Boy	2	(Oct 01, 1966)
Substitute	5	(Apr 16, 1966)
Happy Jack	3	(Jan 21, 1967)
Pictures Of Lily	4	(May 20, 1967)
I Can See For Miles	10	(Nov 18, 1967)
Pinball Wizard	4	(Apr 26, 1969)
Won't Get Fooled Again	9	(Aug 14, 1971)
Join Together	9	(Jul 22, 1972)
Squeeze Box	10	(Feb 28, 1976)
Substitute	7	(Nov 20, 1976)
You Better You Bet	9	(Mar 21, 1981)

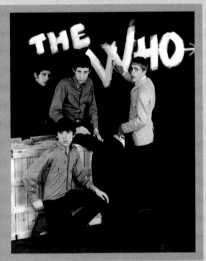

Above: In 1965 the band released the Mod anthem 'My Generation'.

SELL-OUT

Two days after The Who had begun their 25th anniversary UK tour in October 1989, Pete Townshend replied to Mick Jagger's comment that the band was touring for the sake of money, saying "Mick needs a lot more than I do – his last album was a flop."

Left: The Who lost drummer Keith Moon (second from left) to a drug overdose in 1978.

TOMMY

The all-star lineup featured:

Elton John	The Pinball Wizard
Steve Winwood	The Hawker
Patti LaBelle	The Acid Queen
Phil Collins	Uncle Ernie
Billy Idol	Kevin

The first of two all-star stagings of Pete Townshend's first rock opera, *Tommy*, took place at the Universal Amphitheatre in Universal City, California on August 24, 1989.

JAMES BROWN

Abandoned by his mother at the age of four and raised by an aunt, Handsome 'Honey' Washington in her brothel at 944, Twiggs Avenue in Augusta, Georgia, James Joseph Brown quit school at 12, having already formed his first singing group, the Cremona Trio. During his delinquent teenage years in Augusta, Brown served a hard labor stretch in a state corrective institution for petty theft before teaming with R&B/gospel pianist, Bobby Byrd to focus on a career in music. His first recording was 'Please, Please Please' recorded at Macon, Georgia radio station, WIBB in November, 1955.

HIS BEST-SELLING ALBUMS

1	20 All-Time Greatest Hits	1991
2	The James Brown Show	1963
3	Pure Dynamite	1964
4	Live At The Apollo Vol. 2	1968
5	The Payback	1974
6	Get Up I Feel Like Being A Sex Machine	1970
7	Papa's Got A Brand New Bag	1966
8	It's A Mother	1969
9	Say It Loud – I'm Black And I'm Proud	1969
10	Popcorn	1969

Recorded on October 24, 1962 at the legendary New York venue, *Live At The Apollo* – although not selling as many copies as its 1968 sequel – is widely regarded as the greatest live album ever released. It was added to the National Recording Registry by the Library of Congress in 2004.

Below: At the Clyde Auditorium, Glasgow, in 1998.

MONIKERS

Brown had more nicknames than top 10 hits. Here are some of them:

The Godfather of Soul
The Hardest Working Man In Show Business
I Feel Good
The King of Funk
Minister of the New New Super Heavy Funk
Mr. Dynamite
Mr. Please Please Please Please Her
Sex Machine
Soul Brother Number One

Above: The Godfather of Soul plays The Park West, Chicago, in 1985.

HIS TOP 10 US SINGLES

In a chart career spanning 1958 to 1986, during which he notched up 92 Hot 100 hits, James Brown only managed to make the top 10 on seven occasions:

	Peak position	
Papa's Got A Brand New Bag	8	(Sep 04, 1965)
I Got You (I Feel Good)	3	(Dec 18, 1965)
It's A Man's Man's Man's World	8	(Jun 04, 1966)
Cold Sweat	7	(Aug 26, 1967)
I Got The Feelin'	6	(Apr 27, 1968)
Say It Loud (I'm Black And I'm Proud)	10	(Oct 19, 1968)
Living In America	4	(Mar 01, 1986)

I GOT THE FEELING

On February 25, 1997 renowned ladies' man Brown, following a performance at a Victoria Secrets show earlier in the month, proposed to talk-show host Rolonda Watts during the taping of her *Rolonda* TV show. Brown said: "You know I'm crazy about you, so how about tying the knot?" In reply, Watts said: "We're going to continue this discussion on the phone later, James."

JAMES BROWN DAY

On July 23, 1969, Los Angeles declared James Brown Day, in honour of his sellout concert at the Great Western Forum in Inglewood. Mayor Sam Yorty was late to hand Brown the proclamation and so the singer walked out.

KEEPING THE PEACE

On the evening of April 5, 1968, following the assassination of Martin Luther King, which spawned riots in 30 US cities, James Brown made an appeal on national television for calm and rational behaviour, a plea broadcast from the Boston Garden in Massachusetts. His peace-keeping efforts received official commendation from Vice-President Hubert H. Humphrey.

ARETHA FRANKLIN

Born on March 25, 1942 in Memphis, Tennessee, Aretha Louise Franklin was the fourth of six children raised by their father, the 'Million Dollar Voice' Reverend C.L. Franklin, pastor of New Bethel Church in Detroit. Having learnt piano by listening to Eddie Heywood records, but rejecting the offer of professional lessons from her father, Franklin was taught to sing by family friends and gospel greats – Mahalia Jackson and the Ward Sisters, Frances Steadman and Marion Williams – though her biggest influence was her father's friend, hymn writer and gospel singer Clara Ward.

HER BEST-SELLING ALBUMS

1	Amazing Grace	1972
2	Who's Zoomin' Who?	1985
3	Greatest Hits (1980-1994)	1994
4	The Very Best Of Aretha Franklin – The 60's	1994
5	I Never Loved A Man The Way I Love You	1967
6	Aretha: Lady Soul	1968
7	Aretha Now	1968
8	Aretha Franklin – Live At Fillmore Street	1971
9	Young, Gifted And Black	1972
10	Jump To It	1982

HER BEST-SELLING SINGLES IN THE US

1	I Knew You Were Waiting (For Me) (with George Michael)	1987
2	Respect	1967
3	Until You Come Back To Me (That's What I'm Gonna Do)	1974
4	Chain Of Fools	1968
5	Spanish Harlem	1971
6	Baby I Love You	1967
7	(Sweet Sweet Baby) Since You've Been Gone	1968
8	Day Dreaming	1968
9	Bridge Over Troubled Water	1971
10	Think	1968

The Queen of Soul's 2010 album, *A Woman Falling Out of Love* was her first (non-Christmas) studio outing in seven years – and the first to be released on her own label. Franklin's prior album recording output was released on three major labels: Columbia Records (1960–67), Atlantic Records (1967-79) and Arista Records (1980-2008).

Above: The Queen of Soul on the *Andy Williams Show* in 1965.

Below: By the age of 18, Aretha had already given birth to two sons.

Following top 20 success on a duet with Annie Lennox – 'Sisters Are Doin' It For Themselves' – the previous year, Aretha's collaboration with George Michael on their 1987 smash, 'I Knew You Were Waiting For Me' became her second US chart-topper, some 20 years after her first, the iconic R&B belter, 'Respect'.

BLUES BROTHERS

Aretha Franklin made a popular cameo appearance as a waitress in the 1980 comedy film *The Blues Brothers* – in which she also performed 'Think'.

RESPECT

Keith Richards inducted Franklin into the *Rock and Roll Hall of Fame* at the second annual dinner on January 21, 1987 at New York's Waldorf Astoria Hotel.

FEBRUARY 15

It turns out that February 15 has been a significant day in Aretha Franklin's life. In 1969 singer Vickie Jones was arrested on fraud charges for impersonating the Queen of Soul in concert at Fort Myers, Florida (no one in the audience asked for their money back, however) and 30 years later, in 1999, the *Detroit Free Press* reported that Franklin had financial debts. Over the previous 11 years more than 30 lawsuits had been filed against her. She released a statement the following day saying that the article was "malicious."

JIMI HENDRIX

Johnny Allen Hendrix was born on November 27, 1942 in Seattle and grew up in a dysfunctional, poverty-stricken family environment, his parents divorcing when he was nine. A natural southpaw, the musically-fascinated boy was a quick and devoted learner, able to play right-handed guitars left-handed. Inspired by an Elvis Presley concert in 1957, Hendrix also learnt to mimic the stage antics of other rock 'n' roll pioneers, notably Little Richard and Chuck Berry.

HIS HIT SINGLES IN THE US

	Peak position	
Purple Haze	65	(Oct 14, 1967)
Foxey Lady	67	(Jan 13, 1968)
All Along The Watchtower	20	(Oct 19, 1968)
Up From The Skies	82	(Mar 30, 1968)
Crosstown Traffic	52	(Dec 21, 1968)
Freedom	59	(May 08, 1971)
Dolly Dagger	74	(Nov 27, 1971)

HIS BEST-SELLING ALBUMS

1	Are You Experienced?	1968
2	Live At Woodstock	1999
3	The Ultimate Experience	1993
4	Band Of Gypsys	1970
5	Electric Ladyland	1968
6	Smash Hits	1969
7	Experience Hendrix – The Best Of Jimi Hendrix	1999
8	Axis: Bold As Love	1968
9	The Cry Of Love	1971
10	Blues	1994

EXPERIENCE THE MILITARY

Hendrix quit high-school in his senior year before joining the US Army on May 3, 1961, serving for one year as a supply clerk in the 101st Airborne Paratroopers Division. During that time he teamed up with fellow soldier Billy Cox, fronting the R&B combo, the King Kasuals.

FIRE – THE BARBEQUE

On May 29, 1967 The Jimi Hendrix Experience topped the bill of Barbeque 67 at the Tulip Bulb Auction Hall in Spalding, Lincolnshire. The admission – at the door – was £1. Posters for the event announced that a Licensed Bar had been applied for, hot dogs would be on sale and that the Discotheque would start at 4pm in covered accommodation with soft, ultraviolet lighting. The bill comprised: The Jimi Hendrix Experience, Cream, Geno Washington & the Ram Jam Band, Pink Floyd, The Move, Zoot Money & His Big Roll Band.

Below right: The Jimi Hendrix Experience play the Marquee Club, London, in 1967.

Right: Hendrix was prone to mood swings that put him at odds with fellow band members.

HIS HIT SINGLES IN THE UK

	Peak position	
Hey Joe	6	(Feb 04, 1967)
Purple Haze	3	(May 06, 1967)
The Wind Cries Mary	6	(Jun 03, 1967)
Burning Of The Midnight Lamp	18	(Sep 09, 1967)
All Along The Watchtower	5	(Nov 30, 1968)
Crosstown Traffic	37	(Apr 19, 1969)
Voodoo Chile	1	(Nov 21, 1970)
Gypsy Eyes/Remember	35	(Nov 13, 1971)
Johnny B. Goode	35	(Feb 26, 1972)
Crosstown Traffic	61	(Apr 21, 1990)
All Along The Watchtower (EP)	52	(Oct 20, 1990)
The Body Shine (EP)	55	(Sep 12, 1998)

AWARDS

Rolling Stone's Performer of the Year	1968
Inducted into the Rock and Roll Hall of Fame	1992
Grammy Lifetime Achievement Award	1992
Hollywood Walk of Fame	1994
Blue Heritage Plaque	1997
Purple Haze Grammy Hall of Fame	2000
Rolling Stone's The Greatest Guitarist of All Time	2003
Inducted into UK Hall of Fame	2005
Are You Experienced? Inducted into the United States National Recording Registry	2006
Music City Walk of Fame	2007

Born on March 30, 1945, Eric Patrick Clapton was educated at Ripley Primary School and St. Bede's Secondary Modern in Surrey. He was given his first guitar - an acoustic Hoyer model – on his 13th birthday by his grandparents, Rose Clapp and her second husband Jack – who raised him after his parents separated. In 1998, Clapton learned that his real father was a Canadian soldier by the name of Edward Fryer. Influenced by US blues, R&B and rock 'n' roll, he learned guitar licks from the records of old blues masters like Blind Lemon Jefferson and Son House.

ROCK AND ROLL HALL OF FAMER

On March 6, 2000 Clapton became the first artist to be inducted into the Rock and Roll Hall of Fame three times when he was honoured for his solo career. He had already been enshrined as a member of The Yardbirds and Cream.

In typically understated fashion, he delivered a succinct acceptance speech: "For me, it's about the music. I'm just the messenger. I carry a message and I hope to be able to do that as long as I live."

ORDER OF THE BLUES EMPIRE

When Clapton received his OBE (Order of the British Empire) from the Prince of Wales at Buckingham Palace in November 1995, he admitted he was "mellowing out with age."

THE KING AND I

On June 6, 1970, Clapton told *Melody Maker* that he would "vote for B.B. King" in the upcoming General Election: "The first thing any new MP should do is apply the mind to producing a self-tuning electric guitar."

HIS TOP 30 UK HIT SINGLES

	Peak position	
I Shot The Sheriff	9	(Aug 17, 1974)
Swing Low Sweet Chariot	19	(Jun 07, 1975)
Behind The Mask	15	(Feb 21, 1987)
Bad Love	25	(Feb 17, 1990)
Wonderful Tonight (Live)	30	(Nov 30, 1991)
Tears In Heaven	5	(Mar 21, 1992)
It's Probably Me (with Sting)	30	(Sep 05, 1992)
Love Can Build A Bridge (with Cher, Chrissie Hynde & Neneh Cherry)	1	(Mar 25, 1995)
Change The World	18	(Jul 20, 1996)
Forever Man (How Many Times) (with the Beatchuggers)	26	(Nov 18, 2000)

GOD'S GUITARS

At a guitar auction at Christie's in June 1999, $5 million was raised for Clapton's Antiguan rehab center. Of the 100 guitars, his 1956 Sunburst Fender, which he used to record 'Layla', fetched $497,500, breaking the $320,000 paid for a Jimi Hendrix guitar.

COME ON YOU BAGGIES

On September 27, 1978, Clapton sponsored a West Bromwich Albion UEFA soccer cup tie against Galatasaray of Turkey and presented each player with a gold copy of his current *Slowhand* album before the kickoff.

Above: Clapton recorded 'Tears in Heaven' after the death of his four-year-old son in 1991.

HIS BEST-SELLING ALBUMS

1	Unplugged	1993
2	Time Pieces/Best Of Eric Clapton	1982
3	Slowhand	1978
4	From The Cradle	1994
5	The Cream Of Clapton	1995
6	Journeyman	1990
7	Clapton Chronicles – The Best Of Eric Clapton	1999
8	Pilgrim	1998
9	Backless	1979
10	Behind The Sun	1985

Although his passport would incorrectly indicate April 6, Nesta Robert Marley was born on February 6, 1954 in Nine Miles, Rhoden Hall in St. Ann Parish, Jamaica. Leaving school at the age of 14 with a passion for playing music, Marley linked up with his childhood friend Bunny Livingston and musicians Peter Tosh and Junior Braithwaite – recording his first single, the self-penned 'Judge Not' for legendary Jamaican producer and label owner Leslie Kong in 1962 before forming the R&B/ska combo, The Wailers two years later.

HIS BEST-SELLING ALBUMS

1	Legend	1984
2	Exodus	1977
3	Kaya	1978
4	Uprising	1980
5	Rastaman Vibration	1976
6	Confrontation	1983
7	Live*	1975
8	Survival	1979
9	Babylon By Bus	1978
10	Songs of Freedom	1992

* Reissued in 1981 as *Live At The Lyceum*

Marley's ninth studio album, *Exodus* was hailed "Album of the Century" in the millennium-ending edition of *Time Magazine* in 1999.

HIS TOP 10 UK HIT SINGLES

	Peak position	
Jammin'/Punky Reggae Party	9	(Feb 04, 1978)
Is This Love	9	(Apr 01, 1978)
Could You Be Loved	5	(Jun 21, 1980)
No Woman, No Cry	8	(Jun 18, 1981)
Buffalo Soldier	4	(Jul 16, 1983)
One Love/People Get Ready (Medley)	5	(Apr 19, 1984)
Iron Lion Zion	5	(Oct 03, 1992)
Sun Is Shining	3	(Sep 25, 1999)
(Bob Marley Vs Funkstar De Luxe)		

Above: Marley's trademark dreadlocks were a symbol of his Rastafarian faith.

ON THE ROAD

Catch A Fire Tour	Apr – Jul 1973
Burnin' Tour	Oct – Nov 1973
Natty Dread Tour	Jun – Jul 1975
Rastaman Vibration Tour	Apr – Jul 1976
Exodus Tour	May – Jun 1977
Kaya Tour	May – Aug 1978
Babylon By Bus Tour	Apr – May 1979
Survival Tour	Oct 1979 – Jan 1980
Uprising Tour	May – Sep 1980

Right: Marley brought Jamaican music and culture to fans all over the world.

SHOOTING

A towering socio-political force in his home country, Marley was shot and wounded in the chest and arm by unknown assailants while at home with his wife Rita and manager Don Taylor on December 3, 1976. All three made a full recovery.

JAMAICAN ROYALTY

His signature hit single, 'No Woman, No Cry' was recorded live at London's Lyceum Theatre on July 19, 1975. With the the full album version clocking in at over seven minutes, the song's composition was credited to Marley's friend Vincent Ford, who worked in a soup kitchen in Kingston, Jamaica. Though likely written by the reggae icon himself, the story goes that Marley credited Ford so the latter could receive royalty income.

THE CLASH

Seminal British punk pioneers, The Clash played their first gig on August 29, 1976 with band founders Mick Jones on guitar and Paul Simonon on bass, short-term drummer Terry Chimes and ex-101ers' member Joe Strummer on vocals. With punk fever running high among the UK's disaffected youth, the band was quickly snapped up by CBS/Columbia Records in January 1977, recording its first album over three weekends with replacement drummer Topper Headon, firmly in the lineup.

THEIR BEST-SELLING ALBUMS

1	Combat Rock	1982
2	London Calling	1979
3	The Story Of The Clash	1988
4	Give 'Em Enough Rope	1979
5	The Clash	1977
6	Sandinista!	1980
7	Cut The Crap	1985
8	The Essential Clash	2003
9	Live At Shea Stadium	2008
10	The Singles	1991

Above: The Clash's lineup in 1978.

Below: By the late '70s Punk had become a worldwide phenomenon.

THEIR BEST-SELLING SINGLES

1	Should I Stay Or Should I Go	1982
2	Rock The Casbah	1982
3	London Calling	1980
4	Bankrobber	1980
5	Train In Vain (Stand By Me)	1980
6	Tommy Gun	1979
7	This Is England	1985
8	English Civil War (Johnny Comes Marching Home)	1979
9	I Fought The Law	1988
10	The Cost Of Living (EP)	1979

JOE STRUMMER'S DEATH

The prospects for a long-desired Clash reunion were permanently dashed with the sudden, unexpected death of frontman Joe Strummer at his home in Somerset on December 22, 2002, from an undiagnosed congenital heart defect.

PARIS CALLING

On the eve of The Clash's UK "Know Your Rights" tour on April 26, 1982, Joe Strummer went missing, causing its cancellation. Eventually tracked down in Paris, France, and at first thought to be a publicity stunt, Strummer initially claimed that he went there because his girlfriend's mother was in jail, and also to take part in the Paris Marathon. The reality was less interesting than the myth, with exhaustion cited as the main cause for his going AWOL.

... AND THE LAW WON

On March 30, 1978 Simonon and Headon were arrested in Camden Town, London, for criminal damage after shooting down racing pigeons with air guns from the roof of Chalk Farm Studios. Four police cars and one helicopter were required to make the arrest. The pair were subsequently fined £800.

THEIR MUSIC VIDEOS

White Riot	1977
Complete Control	1977
Tommy Gun	1978
I Fought the Law	1978
London Calling	1979
Clampdown	1979
Train in Vain	1980
Bankrobber	1980
The Call Up	1980
This Is Radio Clash	1981
Rock the Casbah	1982
Should I Stay Or Should I Go (Live)	1991

All but two of The Clash's videos were directed by punk/reggae DJ and film producer Don Letts.

AC/DC

A pioneering act in the history of heavy metal, AC/DC was formed by Scottish brothers Angus and Malcolm Young in 1973 in Sydney, Australia (to where their family emigrated in 1963), playing their first gig at the Chequers Club in Sydney on New Year's Eve, before securing a residency at the local Hampton Court Hotel the following year. Their debut album, *High Voltage*, was released in 1975. Lead singer Bon Scott died in 1980 and was replaced by Brit Brian Johnson, whose first album with the band was their all-time highest selling *Back in Black*.

THEIR BEST-SELLING ALBUMS

1	Back In Black	1980
2	Highway To Hell	1979
3	Dirty Deeds Done Cheap	1981
4	The Razor's Edge	1990
5	Who Made Who	1986
6	For Those About To Rock We Salute You	1981
7	Live	1992
8	High Voltage	1982
9	Black Ice	2008
10	Let There Be Rock	1977
11	Live Collector's Edition	1992
12	Flick Of The Switch	1983
13	If You Want Blood You've Got It	1978
14	Power Age	1978
15	'74 Jailbreak	1984
16	Ballbreaker	1995
17	Bonfire	1995
18	Stiff Upper Lip	2000
19	Blow Up Your Video	1988
20	Fly On The Wall	1985

THEIR TOP 30 UK HIT SINGLES

	Peak position	
Rock 'n' Roll Damnation	24	(Jul 15, 1978)
Touch Too Much	29	(Mar 01, 1980)
Let's Get It Up	13	(Feb 20, 1982)
For Those About To Rock (We Salute You)	15	(Jul 10, 1982)
Shake Your Foundations	24	(Jan 25, 1986)
Who Made Who	16	(May 31, 1986)
Heatseeker	12	(Jan 23, 1988)
That's The Way I Wanna Rock 'n' Roll	22	(Apr 09, 1988)
Thunderstruck	13	(Sep 29, 1990)
Highway To Hell (Live)	14	(Oct 24, 1992)
Big Gun	23	(Jul 10 1993)

ARIA AWARDS

Hall of Fame	1988
Best Rock Album for *Black Ice*	2009
Highest Selling Album for *Black Ice*	2009

ARIA is the Australian Recording Industry Association.

Right: In 1976 the band were already popular in their native Australia.

BON SCOTT'S DEATH

While recording in Britain, AC/DC's lead singer Bon Scott and musician friend Alistair Kennear spent the evening of February 19, 1980 at the Music Machine in Camden Town, London, watching groups Protex and the Trendies, while consuming a large amount of alcohol. Kennear drove Scott back to his house in East Dulwich, South London, leaving him asleep in the car. Returning the following morning, Kennear found Scott unconscious and drove him to the nearby King's College Hospital, where he was pronounced dead. Ex-Geordie frontman Brian Johnson was recruited as the new AC/DC lead singer two months later.

Left: Brian Johnson was previously the singer in the band Geordie.

FROM RUSSIA WITH METAL

On September 28, 1991 AC/DC, Metallica, The Black Crowes and several Soviet acts performed before a 500,000 crowd at the Tushino Air Field in Moscow. AC/DC's lead singer Brian Johnson observed: "Opera and ballet did not cut the ice in the Cold War years. They used to exchange opera and ballet companies and circuses, but it takes rock 'n' roll to make no more Cold War."

MARVEL-OUS

The 15-cut soundtrack album to the film sequel of Marvel comics' *Iron Man 2* released in 2010 was entirely comprised of new and old recordings by AC/DC.

Having left his family in Los Angeles (to where they emigrated in August 1980 from Denmark), drummer Lars Ulrich went to London in the summer of 1981 and toured with New Wave of British Heavy Metal outfit Diamond Head. Returning to the US in October, he placed a "musicians wanted" ad in *The Recycler* magazine and recruited local singer/rhythm guitarist James Hetfield. Forming Metallica, their first recording was 'Hit The Lights' in 1982 for inclusion on the *Metal Massacre 1* compilation album.

THEIR BEST-SELLING ALBUMS

1	Metallica	1991
2	...And Justice For All	1988
3	Load	1996
4	Master Of Puppets	1986
5	Ride The Lightning	1984
6	Reload	1997
7	S&M	1999
8	Garage Inc.	1998
9	St. Anger	2003
10	Kill 'Em All	1988

Their six best-selling albums have all sold in excess of 4 million copies each in the US and combined 43 million. The group's 1991 opus, *Metallica* featured the monster metal hit, 'Enter Sandman'.

Above: Metallica's frontman James Hetfield in 2009.

Bottom Right: James Hetfield, Kirk Hammett, Lars Ulrich and Cliff Burton in 1984.

THEIR UK HIT SINGLES

CLIFF BURTON'S DEATH

During a European tour in 1986, Metallica's tour bus crashed on the E4 road near Ljunby in Sweden on September 26, killing bassist Cliff Burton. He was posthumously inducted into the Rock and Roll Hall of Fame along with the rest of Metallica on April 4, 2009.

TIPPER GORE

Concerned about the heightened profile of Al Gore's wife, the censorship-heralding Tipper, James Hetfield says in the July 22, 1992 edition *USA Today*: "Her re-emergence makes me want to clean my guns."

ST. ANGER

During a Metallica gig at the Orlando Centroplex in Orlando, Florida on March 16, 1992, fans dangled an usher by his ankles from the balcony during crowd trouble. The band subsequently paid $38,000 for repairs and cleaning, after the audience trashed the building. Arena director Joanne Grant said 'This stuff doesn't happen at a Kenny Rogers concert, but the band was very gracious.'

ROBBIE WILLIAMS

Serving his apprenticeship as the youngest member (at 16) of UK boy band Take That in the early nineties, Robert Peter Williams quit the group in 1995 determined to focus on a solo career. Despite a strong start with a cover version of George Michael's 'Freedom' in 1996, his debut solo album, 1997's *Life Thru A Lens*, was worryingly under-performing until the release of its fourth single, 'Angels'. Co-written by the star with co-producer Guy Chambers, the soaring ballad firmly re-launched Williams' career, spurring multi-platinum sales of the album around Europe.

HIS BEST-SELLING SINGLES

	Peak position	
Angels	4	(Feb 21, 1998)
Rock DJ	1	(Aug 12, 2000)
She's The One/It's Only Us	1	(Nov 20, 1999)
Millennium	1	(Sep 19, 1998)
Kids (with Kylie Minogue)	2	(Oct 21, 2000)
Eternity/The Road To Mandalay	1	(Jul 21, 2001)
Somethin' Stupid (with Nicole Kidman)	1	(Dec 22, 2001)
Freedom	2	(Aug 10, 1996)
Let Me Entertain You	3	(Mar 28, 1998)
No Regrets	4	(Dec 12, 1998)
Bodies	2	(Oct 24, 2009)
You Know Me	6	(Dec 26, 2009)

... FEATURING ROBBIE WILLIAMS

I Started A Joke	The Orb	1998
Are You Gonna Go My Way	Tom Jones	1999
That Old Black Magic	Jane Horrocks	2000
My Culture	1 Giant Leap	2002
Do They Know It's Christmas?	Band Aid 20	2004
Jealousy	Pet Shop Boys	2006
The Only One I Know	Mark Ronson	2007
Please Don't Talk About Me When I'm Gone	Dean Martin	2007
Everybody Hurts	Helping Haiti	2010

In addition to the above guest vocal spots, Williams provided the voice for the Dougal character in the 2005 film, *The Magic Roundabout*, based on the popular children's television series.

Right: Robbie celebrates at the BRIT Awards in 1999.

HIS BEST-SELLING ALBUMS

I've Been Expecting You	1998
Swing When You're Winning	2001
Sing When You're Winning	2000
Life Thru A Lens	1998
Escapology	2002
Greatest Hits	2004
Intensive Care	2005
Reality Killed The Video Star	2009
Live At Knebworth	2003
Rudebox	2006

MISUNDERSTOOD

Despite becoming a multi-platinum selling fixture throughout Europe, Asia and Latin America over the past 15 years, Williams has consistently failed to conquer the world's biggest record market: the US. Several expensive promotional campaigns across the pond have resulted in only a smattering of chart success: 'Angels' (number 53) and 'Millennium' (number 72.)

Right: Performing at the Telstra Dome, Melbourne in 2006.

WILLIAMS – ROBBIE WILLIAMS

Robbie Williams arrived in style at the 19th annual BRIT Awards, abseiling down to the stage at the London's Docklands Arena, as he sang 'Let Me Entertain You'. He also won three of the event's awards – Best British Male Solo Artist, Best British Single ('Millennium') and Best British Video ('Let Me Entertain You'). Receiving one of his trophies, Williams said, "I'm sorry I can't be here in person tonight – I'm doing panto with Céline Dion in Wolverhampton."

COLDPLAY

The British rock quartet was formed in 1997 by four college chums – Chris Martin, Jonny Buckland, Guy Berryman and Will Champion – at University College London in 1997. Before settling on its permanent moniker, the group played under the names Pectoralz and Starfish. Their first recordings – self-financed and self-released – appeared on the 1998 EP *Safety* – of which only 500 copies were pressed. Briefly signed to the indie Fierce Panda label for the *Brothers and Sisters* EP, Coldplay finally inked a major deal with EMI/Parlophone in 1999.

THEIR BEST-SELLING ALBUMS

1	A Rush Of Blood To The Head	2002
2	X&Y	2005
3	Parachutes	2000
4	Viva La Vida Or Death And All His Friends	2008

THEIR UK HIT SINGLES

	Peak position	
Shiver	35	(Mar 18, 2000)
Yellow	4	(Jul 08, 2000)
Trouble	10	(Nov 04, 2000)
In My Place	2	(Aug 17, 2002)
The Scientist	10	(Nov 23, 2002)
Clocks	9	(Apr 05, 2003)
Speed Of Sound	2	(Jun 04, 2005)
Fix You	4	(Sep 17, 2005)
Talk	10	(Dec 31, 2005)
Violet Hill	8	(May 17, 2008)
Viva La Vida	1	(Jun 28, 2008)
Lost	54	(Nov 22, 2008)
Life In Technicolor II	28	(Feb 14, 2009)

Above: The band play to a packed Wembley Stadium in 2009.

VIVA LA CHART-TOPPER

Although a mighty-selling albums band, Coldplay has only topped the UK and US charts on one occasion: both times with the Brian Eno co-produced classic 'Viva La Vida'. It also became the best-selling single on iTunes Music Store in 2008. Swedish pop vocalist Darin scored a domestic number one with his cover version on October 30, 2009.

The minimalist, award-winning video for the band's breakthrough hit 'Yellow' happened by accident: the original plan – to feature the whole band on a sunny day at the beach at Studland Bay in Dorset – was changed due to the funeral of drummer Will Champion's mother.

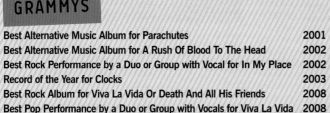

Right: Coldplay released *X&Y* in 2005.

THEIR MUSIC VIDEOS

Bigger Stronger	1999	Talk	2005
Shiver	2000	The Hardest Part	2006
Yellow	2000	Violet Hill	2008
Trouble	2000	Violet Hill (Dancing Politicians)	2008
Don't Panic	2001	Viva La Vida	2008
In My Place	2002	Lost!	2008
The Scientist	2002	Lost+ (featuring Jay-Z)	2008
Clocks	2003	Lovers In Japan	2008
God Put A Smile Upon Your Face	2003	Lost?	2008
Speed Of Sound	2005	Life in Technicolor II	2009
Fix You	2005	Strawberry Swing	2009

AT THE GRAMMYS

Best Alternative Music Album for Parachutes	2001
Best Alternative Music Album for A Rush Of Blood To The Head	2002
Best Rock Performance by a Duo or Group with Vocal for In My Place	2002
Record of the Year for Clocks	2003
Best Rock Album for Viva La Vida Or Death And All His Friends	2008
Best Pop Performance by a Duo or Group with Vocals for Viva La Vida	2008

The group cut three separate videos for *Lost!* the first being a live performance of the song, the second used the same performance but digitally added an appearance by rapper Jay-Z - and the third, "Lost?" was directed by Paul O'Brien, who won a worldwide competition among fans to create a homemade video to an acoustic version of the song.

Manchester City soccer club supporters and siblings Noel Thomas Gallagher and his younger brother Liam were raised – together with their older brother Paul – during their teenage years by their Irish-Catholic mother Margaret in the working-class Manchester suburb of Burnage. Liam had already performed as frontman for local outfit Rain before forming Oasis in 1991. Noel (who was playing with indie outfit Inspiral Carpets) agreed to join on condition the group performed songs written by him.

THEIR BEST-SELLING ALBUMS

1. (What's The Story) Morning Glory?
2. Definitely Maybe
3. Be Here Now
4. Stop The Clocks
5. Heathen Chemistry
6. Don't Believe The Truth
7. Dig Out Your Soul
8. Standing On The Shoulder Of Giants
9. The Master Plan
10. Familiar To Millions

Already certified for 1.5 million sales on pre-orders, Oasis' album *Be Here Now* sold 696,000 copies in its first two days of release in Britain in August 1997, making it the fastest-selling album ever in the UK.

Above: The Gallaghers at Shepherd's Bush Empire in 2001.

Right: The band pose outside Westpoint Arena in 1997.

THEIR BEST-SELLING SINGLES

1	Wonderwall	1995
2	Don't Look Back In Anger	1996
3	Whatever	1994
4	Some Might Say	1995
5	Roll With It	1995
6	Cigarettes And Alcohol	1994
7	Stand By Me	1997
8	D'you Know What I Mean?	1997
9	Live Forever	1994
10	All Around The World	1998

AND THE WINNER IS ...

The band has won a plethora of awards over the years. Here is a sampling:

BRITS

Best British Newcomer	1995
Best British Video ("Wonderwall")	1996
Best British Album ((What's The Story) Morning Glory?)	1996
Best British Group	1996
Outstanding Contribution To Music	2007
BRITs Album of 30 Years ((What's The Story) Morning Glory?)	2010

Ivor Novellos

Songwriter of the Year	1995, 1996

MTV Europe Music Awards

Best UK Act	1994
Best Song (Wonderwall)	1996
Best Group	1996
Best Rock Act	1997

Q Awards

Best New Act	1994
Best Live Act	1995
Best Act In The World Today	1996
Best Act In The World Today	1997
Best Live Act	2000
Best Album (Don't Believe The Truth)	2005
People's Choice Award	2005
Best Act In The World Today	2006
Classic Songwriter Award	2006

DEFINITELY MAYBE

After years of intense sibling rivalry and squabbling, Noel Gallagher announced a permanent split from his brother Liam on August 28, 2009, stating via a public press release that, "with some sadness and great relief to tell you that I quit Oasis tonight. People will write and say what they like, but I simply could not go on working with Liam a day longer."

BRITPOP FEVER

At the height of the popular Britpop rivalry in the mid-nineties, the *NME's* front cover on its August 12, 1995 edition featured side-by-side photos of Liam Gallagher and Blur's Damon Albarn with the heading: "British Heavyweight Championship: Blur Vs. Oasis."

Intent on creating the British equivalent to US boy band mega-unit New Kids On The Block, Manchester-based manager Nigel Martin-Smith held auditions in 1990 which resulted in the recruitment of Gary Barlow, Mark Owen, Robbie Williams, Howard Donald (the only non-teenager at 21) and Jason Orange. Their telegenic looks and catchy dance-pop fare – much of it penned by Barlow – made Take That the biggest UK act of the first half of the 1990s with record sales exceeding 19 million.

GARY BARLOW

Songwriter Gary Barlow – who wrote most of the group's hits – submitted 'Let's Pray For Christmas' as a 15-year old for BBC Television's "Pebble Mill At One" song competition: "A Song For Christmas". It reached the semifinal stage. Among his many non-Take That compositions, Barlow wrote 'This Time' for Shirley Bassey for her 2009 album, *The Performance*.

LOVE AIN'T HERE ANYMORE

After achieving seven Number 1 singles and two Number 1 albums, Take That held a press conference at the Hilton Hotel in Manchester on February 13, 1996 to announce their intention to split after five years together, following farewell commitments. The 24-hour Childline helpline and the Samaritans reported that they were deluged with calls from distraught fans.

BEATLES TRIBUTE

On Valentine's Day 1994, the group performed a medley of Beatles, hits to celebrate the 30th anniversary of the Fab Four's conquest of the US at the 13th annual BRIT Awards, held at London's Alexandra Palace. They also snared trophies for Best Single ('Pray') and Best Video ('Pray').

THEIR BEST-SELLING ALBUMS IN THE UK

1	Beautiful World	2006
2	The Circus	2008
3	Everything Changes	1993
4	Never Forget – The Ultimate Collection	2005
5	Greatest Hits	1996
6	Take That And Party	1993
7	Nobody Else	1995

Following the group's dissolution in 1995, it took the band - still sans Robbie Williams – ten years to reform and begin recording again.

BACK FOR GOOD

On November 25, 2005 – following a *Take That: For The Record* ITV-aired documentary on the group two weeks earlier – Take That, still minus Robbie Williams, announced their reunion and an upcoming 'Ultimate' tour planned for 2006. In May 2006 they signed a new recording contract with Polydor Records.

THEIR BEST-SELLING SINGLES IN THE UK

1	Back For Good	1995
2	How Deep Is Your Love	1996
3	Babe	1993
4	Rule The World	2007
5	Patience	2006
6	Pray	1993
7	Never Forget	1995
8	Shine	2007
9	Sure	1994
10	Relight My Fire	1993
11	Could It Be Magic	1992
12	Love Ain't Here Anymore	1994
13	Why Can't I Wake Up With You	1993
14	Everything Changes	1994
15	Greatest Day	2008

When Take That's 'Pray' entered the UK chart at Number 1 on July 17, 1993, the band became the first act on RCA to debut at the top since Elvis Presley with 'It's Now Or Never' in 1960.

Left: A jubilant Take That at the 2008 BRIT Awards.

AND THE WINNER IS ...

Take That has won five BRITS for Best British Single.

Could It Be Magic	1993
Pray	1994
Back For Good	1996
Patience	2007
Shine	2008

JAY-Z

Shawn Corey Carter was raised by his mother Gloria in the Marcy Houses projects in Brooklyn's Bedford-Stuyvesant area, where he attended the local Eli Whitney High School. Nicknamed Jazzy from an earlier age, he adopted the stage name Jay-Z when he began freestyle rapping in the 1980s. Unable to secure a recording contract after years of trying, he formed his own Roc-A-Fella label in 1996 with co-founders Damon Dash and Kareem Burke: WIBB in November 1955. One of rap music's most revered and successful artists, Jay-Z is today estimated to be worth north of $500 million.

HIS BEST-SELLING ALBUMS

1	Vol. 2 ... Hard Knock Life	1998
2	The Black Album	2003
3	Vol. 3 ... Life And Times Of S. Carter	2000
4	The Blueprint 2 – The Gift And The Curse	2002
5	Kingdom Come	2006
6	The Blueprint	2001
7	The Dynasty – Roc La Familia	2000
8	MTV Ultimate Mash-Ups Presents – Collision Course (with Linkin Park)	2004
9	American Gangster	2007
10	The Blueprint 3	2009
11	The Best Of Both Worlds (with R. Kelly)	2002
12	In My Lifetime, Vol. 1	1997
13	Blueprint 2.1	2003
14	Reasonable Doubt	1996
15	Unfinished Business (with R. Kelly)	2004

... FEATURING – HIS US CHART SUCCESS

Jay-Z has charted 58 times on the US Hot 100. A mere 20 of those hits have been solo efforts. The others have been collaborations. They are:

Can I Get A ...	Amil	Storm	Lenny Kravitz
Sunshine	Babyface & Foxy Brown	Mr. Carter	Lil Wayne
Crazy In Love	Beyoncé	It's Alright	Memphis Bleek
Deja Vu	Beyoncé	Hey Papi	Memphis Bleek & Amil
Upgrade U	Beyoncé	Is That Your Chick?	Memphis Bleek & Missy Elliott
'03 Bonnie & Clyde	Beyoncé Knowles		
Jigga What ...	Big Jaz	Lost One	Chrisette Michele
The City Is Mine	BLACKstreet	Young Forever	Mr. Hudson
Can't Knock The Hustle	Mary J. Blige	Beware Of The Boys	
I'll Be	Foxy Brown	(Mundian To Bach Ke)	Panjabi MC
Heartbreaker	Mariah Carey	Frontin'	Pharrell
All Of My Days	Changing Faces	Love For Free	Rell
Lost!	Coldplay	Umbrella	Rihanna
What We Do	Freeway & Beanie Sigel	Run This Town	Rihanna & Kanye West
Money Ain't A Thang	JD	Guess Who's Back?	Scarface & Beanie Sigel
Big Chips	R. Kelly	Do It Again	
Fiesta	R. Kelly	(Put Ya Hands Up)	Beanie Sigel & Amil
Guilty Until Proven Innocent	R. Kelly	Change The Game	Beanie Sigel & Memphis Bleek
Take You Home With Me A.K.A. Body	R. Kelly	Swagga Like Us	T.I., Kanye West & Lil Wayne
Empire State Of Mind	Alicia Keys	Big Pimpin'	UGK

Jay-Z's business interests include part-ownership of the New Jersey Nets basketball team, the Rocawear clothing line, multimedia company, Roc Nation and The 40/40 Club.

Left: Jay-Z during *The Blueprint 3* tour, Pittsburg, 2010.

Right: Jay-Z with wife Beyoncé.

CHANGE THE GAME

Following an August 9, 2006 meeting with UN Secretary General: Kofi Annan in New York, Jay-Z announced that his comeback world tour would be used to raise awareness about the global water crisis. MTV filmed much of the trek, yielding the November 2006 documentary *Diary Of Jay-Z: Water For Life*.

CRAZY IN LOVE

Sporting a $5 million wedding ring, Beyoncé finally tied the knot with longtime boyfriend (and musical collaborator) Jay-Z on April 4, 2008, in New York City.

EMINEM

Marshall Bruce Mathers III – aka Eminem – was born on October 17, 1972 in Saint Joseph, Missouri and raised by his single-parent mother Deborah. Growing up in the Detroit suburb of Warren, Mathers became a hip-hop devotee after first hearing the Beastie Boys' *Licensed To Ill* album as a teenager. Initially using the moniker M&M (named after the candy) he performed solo at local freestyle amateur rap competitions from the age of 14 before joining his first group, Bassmint Productions.

HIS BEST-SELLING ALBUMS

1	The Marshall Mathers LP	2000
2	The Eminem Show	2002
3	Encore	2004
4	The Slim Shady LP	1999
5	Curtain Call – The Hits	2005
6	Relapse	2009

Left: Marshall Mathers, keeping it real.

The *Marshall Mathers LP* was released in the US on May 23, 2000, celebrated by Eminem signing copies for 500-plus fans at the Virgin Megastore in New York. Considered an 18-track hip-hop classic, it sold 1.76 million domestic copies in its first week, the highest-ever tally for a solo artist in any genre.

HIS BEST-SELLING SINGLES

1	Lose Yourself	2002
2	Without Me	2002
3	Just Lose It	2004
4	When I'm Gone	2005
5	Like Toy Soldiers	2005
6	Mockingbird	2005
7	The Real Slim Shady	2000
8	Stan	2000
9	Cleanin' Out My Closet	2002
10	My Name Is	1999

List does not include singles with other artists.

Left: Performing in London (with Dr Dre) in 2000.

In addition to becoming his biggest hit, 'Lose Yourself' also became the first rap song to win an Academy Award, nabbing the Best Original Song category in 2003. Co-written by the artist, the song was recorded for the semi-autobiographical movie, *8 Mile*, which premiered in October 2002.

THE REAL SLIM SHADY

On Valentine's Day 2001 Eminem pleaded guilty to carrying a concealed weapon in Macomb County Court in Michigan. In exchange for the plea, prosecutor Carl Marlinga dropped a felony charge of assault with a deadly weapon. He was sentenced on April 10, placed on two years' probation and fined $2,500. Judge Antonio Viviano also required the rapper to refrain from excessive alcohol or drug use for two years to undergo counselling.

NUMBER ONE SINGLES BY COUNTRY

Australia, Ireland, New Zealand, United Kingdom	7
Austria, Switzerland	4
Germany, Italy, Sweden, United States	2

MARSHALL, STAN AND ELTON

The opening highlight of the MTV Video Music Awards on February 21, 2001 was the controversial pairing of the openly-gay Elton John and the seemingly homophobic Eminem, performing the latter's 'Stan'. With Elton inserting the piano and vocal rolls from the single's use of Dido's 'Thank You', Eminem delivered the first verse lying on a bed, wearing a blue jumpsuit.

Above: Slim Shady at the MTV Europe Music Awards, Dublin, in 1999.

MARIAH CAREY

Singing since the age of four, Mariah Carey was named after *They Call The Wind Mariah*, a cut from the Lerner and Loewe musical *Paint Your Wagon* – which also included the song 'Wand'rin' Star' by Lee Marvin, which happened to be Number One in the UK on the day Carey was born. She began writing songs while still attending Harborfields High school at 16 and was signed to CBS/Columbia Records at the age of 18 while working as a waitress and coat-check girl in New York by its president, Tommy Mottola – who also became her first husband.

HER NUMBER ONE HIT SINGLES IN THE US

I'll Be There	Jun 20, 1992
Touch My Body	Apr 12, 2008
Fantasy	Sep 30, 1995
Don't Forget About Us	Dec 31, 2005
We Belong Together	Jun 04, 2005
Love Takes Time	Nov 10, 1990
Vision Of Love	Aug 04, 1990
Someday	Mar 09, 1991
Dreamlover	Sep 11, 1993
Thank God I Found You (featuring Joe & 98 Degrees)	Feb 19, 2000
Always Be My Baby	May 04, 1996
One Sweet Day (with Boyz II Men)	Dec 02, 1995
I Don't Wanna Cry	May 25, 1991
Emotions	Oct 12, 1991
Honey	Sep 13, 1997
Heartbreaker (featuring Jay-Z)	Oct 09, 1999
Hero	Dec 25, 1993
My All	May 23, 1998

Distinguishing Carey's catalogue from her contemporary, Whitney Houston, she has written or co-written the great majority of her work. When 'Touch My Body' hit the top spot in the US in 2008, Carey overtook Elvis Presley as the solo artist with the most number ones of all-time with 18. Carey has only had two Number One hit singles in the UK – 'Without You' (February 19, 1994) and 'Against All Odds' (September 30, 2000).

HER BEST-SELLING ALBUMS

1	Music Box	1993
2	Mariah Carey	1990
3	Daydream	1995
4	The Emancipation Of Mimi	2005
5	#1's	1998
6	Butterfly	1997
7	Merry Christmas	1994
8	Emotions	1991
9	MTV Unplugged (EP)	1992
10	Rainbow	1999
11	Charmbracelet	2002
12	Greatest Hits	2001
13	E=mc2	2008
14	Glitter	2001
15	Memoirs Of An Imperfect Angel	2009
16	The Ballads	2008
17	The Remixes	2003

Right: Performing in Toronto, Canada, in 2010.

THE FIRST MINIDISC

In December 1992 – when Sony first introduced MiniDisc players and recording titles to the retail market in the US – Carey's *MTV Unplugged (EP)* became the first MiniDisc title to be pressed for commercial release.

SHOW ME THE MONEY

In January 2002, nine months after signing an unprecedented multi-album, multi-million-dollar recording agreement with the Virgin Music Group Worldwide and two weeks after EMI Records denied she was being dropped from its Virgin subsidiary, Carey received a $28 million (£19 million) buyout from the company. By the end of May, she had a new home signing with the Island/Def Jam label.

AT THE MOVIES

The Bachelor	Ilana	1999
Glitter	Billie Frank	2001
WiseGirls	Raychel	2002
Death Of A Dynasty	Herself	2003
State Property 2	Dame's Wifey	2005
You Don't Mess With The Zohan	Herself	2008
Tennessee	Krystal	2009
Precious	Mrs. Weiss	2009

Although Carey's film career has suffered its share of poor reviews (notably winning the Golden Raspberry Award for Worst Actress for her performance in *Glitter*) her eighth role, an unglamorous, gritty portrayal of social worker Mrs. Weiss in 2009's *Precious* won top notices.

Beyoncé Giselle Knowles was born in Houston, Texas on September 4, 1981. A gifted performer from an early age, she won her first talent show at the age of seven, performing John Lennon's 'Imagine'. Subsequently attending Houston's High School for the Performing Arts, she soon joined her first all-girl singing troupe Girl's Tyme, which evolved into Destiny's Child by 1993 when Beyoncé was still only 12. Signed to Columbia/Sony four years later, the group recorded its first song, 'Killing Time' for inclusion on the soundtrack to the first *Men In Black* movie in 1997.

HER BEST-SELLING ALBUMS

1 Dangerously In Love   2003
2 B'Day   2006
3 I Am Sasha Fierce   2008
4 Beyoncé – Live At Wembley   2004
5 Above And Beyoncé – Video
   Collection And Dance Mixes   2009

HER NUMBER ONE SINGLES IN THE US

Crazy In Love (featuring Jay-Z)	Jul 12, 2003
Baby Boy (featuring Sean Paul)	Oct 04, 2003
Check On It (featuring Slim Thug)	Feb 04, 2006
Irreplaceable	Dec 16, 2006
Single Ladies (Put A Ring On It)	Dec 13, 2008

DESTINY'S CHILD'S BEST-SELLING ALBUMS IN THE US

1 The Writing's On The Wall 2000
2 Survivor   2001
3 Destiny Fulfilled   2004
4 Destiny's Child   1998
5 #1's   2005
6 8 Days Of Christmas   2001
7 This Is The Remix   2002

Beyoncé recorded four studio albums with the all-female R&B group Destiny's Child, all of which went platinum in the US. Their sophomore set, *The Writing's On The Wall*, included four hit singles and eventually sold more than eight million domestic copies.

HOPE FOR HAITI

On January 22, 2010 Beyoncé was one of dozens of top artists to perform live on the George Clooney/MTV-organised "Hope For Haiti" fundraiser. Appearing in London and accompanied by Coldplay's Chris Martin on piano, she performed a lyrically revised version of her own smash, 'Halo' (which she originally co-wrote and co-produced for her 2008 album, *I Am ... Sasha Fierce*).

Above: Performing at the World Music Awards in 2010.

Below: Turning up the heat in Brazil.

AT THE MOVIES

Carmen – A Hip Hopera (TV film)	2001
Austin Powers In Goldmember	2002
The Fighting Temptations	2003
The Pink Panther	2006
Dreamgirls	2006
Cadillac Records	2008
Obsessed	2009

In addition to her multi-platinum recording career, Beyoncé Knowles has found considerable success on film and is set to continue her acting career in movie remakes of *A Star Is Born* and *Gilligan's Island*.

BEYONCE THE BRAND

With her good looks, strong hooks and savvy business mind, the hardworking diva has been a pioneer in the branding industry, lending her name, face and music to a wide range of commercial ventures, including campaigns for Pepsi, L'Oréal, Tommy Hilfiger and Armani. Beyoncé also launched her own fragrance, 'Heat' in 2010.

FESTIVALS

Although a handful of music festivals had been held for several years – mostly confined to specific genres (notably the Newport Jazz Festival since 1954 and the Newport Folk Festival (since 1959) – it was not until the Monterey International Pop Music Festival in 1967 that rock music got its due. Soon followed by Woodstock and the Isle of Wight event in the UK, large open-air music fests, usually held over three-day weekends with multi-artist lineups, became increasingly popular and financially rewarding.

MONTEREY 1967

Friday, June 16
The Association • The Paupers • Lou Rawls • Beverly • Johnny Rivers • Eric Burdon & the Animals • Simon & Garfunkel

Saturday, June 17
Canned Heat • Big Brother & the Holding Company • Country Joe and the Fish • Al Kooper • The Butterfield Blues Band • The Electric Flag • Quicksilver Messenger Service • Steve Miller Band • Moby Grape • Hugh Masekela • The Byrds • Laura Nyro • Jefferson Airplane • Booker T. & the M.G.s • Otis Redding

Sunday, June 18
Ravi Shankar • The Blues Project • Big Brother & the Holding Company • The Group With No Name • Buffalo Springfield • The Who • The Grateful Dead • The Jimi Hendrix Experience • Scott McKenzie • The Mamas & the Papas

Right: Joe Cocker at Woodstock.

Below: Otis Redding plays Monterey in 1967.

WOODSTOCK 1969

Friday, August 15
Richie Havens • Swami Satchidananda • Sweetwater • The Incredible String Band • Bert Sommer • Tim Hardin • Ravi Shankar • Melanie • Arlo Guthrie • Joan Baez

Saturday, August 16
Quill • The Keef Hartley Band • Country Joe McDonald • John Sebastian • Santana • Canned Heat • Mountain • The Grateful Dead • Creedence Clearwater Revival • Janis Joplin with the Kozmic Blues Band • Sly & the Family Stone • The Who • Jefferson Airplane

Sunday, August 17 to Monday, August 18
The Grease Band • Joe Cocker • Country Joe & the Fish • Ten Years After • The Band • Blood, Sweat & Tears • Johnny & Edgar Winter • Crosby, Stills, Nash & Young • The Paul Butterfield Blues Band • Sha-Na-Na • Jimi Hendrix

A three-day festival staged from June 16–18 at the Monterey County Fairgrounds in California, "Monterey" was a watershed event with an estimated 90,000-strong audience in attendance on the final day. Inaugurating the "Summer of Love", it came to define '60s hippie counterculture, an historic musical celebration which included the first major US performances by both The Who and Jimi Hendrix and other show-stopping sets by the likes of Otis Redding and Janis Joplin. Taking less than two months to organize, the festival's board included members of The Beach Boys and The Beatles – neither of whom performed.

The "Woodstock Music and Art Fair" got underway at 5.07 p.m. on August 15, 1969 on Max Yasgur's farm in Bethel, Sullivan County, New York (actually 70 miles from the town of Woodstock). With an estimated 450,000 music fans – most without tickets – attending what was the largest rock festival/cultural exposition to date, 'Woodstock''s legendary musical highlights were accompanied by historic traffic jams, three (non-malicious) deaths, two births and four miscarriages, innumerable conceptions, and the consumption of vast quantities of drugs and alcohol.

ISLE OF WIGHT 1969

Above: Bob Dylan at the 1969 Isle of Wight Festival.

Organized by Ron, Ray and Bill Foulk, the first Isle of Wight Festival of Music took place in 1968, though it wasn't until the following year – with Bob Dylan and The Who in the lineup – that the event became legendary. With only 10,000 music fans attending the inaugural event, 1969's throng swelled to some 150,000. Staged in the island's village of Wootton, and showcasing 28 acts over 3 days, The Who's set included nearly all of the songs from its recent rock opera release, Tommy.

BOB DYLAN'S ISLE OF WIGHT 1969 SET LIST

She Belongs To Me	Highway 61 Revisited
I Threw It All Away	One Too Many Mornings
Maggie's Farm	I Pity The Poor Immigrant
Wild Mountain Thyme	Like A Rolling Stone
It Ain't Me Babe	I'll Be Your Baby Tonight
To Ramona	The Mighty Quinn
Mr. Tambourine Man	Minstrel Boy (encore)
I Dreamed I Saw St.	Rainy Day Women, Nos.
Augustine	12 & 35 (encore)
Lay Lady Lay	

Dylan's Isle of Wight appearance with the Band was watched by some 200,000 people, including Beatles John Lennon, George Harrison and Ringo Starr, Rolling Stones Keith Richard, Bill Wyman and Charlie Watts were also in the audience, as were Traffic's Stevie Winwood and Jim Capaldi.

ISLE OF WIGHT 1970

Wednesday, August 26
Redbone • Might Baby • Judas Jump • Kathy Smith

Thursday, August 27
The Groundhogs • Andy Roberts & Everyone • Supertramp • Black Widow • Howl • Terry Reid

Friday, August 28
Arrival • Taste • Chicago • Cactus • Family • Tony Joe White • Lighthouse • Procol Harum • The Voices of East Harlem • Melanie

Saturday, August 29
John Sebastian • Shawn Phillips • Emerson, Lake & Palmer • Ten Years After • The Doors • Joni Mitchell • Tiny Tim • Miles Davis • The Who • Sly & the Family Stone

Sunday, August 30
Kris Kristofferson • Ralph McTell • Heaven • Free • Donovan • Pentangle • The Moody Blues • Jethro Tull • Jimi Hendrix Experience • Joan Baez • Richie Havens • Leonard Cohen with the Army

Highlighted by an iconic performance by Jimi Hendrix, this year's event was held on Afton Down on the Isle's western side. It attracted huge numbers, estimated somewhere between 600,000 and 750,000. Despite the massive attendance, logistical problems and commercial shortcomings meant that an annual music festival would not return to the Isle of Wight until 2002.

Left: Jimi Hendrix at the 1970 Isle of Wight festival.

Left: Leonard Cohen plays the Isle of Wight in 1970.

ALTAMONT DECEMBER 6, 1969

Aiming to repeat their successful Hyde Park open-air concert in London in July 1969, the Rolling Stones closed their US tour headlining a free concert at the Altamont Speedway track in Livermore, California – an event which also featured Santana, The Flying Burrito Brothers, Crosby Still & Nash and Jefferson Airplane. With an estimated crowd of some 300,000, the event hired San Francisco-based Hell's Angels to handle security who – fuelled by a mixture of alcohol and drugs – provoked angry, violent scenes among concertgoers. In the confused atmosphere, 18-year-old black youth Meredith Hunter, wearing a lime green suit, was stabbed to death by Hell's Angels after he pulled out a gun near the front of the stage midway through the Stones' performance of 'Under My Thumb'. The group rushed through its remaining numbers before fleeing in a helicopter. Three other attendees died during the evening: two were run over in their sleeping bags, with one other person drowning in a nearby lake. Earlier in the show, Jefferson Airplane's Marty Balin was attacked halfway through a song, again by one of the Hell's Angels. The Grateful Dead had already pulled out of a scheduled appearance, citing "bad vibes." This disastrous concert was subsequently viewed by many as an epitaph to the peace and love "Flower Power" movement of the late 60s – and the end of an ideological era.

THE OTHER STAGES AT GLASTONBURY 2009

In addition to the main Pyramid Stage, the 2009 festival featured 20 other performing areas:
The Other Stage • Jazz World • The John Peel Stage • The Acoustic Stage • The Park Stage • The Queen's Head • The East Dance • The West Dance • The Avalon • The Glade • The Croissant Neuf • Club Dada • The Rabbit Hole • The Guardian Lounge • The Bandstand • The Stonebridge Bar • Arcadia • BBC Introducing • The Bimble Inn • Poetry & Words 2009

Headliners in 2009 on the John Peel Stage (renamed in 2005 after the legendary DJ who died in 2004) were the Doves (Friday), Jarvis Cocker (Saturday) and Echo & the Bunnymen (Sunday). Non-electric strummers on the Acoustic Stage included veterans like Ray Davies and Roger McGuinn, alongside relative newcomers Jason Mraz, Ben Taylor (James' son), Sharon Corr and Imelda May.

GLASTONBURY 1970

Organized by local dairy farmer Michael Eavis, the first annual Glastonbury Festival took place on September 19–20, 1970. Billed as the "Pop Folk & Blues" festival, it was held at Worthy Farm in Pilton near Shepton Mallet in Somerset. The 1,500 or so attendees were offered free farm milk, sheltered fields for camping and an Ox roast. Tickets cost £1.

Having evolved into Britain's most famous and best-attended summer rock festival, Glastonbury now uses more than three million gallons of drinking water for its regular 100,000-plus attendees, 3,000 toilets and more than 30 megawatts of electricity. The standard festival ticket price for 2010 was £185.

GLASTONBURY FESTIVAL 2009

Headliners on the Pyramid Stage:

Friday, June 26
Neil Young • The Specials • Lily Allen • The Fleet Foxes • N*E*R*D • Regina Spektor • Gabriella Cilmi • Björn Again

Saturday, June 27
Bruce Springsteen • Kasabian • Crosby, Stills & Nash • Dizzee Rascal • Spinal Tap • The Eagles of Death Metal • Tinariwen • VV Brown

Sunday, June 28
Blur • Nick Cave & the Bad Seeds • Madness • Tom Jones • Amadou & Mariam • Tony Christie • Status Quo • The Easy Star All-Stars

Right: Damon Albarn and Blur feel heavy metal at Glastonbury in 2009.

Left: Katy Perry makes a point at the Hurricane Festival in 2009.

V96

The first V Festival took place over the weekend of August 17 and 18, 1996. Performers were featured on three stages – the V Stage, the Edge Park Second Stage and the Dance Arena.

V Stage
Pulp • Paul Weller • Supergrass • The Charlatans • Cast • The Lightning Seeds • Gary Numan • Shed Seven • Stereolab • Incognito • Jonathan Richman • The Mike Flowers Pops • Longpigs

Edge Park – Second Stage
Elastica • Sleeper • Heavy Stereo • Menswear • Fluffy • The Cardigans • Super Furry Animals • The Wannadies • Denim • Kula Shaker • Gorky's Zygotic Mynci • Space • Tiger • Pusherman • Orbital

Dance Arena
Tricky • Morcheeba • Lamb • Aloof • Mad Professor

Sponsored by the Virgin Group, the V Festival has been held annually since 1996 and now uses two parks: Hylands Park in Chelmsford, Essex and Weston Park, South Staffordshire over an August weekend.

HURRICANE FESTIVAL

Listed below are the lineups for the inaugural festival in 1973 and the more recent 2009 lineup.

1973
Argent • Buddy Miles • Chicago • Chuck Berry • Jerry Lee Lewis • East of Eden • Epitaph • Ian Carr with Nucleus • Osibisa • Karthago • Lou Reed • Manfred Mann's Earth Band • Odin Bronco • Richie Havens • Soft Machine • Ten Years After • Vinegar Joe • Wishbone Ash

2009
Kraftwerk • Kings of Leon • Culcha Candela • Faith No More • Nick Cave & the Bad Seeds • Tomete • Die Ärzte • Nine Inch Nails • Friendly Fires • Moby • Franz Ferdinand • Duffy • The Pixies • Ben Harper • Keane • Lily Allen

The Hurricane Festival was first held in 1973 in Germany, and was then revived in 1997, since when it has been held annually. This rock fest is held over three days every June in Scheebel, Bremen, Germany.

V2009

The 14th annual V Festival took place on August 22–23, 2009.

Hylands Park Saturday/Weston Park Sunday
V Stage
The Killers • Razorlight • The Specials • Lily Allen • The Script • Taylor Swift • Starsailor • McFly

4Music
Fatboy Slim • Pendulum • The Ting Tings • The Wombats • Dizzee Rascal • The Noisettes • The Red Light Company • Jet • Mr Hudson • Underline The Sky

The Arena
2ManyDJs • Calvin Harris • The Happy Mondays • The Saturdays • Will Young • Ladyhawke • N-Dubz • Asher Roth • Tinchy Stryder • Pixie Lott • Gabriella Cilmi • Matt Trakker

Virgin Media Union
Peter Doherty • Alphabeat • Sunshine Underground • The Howling Bells • Pete Murray • Goldie Lookin Chain • VV Brown • Kid British • Raygun • Wallis Bird • Zarif • Exit Calm

Hylands Park Saturday/Weston Park Sunday

V Stage
Oasis (Staffordshire only) • Snow Patrol • Elbow • James • Biffy Clyro • James Morrison • Ocean Colour Scene • Born Again

4Music
Keane • The Enemy • Paolo Nutini • Katy Perry • Athlete • Alesha Dixon • The Proclaimers • The Lightning Seeds • King Blues • The Last Republic

The Arena
MGMT • Lady Gaga • The Streets • Human League • Lemar • Natalie Imbruglia • Daniel Merriweather • Sneaky Sound System • Ben's Brother • Blizzard

Virgin Media Union
British Sea Power • Twang • The Mystery Jets • Gary Go • Seth Lakeman • Joe Lean & Jing Jang Jong • Mike Snow • Vagabond • The Gay Blades • One Eskimo • Iain Archer

Above: The Killers at V2009.

THE BATH FESTIVAL OF BLUES AND PROGRESSIVE MUSIC

In order of appearance:

Saturday, June 27
Formerly Fat Harry • The Maynard Ferguson Big Band • The Keef Hartley Band • Donovan • Joe Jammer • Fairport Convention • Colosseum • It's A Beautiful Day

Sunday, June 28
Steppenwolf • Johnny Winter • Pink Floyd • John Mayall • Canned Heat • Joe Jammer • Donovan • Frank Zappa • Santana • The Flock • Led Zeppelin • Hot Tuna

Monday, June 29
Country Joe McDonald (12.05 a.m.) • Jefferson Airplane • The Byrds • Dr. John

Conceived by husband and wife team, Freddy and Wendy Bannister (who had organized an embryonic event known as the Bath Festival of Blues the previous year), the Bath Festival of Blues and Progressive Music '70 was staged at the West Showground in Shepton Mallet, Somerset in England between June 27–29, 1970. Attracting a stellar lineup of top transatlantic acts, the event finally ended with Dr. John performing at 6.30 a.m. on Monday morning.

Above: Led Zeppelin rock Knebworth in 1979.

Below: Ronnie Wood and Keith Richards were The New Barbarians in 1979.

MOST ARTIST APPEARANCES AT OZZFEST

These are the "Ozzfest" acts which have most frequently performed from 1996–2008:

Ozzy Osbourne	8	DevilDriver	3
The Black Label Society	6	The Coal Chamber	3
Hatebreed	6	Marilyn Manson	3
Black Sabbath	5	Slayer	3
System of a Down	4	The Fear Factory	3
The Disturbed	4	Static-X	3
Slipknot	3	Shadows Fall	3
The Drowning Pool	3	Otep	3
Rob Zombie	3		

Above: Ozzy at Ozzfest in 2001.

Created by heavy metal legend Ozzy Osbourne and his manager wife Sharon in 1996, "Ozzfest" evolved into one of the most successful hard rock caravan tours of the modern era. Its first outing was, however, a modest two-day, two-venue festival, held on October 25 and 26 in Phoenix, Arizona and Devore, California.

KNEBWORTH PARK FESTIVAL 1979

Major rock concerts have been held periodically at the stately Knebworth House since 1974 when the Allman Brothers headlined the bill. Following 1978's event, self-effacingly billed as "Oh God Not Another Boring Old Knebworth" (which featured Dave Edmunds, Peter Gabriel and Frank Zappa among others), Led Zeppelin's pair of performances in August 1979 is still regarded as the unusual venue's most iconic affair – and marked their first UK concerts in four years.

HEADLINERS AT THE READING AND LEEDS FESTIVALS

1961
Humphrey Lyttelton • Kenny Ball • Roger Damen • John Frodsham • The Clyde Valley Stompers • Dick Charlesworth • Charlie Barnes • Tubby Hayes • Ken Colyer
1962
The Rolling Stones • Long John Baldry • Muddy Waters
1963
The Yardbirds • Manfred Mann • The Rolling Stones
1964
The Yardbirds • Manfred Mann • The Animals
1965
The Who • The Yardbirds • Cream
1966
The Small Faces • Paul Jones • Cream
1967
Tyrannosaurus Rex • Jethro Tull • The Nice
1968
Pink Floyd • The Who • The Nice
1969
The Groundhogs • Cat Stevens • Deep Purple
1970
Arthur Brown • East of Eden • Colosseum
1971
Curved Air • The Faces • Ten Years After
1972
Rory Gallagher • The Faces • Genesis
1973
Alex Harvey • 10cc • Traffic
1974
Hawkwind • Yes • Wishbone Ash
1975
Gong • Rory Gallagher • Osibisa
1976
Golden Earring • Thin Lizzy • Alex Harvey
1977
The Jam • Status Quo • Patti Smith
1978
The Police • Thin Lizzy • Peter Gabriel
1979
Rory Gallagher • UFO • Whitesnake
1980
Girlschool • Gillan • The Kinks
1981
Budgie • Iron Maiden • Michael Schenker
1982
The Stranglers • Black Sabbath • Thin Lizzy*
1986
Killing Joke • Hawkwind • Saxon
1987
The Mission • Status Quo • Alice Cooper

1988
The Ramones • Starship • Squeeze
1989
New Order • The Pogues • The Mission
1990
The Cramps • The Inspiral Carpets • The Pixies
1991
Iggy Pop • James • Sisters of Mercy
1992
The Wonderstuff • Public Enemy • Nirvana
1993
Porno For Pyros • The The • New Order
1994
Cypress Hill • Primal Scream • Red Hot Chili Peppers
1995
The Smashing Pumpkins • Björk • Neil Young
1996
Prodigy • Black Grape • The Stone Roses
1997
Suede • The Manic Street Preachers • Metallica
1998
Jimmy Page & Robert Plant • The Beastie Boys • Garbage
1999
The Charlatans • Blur • Red Hot Chili Peppers
2000
Oasis • Pulp • Stereophonics
2001
Travis • The Manic Street Preachers • Eminem
2002
The Strokes • The Foo Fighters • Guns n' Roses • The Prodigy
2003
Linkin Park • Blur • Metallica
2004
The Darkness • The White Stripes • Green Day
2005
The Pixies • Foo Fighters • Iron Maiden
2006
Franz Ferdinand • Muse • Pearl Jam
2007
Razorlight • Red Hot Chili Peppers • The Smashing Pumpkins
2008
Rage Against The Machine • The Killers • Metallica
2009
Kings of Leon • Arctic Monkeys • Radiohead

*There were no festivals between 1983 and 1985.

Above: Kurt Cobain of Nirvana at Reading in 1992.

Below: Radiohead's Thom Yorke at Reading in 2009.

Taking place over Britain's annual Bank Holiday weekend in August, the Reading and Leeds Festivals are twin events run by one promoter (Festival Republic) staged in their respective cities. Their roots go back to the first National Jazz Festival held in 1961 at the Richmond Athletic Ground, organized by the founder of the infamous Marquee Club in London, Harold Pendleton.

BIG DAY OUT FESTIVAL

1992
The Beasts of Bourbon • Box the Jesuit • The Celibate Rifles • The Clouds • Club Hoy • The Cosmic Psychos • Died Pretty • The Falling Joys • Dave Graney & the Coral Snakes • Hellmen • The Hard Ons with Henry Rollins • Massappeal • The Meanies • Nirvana • Ratcat • The Ruptured Spleans • Smudge • The Sound Unlimited Posse • The Village Idiots • The Violent Femmes • Welcome Mat • Yothu Yindi • You Am I

2010
Staged across six-sites, the BDO festival now includes dates in New Zealand:
Friday, January 15: Auckland, NZ
Sunday, January 17, Gold Coast
Friday, January 22, Sydney
Saturday, January 23, Sydney
Tuesday, January 26, Melbourne
Friday, January 29, Adelaide
Sunday, January 31, Perth

Muse • Powderfinger • Lily Allen • Eskimo Joe • Groove Armada • Grinspoon • The Mars Volta • Ladyhawke • Dizzee Rascal • Karnivool • Peaches • The Temper Trap • Kasabian • The Midnight Juggernauts • Rise Against • Magic Dirt • Mastodon • Lisa Mitchell • The Horrors • Bluejuice • Calvin Harris • Kisschasy • The Decemberists • Tame Impala • Girl Talk • Jet • Sasha • Devendra Banhart • Passion Pit • Simian Mobile Disco • Silent Disco • The Hilltop Hoods • Decoder Ring • Itch-E & Scratch-E • Maya Jupiter • Miami Horror • MDX • Sugar Army • Sam La More • The Scare • The Middle East • The Wagons • Phrase • Grrilla Step • Fear Factory • Dead Prez • Tumbleweed • Blowfly • DJ Chucuchu • Poirier featuring MC Zulu • Teleprompter

Inaugurated in Sydney in 1992, "Big Day Out" has become Australia's largest and most popular annual music festival. Now held over a three-week period at the end of January across the country, BDO staged its 100th show in 2010 with more than 700 combined artists and crew involved.

Above: Lily Allen flies the flag at Australia's "Big Day Out".

FIRST MONSTERS OF ROCK FESTIVAL LINEUP

Initially held each August at the Castle Donington Racetrack in Leicestershire, England, "Monsters of Rock" became Britain's most prominent heavy metal festival during the 80s and 90s.

Right: Kiss at the last UK "Monsters of Rock" festival.

LAST MONSTERS OF ROCK FESTIVAL LINEUP IN THE UK

August 17, 1996
Kiss • Ozzy Osbourne • Sepultura • Biohazard • Dog Eat Dog • Paradise Lost • The Fear Factory • KoRn • Type O Negative • Everclear • 3 Colours Red • Honeycrack • Cecil

After 1996, the "Monsters of Rock" became an international festival, staged in Argentina, Belgium, Chile, Brazil, France, Germany, Hungary, Italy, Holland, Poland, Russia, Spain, Sweden and the US. In 2003, a new annual UK rock fest, the "Download Festival" was held in Donington.

T IN THE PARK 2009

The 2009 event held between Friday, July 10-Sunday July 12, featured 180 acts – here are the lineups for those who performed on the main stage on each day:

Friday, July 10
Kings of Leon • Franz Ferdinand • Maxïmo Park • James Morrison

Saturday, July 11
The Killers • Razorlight • The Specials • James • Paolo Nutini • Lady Gaga • Calvin Harris • Björn Again

Sunday, July 12
Blur • Snow Patrol • Elbow • Bloc Party • The Script • Seasick Steve • Squeeze • The Parsonage •

Named after the first letter of its title sponsor, the Scottish brewery Tennents, the first T In The Park Festival took place at Strathclyde Park, Lanarkshire, Scotland in 1992 but is now held at an airfield in Balado, near Loch Leven, Perth, Scotland.

The first Lollapalooza Tour – showcasing a diverse, genre-bending roster of alternative acts – took place July 18–August 28, 1991 in North America. Created by Jane's Addiction frontman, Perry Farrell, it initially ran as a highly successful caravan from 1991 until 1997 before being revived in 2003.

Above: Jane's Addiction head the first Lollapalooza tour in 1991.

Below: Dave Gahan of Depeche Mode plays Lollapalooza in 2009.

LOLLAPALOOZA 2009

Grant Park • Chicago • August 7 – 9, 2009

Chicago 2016 Stage
Friday: The Gaslight Anthem • Sound Tribe Sector 9 • The Thievery Corporation • Depeche Mode.
Saturday: The Living Things • Atmosphere • Coheed & Cambria • Rise Against • Tool.
Sunday: Ra Ra Riot • The Airborne Toxic Event • Vampire Weekend • Snoop Dogg • The Killers.

Budweiser Stage
Friday: The Manchester Orchestra • White Lies • Ben Folds • The Decemberists • Kings of Leon.
Saturday: Delta Spirit • Los Campesinos! • Arctic Monkeys • TV on the Radio • The Yeah Yeah Yeahs.
Sunday: Friendly Fires • The Kaiser Chiefs • Neko Case • Lou Reed • Jane's Addiction.

Vitaminwater Stage
Friday: The Henry Clay People • Black Joe Lewis & the Honeybears • The Heartless Bastards • The Crystal Castles • of Montreal.
Saturday: The Low Anthem • Miike Snow • Gomez • Glasvegas • Animal Collective.
Sunday: Alberta Cross • Bat for Lashes • Dan Deacon • The Cold War Kids • The Silversun Pickups.

Playstation Stage
Friday: Hockey • Zap Mama • Bon Iver • The Fleet Foxes • Andrew Bird.
Saturday: Ezra Furman & the Harpoons • Federico Aubele • Robert Earl Keen • Santigold • Ben Harper & Relentless7.
Sunday: The Sam Roberts Band • Portugal • The Man • The Raveonettes • Dan Auerbach • The Band of Horses.

Citi Stage
Friday: The Other Lives • The Knux • Amazing Baby • The Virgins • Asher Roth • Peter Bjorn & John.

Saturday: thenewno2 • The Constantines • Ida Maria • The Chairlift • No Age • Lykke Li.
Sunday: Carney • Davy Knowles & Back Door Slam • Cage the Elephant • The Gang Gang Dance • Passion Pit • Deerhunter.

Perry's Stage
Friday: DJ Pasha (Last Band Standing Winner) • Nick Catchdubs • DJ Mel • Dark Wave Disco • Hollywood Holt • The Bloody Beetroots (DJ Set) • A-Trak • Simian Mobile Disco (DJ Set) • The Crookers • Kid Cudi.
Saturday: Punky Fresh (Last Band Standing Winner) • Moneypenny • Kaskade • Animal Collective (DJ Set) • Prophit • Perry Farrell & Special Guest • Hercules & Love Affair (DJ Set) • The LA Riots • Diplo • Bassnectar.
Sunday: Yello Fever • Car Stereo (Wars) • He Say • She Say • The Hood Internet • The Glitch Mob • Boys Noize • MSTRKRFT • Deadmau5.

BMI Stage
Friday: April Smith • Gringo Star • The Builders & the Butchers • Kevin Devine • Eric Church.
Saturday: Band of Skulls • Dirty Sweet • Langhorne Slim • Joe Pug • Blind Pilot.
Sunday: Mike's Pawn Shop • Esser • The Greencards • Priscilla Renea • Ke$ha.

Kidz Stage
Friday: Yuto Miyazawa • Paul Green's School of Rock All-Stars • Frances England • Secret Agent 23 Skidoo • Zach Gill (from ALO) • Special Guest • Lunch Money.
Saturday: Frances England • Zach Gill (from ALO) • Quinn Sullivan • Secret Agent 23 Skidoo • Care Bears on Fire • Special Guest • Ralph's World.
Sunday: Care Bears on Fire • Q Brothers • Ralph's World • Peter DiStefano & Tor Hyams • Perry Farrell • Paul Green's School of Rock All-Stars with Perry Farrell.

FAMOUS FINAL GIGS

Many legendary groups have split either due to fragile or combative egos, band member deaths or debilitating dependencies on drugs and alcohol: longevity for many is far from assured and their final gigs become iconic moments in rock lore. Few acts (Queen, Led Zeppelin, the Police, INXS) have managed to resist the lucrative urge to reunite or simply carry on, but among the most-desired reunions still possible is one by 80s icons The Smiths, although key members Johnny Marr and Morrisey have turned down many offers already.

THE BEATLES – CANDLESTICK PARK, SAN FRANCISCO

Chronological set list:

Rock And Roll Music
She's A Woman
If I Needed Someone
Day Tripper
Baby's In Black
I Feel Fine

Yesterday
I Wanna Be Your Man
Nowhere Man
Paperback Writer
Long Tall Sally

On Monday, August 29, 1966 – seven years to the day since John Lennon, Paul McCartney and George Harrison performed together for the first time at the opening of the Casbah Coffee Club in Liverpool – the final Beatles concert took place at Candlestick Park in San Francisco. Twenty-five thousand screaming fans saw their 11-song set close with Little Richard's 'Long Tall Sally'.

LED ZEPPELIN – EISSPORTHALLE, BERLIN

Chronological set list:

Train Kept A Rollin'
Nobody's Fault But Mine
(Out On The Tiles Intro)
Black Dog
In The Evening
Rain Song
Hot Dog
All My Love

Trampled Underfoot
Since I've Been Loving You
White Summer –
   Black Mountainside
Kashmir
Stairway To Heaven
Rock And Roll
Whole Lotta Love

The iconic hard rock quartet's final concert with its original lineup prior to drummer John Bonham's death was played at the Eissporthalle, Berlin, West Germany on July 7, 1980. Robert Plant, Jimmy Page and John Paul Jones would reunite – with Phil Collins filling in on drums – at Live Aid in 1985.

THE LAST WALTZ

In order of performance:

The Band • Ronnie Hawkins • Dr. John • Bobby Charles with Dr. John • Paul Butterfield • Muddy Waters • Eric Clapton • Neil Young • Joni Mitchell • Van Morrison • The Band with Neil Young and Joni Mitchell • The Band • Bob Dylan • The Band with Ronnie Wood and Ringo Starr

First finale jam: Neil Young • Ronnie Wood • Eric Clapton • Robbie Robertson • Paul Butterfield • Dr. John • Garth Hudson • Rick Danko • Ringo Starr and Levon Helm

Second finale jam: Neil Young • Ronnie Wood • Eric Clapton • Stephen Stills • Paul Butterfield • Dr. John • Garth Hudson • Carl Radle • Ringo Starr and Levon Helm.

After 16 years together, The Band made their final appearance together on November 25, 1976 at San Francisco's Winterland Ballroom – the scene of their first concert as The Band. A grand affair – organized by promoter Bill Graham which included a buffet, chandeliers and an orchestra – it cost $25 a ticket and was dubbed "The Last Waltz".

Right: *The Last Waltz* was made into a documentary by director Martin Scorsese.

PINK FLOYD'S LAST "THE WALL" CONCERT

Chronological set list:

Billed as "LiveWall", Pink Floyd's final concert with its seminal lineup intact – including Roger Waters – took place at Earls Court Arena in London on June 17, 1981. The main driving force behind both *Dark Side of the Moon* and *The Wall* projects, Waters awkwardly reunited with his erstwhile colleagues for four songs at Live 8 in 2005.

WHAM! – THE FINAL!

Chronological set list:

Everything She Wants	Where Did Your Heart Go?
Club Tropicana	Why?
Heartbeat	Last Christmas
Battlestations	Wham Rap
Bad Boys	A Different Corner
If You Were There	Freedom
The Edge Of Heaven	Careless Whisper
Candle In The Wind	Young Guns (Go For It)
(with Elton John)	Wake Me Up Before You
Credit Card Baby	Go-Go
Like A Baby	I'm Your Man (with Simon
Love Machine	Le Bon and Elton John)

Right: The beginning of George Michael's incredibly successful solo career.

At the height of their career as the world's most successful pop duo, George Michael and Andrew Ridgeley – aka Wham! – staged a farewell fling at London's Wembley Stadium on June 28, 1986 in front of a sellout crowd of 73,000.

QUEEN – KNEBWORTH PARK

Chronological set list:

One Vision	Love Of My Life
Tie Your Mother Down	Is This The World We Created?
In the Lap Of The Gods	(You're So Square) Baby
Seven Seas Of Rhye	Hello Mary Lou
Tear It Up	Tutti Frutti
A Kind Of Magic	Bohemian Rhapsody
Vocal improvisation	Hammer To Fall
Under Pressure	Crazy Little Thing Called Love
Another One Bites The Dust	Radio Ga Ga
Who Wants To Live Forever	We Will Rock You
I Want To Break Free	Friends Will Be Friends
Band Jam	We Are The Champions
Brighton Rock solo	God Save The Queen
Now I'm Here	

Queen's Knebworth Park, Hertfordshire concert on August 9, 1986 was the final date of their "Magic Tour", which saw them supported by Belouis Some and Status Quo. Tickets cost £14.95 in advance or £16.00 on the day. At the time no one knew that it would be the band's last hurrah in its original lineup: lead singer, Freddie Mercury was subsequently diagnosed with AIDS the following spring.

NIRVANA – TERMINAL EINS

Chronological set list:

My Best Friend's Girl	Pennyroyal Tea
Moving In Stereo jam	School
Radio Friendly Unit Shifter	Polly [acoustic]
Drain You	Very Ape
Breed	Lounge Act
Serve The Servants	Rape Me
Come As You Are [aborted	Territorial Pissings
due to a power failure]	The Man Who Sold The
Come As You Are	World
Sliver	All Apologies
Dumb	On A Plain
In Bloom	Blew
About A Girl	Heart-Shaped Box
Lithium	

'My Best Friend's Girl' and 'Moving In Stereo Jam' were both covers of The Cars songs. 'The Man Who Sold The World' was a version of the David Bowie hit.

Grunge icons Nirvana were scheduled to play two gigs during a 1994 European tour at Terminal Eins, Flughafen in München-Riem, Germany – but only the first was performed – and it would prove to be their last-ever concert. Frontman Kurt Cobain committed suicide four weeks later.

CHARITABLE DEEDS

Over the past 40 years rock music and charitable fundraising – especially for emergency relief efforts for tragedies around the world – have become close cousins. While the high watermark may be Bob Geldof's historic Band Aid/Live Aid initiatives in the mid-eighties, the first major music event staged to raise awareness and money for a worthwhile cause was the George Harrison-conceived Concert For Bangla Desh. The most recent example of musicians on both sides of the Atlantic stepping up for a worthy cause was to raise funds for victims of the tragic Haiti earthquake in January 2010.

THE CONCERT FOR BANGLA DESH

With two shows held on one day at New York's Madison Square Garden on Sunday, August 1, 1971, The Concert For Bangla Desh was organized by ex-Beatle George Harrison after a personal plea for help from his musician friend Ravi Shankar to aid victims of famine and war in Bangla Desh. The lineup included Harrison, Eric Clapton, Bob Dylan (in his only major live appearance of the year), Billy Preston, Leon Russell, Ringo Starr and Shankar, with musical backing from Badfinger, Jesse Ed Davis, Jim Horn, Jim Keltner, Don Nix and Carl Radle. Due to legal problems, the proceeds from what was the largest benefit concert staged to date were frozen with Harrison writing his own cheque to maintain the fund. The unique event was filmed for posterity and recorded for subsequent release, its triple album boxed set hitting US Number 2 and UK Number 1 the following year.

THE FEATURED SINGERS ON BAND AID'S 'DO THEY KNOW IT'S CHRISTMAS?'

Taped on November 25, 1984 at SARM West Studios in Notting Hill, West London, the historic Band Aid recording assembled by Bob Geldof and Midge Ure featured 47 invited musicians. However, only the following were given "lead" vocal roles:

Paul Young • Boy George • George Michael • Simon LeBon • Sting • Tony Hadley • Bono • Paul Weller • Glenn Gregory • Midge Ure

LIVE AID

LIVE AID PERFORMERS AT LONDON'S WEMBLEY STADIUM
Status Quo • The Style Council • The Boomtown Rats • Adam Ant • Ultravox • Spandau Ballet • Elvis Costello • Nik Kershaw • Sade • Sting & Phil Collins • Howard Jones • Bryan Ferry • Paul Young • U2 • Dire Straits • Queen • David Bowie • The Who • Elton John • Freddie Mercury & Brian May • Paul McCartney • Band Aid

LIVE AID PERFORMERS AT PHILADELPHIA'S JFK STADIUM
Joan Baez • The Hooters • The Four Tops • Billy Ocean • Black Sabbath • Run-DMC • Rick Springfield • REO Speedwagon • Crosby, Stills & Nash • Judas Priest • Bryan Adams • The Beach Boys • George Thorogood & the Destroyers • Simple Minds • The Pretenders • Santana & Pat Metheny • Ashford & Simpson • Madonna • Tom Petty & the Heartbreakers • Kenny Loggins • The Cars • Neil Young • Power Station • Thompson Twins • Eric Clapton • Phil Collins • Led Zeppelin • Crosby, Stills, Nash & Young • Duran Duran • Patti LaBelle • Hall & Oates • Mick Jagger • Bob Dylan, Keith Richards & Ronnie Wood • USA for Africa

Below: Bob Geldof leads an all-star lineup at "Live Aid" in 1985.

On Saturday, July 13, 1985 at 12.01 p. m., Status Quo opened the "Live Aid" benefit concert extravaganza with 'Rockin' All Over The World', organized once again by Bob Geldof and Midge Ure, helped by legendary rock promoters Harvey Goldsmith and Bill Graham, as a follow-up to the Band Aid project. Switching alternately between joint venues – Wembley Stadium in London, in the presence of the Prince and Princess of Wales, and the JFK Stadium in Philadelphia – the world's biggest rock acts participated in a global fundraising effort which raised some $70 million.

Left: Kim Carnes, Michael Jackson and Diana Ross share a smile on the video of 'We Are The World'.

THE FEATURED SINGERS ON USA FOR AFRICA'S 'WE ARE THE WORLD'

Lionel Richie • Stevie Wonder • Paul Simon • Kenny Rogers • James Ingram • Tina Turner • Billy Joel • Michael Jackson • Diana Ross • Dionne Warwick • Willie Nelson • Al Jarreau • Bruce Springsteen • Kenny Loggins • Steve Perry • Daryl Hall • Huey Lewis • Cyndi Lauper • Kim Carnes • Bob Dylan • Ray Charles

Following the Los Angeles-held American Music Awards celebrations on January 28, 1985, at 10:00 p.m., 46 top recording artists arrived at the A&M Studios in Hollywood, greeted by a warning notice from producer Quincy Jones to "check your egos at the door." They were there at the behest of Jones, Harry Belafonte (inspired by the efforts of Bob Geldof's Band Aid single) and Ken Kragen (Kenny Rogers' manager). They recorded 'We Are The World'.

HOPE FOR HAITI NOW – BEST-SELLING DOWNLOADS

Here are the ten bestsellers:

1	Hallelujah	Justin Timberlake, Matt Morris and Charlie Sexton
2	Stranded	Jay-Z, Bono and Rihanna
3	Lean On Me	Sheryl Crow, Kid Rock and Keith Urban
4	Breathless	Taylor Swift
5	Let It Be	Jennifer Hudson, the Roots
6	A Message 2010	Coldplay
7	Halo	Beyoncé and Chris Martin
8	Lift Me Up	Christina Aguilera
9	I'll Stand By You	Shakira and the Roots
10	Like A Prayer	Madonna

In their first week on sale, the 19 tracks made available collectively sold 792,000 copies.

All of the performances from the "Hope For Haiti Now – A Global Benefit for Earthquake Relief" live telethon organized by actor, George Clooney and MTV on January 22, 2010 were immediately released as individual digital download tracks the following day.

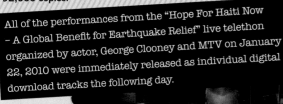

Right: Model Molly Sims, Ricky Martin and Justin Timberlake have "Hope For Haiti Now".

HELPING HAITI

Performers in order of appearance:

Leona Lewis • Rod Stewart • Mariah Carey • Cheryl Cole • Mika • Michael Bublé • Joe McElderry • Miley Cyrus • James Blunt • Gary Barlow (Take That) • Mark Owen (Take That) • Jon Bon Jovi • James Morrison • Alexandra Burke • Susan Boyle • Aston Merrygold (JLS) • Marvin Humes (JLS) • Shane Filan (Westlife) • Mark Feehily (Westlife) • Kylie Minogue • Robbie Williams

In January 2010, and at the request of British Prime Minister Gordon Brown, pop impresario Simon Cowell arranged to assemble an all-star cast to record a charity single for the relief effort in Haiti following its devastating earthquake. Cowell chose the R.E.M. ballad, 'Everybody Hurts'. The recording was first aired on February 2, 2010 and released online and to retail on February 7. Proceeds were divided between the *Sun* newspaper's Helping Haiti fund and the Disasters Emergency Committee.

THE FEATURED SINGERS ON 'WE ARE THE WORLD 25' FOR HAITI

Akon • Bono • India.Arie • Patti Austin • Tony Bennett • Justin Bieber • Bizzy Bone (Bone Thugs-N-Harmony) • Ethan Bortnick • Brandy • Jeff Bridges • Toni Braxton • Zac Brown • Kristian Bush • Natalie Cole • Harry Connick Jr. • Kid Cudi • Miley Cyrus • Céline Dion • Snoop Dogg • Drake • Earth Wind & Fire • Faith Evans • Melanie Fiona • Jamie Foxx • Sean Garrett • Tyrese Gibson • Josh Groban • Anthony Hamilton • Keri Hilson • Julianne Hough • Jennifer Hudson • Enrique Iglesias • LL Cool J • Janet Jackson • Randy Jackson • Taj Jackson • Taryll Jackson • TJ Jackson • Al Jardine • Joe Jonas • Kevin Jonas • Nick Jonas • Rashida Jones • Gladys Knight • Adam Levine • Jimmy Jean-Louis • Benji Madden • Joel Madden • Mary Mary • Katharine McPhee • Jason Mraz • Mya • Jennifer Nettles • Orianthi • Freda Payne • P!nk • A.R. Rahman • Nicole Richie • Raphael Saadiq • Carlos Santana • Nicole Scherzinger • Isaac Slade • Trey Songz • Musiq Soulchild • Jordin Sparks • Barbra Streisand • T-Pain • Robin Thicke • Rob Thomas • Usher • Vince Vaughn • Lil Wayne • Kanye West • will.i.am • Ann Wilson • Brian Wilson • Nancy Wilson • BeBe Winans

Officially released as 'We Are The World 25 For Haiti', Quincy Jones and Lionel Richie reprised their historic efforts from 25 years earlier by assembling a new cast of A-list musicians for an updated version recorded on February 1, 2010. More than 70 artists participated during a marathon 14-hour session. Its accompanying video premiered on February 12 during coverage of the opening ceremony of the 2010 Winter Olympics.

MTV MUSIC TELEVISION

LIVE 8

On May 31, 2005 – some twenty years after "Live Aid" – organizers Bob Geldof and Midge Ure announced the upcoming "Live 8" event: an ambitious plan to simultaneously stage ten concerts around the world on one day, July 2 - to raise awareness (not money) in support of the "Make Poverty History" campaign, and in advance of the July 6 G8 Conference political/business gathering in Scotland.

HYDE PARK, LONDON, ENGLAND

The African Children's Choir • Annie Lennox • Bob Geldof • Coldplay • Dido • Elton John • Joss Stone • Keane • The Killers • Madonna • Mariah Carey • Ms. Dynamite • Paul McCartney • Pink Floyd • Razorlight • R.E.M. • Robbie Williams • Scissor Sisters • Snoop Dogg • Snow Patrol • Stereophonics • Sting • Travis • U2 • UB40 • Velvet Revolver • The Who

Above: The Who rock Hyde Park, London.

PALAIS DE VERSAILLES, FRANCE

Andrea Bocelli with the Philarmonie der Nationen • Amel Bent • Axelle Red • Calogero • Cerrone and Nile Rodgers • Craig David • The Cure • David Hallyday • Diam's • Dido • Disiz La Peste • Faudel • Florent Pagny • Kool Shen • Kyo • Louis Bertignac • Matt Copora • Muse • Placebo • Raphael • Shakira • Sheryl Crow • Tina Arena • Yannick Noah • Youssou N'Dour

SIEGESSAULE, BERLIN, GERMANY

A-ha • Audioslave • Bap • Brian Wilson • Chris de Burgh • Crosby Stills & Nash • Die Toten Hosen • Faithless • Green Day • Herbert Grönemeyer • Joana Zimmer • Juan Diego Florez • Juli • Katherine Jenkins • Reamonn • Renee Olstead • Roxy Music • Sasha • Silbermond • Soehne Mannheims • Wir Sind Helden

CIRCUS MAXIMUS, ROME, ITALY

Antonello Venditti • Articolo 31 • Biagio Antonacci • Claudio Baglioni • Duran Duran • Elisa • Faith Hill • Francesco De Gregori • Gemelli Diversi • Irene Grandi • Jovanotti • Laura Pausini • Le Vibrazioni • Ligabue • Max Pezzali • Negramaro • Negrita • Nek • Noa • Piero Pelu • Pino Daniele • Povia • Renato Zero • Tim McGraw • Tiromancino • Velvet

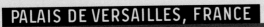

Right: Green Day make some noise in Berlin.

MUSEUM OF ART, PHILADELPHIA, US

Alicia Keys • The Black Eyed Peas • Bon Jovi • Dave Matthews Band • Def Leppard • Destiny's Child • Jay-Z • Josh Groban • The Kaiser Chiefs • Keith Urban • Linkin Park • Maroon 5 • P. Diddy • Rob Thomas • Sarah McLachlan • Stevie Wonder • Toby Keith

Left: The Black Eyed Peas get the party started in Philadelphia.

PARK PLACE, BARRIE, CANADA

The African Guitar Summit • Barenaked Ladies • Blue Rodeo • Bruce Cockburn • Bryan Adams • The Bachman Cummings Band • Deep Purple • DMC • DobaCaracol featuring K'naan • Gordon Lightfoot • Great Big Sea • Jann Arden • Jet • Les Trois Accords • Mötley Crüe • Our Lady Peace • Sam Roberts • Simple Plan • Tegan & Sara • The Tragically Hip • Tom Cochrane

MAKUHARI MESSE, TOKYO, JAPAN

Björk • Def Tech • Dreams Come True • Good Charlotte • McFly • Rize

MARY FITZGERALD SQUARE, NEWTOWN, JOHANNESBURG, SOUTH AFRICA

4Peace Ensemble • Jabu Khanyile and Bayete • Lindiwe • Lucky Dube • Mahotella Queens • Malaika • Orchestre Baobab • Oumou Sengare • Vusi Mahlasela • Zola

RED SQUARE, MOSCOW, RUSSIA

Agata Kristy • Aliona Sviridova • B-2 • Delphin • Garik Sukachev • Jungo • Linda • Moral Code X • Pet Shop Boys • The Red Elvises

EDEN PROJECT, ST. BLAZEY, CORNWALL, ENGLAND

Ayub Ogada & Uno • Mariza • Thomas Mapfumo & the Blacks Unlimited • Coco Mbassi • Modou Diouf & O Fogum • Youssou N'Dour & Le Super Étoile de Dakar • Geoffrey Oryema • Angelique Kidjo • Tinariwen • Kanda Bongo Man • Daara J • Chartwell Dutiro • Maryam Mursal • Siyaya • Emmanuel Jal • Coco Mbassi • Ayub Ogada • Chartwell Dutiro • Frititi • Akim El Sikameya

Organized by Peter Gabriel, the tenth Live 8 event was also known as "Live 8 Africa Calling", and featured top World Music artists from that continent.

Above: Björk in Tokyo.

Left: Sting in London.

SONGS PERFORMED AT BOTH LIVE AID AND LIVE 8

Title	Live Aid	Live 8
Message In A Bottle	Sting	Sting
Driven To Tears	Sting	Sting
Every Breath You Take	Sting & Phil Collins	Sting
Good Vibrations	The Beach Boys	Brian Wilson
Jealous Guy	Bryan Ferry	Roxy Music
I Don't Like Mondays	Boomtown Rats	Bob Geldof
Rat Trap	Boomtown Rats	Bob Geldof
Rockin' All Over The World	Status Quo	Coldplay
Save A Prayer	Duran Duran	Duran Duran
Tears Are Not Enough	Bryan Adams	Bryan Adams
Vienna	Ultravox	Midge Ure
We Are The Champions	Queen	Green Day
We Will Rock You	Queen	Robbie Williams
Won't Get Fooled Again	The Who	The Who

EDINBURGH 50,000 – THE FINAL PUSH, JULY 6 2005

Hosted by Lenny Henry, the performers and presenters were:

The Proclaimers • Jamie Cullum • Natasha Bedingfield • Wet Wet Wet • Davina McCall • Peter Kay • McFly • Eddie Izzard • Giant Leap featuring Will Young, Maxi Jazz, Neneh Cherry • Geoffrey Oryema and Mahotella Queens • Sugababes • Bono • Nelson Mandela (a spoken prerecorded message from South Africa) • George Clooney • Annie Lennox • Coumi Nidu (Action Against Poverty) • Susan Sarandon (presenter) • Bob Geldof and Campino • The Thrills • Claudia Schiffer and Herbert Grönemeyer • Midge Ure • Chris Evans • Feeder • Wangari Maathai (presenter) • Youssou N'Dour and Neneh Cherry • Embrace • Beverley Knight • Texas • Katherine Jenkins • Snow Patrol • Ronan Keating • Travis • The Corrs • James Brown

An eleventh concert, "Edinburgh 50,000 – The Final Push", took place at Murrayfield Stadium in the Scottish capital four days later on July 6, the closest location to the G8 summit, which began that day.

Although a smattering of nascent music awards ceremonies preceded it (notably the British songwriters' Ivor Novello Awards in 1955), the Grammy Awards was the first major event established to recognise excellence in popular music. On May 28, 1957 the National Academy of Recording Arts and Sciences (NARAS) was established in Los Angeles by a group of five label executives who recognised the need to create an organization that would represent creative people engaged in the business of making music – and put on an awards show which became the Grammys.

THE GRAMMY AWARDS

The first Grammy Awards took place on May 4, 1959 in the Grand Ballroom of the Beverly Hilton Hotel. With 500 music industry attendees paying $15 each for dinner, winners included Domenico Modugno's 'Nel Blu Dipinto Di Blu' ('Volare') (Record of the Year and Song of the Year) and Henry Mancini's *The Music From Peter Gunn* (Album of the Year).

BEST NEW ARTIST
WINNERS OF THE 1960S

1960	Bobby Darin
1961	Bob Newhart
1962	Peter Nero
1963	Robert Goulet
1964	The Swingle Singers
1965	The Beatles
1966	Tom Jones
1967	No award
1968	Bobbie Gentry
1969	Jose Feliciano

BEST NEW ARTIST
WINNERS OF THE 1970S

A Taste Of Honey – who only scored two top 10 US hits including the disco novelty 'Boogie Oogie Oogie' – beat out the following Best New Artist nominees in 1979: The Cars, Elvis Costello, Toto and Chris Rea.

BEST NEW ARTIST
WINNERS OF THE 1980S

1980	Rickie Lee Jones
1981	Christopher Cross
1982	Sheena Easton
1983	Men At Work
1984	Culture Club
1985	Cyndi Lauper
1986	Sade
1987	Bruce Hornsby & the Range
1988	Jody Watley
1989	Tracy Chapman

1960 marked the first year that the Best New Artist category was added to the Grammy Awards.

Left: Judy Holliday with Peter Nero.

Right: Christopher Cross.

Singer-songwriter Christopher Cross' self-titled debut album garnered five Grammys at the 1981 ceremony including Best New Artist. Despite recording several similarly harmonic follow-up albums, Cross failed to receive any further Grammy nods.

BEST NEW ARTIST
WINNERS OF THE 1990S

1990	Milli Vanilli
1991	Mariah Carey
1992	Marc Cohn
1993	Arrested Development
1994	Toni Braxton
1995	Sheryl Crow
1996	Hootie & the Blowfish
1997	LeAnn Rimes
1998	Paula Cole
1999	Lauryn Hill

Of all the Grammy controversies over the years, none has surpassed the Best New Artist Award given to Milli Vanilli in 1990. The honour was revoked when it was revealed on November 16, 1990 that the pop/dance duo of Fab Morvan and Rob Pilatus were not the singers used by producer Frank Farian on their recordings.

BEST NEW ARTIST
WINNERS OF THE 2000S

2000	Christina Aguilera
2001	Shelby Lynne
2002	Alicia Keys
2003	Norah Jones
2004	Evanescence
2005	Maroon 5
2006	John Legend
2007	Carrie Underwood
2008	Amy Winehouse
2009	Adele
2010	The Zac Brown Band

Below: Christina Aguilera.

Left: Lauryn Hill.   Above: Amy Winehouse.

HIGHEST GRAMMY AWARDS
US TV RATINGS 2000-10

Audience totals in millions. The highest-ever rating was 51.7 million in 1984 when Michael Jackson's *Thriller* dominated the event.

HAL BLAINE'S RECORD-BREAKING GRAMMY STREAK

Legendary session drummer Hal Blaine performed on six consecutive recordings that won the Record of the Year category at the Grammy Awards:

Herb Alpert & the Tijuana Brass' A Taste of Honey	1966
Frank Sinatra's Strangers in the Night	1967
The 5th Dimension's Up, Up and Away	1968
Simon & Garfunkel's Mrs. Robinson	1969
The 5th Dimension's Aquarius/Let the Sunshine In	1970
Simon & Garfunkel's Bridge Over Troubled Water	1971

Above: Hal Blaine.

MTV
MUSIC TELEVISION

ARTISTS WITH MOST WINS

Artist	Wins	Artist	Wins
Georg Solti	31	Eric Clapton	17
Quincy Jones	27	Michael Jackson	17
Alison Krauss	27	Al Schmitt	17
U2	22	Leonard Bernstein	16
Stevie Wonder	22	Beyoncé	16
Vince Gill	20	Michael Brecker	16
Henry Mancini	20	Chick Corea	16
Bruce Springsteen	20	David Foster	16
Aretha Franklin	18	B.B. King	16
Pat Metheny	18	Yo-Yo Ma	16
Jimmy Sturr	18	Sting	16
Ray Charles	17		

Although contemporary music artists dominate the rest of the most-honoured list, Hungarian/British classical music conductor Sir Georg Solti holds the all-time record. The Beatles only won eight Grammys during their career (and another five since 1972).

MOST WINS BY GROUPS

Group	Wins	Group	Wins
U2	22	The Eagles	7
Dixie Chicks	18	Foo Fighters	7
The Beatles	13	OutKast	7
Metallica	10	Police	7
Santana	9	Red Hot Chili Peppers	7
Coldplay	8	The Black Eyed Peas	7

MOST WINS BY PRODUCERS

Producer	Wins	Producer	Wins
Quincy Jones	27	Arif Mardin	11
David Foster	15	Babyface	10
Phil Ramone	13	T-Bone Burnett	10

Producer icon Quincy Jones has been nominated for a staggering 79 Grammys over his unique career, more than twice of any other nominee.

Above: Michael Jackson celebrates with Quincy Jones.
Right: Robert Plant and Alison Krauss.

MOST WINS BY MALE ARTISTS

Michael Jackson and Carlos Santana share the honour for the most number of Grammys won in a single night – eight.

Above: Stevie Wonder with Helen Reddy and Alice Cooper.

MOST WINS BY FEMALE ARTISTS

Artist	Wins	Artist	Wins
Alison Krauss	27	Linda Ronstadt	10
Aretha Franklin	18	Mary J. Blige	9
Beyoncé	16	Sheryl Crow	9
Ella Fitzgerald	13	Norah Jones	9
Emmylou Harris	12	Madonna	9
Alicia Keys	12	Barbra Streisand	9
Chaka Khan	10		

Beyoncé holds the record for the most number of trophies lifted in one night by a female artist – six, all nabbed at the 2010 Awards.

MOST NUMBER OF GRAMMY NOMINATIONS WITHOUT A WIN

Brian McKnight	16	Tori Amos	8
Joe Satriani	15	Avril Lavigne	8
Björk	13	Megadeth	8
Snoop Dogg	12	*NSync	8
Vanessa Williams	11	Alice In Chains	7
Alan Parsons	10		

Smooth R&B crooner, Brian McKnight's biggest US hit was his number three-peaking duet, 'Love Is', with Vanessa Williams.

Left: Grammy-nominated Brian McKnight.

RECORD OF THE YEAR – 2000S

2000	Smooth	Santana featuring Rob Thomas
2001	Beautiful Day	U2
2002	Walk On	U2
2003	Don't Know Why	Norah Jones
2004	Clocks	Coldplay
2005	Here We Go Again	Ray Charles & Norah Jones
2006	Boulevard Of Dreams	Green Day
2007	Not Ready To Make Nice	The Dixie Chicks
2008	Rehab	Amy Winehouse
2009	Please Read The Letter	Alison Krauss & Robert Plant
2010	Use Somebody	Kings of Leon

A popular collaboration between its co-writer, Rob Thomas (Matchbox Twenty's lead singer) and rock guitar veteran Carlos Santana, Smooth's video featured slinky dancing by Thomas' wife, Marisol.

THE GRAMMY LEGEND AWARD

Andrew Lloyd Webber	1990	Barbra Streisand	1992
Liza Minnelli	1990	Michael Jackson	1993
Willie Nelson	1990	Curtis Mayfield	1994
Smokey Robinson	1990	Frank Sinatra	1994
Johnny Cash	1991	Luciano Pavarotti	1998
Aretha Franklin	1991	Elton John	1999
Billy Joel	1991	The Bee Gees	2003
Quincy Jones	1991		

Also known as the Grammy Living Legend Award, this prestigious honour has only been handed out intermittently since its introduction in 2000.

Left: Norah Jones cleaned up at the 2003 Grammys.

ALBUM OF THE YEAR – 2000S

2000	Supernatural	Santana
2001	Two Against Nature	Steely Dan
2002	O Brother, Where Art Thou?	Soundtrack
2003	Come Away With Me	Norah Jones
2004	Speakerboxxx/The Love Below	OutKast
2005	Genius Loves Company	Ray Charles & Various Artists
2006	How To Dismantle An Atomic Bomb	U2
2007	Taking The Long Way	The Dixie Chicks
2008	River: The Joni Letters	Herbie Hancock
2009	Raising Sand	Robert Plant & Alison Krauss
2010	Fearless	Taylor Swift

The Album of the Year category often rewards artistic endeavour over commercial success, as evidenced by wins for Steely Dan and Herbie Hancock.

Organized by the British Phonographic Industry (BPI) trade body, the first BRIT Awards – then known as the Britannia Music Awards – were held on October 18, 1977 at the Wembley Conference Centre in London to celebrate the Queen's Silver Jubilee and honour the best in British music since 1952. It was not until 1982, however, that it became an annual event with relevant, annual categories.

THE BEST BRITISH GROUP WINNERS

1982	Police	1996	Oasis
1983	Dire Straits	1997	Manic Street Preachers
1984	Culture Club	1998	Verve
1985	Wham!	1999	Manic Street Preachers
1986	Dire Straits	2000	Travis
1987	Five Star	2001	Coldplay
1988	Pet Shop Boys	2002	Travis
1989	Erasure	2003	Coldplay
1990	The Fine Young Cannibals	2004	Darkness
1991	Cure	2005	Franz Ferdinand
1992	KLF & Simply Red	2006	Kaiser Chiefs
	(joint winners)	2007	Arctic Monkeys
1993	Simply Red	2008	Arctic Monkeys
1994	Stereo MCs	2009	Elbow
1995	Blur	2010	Kasabian

Arguably the most controversial performance by a Best British Group winner was KLF in 1992 during which they fired machine guns – with blank bullets – at the music biz audience. The ever-controversial acid house duo then delivered a dead sheep to attendees at the after-awards party.

Left: A gentrified Arctic Monkeys at the 2008 BRITs.

THE BEST BRITISH SINGLE WINNERS

1982	Tainted Love	Soft Cell
1983	Come On Eileen	Dexy's Midnight Runners
1984	Karma Chameleon	Culture Club
1985	Relax	Frankie Goes To Hollywood
1986	Everybody Wants To Rule The World	Tears For Fears
1987	West End Boys	Pet Shop Boys
1988	Never Gonna Give You Up	Rick Astley
1989	Perfect	Fairground Attraction
1990	Another Day In Paradise	Phil Collins
1991	Enjoy The Silence	Depeche Mode
1992	These Are The Days Of Our Lives	Queen
1993	Could It Be Magic	Take That
1994	Pray	Take That
1995	Parklife	Blur
1996	Back For Good	Take That
1997	Wannabe	Spice Girls
1998	Never Ever	All Saints
1999	Angels	Robbie Williams
2000	She's The One	Robbie Williams
2001	Rock DJ	Robbie Williams
2002	Don't Stop Movin'	S Club 7
2003	Just A Little	Liberty X
2004	White Flag	Dido
2005	Your Game	Will Young
2006	Speed Of Sound	Coldplay
2007	Patience	Take That
2008	Shine	Take That
2009	The Promise	Girls Aloud
2010	Beat Again	JLS

Left: Take That 'Back For Good' in 1996.

Robbie Williams	12	Michael Jackson	6
Annie Lennox	8	Phil Collins	5
Take That	7	Prince	5
U2	7	Oasis	5
Coldplay	6	Arctic Monkeys	5

The totals for Robbie Williams, Annie Lennox (solo and as a member of Eurythmics), U2, Oasis and the Spice Girls have all included the award for Outstanding Contribution to British Music. Lennox has won Best British Female Solo Artist a record six times.

Above: U2's victory performance at the 2001 BRITs.

Above: BRIT-favourite, Robbie Williams.

THE OUTSTANDING CONTRIBUTION TO BRITISH MUSIC

1982	John Lennon	1996	David Bowie
1983	The Beatles	1997	The Bee Gees
1984	George Martin	1998	Fleetwood Mac
1985	The Police	1999	Eurythmics
1986	Elton John	2000	Spice Girls
	Wham!	2001	U2
1987	Eric Clapton	2002	Sting
1988	The Who	2003	Tom Jones
1989	Cliff Richard	2004	Duran Duran
1990	Queen	2005	Bob Geldof
1991	Status Quo	2006	Paul Weller
1992	Freddie Mercury	2007	Oasis
1993	Rod Stewart	2008	Paul McCartney
1994	Van Morrison	2009	The Pet Shop Boys
1995	Elton John	2010	Robbie Williams

Three Irish acts have won the Outstanding Contribution to British Music: Van Morrison, U2 and Bob Geldof.

BRIT AWARD WINNERS 2010

British Female Solo Artist	Lily Allen
British Male Solo Artist	Dizzee Rascal
British Breakthrough Act	JLS
British Group	Kasabian
British Album	Florence + the Machine's *Lungs*
British Single	JLS' Beat Again
British Producer	Paul Epworth
Critics' Choice	Ellie Goulding
BRITS Album of 30 Years	Oasis' '(What's The Story) Morning Glory?'
The BRITs Hits 30	Spice Girls' 'Wannabe/ Who Do You Think You Are?'
International Female Solo Artist	Lady Gaga
International Male Solo Artist	Jay-Z
International Album	Lady Gaga's *The Fame*
International Breakthrough Act	Lady Gaga
Outstanding Contribution Award	Robbie Williams

Robbie Williams celebrated his Outstanding Contribution achievement by performing a medley of hits including 'Angels' and 'Millennium'.

BRITANNIA AWARDS 1977

On October 18, 1977 – a year which marked both the centenary of recorded sound and the Queen's Silver Jubilee – the UK record industry presented a series of awards.

THE AWARDS

Best British Album	The Beatles
Best British Group	The Beatles
Best British Male Singer	Cliff Richard
Best British Female Singer	Shirley Bassey
Best British Male Newcomer	Graham Parker
Best British Female Newcomer	Julie Covington
Best British Single	Procol Harum's 'A Whiter Shade Of Pale' Queen's 'Bohemian Rhapsody'
Best British Album	The Beatles' *Sgt. Pepper's Lonely Hearts Club Band*
Best British Producer	George Martin
Outstanding Contribution	L.G. Wood & The Beatles

THE PERFORMANCES

Cliff Richard's 'Miss You Nights'
George Martin's 'A Hard Day's Night'
Julie Covington's 'Only Women Bleed'
Procol Harum's 'A Whiter Shade Of Pale'
Simon & Garfunkel's 'Old Friends'

A fair number of nominees and winners failed to attend, though onstage performances by those who did show up – notably Simon & Garfunkel and Cliff Richard – provided the event with its highlights.

In addition to the major Grammy and BRIT celebrations held on either side of the Atlantic, more than a dozen other countries hold meaningful annual music celebrations including the Porin Awards (Croatia), the Danish Music Awards (Denmark), the Hungarian Music Awards (Hungary), the Fryderyk (Poland) and the Emma (Finland).

ARIA

The Australian Recording Industry Association (ARIA) Music Awards have been held annually since 1987.

ARIA SINGLE OF THE YEAR

2000	Don't Call Me Baby	Madison Avenue
2001	My Happiness	Powderfinger
2002	Can't Get You Out Of My Head	Kylie Minogue
2003	Born To Try	Delta Goodrem
2004	Are You Gonna Be My Girl	Jet
2005	Catch My Disease	Ben Lee
2006	Black Fingernails, Red Wine	Eskimo Joe
2007	Straight Lines	Silverchair
2008	Sweet About Me	Gabriella Cilmi
2009	Walking On A Dream	Empire of the Sun

Empire of Sun is the electronic duo of Luke Steele and Nick Littlemore. Their 2009 winner, 'Walking On A Dream' was their first release.

ACTS WHO HAVE WON THE MOST ARIAS

Silverchair	21	Crowded House	11
John Farnham	19	Midnight Oil	11
Kylie Minogue	16	You Am I	10
Powderfinger	15	Delta Goodrem	9
Savage Garden	14		

Up to 2009, Aussie alt-rockers Silverchair have been nominated 49 times, ten more than runner-up, John Farnham.

Left: The lovely Delta Goodrem.

ECHO

The ECHO Deutscher Musikpreis began as an annual event in 1992, organized by the German music trade body Deutsche Phono-Academie.

BEST INTERNATIONAL GROUP WINNERS

1992	Queen	2002	Destiny's Child
1993	Genesis	2003	Red Hot Chili
1994	Ace of Base		Peppers
1995	Pink Floyd	2004	Evanescence
1996	The Kelly Family	2005	Green Day
1997	The Fugees	2006	Coldplay
1998	Backstreet Boys	2007	Pussycat Dolls
1999	Lighthouse Family	2008	Nightwish
2000	Buena Vista Social	2009	Coldplay
	Club & Ry Cooder	2010	Depeche Mode
2001	Bon Jovi		

HONORARY LIFETIME ACHIEVEMENT INDUCTEES

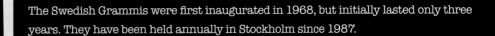

The Swedish Grammis were first inaugurated in 1968, but initially lasted only three years. They have been held annually in Stockholm since 1987.

SONG OF THE YEAR

2000	It Takes a Fool to Remain Sane	The Ark
2001	Come Along	Titiyo
2002	Dom andra	Kent
2003	Här kommer alla känslorna (på en och samma gång)	Per Gessle
2004	Ingen vill veta var du köpt din tröja	Raymond & Maria
2005	Money For Nothing	Darin
2006	7milakliv	Martin Stenmarck
2007	Om du lämnade mig nu	Lars Winnerbäck & Miss Li
2008	Jennie Let Me Love You	E.M.D.
2009	Om du lämnade mig nu	Lars Winnerbäck
2010	Dance With Somebody	Mando Diao

Left: Gustaf Norén of Mando Diao.

Honouring the best in Canadian music, the Juno Awards trace their history back to the Gold Leaf Awards which began in 1970, organized by music magazine, *RPM*.

SINGLE OF THE YEAR

Above: Valerie Poxleitner aka Lights.

NEW ARTIST OF THE YEAR

2003	Avril Lavigne	2007	Tomi Swick
2004	Michael Bublé	2008	Serena Ryder
2005	Feist	2009	Lights
2006	Daniel Powter	2010	Drake

This category replaced the Best New Solo Artist category in 2003.

Left: The phenomenal Michael Bublé.

MUSIC TELEVISION

Honouring achievements in the Irish music industry, The Meteor Ireland Music Awards replaced the trade association-organized IRMA Ireland Music Awards in 2001.

BEST IRISH ALBUM

Above: U2's Adam Clayton.

2001	Westlife	2006	Westlife
2002	Westlife	2007	Westlife
2003	Westlife	2008	Westlife
2004	Westlife	2009	Westlife
2005	Westlife	2010	Westlife

U2's *All That You Can't Leave Behind* did indeed win this category two years running. The country's most beloved band – and biggest musical export – has also won the Meteor Best Band Award four times: 2001–03 and again in 2006.

The first and only global music awards ceremony, the World Music Awards has been staged each year in Monte-Carlo since 1989. Its patron is Albert II, Prince of Monaco.

LIFETIME ACHIEVEMENT AWARD

Barry White • The Bee Gees • Beyoncé • Bon Jovi • Carlos Santana • Céline Dion • Chaka Khan • Cher • Cliff Richard • David Bowie • Deep Purple • Diana Ross • Elton John • George Benson • Gloria Gaynor • Janet Jackson • Julio Iglesias • L.A. Reid • Lionel Richie • Luciano Pavarotti • Madonna • Mariah Carey • Michael Jackson • Placido Domingo • Prince • Ray Charles • Ringo Starr • Rod Stewart • Status Quo • Stevie Wonder • Tina Turner • Tony Bennett • Whitney Houston.

RECIPIENTS OF THE CHOPARD DIAMOND AWARD

This honour is occasionally bestowed at the World Music Awards on artists whose global record sales exceed 100 million copies according to the International Federation of the Phonographic Industry. To date, only six acts have been crowned.

The American Music Awards is a major annual event produced by Dick Clark Productions since 1973 as a populist rival to the Grammy Awards.

AMERICAN MUSIC AWARD WINNERS 2009

Artist of the Year	Taylor Swift
Breakthrough Artist	Gloriana
International Artist	Whitney Houston
Favorite Pop/Rock Male Artist	Michael Jackson
Favorite Pop/Rock Female Artist	Taylor Swift
Favorite Pop/Rock Band, Duo or Group	Black Eyed Peas
Favorite Pop/Rock Album	*Number Ones: Michael Jackson*
Favorite Rap/Hip-Hop Male Artist	Jay-Z
Favorite Soundtrack	Twilight
Favorite Alternative Rock Artist	Kings of Leon

Right : American favourites, The Black Eyed Peas.

Inaugurated in 2000, the Latin Grammys were the first genre spin-off awards show from the main Grammys, a stand-alone event first held at the Staples Center in Los Angeles.

RECORD OF THE YEAR

Left: Alejandro Cruz.

Perennial winner Spanish singer-songwriter Alejandro Sanz has won 14 Latin Grammys, trailing only Colombian-born rocker Juanes, who has lifted 17 trophies. Christina Aguilera was the first American-born winner.

SOUL TRAIN MUSIC AWARDS

The *Soul Train* Music Awards' most prestigious honour is the occasional Quincy Jones Award For Outstanding Career Achievements, which was first bestowed in 1998.

QUINCY JONES AWARD FOR OUTSTANDING CAREER ACHIEVEMENTS

1998	Whitney Houston	2003	LL Cool J,	2005	Ice Cube
1999	Luther Vandross		Mariah Carey	2006	Jamie Foxx,
2001	The Isley Brothers	2004	Janet Jackson,		Destiny's Child
2002	O'Jays		R. Kelly	2007	Jermaine Dupri

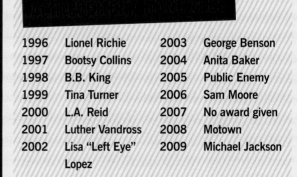

Right: Mariah Carey's outstanding achievements were acknowledged in 2003.

MOBO

The Music of Black Origin Awards (MOBO) were established by TV presenter Andy Ruffell and entrepreneur Kanya King in London in 1996.

BEST SINGLE

Left: British singer and rapper, Estelle.

2000	Fill Me In	Craig David
2001	Independent Women Part 1	Destiny's Child
2002	It Takes More	Ms Dynamite
2003	In Da Club	50 Cent
2004	Thank You	Jamelia
2005	Pow (Forward)	Lethal Bizzle
2006	Deja Vu	Beyoncé featuring Jay-Z
2007	Because Of You	Ne-Yo
2008	Dance Wiv Me	Estelle
2009	Beat Again	JLS

MOBO LIFETIME ACHIEVEMENT HONOURS

1996	Lionel Richie	2003	George Benson
1997	Bootsy Collins	2004	Anita Baker
1998	B.B. King	2005	Public Enemy
1999	Tina Turner	2006	Sam Moore
2000	L.A. Reid	2007	No award given
2001	Luther Vandross	2008	Motown
2002	Lisa "Left Eye" Lopez	2009	Michael Jackson

MTV
MUSIC TELEVISION

Beginning in 1991, the National Academy of Recording Arts and Sciences (NARAS) – the organization behind the Grammys – has honoured one iconic musician for his/her contributions to philanthropy and social causes. The accompanying high-ticket dinner ceremony – held just before the Grammy Awards – also raises funds for NARAS' nonprofit healthcare body, MusiCares.

Right: Neil Young's musical career spans 50 years.

MUSICARES PERSON OF THE YEAR

1991	David Crosby	1998	Luciano	2004	Sting
1992	Bonnie Raitt		Pavarotti	2005	Brian Wilson
1993	Natalie Cole	1999	Stevie Wonder	2006	James Taylor
1994	Gloria Estefan	2000	Elton John	2007	Don Henley
1995	Tony Bennett	2001	Paul Simon	2008	Aretha Franklin
1996	Quincy Jones	2002	Billy Joel	2009	Neil Diamond
1997	Phil Collins	2003	Bono	2010	Neil Young

Q AWARDS

Devised as a "serious music lovers'" alternative to the more mainstream BRITs, the annual Q Awards – often raucous and celebrity-packed – were created in Britain in 1990 by revered rock magazine, Q. Here are the winners in the major categories since 2000.

BEST ACT IN THE WORLD TODAY

2000	Travis	2005	Coldplay
2001	Radiohead	2006	Oasis
2002	Coldplay	2007	Arctic Monkeys
2003	Radiohead	2008	Coldplay
2004	Red Hot Chili Peppers	2009	Muse

Right: Kasbian's frontman Tom Meighan.

BEST ALBUM

2000	Parachutes	Coldplay
2001	The Invisible Band	Travis
2002	A Rush Of Blood To The Head	Coldplay
2003	Think Tank	Blur
2004	Hope and Fears	Keane
2005	Don't Believe The Truth	Oasis
2006	Whatever People Say I Am, That's What I'm Not	Arctic Monkeys
2007	Back To Black	Amy Winehouse
2008	Viva La Vida Or Death And All His Friends	Coldplay
2009	West Ryder Pauper Lunatic Asylum	Kasabian

Below: The iconic Sir Paul McCartney.

Q ICON

2000	Joe Strummer (known as the Q Inspiration Award)
2001	Brian Eno (Q Special Award)
2002	Depeche Mode (known as the Q Special Award)
2003	Jane's Addiction
2004	U2
2005	Jimmy Page
2006	Jeff Lynne
2007	Paul McCartney
2008	Adam Ant
2009	Marianne Faithfull

The Mercury Prize (originally known as the Mercury Music Prize) was established in 1992 by the British Phonographic Industry (BPI) and the British Association of Record Dealers (BARD) as an alternative to the annual BRIT Awards – and makes only one award, for the best British album of the year. In the words of the organizers, the prize exists "solely to champion music in the UK." Each July, 12 albums are nominated, chosen by a panel of music industry figures, from musicians to journalists to executives. The winner is announced in September.

THE WINNERS

1992	Screamadelica	Primal Scream
1993	Suede	Suede
1994	Elegant Slumming	M People
1995	Dummy	Portishead
1996	Different Class	Pulp
1997	New Forms	Roni Size/Reprazent
1998	Bring It On	Gomez
1999	OK	Talvin Singh
2000	The Hour Of Bewilderbeast	Badly Drawn Boy
2001	Stories From The City, Stories From The Sea	PJ Harvey
2002	A Little Deeper	Ms. Dynamite
2003	Boy In Da Corner	Dizzee Rascal
2004	Franz Ferdinand	Franz Ferdinand
2005	I Am A Bird Now	Antony & the Johnsons
2006	Whatever People Say I Am, That's What I'm Not	Arctic Monkeys
2007	Myths Of The Near Future	The Klaxons
2008	The Seldom Seen Kid	Elbow
2009	Speech Therapy	Speech Debelle

Above: Pulp take the Mercury Prize in 1996.

Between them, the 18 winners have only managed a combined 17 chart albums since their win. Radiohead has been nominated four times, but never managed to win.

The Polar Music Prize was created by the late Stig "Stikkan" Anderson, the manager, publisher and co-lyricist for Abba. Bowing in 1989 and presented in Sweden by the royal family, its name is derived from Anderson's record label, Polar Records.

THE LAUREATES

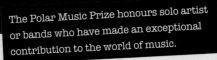

The Polar Music Prize honours solo artist or bands who have made an exceptional contribution to the world of music.

Right: Polar Music Prize winner Peter Gabriel in 2009.

THE ROCK AND ROLL HALL OF FAME

The Rock and Roll Hall of Fame Foundation was formed in the United States in 1983 by leading music industry figures including *Rolling Stone* publisher Jann Wenner, Sire Records boss Seymour Stein and Atlantic Records co-founder Ahmet Ertegun.

Right: Chuck Berry entered the Hall of Fame in 1986.

1986

Chuck Berry • James Brown • Ray Charles • Sam Cooke • Fats Domino • The Everly Brothers • Buddy Holly • Jerry Lee Lewis • Little Richard • Elvis Presley

With votes cast by a select number of music industry executives, rock critics and musicians, eligibility for induction into the Hall of Fame requires a 25-year period to have passed since an act released its first recording.

1987

1988

The Beach Boys • The Beatles • The Drifters • Bob Dylan • The Supremes

1989

Dion • Otis Redding • The Rolling Stones • The Temptations • Stevie Wonder

1990

1991

LaVern Baker • The Byrds • John Lee Hooker • The Impressions • Wilson Pickett • Jimmy Reed • Ike & Tina Turner

1992

Bobby "Blue" Bland • Booker T. & the M.G.s • Johnny Cash • The Isley Brothers • The Jimi Hendrix Experience • Sam & Dave

1993

Ruth Brown • Cream • Creedence Clearwater Revival • The Doors • Frankie Lymon & the Teenagers • Etta James • Van Morrison • Sly & the Family Stone

1994

The Animals • The Band • Duane Eddy • The Grateful Dead • Elton John • John Lennon • Bob Marley • Rod Stewart

1995

THE MUSEUM

In addition to annually honouring rock legends, the Foundation also raised funds to build a permanent *Rock and Roll Hall of Fame* Museum. It finally opened its doors on September 2, 1995, on the shores of Lake Erie in Cleveland, Ohio, the broadcast home of pioneering 50s rock 'n' roll deejay, Alan 'Moondog' Freed.

1996

David Bowie • Gladys Knight & the Pips • Jefferson Airplane • Little Willie John • Pink Floyd • The Shirelles • The Velvet Underground

Left: The Byrds in 1991.

1997

The Bee Gees • Buffalo Springfield • Crosby, Stills & Nash • The Jackson 5 • Joni Mitchell • Parliament/Funkadelic • The Rascals

1998

The Eagles • Fleetwood Mac • The Mamas & the Papas • Lloyd Price • Santana • Gene Vincent

1999

Billy Joel • Curtis Mayfield • Paul McCartney • Del Shannon • Dusty Springfield • Bruce Springsteen • The Staple Singers

2000

With this year's solo honour, Eric Clapton became the first musician to be welcomed into the *Rock and Roll Hall of Fame* for three separate bodies of work – previously inducted as a member of Cream and the Yardbirds.

2001

Aerosmith • Solomon Burke • The Flamingos • Michael Jackson • Queen • Paul Simon • Steely Dan • Ritchie Valens

2002

Isaac Hayes • Brenda Lee • Tom Petty & the Heartbreakers • Gene Pitney • The Ramones • Talking Heads

2003

AC/DC • The Clash • Elvis Costello & the Attractions • The Police • The Righteous Brothers

2004

Jackson Browne • The Dells • George Harrison • Prince • Bob Seger • Traffic • ZZ Top

2005

2006

Black Sabbath • Blondie • Miles Davis • Lynyrd Skynyrd • The Sex Pistols

Left: Grandmaster Flash & the Furious Five with Jay-Z in 2007.

2007

Grandmaster Flash & the Furious Five • R.E.M. • The Ronettes • Patti Smith • Van Halen

Rap pioneers Grandmaster Flash & the Furious Five – led by Barbados-born DJ Joseph Saddler – became the first hip-hop act to be inducted.

2008

2009

Jeff Beck • Little Anthony & the Imperials • Metallica • Run-DMC • Bobby Womack

25TH ANNIVERSARY CONCERTS

On October 29 and 30, 2009, the *Rock and Roll Hall of Fame* held two marathon concerts at New York's Madison Square Garden to celebrate its 25th anniversary. Performers included Paul Simon, Bruce Springsteen, Jeff Beck, Aretha Franklin, Stevie Wonder, Sting, U2, Patti Smith, Bruce Springsteen & the E Street Band, John Fogerty, Darlene Love, Tom Morello, Sam Moore, Jackson Browne, Peter Wolf, Billy Joel, Simon & Garfunkel, Metallica, Fergie, Lou Reed, Ray Davies, Ozzy Osbourne, Crosby, Stills & Nash and Mick Jagger.

2010

Abba • Genesis • Jimmy Cliff • The Hollies • The Stooges

Of the 169 inductees over its 25-year history, the preponderance have been American. There have been 33 British inductees, three Canadian, two Jamaican and one each from Australia, Ireland and Sweden.

MTV
MUSIC TELEVISION™

Many music genres (mostly based in the States) have begun their own Hall of Fame, including the Country Music Hall of Fame, the Gospel Music Hall of Fame and the Blues Hall of Fame – even those for Polka, Bluegrass, Jazz and Rockabilly.

ARIA HALL OF FAME

1988	AC/DC • Joan Sutherland • Johnny O'Keefe • Slim Dusty • Col Joye • Harry Vanda & George Young
1989	Ross Wilson • Nellie Melba,
1990	Percy Grainger • Sherbet
1991	Billy Thorpe • Glenn Shorrock • Don Burrows
1992	The Skyhooks • Pete Dawson
1993	Cold Chisel • Peter Allen
1994	Men At Work
1995	The Seekers
1996	Australian Crawl • Horrie Dargie
1997	The Bee Gees • Paul Kelly • Graeme Bell
1998	The Masters Apprentices • The Angels
1999	Richard Clapton • Jimmy Little
2000	No award given
2001	INXS • The Saints
2002	Olivia Newton John
2003	John Farnham
2004	The Little River Band
2005	Split Enz • Renee Geyer • Normie Rowe • Smoky Dawson • The Easybeats • Hunters & Collectors • Jimmy Barnes
2006	Midnight Oil • The Divinyls • Rose Tattoo • Helen Reddy • Daddy Cool • Icehouse and Lobby Loyde
2007	Nick Cave • Frank Ifield • Hoodoo Gurus • Marcia Hines • Jo Jo Zep & the Falcons • Brian Cadd • Radio Birdman
2008	Dragon • Max Merritt • Rolf Harris • Russell Morris • The Triffids
2009	John Paul Young • Mental As Anything • Little Pattie • The Dingoes • Kev Carmody

ARIA – the Australian Recording Industry Association – inducts Australian musicians and singers into its Hall of Fame at its annual ARIA Awards.

CANADIAN MUSIC HALL OF FAME

1978	Guy Lombardo • Oscar Peterson
1979	Hank Snow
1980	Paul Anka
1981	Joni Mitchell
1982	Neil Young
1983	Glenn Gould
1984	The Crewcuts • The Diamonds • The Four Lads
1985	Wilf Carter
1986	Gordon Lightfoot
1987	The Guess Who
1989	The Band
1990	Maureen Forrester
1991	Leonard Cohen
1992	Ian & Sylvia
1993	Anne Murray
1994	Rush
1995	Buffy Sainte-Marie
1996	David Clayton-Thomas •
	Denny Doherty • John Kay • Domenic Troiano • Zal Yanovsky
1997	Gil Evans • Lenny Breau • Maynard Ferguson • Moe Koffman • Rob McConnell
1998	David Foster
1999	Luc Plamondon
2000	Bruce Fairbairn
2001	Bruce Cockburn
2002	Daniel Lanois
2003	Tom Cochrane
2004	Bob Ezrin
2005	The Tragically Hip
2006	Bryan Adams
2007	Bob Rock
2008	Triumph
2009	Loverboy
2010	April Wine

The Canadian Music Hall of Fame honour is bestowed by the Canadian Academy of Recording Arts and Sciences at the annual Juno Awards.

UK MUSIC HALL OF FAME

Remarkably for such an influential music nation, the half-hearted UK Music Hall of Fame not only had a slow take-off (beginning in 2004), it also had a quick crash landing – unable to find funding or a broadcast partner after Channel 4 dropped the ceremony in 2007.

KERRANG! MAGAZINE HALL OF FAME RECIPIENTS

1999	Jimmy Page	2005	Iron Maiden
2000	Marilyn Manson	2006	Slayer
2001	Iggy Pop	2007	Judas Priest
2002	Foo Fighters	2008	Rage Against The Machine
2003	Metallica		
2004	Green Day	2009	Limp Bizkit

Britain's longest-running heavy metal/hard rock magazine, Kerrang!, was first published on June 6, 1981 as a spin-off supplement for the popular weekly music newspaper, Sounds.

THE SILVER CLEF AWARD

The Silver Clef Award was established in 1976 by a group of British musicians and managers as an annual luncheon to raise awareness and funds for the Nordoff-Robbins Music Therapy Centre in London and to celebrate the best in British music.

SILVER CLEF HONOURS

Year	Artist	Year	Artist
1976	The Who	1992	Def Leppard
1977	Genesis	1993	Eric Clapton
1978	Cliff Richard & the Shadows	1994	Sting
		1995	Take That
1979	Elton John	1996	Wet Wet Wet
1980	Pink Floyd	1997	Elvis Costello
1981	Status Quo	1998	Jamiroquai
1982	The Rolling Stones	1999	M People
		2000	Eurythmics
1983	Eric Clapton	2001	Tom Jones
1984	Queen	2002	Dido
1985	Dire Straits	2003	Coldplay
1986	Phil Collins	2004	Morrissey
1987	David Bowie	2006	Ozzy & Sharon Osbourne
1988	Paul McCartney		
1989	George Michael	2007	Paul Weller
1990	Robert Plant	2008	Oasis
1991	Rod Stewart	2009	Take That

Eric Clapton (1983 and 1993) and Take That (1995 and 2009) are both twice-winners of the Silver Clef. No award was given in 2005.

BEST NEWCOMER AWARD

SPECIAL ACHIEVEMENT AWARD

Year	Recipient	Year	Recipient
1992	Alan Freeman	2002	Lulu
1992	The Bee Gees	2003	Ray Davies
1995	George Martin	2004	Iron Maiden
1997	Chris Barber	2005	The Who
1998	Deep Purple	2006	Gary Farrow
1999	Pete King	2007	Rod Stewart
2000	Burt Bacharach & Hal David	2008	Squeeze
2001	Jerry Leiber & Mike Stoller	2009	Madness

It was renamed the Icon Award in 2007.

SPECIAL HONOURS

The Nordoff-Robbins Silver Clef Awards have also bestowed several (often short-lived) special honours to musicians over the year. These include the World Peace Award given only to John Lennon in 1997, the Silver Accolade Award to Cliff Richard in 1998 and Madness the following year, and the 30th Anniversary Award to The Who in 2005. The following have also been crowned with the Silver Clef Lifetime Achievement Award: U2 (2005), the Eagles (2006) and Nordoff-Robbins co-founder Clive Robbins (2007). In 2008, they introduced a Download of the Year category given to Estelle, with N-Dubz winning in 2009. Three Ambassadors of Rock honours have also been awarded: Bryan Ferry (2007), Bryan Adams (2008) and Queen (2009).

INTERNATIONAL AWARD

Above: Beach Boy and International Award winner, Brian Wilson.

THE IVOR NOVELLO AWARDS

Widely regarded as the most prestigious prize in UK music, the Ivor Novello Awards celebrate the best in British songwriting and composition. Named after the famous Welsh composer, singer and actor, the Ivors were introduced in 1955 – and are the oldest meaningful awards ceremony in popular music.

SONGWRITER OF THE YEAR

The first Songwriter of the Year Award was presented in 1969. The given year for each award is for the previous year of achievement (not the year the honour was bestowed).

Below: Dido, Songwriter of the Year in 2001.

Left : Michael Holbrook Penniman Jr. aka: Mika.

At an emotional ceremony in 1985, George Michael wept openly upon receiving his first "Songwriter of the Year" award (for the 1984 year), presented to him by Elton John. At age 21, Michael was the youngest-ever recipient of this much-coveted trophy.

THE FIRST IVOR NOVELLO AWARDS, 1955

At the year's first ceremony, eight prizes were handed out:

The Year's Most Popular Song	Ev'rywhere by Tolchard Evans & Larry Kahn
The Year's Outstanding Popular Song	In Love For The Very First Time by Jack Woodman & Paddy Roberts
The Year's Outstanding Comedy Song	Got'n Idea by Jack Woodman & Paddy Roberts
The Year's Most Effective Musical Play Score	Salad Days by Julian Slade & Dorothy Reynolds
The Year's Outstanding Swing Composition	Big City Suite by Ralph Dollimore
The Year's Outstanding Piece of Light Orchestral Music	The Dam Busters by Eric Coates
Outstanding Services in the Field of Popular Music	Jack Payne
Special Award	Haydn Wood

OUTSTANDING SONG COLLECTION

1996	Richard Thompson
1997	Sharleen Spiteri & John McElhone
1998	Jason Kay, Simon Katz, Derrick McKenzie, Toby Smith, Wallis Buchanan & Stuart Zender
1999	Cathal Smyth, Michael Barson, Lee Thompson, Graham McPherson, Daniel Woodgate, Christopher Foreman & Mark Bedford
2000	Roy Wood
2001	Mick Hucknall
2002	Bono, The Edge, Larry Mullen Jr. & Adam Clayton
2003	Eric Stewart, Kevin Godley, Lol Crème & Graham Gouldman
2004	Brian May, Freddie Mercury, John Deacon & Roger Taylor
2005	Philip Cunningham, Gillian Gilbert, Peter Hook, Stephen Morris & Bernard Sumner
2006	Yusuf Islam
2007	Gabrielle
2008	Vince Clarke

The majority of the Ivor Novello Award categories are judged and presented by members from the songwriting and composing community – one of the exceptions being the Most Performed Work, which is based on airplay and public performance data supplied by the PRS/MCPS.

Above: Vince Clarke penned hits for Depeche Mode, Yazoo and Erasure.

MOST PERFORMED WORK OF THE YEAR

1956	My September Love
1957	We Will Make Love
1958	Trudie
1959	Side Saddle
1960	As Long As He Needs Me
1961	My Kind Of Girl
1962	Stranger On The Shore
1963	She Loves You
1964	Can't Buy Me Love
1965	I'll Never Find Another You
1966	Michelle
1967	Puppet On A String
1968	Congratulations
1969	Get Back
1970	Yellow River
1971	My Sweet Lord
1972	Beg Steal Or Borrow
1973	Get Down
1974	The Wombling Song
1975	I'm Not In Love
1976	Save Your Kisses For Me
1977	Don't Cry For Me Argentina
1978	Night Fever
1979	Bright Eyes
1980	Together We Are Beautiful
1981	You Drive Me Crazy
1982	Golden Brown
1983	Every Breath You Take
1984	Careless Whisper
1985	Easy Lover
1986	Chain Reaction
1987	Never Gonna Give You Up
1988	I Should Be So Lucky
1989	This Time I Know It's For Real
1990	Blue Savannah
1991	I'm Too Sexy
1992	Deeply Dippy
1993	Ordinary World
1994	Love Is All Around
1995	Back For Good
1996	Fast Love
1997	I'll Be Missing You
1998	Angels
1999	Beautiful Stranger
2000	Pure Shores
2001	Can't Get You Out Of My Head
2002	Just A Little
2003	Superstar
2004	Toxic
2005	You're Beautiful
2006	I Don't Feel Like Dancin'
2007	Shine
2008	Mercy
2009	The Fear

MOST IVOR NOVELLO WINS

Paul McCartney	19	Matt Aitken, Mike Stock & Pete Waterman	8
John Lennon	15	Bernie Taupin	8
Andrew Lloyd Webber	14	Lionel Bart	7
Elton John	12	Leslie Bricusse	7
Barry & Robin Gibb	12	George Fenton	7
Tim Rice	11	Don Black	6
Maurice Gibb	11	Phil Collins	6
Tony Macaulay	8	Michael Kamen	6
Sting	8	George Michael	6

Right: Sir Paul shows off one of his many Ivor Novello trophies.

Sir Paul McCartney on the Ivors:
"I remember coming here the very first time with my mates John, George and Ringo. Sitting back there just as little kids we were. And it was just fantastic to be part of this songwriting thing. It was always the greatest award – the greatest thing to get for songwriters. I think it still is."

THE STATUETTE

The actual Ivor Novello trophy is a solid bronze sculpture of Euterpe, the Muse of poetry.

With the idea to establish a national organisation to recognize the achievements of America's top songwriters, Johnny Mercer, Howard Richmond and Abe Colman set up the Songwriters Hall of Fame in New York in 1969 as the showpiece for their National Academy of Popular Music.

Left: Peter Yarrow, Paul Stookey and Mary Travers.

THE SAMMY CAHN LIFETIME ACHIEVEMENT AWARD

1980	Ethel Merman
1981	Tony Bennett
1982	Dinah Shore
1983	Willie Nelson
1984	Benny Goodman
1985	John Hammond
1987	Jerry Wexler
1988	Dick Clark
1989	Quincy Jones
1990	B. B. King
1991	Gene Autry
1992	Nat King Cole
1993	Ray Charles
1994	Lena Horne
1995	Steve Lawrence & Eydie Gorme
1996	Frankie Laine
1997	Vic Damone
1998	Berry Gordy
1999	Kenny Rogers
2000	Neil Diamond
2001	Gloria & Emilio Estefan
2002	Stevie Wonder
2003	Patti LaBelle
2004	Neil Sedaka
2005	Les Paul
2006	Peter, Paul & Mary

The much coveted Lifetime Achievement honour is presented to "a music veteran who is also a non-songwriter" and is named after the legendary Broadway lyricist and songwriter, Sammy Cahn.

THE JOHNNY MERCER AWARD

The Johnny Mercer Award, named after the iconic lyricist and songwriter, celebrates "a writer or writers already inducted into the Songwriters Hall of Fame and judged by the Nominating Committee as having established a history of outstanding creative works."

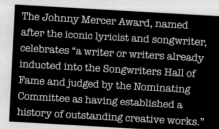

Above: Ethel Merman with Sammy Cahn.

Right: The first Johnny Mercer Award winner, Frank Sinatra.

THE HOWIE RICHMOND HITMAKER AWARD

1981	Chuck Berry	1999	Natalie Cole
1983	Rosemary Clooney/	2000	Johnny Mathis
	Margaret Whiting	2001	Dionne Warwick
1990	Whitney Houston	2002	Garth Brooks
1991	Barry Manilow	2003	Clive Davis
1995	Michael Bolton	2008	Anne Murray
1996	Gloria Estefan	2009	Tom Jones
1998	Diana Ross		

The Howie Richmond Hitmaker Award, named after one of the Hall's three co-founders, is "specifically tailored for artists or "star makers" in the music industry who have been responsible for a substantial number of hit songs for an extended period, and who recognize the importance of songs and their writers."

Right: Welsh hitmaker, Tom Jones.

Above: Diana Ross in 1998.

THE HAL DAVID STARLIGHT AWARD

2004	Rob Thomas	2007	John Legend
2005	Alicia Keys	2008	John Rzeznick
2006	John Mayer	2009	Jason Mraz

Introduced in 2004 and named after the Chairman of the Songwriters Hall of Fame, legendary lyricist Hal David, the Starlight Award is given to "gifted songwriters who are at an apex in their careers and are making a significant impact in the music industry via their original songs."

Above: 2006 Hal David Starlight Award winner, John Mayer.

THE TOWERING SONG AWARD

1995	As Time Goes By	2003	I Left My Heart In San Francisco
1996	Happy Birthday To You	2004	What The World Needs Now Is Love
1997	How High The Moon	2005	You've Lost That Lovin' Feelin'
1998	The Christmas Song	2006	When The Saints Go Marching In
1999	Fly Me To The Moon	2008	Take Me Out To The Ball Game
2000	All Of Me/You Are My Sunshine	2009	Moon River
2001	Let Me Call You Sweetheart		
2002	You're A Grand Old Flag		

An occasional award not presented annually, the Towering Song Award "honors outstanding songs by writers who may not have an extensive catalog of hits and who have not been inducted into the Songwriters Hall of Fame."

GENRES

In the same way that rock 'n' roll was created in the early fifties by a percolating brew of different music genres including country, rhythm & blues, gospel, swing and bluegrass, its subsequent evolution has spawned other distinct new music sub-groups including surf, folk, pop, bubblegum, punk, disco, new wave, heavy metal, rap, electronica, garage, grunge, house, world, acid, crunk and latin – to name a few.

THE BEST-SELLING COUNTRY ALBUMS OF ALL-TIME IN THE US

1	Come On Over	Shania Twain	1997
2	No Fences	Garth Brooks	1992
3	Ropin' The Wind	Garth Brooks	1991
4	Greatest Hits	Kenny Rogers	1980
5	The Woman In Me	Shania Twain	1995
6	Wide Open Spaces	Dixie Chicks	1999
7	Double Live	Garth Brooks	1998
8	Up!	Shania Twain	2002
9	Fly	The Dixie Chicks	1999
10	Greatest Hits	Patsy Cline	1967

Above: Shania Twain at the start of her *Up!* World Tour in 2004.

Come On Over was a rare country pop crossover success – owing much of its mainstream appeal to the involvement of co-writer/producer Robert John "Mutt" Lange – who married Shania Twain, a union which lasted until 2008.

THE BEST-SELLING HEAVY METAL ALBUMS OF ALL-TIME IN THE US

1	Led Zeppelin IV	Led Zeppelin	1971
2	Back In Black	AC/DC	1980
3	Appetite For Destruction	Guns N' Roses	1988
4	Boston	Boston	1976
5	Physical Graffiti	Led Zeppelin	1975
6	Journey's Greatest Hits	Journey	1989
7	Metallica	Metallica	1991
8	Bat Out Of Hell	Meat Loaf	1978
9	Hysteria	Def Leppard	1988
10	Slippery When Wet	Bon Jovi	1986
11	Led Zeppelin II	Led Zeppelin	1969

Robert John "Mutt" Lange is also influential here – the only producer to have helmed two separate albums on this mighty metal list: *Back In Black* and *Hysteria*.

THE BEST-SELLING R&B ALBUMS OF ALL-TIME IN THE US

1	Thriller	Michael Jackson	1983
2	The Bodyguard (Soundtrack)	Whitney Houston/ Various Artists	1992
3	Music From Purple Rain	Prince & the Revolution	1984
4	Whitney Houston	Whitney Houston	1986
5	II	Boyz II Men	1994
6	CrazySexyCool	TLC	1995
7	Can't Slow Down	Lionel Richie	1983
8	Music Box	Mariah Carey	1993
9	Confessions	Usher	2004
10	Daydream	Mariah Carey	1995

Boyz II Men's second solo album became Motown's best-selling album of all-time in the US, its success spurred by four top-notch soul ballads: 'I'll Make Love To You', 'On Bended Knee', 'Thank You' and 'Water Runs Dry'.

THE BEST-SELLING RAP ALBUMS OF ALL TIME IN THE US

1	Speakerboxxx/The Love Below	OutKast	2003
2	Please Hammer Don't Hurt 'Em	MC Hammer	1990
3	Life After Death	The Notorious B.I.G.	1997
4	The Marshall Mathers LP	Eminem	2000
5	The Eminem Show	Eminem	2002
6	Licensed To Ill	The Beastie Boys	1987
7	All Eyez On Me	2Pac	1996
8	Greatest Hits	2Pac	1998
9	Big Willie Style	Will Smith	1998
10	The Miseducation Of Lauryn Hill	Lauryn Hill	1998

OutKast is the Atlanta-based duo of Antwan "Big Boi" Patton and snappy dresser André "André 3000" Benjamin. Their 2003-released bestseller was essentially a pairing of two solo albums under the OutKast moniker.

THE BEST-SELLING COUNTRY ALBUMS OF ALL TIME IN THE UK

1	Come On Over	Shania Twain	1998
2	Up!	Shania Twain	2002
3	Greatest Hits	Shania Twain	2004
4	Glen Campbell's Twenty Golden Greats	Glen Campbell	1976
5	Greatest Hits	Glen Campbell	1971
6	Johnny Cash at San Quentin	Johnny Cash	1969
7	40 Golden Greats	Jim Reeves	1975
8	The Woman In Me	Shania Twain	2000
9	Images	Don Williams	1978
10	Johnny Cash Live at Folsom Prison	Johnny Cash	1968

Country music's appeal in the UK (and the rest of Europe) has always been modest although albums with strong pop crossover content (Shania Twain, Glen Campbell) or short-lived, TV-advertised greatest hits collections (Jim Reeves) occasionally fare well.

THE BEST-SELLING R&B ALBUMS OF ALL TIME IN THE UK

1	Thriller	Michael Jackson	1983
2	Bad	Michael Jackson	1987
3	Back To Black	Amy Winehouse	2007
4	Legend	Bob Marley & the Wailers	1984
5	Spirit	Leona Lewis	2007
6	Whitney	Whitney Houston	1987
7	The Bodyguard (Soundtrack)	Whitney Houston/ Various Artists	1994
8	Simply The Best	Tina Turner	1991
9	Dangerous	Michael Jackson	1991
10	Can't Slow Down	Lionel Richie	1982
11	Number Ones	Michael Jackson	2009

Right: Best-selling rockers, Bon Jovi.

THE BEST-SELLING HEAVY METAL ALBUMS OF ALL TIME IN THE UK

1	Bat Out of Hell	Meat Loaf	1978
2	Appetite for Destruction	Guns N' Roses	1987
3	Cross Road – The Best of Bon Jovi	Bon Jovi	1994
4	Bat Out of Hell II – Back to Hell	Meat Loaf	1993
5	Led Zeppelin IV	Led Zeppelin	1971
6	Led Zeppelin II	Led Zeppelin	1969
7	Eliminator	ZZ Top	1983
8	[Hybrid Theory]	Linkin Park	2001
9	Slippery When Wet	Bon Jovi	1986
10	Greatest Hits	Guns N' Roses	2004

Unlike its 1993 sequel, which made Number 1 in the UK, *Bat Out of Hell* only ever peaked at Number 9, but logged an impressive 470-plus weeks on the chart, an achievement split over three decades.
Between 1969 and 1979, Led Zeppelin hit the top spot with eight consecutive albums, from *Led Zeppelin II* to *In Through The Out Door*.

Right: MC Hammer playing Wembley Arena in 1991.

THE BEST-SELLING RAP ALBUMS OF ALL TIME IN THE UK

1	The Marshall Mathers LP	Eminem	2000
2	The Eminem Show	Eminem	2002
3	The Score	The Fugees	1996
4	Encore	Eminem	2004
5	Curtain Call – The Hits	Eminem	2005
6	The Slim Shady LP	Eminem	2000
7	Speakerboxx/The Love Below	OutKast	2004
8	Big Willie Style	Will Smith	1999
9	Nellyville	Nelly	2002
10	Please Hammer Don't Hurt 'Em	MC Hammer	1990

Despite the multi-platinum global success of MC Hammer's album, he somehow managed to blow a substantial eight-figure fortune, filing for bankruptcy in 1996.

MTV
MUSIC TELEVISION

THE BEST-SELLING ALBUMS OF ALL-TIME IN THE UK BY UK GROUPS

1	Greatest Hits	Queen	1981
2	Sgt. Pepper's Lonely Hearts Club Band	The Beatles	1967
3	(What's The Story?) Morning Glory	Oasis	1995
4	Brothers In Arms	Dire Straits	1985
5	Dark Side of the Moon	Pink Floyd	1973
6	Greatest Hits II	Queen	1991
7	Stars	Simply Red	1991
8	Urban Hymns	The Verve	1997
9	Spice	Spice Girls	1996
10	1	The Beatles	2000
11	A Rush Of Blood To The Head	Coldplay	2002
12	Hopes And Fears	Keane	2004
13	The Man Who	Travis	1999
14	Beautiful World	Take That	2006
15	X&Y	Coldplay	2005
16	Parachutes	Coldplay	2000
17	Abbey Road	The Beatles	1969
18	A New Flame	Simply Red	1989
19	Carry On Up The Charts – The Best Of	Beautiful South	1994
20	The Greatest Hits	Texas	2000

Although *Sgt. Pepper's Lonely Hearts Club Band* is less than 100,000 shy of the mark, *Greatest Hits* by Queen is the only album by a British group to have sold in excess of five million copies on home turf.

THE BEST-SELLING ALBUMS OF ALL TIME IN THE UK BY UK FEMALE SOLO ARTISTS

1	Back To Black	Amy Winehouse	2007
2	No Angel	Dido	2001
3	Life For Rent	Dido	2003
4	Spirit	Leona Lewis	2007
5	Rockferry	Duffy	2008
6	Eye To The Telescope	KT Tunstall	2005
7	Rise	Gabrielle	2000
8	The Whole Story	Kate Bush	1987
9	So Close	Dina Carroll	1993
10	Dreams Can Come True – Greatest Hits	Gabrielle	2001
11	Frank	Amy Winehouse	2004
12	Diva	Annie Lennox	1991
13	Alf	Alison Moyet	1985
14	Alright, Still	Lily Allen	2006
15	Mind, Body & Soul	Joss Stone	2004
16	The Soul Sessions	Joss Stone	2004
17	Northern Star	Melanie C	2000
18	Affection	Lisa Stansfield	1989
19	This Is The Life	Amy MacDonald	2008
20	19	Adele	2008

The top four albums have all sold over two and a half million copies in Britain.

Right: Amy Winehouse at Glastonbury in 2008.

Below: James Blunt.

THE BEST-SELLING ALBUMS OF ALL TIME IN THE UK BY UK MALE SOLO ARTISTS

1	Back To Bedlam	James Blunt	2005
2	White Ladder	David Gray	2001
3	... But Seriously	Phil Collins	1989
4	Tubular Bells	Mike Oldfield	1974
5	I've Been Expecting You	Robbie Williams	1998
6	Ladies And Gentleman Best Of George Michael	George Michael	1998
7	Swing When You're Winning	Robbie Williams	2001
8	The Very Best Of Elton John	Elton John	1990
9	Life Thru A Lens	Robbie Williams	1998
10	Escapology	Robbie Williams	2002
11	Greatest Hits	Robbie Williams	2004
12	No Jacket Required	Phil Collins	1985
13	Born To Do It	Craig David	2000
14	Older	George Michael	1996
15	The Road To Hell	Chris Rea	1989
16	Sing When You're Winning	Robbie Williams	2000
17	Face Value	Phil Collins	1981
18	The Best Of Rod Stewart	Rod Stewart	1989
19	Intensive Care	Robbie Williams	2005
20	Stanley Road	Paul Weller	1995

Sensitive singer-songwriter James Hillier Blount (aka James Blunt) was an officer in a Cavalry Regiment of the British Army and made a tour of duty in Kosovo with NATO in 1999, before pursuing a music career in 2002, which resulted in his debut album being released the following year. By the decade's end it had sold more than three million domestic copies.

THE BEST-SELLING DUET SINGLES OF ALL TIME IN THE UK

You're The One That I Want	John Travolta & Olivia Newton-John	1978
Unchained Melody/ (There'll Be Bluebirds Over The) White Cliffs Of Dover	Robson Green & Jerome Flynn	1995
Summer Nights	John Travolta & Olivia Newton-John	1978
Last Christmas	Wham!	1984
I'll Be Missing You	Puff Daddy & Faith Evans	1997
Gangsta's Paradise	Coolio featuring LV	1995
Is This The Way To Amarillo?	Tony Christie featuring Peter Kay	2005
It Wasn't Me	Shaggy featuring RikRok	2001
I Believe/Up On The Roof	Robson & Jerome	1995
Especially For You	Kylie Minogue & Jason Donovan	1988

THE BEST-SELLING SINGLES OF ALL TIME IN THE UK BY UK MALE SOLO ARTISTS

Candle In The Wind 1997/ Something About The Way You Look Tonight	Elton John	1997
Anything Is Possible/Evergreen	Will Young	2002
Tears	Ken Dodd	1965
Imagine	John Lennon	1975
Careless Whisper	George Michael	1984
Unchained Melody	Gareth Gates	2002
Green Green Grass Of Home	Tom Jones	1966
The Last Waltz	Engelbert Humperdinck	1967
I Love You Love Me Love	Gary Glitter	1973
Stranger On The Shore	Mr. Acker Bilk	1961

Left: Will Young, performing at the Hammersmith Apollo in 2010.

Right: Olivia Newton-John and John Travolta, stars of the 1978 film *Grease*.

Penned by former Shadows guitarist John Farrar, 'You're The One That I Want' featured in the perennial movie musical blockbuster *Grease* in 1978.

THE BEST-SELLING R&B SINGLES OF ALL TIME IN THE UK

I Just Called To Say I Love You	Stevie Wonder	1984
I'll Be Missing You	Puff Daddy & Faith Evans	1997
I Will Always Love You	Whitney Houston	1992
Killing Me Softly	Fugees	1996
Gangsta's Paradise	Coolio featuring LV	1995
It Wasn't Me	Shaggy featuring RikRok	2001
It's Like That	Run-DMC Vs. Jason Nevins	1998
Earth Song	Michael Jackson	1995
Ghostbusters	Ray Parker Jr.	1984
Ride On Time	Black Box	1989

R&B icon Stevie Wonder features prominently: in addition to holding the top slot, his 1976 song, 'Pastime Paradise' provided the sampled rhythm track for rapper Coolio's 1995 smash, 'Gangsta's Paradise'.

THE BEST-SELLING INSTRUMENTAL SINGLES OF ALL TIME IN THE UK

Stranger On The Shore	Mr. Acker Bilk	1962
Eye Level	The Simon Park Orchestra	1972
Telstar	The Tornados	1962
Amazing Grace	Royal Scots Dragoon Guards	1972
Albatross	Fleetwood Mac	1969
Apache	The Shadows	1960
Wonderful Land	The Shadows	1962
Side Saddle	Russ Conway	1959
The Theme From A Summer Place	Percy Faith & His Orchestra	1960
The Good, The Bad And The Ugly	Hugo Montenegro His Orchestra & Chorus	1968

British clarinet player Acker Bilk composed 'Stranger On The Shore' in 1961 for his daughter Jenny. Its phenomenal sales success came as the theme song to the BBC drama series of the same name.

MTV
MUSIC TELEVISION™

The first meaningful weekly popular music chart – a Top 12 Singles list – was compiled and published by the British music paper, the *New Musical Express* on November 14, 1952. An extended top 50 was introduced by UK music trade publication, *Record Retailer*, on March 10, 1960. Across the pond, *Billboard* Magazine inaugurated its own Hot 100 singles chart on August 4, 1958, having compiled its first top 5 Popular Albums list in 1945. *Melody Maker* published the first UK album chart on November 8, 1958.

MOST WEEKS ATOP THE UK ALBUM CHART

South Pacific	Soundtrack	115
The Sound of Music	Soundtrack	70
Bridge Over Troubled Water	Simon & Garfunkel	33
Please Please Me	The Beatles	30
Sgt. Pepper's Lonely Hearts Club Band	The Beatles	27
G.I. Blues	Elvis Presley/Soundtrack	22
With The Beatles	The Beatles	21
A Hard Day's Night	The Beatles/Soundtrack	21
Blue Hawaii	Elvis Presley/Soundtrack	18
Saturday Night Fever	Soundtrack	18
Abbey Road	The Beatles	17
The Singles 1970 – 1973	The Carpenters	17
… But Seriously	Phil Collins	15

The Beatles' *Please Please Me*, *With The Beatles* and *A Hard Day's Night* and the *Saturday Night Fever* soundtrack were the only continuous chart runs. Evergreen musical *South Pacific* was written by American composer Richard Rodgers and lyricist Oscar Hammerstein II, making its theatrical Broadway bow on April 7, 1949 at the Majestic Theatre.

MOST NUMBER ONE ALBUMS IN THE UK

The Beatles	15	R.E.M.	8
Madonna	10	Bob Dylan	7
The Rolling Stones	10	Paul McCartney	7
U2	10	Cliff Richard	7
Abba	9	Rod Stewart	7
Michael Jackson	9	Genesis	6
Queen	9	Elton John	6
David Bowie	8	The Police	6
Led Zeppelin	8	Simply Red	5
Elvis Presley	8		

Right: Fleetwood Mac in 1978.

MOST WEEKS IN THE UK ALBUM CHART

Rumours	Fleetwood Mac	478
Bat Out Of Hell	Meat Loaf	473
Greatest Hits	Queen	472
Gold – Greatest Hits	Abba	438
The Sound Of Music	Soundtrack	384
Dark Side Of The Moon	Pink Floyd	370
Legend	Bob Marley & the Wailers	370
Bridge Over Troubled Water	Simon & Garfunkel	307
Jeff Wayne's Musical Version Of The War Of The Worlds	Various Artists	285
Greatest Hits	Simon & Garfunkel	283
South Pacific	Soundtrack	276
Tubular Bells	Mike Oldfield	276
Face Value	Phil Collins	274
Making Movies	Dire Straits	252
The Immaculate Collection	Madonna	242
Brothers In Arms	Dire Straits	241
U2 Live – Under A Blood Red Sky	U2	203
Thriller	Michael Jackson	201

Lyrically fuelled by the disintegrating relationships and affairs afflicting the five members of the group, Fleetwood Mac's *Rumours* was originally released in February 1977. Clocking in at just 39.03 minutes, the 11-track classic remained on the UK albums survey for more than a combined nine years.

MOST WEEKS ATOP THE US ALBUM CHART

West Side Story	Soundtrack	54
Thriller	Michael Jackson	37
Calypso	Harry Belafonte	31
South Pacific	Soundtrack	31
Rumours	Fleetwood Mac	31
Saturday Night Fever	Soundtrack	24
Music From Purple Rain	Prince & the Revolution	24
Please Hammer Don't Hurt 'Em	MC Hammer	21
Blue Hawaii	Elvis Presley	20
The Bodyguard	Whitney Houston/ Soundtrack	20
Love Me Or Leave Me	Doris Day	19
More Of The Monkees	The Monkees	18
Dirty Dancing	Soundtrack	18
Ropin' The Wind	Garth Brooks	18
Synchronicity	The Police	17
Some Gave All	Billy Ray Cyrus	17
The Sound Of Music	Broadway Cast	16
Days Of Wine And Roses	Andy Williams	16
To The Extreme	Vanilla Ice	16
Titanic	Soundtrack	16
My Fair Lady	Broadway Cast	15
The Kingston Trio At Large	The Kingston Trio	15
Sgt. Pepper's Lonely Hearts Club Band	The Beatles	15
Tapestry	Carole King	15
The Wall	Pink Floyd	15
Hi Infidelity	REO Speedwagon	15
Business As Usual	Men At Work	15

The power of film: including Elvis Presley's *Blue Hawaii* and Prince's *Purple Rain*, six of the top ten are film soundtracks.

MOST NUMBER ONE ALBUMS IN THE US

The Beatles	19	The Eagles	6	
Jay-Z	11	Janet Jackson	6	
Elvis Presley	10	Michael Jackson	6	
The Rolling Stones	9	R. Kelly	6	
Bruce Springsteen	9	Herb Alpert & the Tijuana Brass	5	
Barbra Streisand	9	Chicago	5	
Garth Brooks	8	The Kingston Trio	5	
Elton John	7	Pink Floyd	5	
Paul McCartney/Wings	7	Frank Sinatra	5	
Mariah Carey	7	Van Halen	5	
Led Zeppelin	7			
U2	7			

Left: The Beatles in 1963.

Below: Easy-listening superstar, Johnny Mathis

MOST WEEKS ON THE US ALBUM CHART

Dark Side Of The Moon	Pink Floyd	742
Johnny's Greatest Hits	Johnny Mathis	490
My Fair Lady	Original Cast	480
Highlights From The Phantom Of The Opera	Original Cast	331
Oklahoma!	Soundtrack	305
Tapestry	Carole King	302
Heavenly	Johnny Mathis	295
MCMXC AD	Enigma	282
Metallica	Metallica	281
The King And I	Soundtrack	277
Hymns	Tennessee Ernie Ford	277
The Sound Of Music	Original Cast	276
Camelot	Original Cast	265
South Pacific	Soundtrack	262
Four Symbols	Led Zeppelin	259
The Phantom Of The Opera	Original Cast	255
Nevermind	Nirvana	252
Ten	Pearl Jam	250
The Music Man	Original Cast	245
Hot Rocks 1964 – 1971	The Rolling Stones	243
The Best Of Van Morrison	Van Morrison	242
Shepherd Moons	Enya	238
The Sound Of Music	Soundtrack	233
Film Encores	Mantovani & His Orchestra	231
No Fences	Garth Brooks	224
Garth Brooks	Garth Brooks	224
Breathless	Kenny G	214
Greatest Hits	Queen	207
Fiddler On The Roof	Original Cast	206
Sing Along With Mitch	Mitch Miller & the Gang	204
Soul Provider	Michael Bolton	202

Way ahead of the competition, Pink Floyd's iconic sixth studio album spent a remarkable 14-plus years combined residence on the US chart.

CHART-TOPPING ARTISTS IN THE US

Of the nine artists who have had ten or more American chart-toppers, only The Beatles – at the top – are a foreign act. Their tally was achieved in just over six years, a year more than The Supremes. The longest span is Michael Jackson's at just under 23 years.

THE BEATLES (20)

I Want To Hold Your Hand	Feb 01, 1964
She Loves You	Mar 21, 1964
Can't Buy Me Love	Apr 04, 1964
Love Me Do	May 30, 1964
A Hard Day's Night	Aug 01, 1964
I Feel Fine	Dec 26, 1964
Eight Days A Week	Mar 13, 1965
Ticket To Ride	May 22, 1965
Help!	Sep 04, 1965
Yesterday	Oct 09, 1965
We Can Work It Out	Jan 08, 1966
Paperback Writer	Jun 25, 1966
Penny Lane	Mar 18, 1967
All You Need Is Love	Aug 19, 1967
Hello, Goodbye	Dec 30, 1967
Hey Jude	Sep 28, 1968
Get Back (featuring Billy Preston)	May 24, 1969
Come Together/Something	Nov 29, 1969
Let It Be	Apr 11, 1970
The Long And Winding Road/ For You Blue	Jun 13, 1970

Above: Mariah Carey.

The Beatles' record-breaking haul is all the more remarkable for occurring during a meagre seven-year period, an unmatched average of nearly three per year.

MARIAH CAREY (18)

Vision Of Love	Aug 04, 1990
Love Takes Time	Nov 10, 1990
Someday	Mar 09, 1991
I Don't Wanna Cry	May 25, 1991
Emotions	Oct 12, 1991
I'll Be There	Jun 20, 1992
Dreamlover	Sep 11, 1993
Hero	Dec 25, 1993
Fantasy	Sep 30, 1995
One Sweet Day (with Boyz II Men)	Dec 02, 1995
Always Be My Baby	May 04, 1996
Honey	Sep 13, 1997
My All	May 23, 1998
Heartbreaker (featuring Jay-Z)	Oct 09, 1999
Thank God I Found You (featuring Joe & 98 Degrees)	Feb 19, 2000
We Belong Together	Jun 04, 2005
Don't Forget About Us	Dec 31, 2005
Touch My Body	Apr 12, 2008

Carey's impressive tally includes three collaborations, notably 'One Sweet Day' with Boyz II Men, which spent a record-breaking 16 consecutive weeks in pole position.

ELVIS PRESLEY (17)

Heartbreak Hotel/I Was The One	Apr 21, 1956
I Want You, I Need You, I Love You/ My Baby Left Me	July 28, 1956
Hound Dog/Don't Be Cruel	Aug 18, 1956
Love Me Tender	Nov 03, 1956
Too Much/Playing For Keeps	Feb 09, 1957
All Shook Up	Apr 13, 1957
(Let Me Be Your) Teddy Bear/ Loving You	Jul 13, 1957
Jailhouse Rock/Treat Me Nice	Oct 26, 1957
Don't/I Beg Of You	Feb 15, 1958
Hard Headed Woman/ Don't Ask Me Why	Jul 26, 1958
A Big Hunk O' Love	Aug 15, 1959
Stuck On You	Apr 30, 1960
It's Now Or Never	Aug 20, 1960
Are You Lonesome Tonight?	Dec 03, 1960
Surrender	Mar 25, 1961
Good Luck Charm	Apr 21, 1962
Suspicious Minds	Nov 01, 1969

Left: Elvis Presley.

Elvis' last US chart-topper, 'Suspicious Minds' featured future Grateful Dead member Donna Jean Godchaux on backing vocals.

MICHAEL JACKSON (13)

Ben	Oct 14, 1972
Don't Stop Till You Get Enough	Oct 13, 1979
Rock With You	Jan 19, 1980
Billie Jean	Mar 05, 1983
Beat It	Apr 30, 1983
Say Say Say (with Paul McCartney)	Dec 10, 1983
I Just Can't Stop Loving You (with Siedah Garrett)	Sep 19, 1987
Bad	Oct 24, 1987
The Way You Make Me Feel	Jan 23, 1988
The Man In The Mirror	Mar 26, 1988
Dirty Diana	Jul 02, 1988
Black Or White	Dec 07, 1991
You Are Not Alone	Sep 02, 1995

Always intended as a duet, 'I Just Can't Stop Loving You' was written by Jackson with either Whitney Houston or Barbra Streisand in mind. Following their unavailability, producer Quincy Jones suggested one his protégés, Siedah Garrett.

MADONNA (12)

Like A Virgin	Dec 22, 1984
Crazy For You	May 11, 1985
Live To Tell	Jun 07, 1986
Papa Don't Preach	Aug 16, 1986
Open Your Heart	Feb 07, 1987
Who's That Girl	Aug 22, 1987
Like A Prayer	Apr 22, 1989
Vogue	May 19, 1990
Justify My Love	Jan 05, 1991
This Used To Be My Playground	Aug 08, 1992
Take A Bow	Feb 25, 1995
Music	Sept 16, 2000

Four of Madonna's chart-toppers are from film soundtracks: 'Crazy For You' (*Vision Quest*), 'Live To Tell' (*At Close Range*), 'Who's That Girl' (*Who's That Girl*) and 'This Used To Be My Playground' (*A League Of Their Own*).

Above: Madonna.

WHITNEY HOUSTON (11)

Saving All My Love For You	Oct 26, 1985
How Will I Know	Feb 15, 1986
Greatest Love Of All	May 17, 1986
I Wanna Dance With Somebody (Who Loves Me)	Jun 27, 1987
Didn't We Almost Have It All	Sep 26, 1987
So Emotional	Jan 09, 1988
Where Do Broken Hearts Go	Apr 23, 1988
I'm Your Baby Tonight	Dec 01, 1990
All The Man That I Need	Feb 23, 1991
I Will Always Love You (from *The Bodyguard*)	Nov 28, 1992
Exhale (Shoop Shoop) (from *Waiting To Exhale*)	Nov 25, 1995

Unlike her diva contemporary, Mariah Carey, Houston has never written any of her own hits relying instead on a host of top songwriters recommended to her by longtime executive producer, friend and label boss Clive Davis.

THE SUPREMES (12)

Where Did Our Love Go	Aug 22, 1964
Baby Love	Oct 31, 1964
Come See About Me	Jan 16, 1965
Stop! In The Name Of Love	Mar 27, 1965
Back In My Arms Again	Jun 12, 1965
I Hear A Symphony	Nov 20, 1965
You Can't Hurry Love	Sep 10, 1966
You Keep Me Hangin' On	Nov 19, 1966
Love Is Here And Now You're Gone	Mar 11, 1967
The Happening	May 13, 1967
Love Child*	Nov 30, 1968
Someday We'll Be Together*	Dec 27, 1969

(*Diana Ross & the Supremes)

Originally formed in 1959 as the Primettes, the all-female Motown vocal group The Supremes remain the most successful vocal group of any genre, of all-time.

Below: Janet Jackson.

JANET JACKSON (10)

When I Think Of You	Oct 11, 1986
Miss You Much	Oct 07, 1989
Escapade	Mar 03, 1990
Black Cat	Oct 27, 1990
Love Will Never Do (Without You)	Jan 19, 1991
That's The Way Love Goes	May 15, 1993
Again	Dec 11, 1993
Together Again	Jan 31, 1998
Doesn't Really Matter	Aug 26, 2000
All For You	Apr 14, 2001

With the exception of 'Black Cat', all of Jackson's US chart-toppers have been co-written and produced by the Flyte Tyme production crew of Jimmy Jam and Terry Lewis.

Below: Stevie Wonder.

STEVIE WONDER (10)

Fingertips (Part II)	Aug 10, 1963
Superstition	Jan 27, 1973
You Are The Sunshine Of My Life	May 19, 1973
You Haven't Done Nothin'	Nov 02, 1974
I Wish	Jan 22, 1977
Sir Duke	May 21, 1977
Ebony And Ivory (with Paul McCartney)	May 15, 1982
I Just Called To Say I Love You	Oct 13, 1984
Part-Time Lover	Nov 02, 1985
That's What Friends Are For (with Dionne Warwick, Elton John & Gladys Knight)	Jan 18, 1986

Stevie Wonder penned all of these hits except 'Fingertips', 'Ebony And Ivory' and 'That's What Friends Are For'.

CHART-TOPPING ARTISTS IN THE UK

The disparity of British and American tastes is highlighted with these lists, as half the acts featured mean next to nothing in the United States (Cliff Richard, Westlife and Take That). Take away Presley's re-packaged chart-toppers and he would be tied for the most Number Ones with The Beatles.

ELVIS PRESLEY (21)

All Shook Up	Jul 13, 1957
Jailhouse Rock	Jan 25, 1958
I Got Stung/One Night	Jan 31, 1959
(Now And Then There's)	
A Fool Such As I	May 16, 1959
It's Now Or Never (O Sole Mio)	Nov 05, 1960
Are You Lonesome Tonight?	Jan 28, 1961
Wooden Heart	Mar 25, 1961
Surrender (Torna A Surriento)	Jun 03, 1961
(Marie's The Name)	
His Latest Flame/Little Sister	Nov 11, 1961
Rock-A-Hula Baby	Feb 24, 1962
Good Luck Charm	May 26, 1962
She's Not You	Sep 15, 1962
Return To Sender	Dec 15, 1962
(You're The) Devil In Disguise	Aug 03, 1963
Crying In The Chapel	Jun 19, 1965
The Wonder Of You	Aug 01, 1970
Way Down	Sep 03, 1977
A Little Less Conversation	Jun 22, 2002
Jailhouse Rock	Jan 15, 2005
One Night/I Got Stung	Jan 22, 2005
It's Now Or Never	Feb 05, 2005

After a 25-year gap, Presley once again hit number one in the UK courtesy of a remix of 'A Little Less Conversation' by English DJ Junkie XL for a worldwide Nike World Cup television commercial.

Below: The Beatles in 1963.

THE BEATLES (17)

From Me To You	May 04, 1963
She Loves You	Sep 14, 1963
I Want To Hold Your Hand	Dec 14, 1963
Can't Buy Me Love	Apr 04, 1964
A Hard Day's Night	Jul 25, 1964
I Feel Fine	Dec 12, 1964
Ticket To Ride	Apr 24, 1965
Help!	Aug 07, 1965
Day Tripper/We Can Work It Out	Dec 18, 1965
Paperback Writer	Jun 25, 1966
Yellow Submarine/Eleanor Rigby	Aug 20, 1966
All You Need Is Love	Jul 22, 1967
Hello, Goodbye	Dec 09, 1967
Lady Madonna	Mar 30, 1968
Hey Jude	Sep 14, 1968
Get Back (with Billy Preston)	Apr 26, 1969
The Ballad Of John And Yoko	Jun 14, 1969

American R&B keyboardist Billy Preston holds the enviable record of being the only artist to ever receive a "featuring" credit on a Beatles hit.

CLIFF RICHARD (14)

Living Doll	Aug 01, 1959
Travellin' Light	Oct 31, 1959
Please Don't Tease	Jul 30, 1960
I Love You	Dec 31, 1960
The Young Ones	Jan 13, 1962
The Next Time/Bachelor Boy	Jan 05, 1963
Summer Holiday	Mar 16, 1963
The Minute You're Gone	Apr 17, 1965
Congratulations	Apr 13, 1968
We Don't Talk Anymore	Aug 25, 1979
Living Doll (with the Young Ones	
and featuring Hank Marvin)	Mar 29, 1986
Mistletoe And Wine	Dec 10, 1988
Saviour's Day	Dec 29, 1990
The Millennium Prayer	Dec 04, 1999

Cliff Richard's first six number ones were all credited to Cliff Richard & the Shadows. The Shadows also scored a further five UK chart-toppers without Sir Cliff.

Above: Cliff Richard.

WESTLIFE (14)

Swear It Again	May 01, 1999
If I Let You Go	Aug 21, 1999
Flying Without Wings	Oct 30, 1999
I Have A Dream/Seasons In The Sun	Dec 25, 1999
Fool Again	Apr 08, 2000
Against All Odds (with Mariah Carey)	Sep 30, 2000
My Love	Nov 11, 2000
Uptown Girl	Mar 17, 2001
Queen Of My Heart	Nov 17, 2001
World Of Our Own	Mar 02, 2002
Unbreakable	Nov 16, 2002
Mandy	Nov 29, 2003
You Raise Me Up	Nov 12, 2005
The Rose	Nov 18, 2006

Left: Westlife.

Boy-band Westlife formed in their native Ireland in July 1998 and are the only act to hit number one in the UK with their first seven singles. Westlife also holds the record for achieving ten UK chart-toppers in the shortest time – two years, ten months (149 weeks). Initially a five-piece, they trimmed to a quartet in 2004 with the departure of Brian McFadden.

TAKE THAT (11)

Pray	Jul 17, 1993
Relight My Fire (featuring Lulu)	Oct 09, 1993
Babe	Dec 18, 1993
Everything Changes	Apr 09, 1994
Sure	Oct 15, 1994
Back For Good	Apr 08, 1995
Never Forget	Aug 05, 1995
How Deep Is Your Love	Mar 09, 1996
Patience	Dec 02, 2006
Shine	Mar 10, 2007
Greatest Day	Dec 06, 2008

Few reuniting bands manage to reclaim their former glory days but Take That defied both the odds and the critics by scoring three more chart-toppers following their reunion in 2006.

Below: Take That reunited and strong.

MADONNA (13)

Into The Groove	Aug 03, 1985
Papa Don't Preach	Jul 12, 1986
True Blue	Oct 11, 1986
La Isla Bonita	Apr 25, 1987
Who's That Girl	Jul 25, 1987
Like A Prayer	Mar 25, 1989
Vogue	Apr 14, 1990
Frozen	Mar 07, 1998
American Pie	Mar 11, 2000
Music	Sep 02, 2000
Hung Up	Nov 19, 2005
Sorry	Mar 04, 2006
4 Minutes (featuring Justin Timberlake)	Apr 26, 2008

The most successful female chart-topper in UK chart history, Madonna's record haul comes from a total of 11 studio albums beginning with her eponymous maiden effort in 1983.

MOST NUMBER ONES

The individual with the most number ones is Paul McCartney featuring on 24 in all – 17 times with The Beatles, once with Wings on 'Mull Of Kintyre'/'Girls' School', once with Stevie Wonder on 'Ebony And Ivory' and once as a solo artist with 'Pipes Of Peace'. In addition he has appeared on charity singles with Band Aid, Band Aid 20, Ferry Aid and with The Christians, Holly Johnson, Gerry Marsden, Stock Aitken & Waterman on 'Ferry 'Cross The Mersey'. Four number ones behind McCartney is John Lennon with 20 – 17 with The Beatles and three solo. Robbie Williams has accrued 13 chart-toppers – five solo, seven with Take That and one with actress Nicole Kidman.

SINGLES WHICH SPENT MORE THAN 50 WEEKS ON THE US CHART

			Year	Wks
1	I'm Yours	Jason Mraz	2008	76
2	How Do I Live	LeAnn Rimes	1997	69
3	Foolish Games/You Were Meant For Me	Jewel	1996	65
4	Before He Cheats	Carrie Underwood	2006	64
5	You And Me	Lifehouse	2005	62
6	Macarena (Bayside Boys Mix)	Los Del Rio	1996	60
7	Smooth	Santana featuring Rob Thomas	1999	58
8	How To Save A Life	The Fray	2006	58
9	Higher	Creed	1999	57
10	I Don't Want to Wait	Paula Cole	1997	56
11	The Way You Love Me	Faith Hill	2000	56
12	Use Somebody	Kings of Leon	2009	56
13	Barely Breathing	Duncan Sheik	1996	55
14	Missing	Everything But The Girl	1996	55
15	Amazed	Lonestar	1999	55
16	Hanging By A Moment	Lifehouse	2001	54
17	Unwell	Matchbox Twenty	2003	54
18	Too Close	Next	1998	53
19	Breathe	Faith Hill	2000	53
20	Kryptonite	3 Doors Down	2000	53
21	Drops Of Jupiter (Tell Me)	Train	2001	53
22	Truly Madly Deeply	Savage Garden	1998	52
23	How It's Going To Be	Third Eye Blind	1998	52
24	Here Without You	3 Doors Down	2003	51
25	Viva La Vida	Coldplay	2008	51
26	Someday	Nickelback	2004	50
27	Paralyzer	Finger Eleven	2008	50

Left: Frank Sinatra in the recording studio.

SINGLES WHICH SPENT MORE THAN 50 WEEKS ON THE UK CHART

			Year	Wks
1	My Way	Frank Sinatra	1969	124
2	Chasing Cars	Snow Patrol	2007	91
3	Rule The World	Take That	2007	71
4	Amazing Grace	Judy Collins	1970	66
5	Sex On Fire	Kings of Leon	2008	65
6	Use Somebody	Kings of Leon	2009	60
7	Relax	Frankie Goes To Hollywood	1983	59
8	Rock Around The Clock	Bill Haley & His Comets	1955	57
9	Release Me	Engelbert Humperdinck	1967	56
10	Stranger On The Shore	Mr. Acker Bilk	1961	55
11	Blue Monday	New Order	1983	54
12	Low	Flo Rida featuring T-Pain	2008	53
13	Rehab	Amy Winehouse	2006	51
14	Umbrella	Rihanna featuring Jay-Z	2007	51
15	Whatever	Oasis	1994	50
16	Rockstar	Nickelback	2008	50
17	I'm Yours	Jason Mraz	2009	50

Kings of Leon is the only act to have two different songs each spend more than 60 weeks on the UK chart. The American rock quartet which formed in Nashville in 1999, it is a family affair with brothers Caleb, Nathan and Jared Followill, joined by their cousin Matthew. Uniquely, each of them chooses to be known by their middle name: their respective first names are Anthony, Ivan, Michael and Cameron.

Featured on his third solo album, *We Sing. We Dance. We Steal Things*, singer-songwriter Jason Mraz's 'I'm Yours' also became the third best-selling digital track of all-time in the US with more than 5 million downloads. Despite its record-breaking chart residence, it only peaked at number 6 – though it curiously topped surveys in both Norway and Sweden.

Left: Jason Mraz.

AMERICAN RECORDS WHICH REACHED NO. 1 IN THE UK WITHOUT CHARTING IN THE US

THE 1960S

Three Steps To Heaven	Eddie Cochran	1960
Wooden Heart	Elvis Presley	1961
What A Wonderful World	Louis Armstrong	1968
I'll Never Fall In Love Again	Bobbie Gentry	1969

THE 1970S

Wand'rin Star	Lee Marvin	1970
Daydreamer/The Puppy Song	David Cassidy	1973
If	Telly Savalas	1975
Tears On My Pillow	Johnny Nash	1975
I Can't Give You Anything (But My Love)	The Stylistics	1975
When A Child Is Born (Soleado)	Johnny Mathis	1976
Chanson D'Amour	Manhattan Transfer	1977
Bright Eyes	Art Garfunkel	1979

THE 1980S

Together We Are Beautiful	Fern Kinney	1980
Theme From M*A*S*H	M*A*S*H	1980
Use It Up And Wear It Out	Odyssey	1980
Move Closer	Phyllis Nelson	1985
Reet Petite	Jackie Wilson	1986
Jack Your Body	Steve "Silk" Hurley	1987
First Time	Robin Beck	1988
Something's Gotten Hold Of My Heart	Gene Pitney (with Marc Almond)	1989

THE 1990S

Show Me Heaven	Maria McKee	1990
Do The Bartman	The Simpsons	1991
Without You	Mariah Carey	1994
Love Can Build A Bridge	Cher, Chrissie Hynde, Neneh Cherry with Eric Clapton	1995
(Cher and Chrissie Hynde are both American)		
Don't Stop (Wiggle Wiggle)	The Outhere Brothers	1995
Killing Me Softly	The Fugees	1996
Ready Or Not	The Fugees	1996
Professional Widow	Tori Amos	1997
Don't Speak	No Doubt	1997
Men In Black	Will Smith	1997
It's Like That	Run-DMC Vs. Jason Nevins	1998
U Don't Know Me	Armand Van Helden	1999
King Of My Castle	The Wamdue Project	1999

THE 2000S

Born To Make You Happy	Britney Spears	2000
Against All Odds	Mariah Carey featuring Westlife	2000
Another Chance	Roger Sanchez	2001
Be Faithful	Fatman Scoop	2003
Mad World	Michael Andrews & Gary Jules	2003
Cha Cha Slide (Part 2)	DJ Casper	2004
No Tomorrow	Orson	2006
I Don't Feel Like Dancin'	Scissor Sisters	2006
What A Wonderful World	Eva Cassidy (with Katie Melua)	2007
Killing In The Name	Rage Against The Machine	2009

Above: Lauryn Hill of The Fugees.

BRITISH HITS WHICH REACHED NO. 1 IN THE US WITHOUT CHARTING IN THE UK

Eight Days A Week	The Beatles	1965
Mrs. Brown You've Got A Lovely Daughter	Herman's Hermits	1965
I'm Henry VIII, I Am	Herman's Hermits	1965
To Sir With Love	Lulu	1967
The Long And Winding Road	The Beatles	1970
How Can You Mend A Broken Heart	The Bee Gees	1971
Uncle Albert/Admiral Halsey	Paul & Linda McCartney	1971
Have You Never Been Mellow	Olivia Newton-John	1975
Saturday Night	The Bay City Rollers	1976
(Love Is) Thicker Than Water	Andy Gibb	1978
Wild Wild West	The Escape Club	1988

The Beatles, Herman's Hermits and Paul McCartney's tracks were not released as singles in Britain, and therefore stood no chance of charting. Lulu's 'To Sir With Love' was the British B-side of her single 'Let's Pretend', promoted later as an American A-side when the film of the same name was released stateside. Demonstrating how disparate musical tastes either side of the Atlantic are, there hasn't been anything added to this list in over 30 years.

Right: Herman's Hermits, led by Peter Noone in 1966.

Some of these singles, like Presley's 'Wooden Heart', were not released in the US at the time of their British success. Others were novelties or film tie-ins which seemed to click with British tastes, but were not, however, promoted in America.

YOUNGEST CHART-TOPPING ARTISTS

Teenagers have been topping the charts since the 1950s, but perhaps surprisingly three of these four lists are led by teens from the early 1960s. In the male lists, not one artist from the 1990s appears. Michael Jackson, Stevie Wonder and Paul Anka all topped the charts in their 30s as well, at 37, 35, and 33 respectively. A betting man would probably put money on Kylie Minogue being the first person to make both the Youngest and Oldest lists.

MALE TEENAGE US CHART-TOPPERS

			Years-Months-Days
Fingertips	Stevie Wonder	Aug 10, 1963	13-2-28
Jump	Kris Kross	Apr 25, 1992	13-3-15 (Chris Smith) 13-8-14 (Chris Kelly)
Go Away Little Girl	Donny Osmond	Sept 11, 1971	13-9-2
Ben	Michael Jackson	Oct 14, 1972	14-1-15
He's Got the Whole World In His Hands	Laurie London	Apr 19, 1958	14-3-0
Run It!	Chris Brown	Nov 26, 2005	15-6-21
Diana	Paul Anka	Sep 14, 1957	16-1-16
Itsy Bitsy Teenie Weenie Yellow Polkadot Bikini	Brian Hyland	Aug 13, 1960	16-9-1
Crank That Soulja Boy	Soulja Boy	Sep 15, 2007	17-1-18
Let Me Love You	Mario	Jan 01, 2005	17-4-7
Kiss Kiss	Chris Brown (featuring T-Pain)	Nov 10, 2007	17-6-5
Beautiful Girls	Sean Kingston	Aug 11, 2007	17-6-8
Lonely Boy	Paul Anka	Jul 18, 1959	17-11-18
Poor Little Fool	Ricky Nelson	Aug 09, 1958	18-3-1
Take Good Care Of My Baby	Bobby Vee	Sep 23, 1961	18-4-24
Venus	Frankie Avalon	Mar 14, 1959	19-5-24
Da Doo Ron Ron	Shaun Cassidy	Jul 16, 1977	19-9-19

Left: Chris Brown's debut single went straight to the top of the US charts.

Jimmy Boyd was 12 years, 11 months and 18 days when he topped the chart with 'I Saw Mommy Kissing Santa Claus' in 1952 pre-rock era. Michael Jackson's first US chart-topper, the ballad 'Ben' – written about a rat – was penned by Don Black and Walter Scharf, and originally offered to fellow teen heart-throb, Donny Osmond.

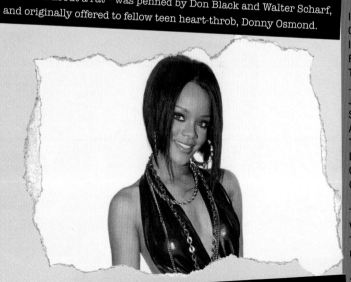

Above: "Good Girl Gone Bad" – R&B star Rihanna.

Lesley's Gore's self-pitying 'It's My Party' was also the first US singles chart-topper for its producer, Quincy Jones. The pair recorded the timeless nugget at Bell Sound Studios in New York on March 30, 1963.

FEMALE TEENAGE US CHART-TOPPERS

			Years-Months-Days
I Will Follow Him	Little Peggy March	Apr 27, 1963	15-1-20
I'm Sorry	Brenda Lee	Jul 23, 1960	15-7-7
I Wanted To Be Wanted (Per Tutta La Vita)	Brenda Lee	Oct 29, 1960	15-10-18
I Think We're Alone Now	Tiffany	Nov 07, 1987	16-1-5
Could've Been	Tiffany	Feb 06, 1988	16-4-4
It's My Party	Lesley Gore	Jun 01, 1963	17-0-30
Foolish Beat	Debbie Gibson	Jun 25, 1988	17-9-25
The First Night	Monica	Oct 03, 1998	17-11-9
... Baby One More Time	Britney Spears	Jan 30, 1990	18-1-28
Johnny Angel	Shelley Fabares	Apr 07, 1962	18-2-19
SOS	Rihanna	May 13, 2006	18-2-24
Angel Of Mine	Monica	Feb 13, 1999	18-3-20
The Boy Is Mine	Monica (with Brandy)	Jun 06, 1998	18-4-18
Lost In Your Eyes	Debbie Gibson	Mar 04, 1989	18-6-4
Genie In A Bottle	Christina Aguilera	Jul 31, 1999	18-7-13
Goodies	Ciara (featuring Peter Pablo)	Sep 11, 2004	18-10-17
To Sir With Love	Lulu	Oct 21, 1967	18-11-18
What A Girl Wants	Christina Aguilera	Jan 15, 2000	19-0-28
The Loco-motion	Little Eva	Aug 25, 1962	19-1-27
Umbrella	Rihanna (featuring Jay-Z)	Jun 09, 2007	19-3-20
The Boy Is Mine	Brandy (with Brandy)	Jun 06, 1998	19-3-26
Come On Over Baby (All I Want Is You)	Christina Aguilera	Oct 14, 2000	19-9-26

MALE TEENAGE UK CHART-TOPPERS

			Years-Months-Days
Long Haired Lover From Liverpool	Little Jimmy Osmond	Dec 23, 1972	9-8-7
Puppy Love	Donny Osmond	Jul 08, 1972	14-7-1
The Twelfth Of Never	Donny Osmond	Mar 31, 1973	15-3-24
Young Love	Donny Osmond	Aug 25, 1973	15-8-18
Diana	Paul Anka	Aug 31, 1957	16-1-1
Beautiful Girls	Sean Kingston	Sep 08, 2007	17-7-5
Unchained Melody	Gareth Gates	Mar 30, 2002	17-8-18
Anyone Of Us (Stupid Mistake)	Gareth Gates	Jul 20, 2002	18-0-8
Nothing's Gonna Change My Love	Glenn Medeiros	Jul 09, 1988	18-0-15
Spirit In The Sky	Gareth Gates (with the Kumars)	Mar 22, 2003	18-8-10
Living Doll	Cliff Richard	Aug 01, 1959	18-9-13
Oopsy Daisy	Chipmunk	Oct 17, 2009	18-10-21
Fill Me In	Craig David	Apr 15, 2000	18-11-10
When You Believe	Leon Jackson	Dec 29, 2007	18-11-29
Travellin' Light	Cliff Richard	Oct 31, 1959	19-0-17
7 Days	Craig David	Aug 05, 2000	19-3-0
What Do You Want?	Adam Faith	Dec 05, 1959	19-5-12
Poor Me	Adam Faith	Mar 05, 1960	19-8-11
Please Don't Tease	Cliff Richard	Jul 30, 1960	19-9-16

Above: Little Jimmy Osmond in 1972.

The ninth and youngest sibling in the Osmond family musical dynasty, Little Jimmy Osmond still pops up regularly on UK stage and television, playing Teen Angel in a West End production of *Grease* in 2009 and on ITV's *Popstar To Operastar* in 2010.

FEMALE TEENAGE UK CHART-TOPPERS

			Years-Months-Days
You Don't Know	Helen Shapiro	Aug 10, 1961	14-10-13
Walkin' Back to Happiness	Helen Shapiro	Oct 19, 1961	15-0-21
Because We Want To	Billie	Jul 05, 1998	15-9-13
Girlfriend	Billie	Oct 11, 1998	16-0-19
I Think We're Alone Now	Tiffany	Jan 30, 1988	16-3-28
... Baby One More Time	Britney Spears	Feb 21, 1999	17-2-19
A Little Peace	Nicole	May 15, 1982	17-6-21
(There's) Always Something There to Remind Me	Sandie Shaw	Oct 22, 1964	17-7-26
Day & Night	Billie Piper	May 21, 2000	17-7-30
Born to Make You Happy	Britney Spears	Jan 23, 2000	18-1-21
Can't Fight the Moonlight	LeAnn Rimes	Nov 19, 2000	18-2-22
Long Live Love	Sandie Shaw	May 27, 1965	18-3-1
Those Were the Days	Mary Hopkin	Sep 25, 1968	18-4-22
Mama Do (Uh Oh, Uh Oh)	Pixie Lott	Jun 14, 2009	18-5-2
Oops!... I Did It Again	Britney Spears	May 07, 2000	18-5-5
You'll Never Stop Me Loving You	Sonia	Jul 22, 1989	18-5-9
All Kinds of Everything	Dana	Apr 18, 1970	18-7-19
Boys and Girls	Pixie Lott	Sep 13, 2009	18-8-1
Genie in a Bottle	Christina Aguilera	Oct 10, 1999	18-9-22
Kiss Kiss	Holly Valance	May 05, 2002	18-11-24
Goodies	Ciara featuring Petey Pablo	Jan 23, 2005	19-2-29
Who's Sorry Now?	Connie Francis	May 16, 1958	19-5-4
Carolina Moon/Stupid Cupid	Connie Francis	Sep 26, 1958	19-9-14
Wuthering Heights	Kate Bush	Mar 11, 1978	19-7-9
I Should Be So Lucky	Kylie Minogue	Feb 20, 1988	19-8-23
Softly, Softly	Ruby Murray	Feb 18, 1955	19-10-20

Above: Pixie Lott.

18-year-old British newcomer Victoria Louise Lott – aka Pixie Lott – scored a number one hit with her first offering, 'Mama Do (Uh Oh, Oh Oh)' in the summer of 2009. The synth-pop smash was co-written and co-produced by veteran hitmaker Phil Thornalley.

OLDEST CHART-TOPPING ARTISTS

Only seven women appear on these lists – all but one of them in their 40s. However, the men's lists comprise 31 artists – two in their 60s and 13 in their 50s. Even in the music business it seems it's a man's world.

OLDEST MALE US CHART-TOPPERS

			Years-Months-Days
Hello, Dolly!	Louis Armstrong	May 09, 1964	63-9-5
Calcutta	Lawrence Welk	Feb 25, 1961	57-11-14
Moonglow and Theme from Picnic	Morris Stoloff	May 26, 1956	57-9-25
Theme From A Summer Place	Percy Faith	Apr 18, 1960	52-0-11
Somethin' Stupid	Frank Sinatra (with Nancy Sinatra)	May 06, 1967	51-4-24
The Stripper	David Rose	Jul 07, 1962	51-0-22
Ringo	Lorne Greene	Dec 05, 1964	50-9-23
Candle in the Wind (1997)/ Something About The Way You Look Tonight (1997)	Elton John	Jan 10, 1998	50-9-16
Strangers In The Night	Frank Sinatra	Jul 02, 1966	50-6-20
All For Love	Rod Stewart (with Bryan Adams & Sting)	Feb 05, 1994	49-0-26
(I've Had) the Time of My Life	Bill Medley (with Jennifer Warnes)	Nov 28, 1987	47-2-9
Everybody Loves Somebody	Dean Martin	Aug 15, 1964	47-1-29
Convoy	C.W. McCall	Jan 10, 1976	47-1-26
The Candy Man	Sammy Davis Jr.	Jun 24, 1972	46-6-16
I'd Do Anything For Love (But I Won't Do That)	Meat Loaf	Dec 04, 1993	46-2-7
Love Theme From Romeo And Juliet	Henry Mancini	Jul 05, 1969	45-2-19
Islands In The Stream	Kenny Rogers (with Dolly Parton)	Nov 05, 1983	45-2-15
Grease	Frankie Valli	Sep 02, 1978	44-3-30
Love Is Blue	Paul Mauriat	Mar 09, 1968	43-0-5
Lady	Kenny Rogers	Dec 20, 1980	42-3-29
The Next Time I Fall	Peter Cetera (with Amy Grant)	Dec 06, 1986	42-2-23
The Most Beautiful Girl	Charlie Rich	Dec 22, 1973	41-11-22
Glory Of Love	Peter Cetera	Aug 09, 1986	41-10-27
My Eyes Adored You	Frankie Valli	Mar 22, 1975	40-9-19

Above: Jazz legend Louis Armstrong in 1967.

Excluded here, Carlos Santana, who as leader of the group Santana scored two Number Ones in 2000 at the age of 53.

Below: Madonna in 2001.

OLDEST FEMALE US CHART-TOPPERS

			Years-Months-Days
Believe	Cher	Apr 03, 1999	52-10-14
What's Love Got To Do With It	Tina Turner	Sep 15, 1984	45-9-20
I Knew You Were Waiting (For Me)	Aretha Franklin (with George Michael)	Apr 25, 1987	44-11-0
The Wind Beneath My Wings	Bette Midler	Jun 10, 1989	43-6-9
Music	Madonna	Oct 07, 2000	42-1-21

Tina Turner's comeback hit, 'What's Love Got To Do With It' also became the title to her 1993 biographical film starring Angela Bassett as the R&B legend.

OLDEST MALE UK CHART-TOPPERS

			Years-Months-Days
What A Wonderful World	Louis Armstrong	May 18, 1968	66-9-14
(Is This The Way To) Amarillo	Tony Christie	May 17, 2005	62-0-23
The Millennium Prayer	Cliff Richard	Dec 18, 1999	59-2-4
Are You Ready For Love?	Elton John	Sep 06, 2003	56-5-12
Chocolate Salty Balls (PS I Love You)	Isaac Hayes (as Chef)	Jan 16, 1999	56-4-27
If	Telly Savalas	Mar 15, 1975	53-1-22
Candle In The Wind 1997	Elton John	Oct 18, 1997	51-6-23
Somethin' Stupid	Frank Sinatra	Apr 22, 1967	51-4-10
Grandad	Clive Dunn	Jan 23, 1971	51-0-14
Strangers In The Night	Frank Sinatra	Jun 18, 1966	50-6-4
Unchained Melody	Righteous Brothers	Nov 24, 1990	50-3-14 (Bobby Hatfield) 50-2-5 (Bill Medley)
She	Charles Aznavour	Jul 20, 1974	50-1-28
Something's Gotten Hold Of My Heart	Gene Pitney	Feb 18, 1989	49-0-1
Stand By Me	Ben E. King	Mar 07, 1987	48-5-7
Theme From Moulin Rouge	Mantovani	Sep 05, 1953	47-9-21
Wand'rin' Star	Lee Marvin	Mar 21, 1970	46-1-2
Sexy Chick	David Guetta (featuring Akon)	Sep 05, 2009	41-9-29
When Love Takes Over	David Guetta (featuring Kelly Rowland)	Jun 27, 2009	41-7-20

Above: French DJ David Guetta.

The ages listed are those of the artists during the final week of their Number One hit. Gene Pitney was just one day past his 49th birthday when his 1989 duet success with ex-Soft Cell frontman Marc Almond finished its chart-topping run. Tom Jones and Robin Gibb were featured artists on Vanessa Jenkins & Bryn West's 2009 chart-topper 'Islands In The Stream', respectively aged 68 years, 9 months and 14 days and 59 years, 2 months and 23 days.

Below: Cher in 1998.

OLDEST UK FEMALE CHART-TOPPERS

			Years-Months-Days
Believe	Cher	Dec 12, 1998	52-6-22
4 Minutes	Madonna	May 17, 2008	49-9-1
Sorry	Madonna	Mar 04, 2006	47-6-16
Hung Up	Madonna	Dec 10, 2005	47-3-24
The Shoop Shoop Song (It's in His Kiss)	Cher	Jun 01, 1991	45-0-12
The Poor People Of Paris	Winifred Atwell	Apr 28, 1956	42-2-1
Music	Madonna	Sep 09, 2000	42-0-24
Chain Reaction	Diana Ross	Mar 22, 1986	41-11-24
American Pie	Madonna	Mar 11, 2000	41-6-24
Let's Have Another Party	Winifred Atwell	Jan 01, 1955	40-10-5

'Believe' marked a remarkable comeback for veteran artiste Cherilyn Sarkisian (Cher) making her the only female singer over 50 to top the UK singles chart. It was also the first chart-topper to use the Auto-Tune vocal effect, which became ubiquitous on dance-pop singles in the noughties. The ages listed are those of the artists during the final week of their Number One hit.

MOST WEEKS ATOP THE UK SINGLES CHART

Title	Artist	Year	Weeks
I Believe	Frankie Laine	1953	18
(Everything I Do) I Do it For You	Bryan Adams	1991	16
Love Is All Around	Wet Wet Wet	1994	15
Bohemian Rhapsody	Queen	1975/1991	14
Rose Marie	Slim Whitman	1955	11
Cara Mia	David Whitfield	1954	10
I Will Always Love You	Whitney Houston	1993	10
Umbrella	Rihanna featuring Jay-Z	2007	10
Here In My Heart	Al Martino	1952	9
Oh Mein Papa	Eddie Calvert	1954	9
Secret Love	Doris Day	1954	9
Diana	Paul Anka	1957	9
Mull Of Kintyre	Wings	1977	9
You're The One That I Want	John Travolta & Olivia Newton-John	1978	9
Two Tribes	Frankie Goes To Hollywood	1984	9
Crazy	Gnarls Barkley	2006	9
Answer Me	Frankie Laine	1953	8
Magic Moments	Perry Como	1958	8
It's Now Or Never	Elvis Presley	1960	8
Wonderful Land	The Shadows	1962	8
Sugar Sugar	The Archies	1969	8
Stay	Shakespear's Sister	1992	8

The totals for 'I Believe', 'Bohemian Rhapsody' and 'Secret Love' are cumulative and include more than one run at the top, in the first case because the single dropped to No. 2 for two weeks in what would otherwise have been a 20-week spell at No. 1, and in the second case through a return to the top for a second lengthy run 16 years after its first. All other totals are for consecutive chart-topping weeks.

ARTISTS WITH MOST UK HITS WITHOUT REACHING THE TOP

Artist	Hits	Artist	Hits
Depeche Mode (4)	47	Orchestral Manoeuvres In The Dark (3)	30
Bon Jovi (2)	39	Billy Fury (2)	29
Janet Jackson (2)	39	AC/DC (12)	28
The Stranglers (2)	39	Kim Wilde (2)	29
R.E.M. (3)	38	Siouxsie & the Banshees (3)	29
Morrissey (3)	37	Texas (3)	27
Nat King Cole (2)	35	Bruce Springsteen (2)	26
Elvis Costello (2)	34	Bananarama (3)	29
Luther Vandross (2)	34	Mary J. Blige (2)	29
The Cure (5)	33	Level 42 (3)	29
New Order (3)	33	Genesis (4)	29
Chris Rea (10)	33	Electric Light Orchestra (3)	28
Sting (2)	33	The Charlatans (3)	27
Paul Weller (5)	33	Marillion (2)	27
Tina Turner (3)	32	Def Leppard (2)	26
The Who (2)	31		
Gloria Estefan (6)	30		

Highest position reached in brackets.

MOST WEEKS ATOP THE US SINGLES CHART

Title	Artist	Year	Weeks
One Sweet Day	Mariah Carey & Boyz II Men	1995	16
I Will Always Love You	Whitney Houston	1992	14
I'll Make Love To You	Boyz II Men	1994	14
Macarena (Bayside Boys Mix)	Los Del Rio	1996	14
Candle In The Wind/Something About The Way You Look Tonight	Elton John	1997	14
We Belong Together	Mariah Carey	2005	14
I Gotta Feeling	The Black Eyed Peas	2009	14
End Of The Road	Boyz II Men	1992	13
The Boy Is Mine	Brandy & Monica	1998	13
Smooth	Santana featuring Rob Thomas	1999	12
Lose Yourself	Eminem	2002	12
Yeah!	Usher featuring Lil Jon & Ludacris	2004	12
Boom Boom Pow	The Black Eyed Peas	2009	12
Don't Be Cruel/Hound Dog	Elvis Presley	1956	11
I Swear	All-4-One	1994	11
Un-break My Heart	Toni Braxton	1996	11
I'll Be Missing You	Puff Daddy & Faith Evans featuring 112	1997	11
Independent Women Part 1	Destiny's Child	2000	11
Cherry Pink And Apple Blossom White	Perez Prado	1955	10
You Light Up My Life	Debby Boone	1977	10
Physical	Olivia Newton-John	1981	10
Maria Maria	Santana featuring Product G&B	2000	10
Foolish	Ashanti	2002	10
Dilemma	Nelly featuring Kelly Rowland	2002	10
Gold Digger	Kanye West featuring Jamie Foxx	2005	10
Irreplaceable	Beyoncé	2006	10
Low	Flo Rida featuring T-Pain	2009	10

1981 holds the record for the year with the greatest number of singles (three) hosting runs of two months or more.

Left: Depeche Mode's frontman, Dave Gahan, in 2003.

British synth-rock pioneers Depeche Mode have charted steadily since their first single, 'Dreaming Of Me' made UK Number 57 in 1981. The group's entire British catalogue, spanning nearly 30 years, has been released by Mute Records.

POSTHUMOUS UK NUMBER ONES

Song	Artist (death)	Date
It Doesn't Matter Anymore	Buddy Holly (Feb 03, 1959)	Apr 25, 1959
Three Steps To Heaven	Eddie Cochran (Apr 17, 1960)	Jun 25, 1960
Distant Drums	Jim Reeves (Jul 31, 1964)	Sep 24, 1966
Voodoo Chile	Jimi Hendrix (Sep 18, 1970)	Nov 21, 1970
Way Down	Elvis Presley (Aug 16, 1977)	Sep 03, 1977
(Just Like) Starting Over	John Lennon (Dec 08, 1980)	Dec 20, 1980
Imagine	John Lennon (Dec 08, 1980)	Jan 10, 1981
Woman	John Lennon (Dec 08, 1980)	Feb 07, 1981
Reet Petite (The Finest Girl You Ever Want To Meet)	Jackie Wilson (Jan 21, 1984)	Dec 27, 1986
Living On My Own	Freddie Mercury (Nov 24, 1991)	Aug 14, 1993
More Than A Woman	Aaliyah (Aug 25, 2001)	Jan 19, 2002
My Sweet Lord	George Harrison (Nov 29, 2001)	Jan 26, 2002
A Little Less Conversation	Elvis (Aug 16, 1977) Vs. JXL	Jun 22, 2002
Jailhouse Rock	Elvis Presley (Aug 16, 1977)	Jan 15, 2005
One Night/i Got Stung	Elvis Presley (Aug 16, 1977)	Jan 22, 2005
It's Now Or Never	Elvis Presley (Aug 16, 1977)	Feb 05, 2005
Ghetto Gospel	2Pac (Sep 13, 1996)	July 02, 2005
Nasty Girl	The Notorious B.I.G. (Mar 09, 97)	Feb 04, 2006
What A Wonderful World	Eva Cassidy (Nov 02, 1996) (with Katie Melua)	Dec 22, 2007

ARTISTS WITH MOST US HITS WITHOUT REACHING THE TOP

Artist		Artist	
James Brown (2)	91	Tom Jones (2)	29
Fats Domino (4)	57	Bobby Rydell (2)	29
Jackie Wilson (4)	49	George Strait (11)	29
Brook Benton (2)	46	Duane Eddy (4)	27
Johnny Cash (2)	44	The Pointer Sisters (2)	27
Nat King Cole (2)	43	Rascal Flatts (6)	27
The Isley Brothers (2)	41	The Spinners (2)	27
Andy Williams (2)	41	Bruce Springsteen (2)	27
The Impressions (4)	39	Joe Tex (2)	27
Wilson Pickett (8)	39	Brooks & Dunn (25)	26
Tim McGraw (3)	39	Solomon Burke (22)	26
Jerry Butler (4)	37	Duane Eddy (4)	26
Bobby Bland (22)	36	Journey (2)	26
Glee Cast (4)	34	Electric Light Orchestra (4)	25
Al Martino (3)	34	Johnny Tillotson (2)	25
Kenny Chesney (22)	32	Taylor Swift (2)	25
B.B. King (15)	32		
Patti Page (5)	32		
George Strait (11)	31	Highest position reached in brackets.	
Toby Keith (22)	30		
Joe Simon (8)	30		

The shortest period of time for a single to reach the top after the artist's death is John Lennon's '(Just Like) Starting Over', which hit Number One eight days after his shooting. Elvis Presley holds the record for most posthumous chart-toppers with four. George Harrison replaced Aaliyah at the summit in 2001, marking the only time in UK chart history that one posthumous act has replaced another at the top. Of the 19 records included in this list, Lennon's 'Imagine' is the biggest-selling. Elton John has scored hits with two posthumous acts – John Lennon and 2Pac.

Top Left: James Brown in Las Vegas, 2002.

Right: Elvis gets his fans "all shook up".

James Brown beats all comers having nabbed nearly 100 Hot 100 entries since 1956, but not once making pole position. His biggest success at number two was 1965's 'I Got You (I Feel Good)'.

POSTHUMOUS US NUMBER ONES

Song	Artist (death)	Date
(Sittin' On) The Dock Of The Bay	Otis Redding (Dec 10, 1967)	Mar 16, 1968
Me And Bobby McGee	Janis Joplin (Oct 04, 1970)	Mar 20, 1971
Time In A Bottle	Jim Croce (Sep 20, 1973)	Dec 29, 1973
(Just Like) Starting Over	John Lennon (Dec 08, 1980)	Dec 27, 1980
Hypnotize	The Notorious B.I.G. (Mar 09, 1977)	May 03, 1997
Mo Money Mo Problems (feat. Puff Daddy & Mase)	The Notorious B.I.G. (Mar 09, 1977)	Aug 30, 1997
Slow Motion (with Juvenile)	Soulja Slim (Nov 26, 2003)	Aug 07, 2004
Lollipop (with Lil Wayne)	Static Major (Feb 25, 2008)	May 03, 2008

Otis Redding's soul classic was originally recorded on November 22, 1967 at the legendary Stax recording studio in Memphis. He died 18 days later on December 10 – and the single was released just four weeks after that tragedy, on January 8, 1968.

UK NUMBER ONES BY DIFFERENT ARTISTS

Answer Me	David Whitfield (1953)
	Frankie Laine (1953)
Cherry Pink And Apple Blossom White	Perez Prado (1953)
	Eddie Calvert (1955)
Unchained Melody	Jimmy Young (1955)
	The Righteous Brothers (1990)
	Robson & Jerome (1995)
	Gareth Gates (2002)
Singing The Blues	Guy Mitchell (1957)
	Tommy Steele (1957)
Young Love	Tab Hunter (1957)
	Donny Osmond (1973)
Mary's Boy Child	Harry Belafonte (1957)
	Boney M. (1978)
Living Doll	Cliff Richard and The Drifters (1959)
	Cliff Richard & the Young Ones featuring Hank Marvin (1986)
Can't Help Falling In Love	Elvis Presley (1962)
	UB40 (1993)
You'll Never Walk Alone	Gerry & the Pacemakers (1963)
	The Crowd (1985)
	Robson & Jerome (1996)
I Got You Babe	Sonny & Cher (1965)
	UB40 and Chrissie Hynde (1985)
Somethin' Stupid	Frank Sinatra & Nancy Sinatra (1967)
	Robbie Williams & Nicole Kidman (2001)
Baby Come Back	The Equals (1967)
	Pato Banton featuring UB40 (1994)
What A Wonderful World	Louis Armstrong (1968)
	Katie Melua & Eva Cassidy (2007)
With A Little Help From My Friends	Joe Cocker (1968)
	Wet Wet Wet (1988)
	Sam & Mark (2004)
Spirit In The Sky	Norman Greenbaum (1971)
	Doctor & the Medics (1986)
	Gareth Gates & the Kumars (2003)
Without You	Harry Nilsson (1972)
	Mariah Carey (1994)
Seasons In The Sun	Terry Jacks (1974)
	Westlife (1999)
Tragedy	The Bee Gees (1979)
	Steps (1999)
The Tide Is High	Blondie (1980)
	Atomic Kitten (2002)
Uptown Girl	Billy Joel (1983)
	Westlife (2001)
Do They Know It's Christmas?	Band Aid (1985)
	Band Aid II (1989)
	Band Aid 20 (2004)
Eternal Flame	The Bangles (1989)
	Atomic Kitten (2001)
You Are Not Alone	Michael Jackson (1995)
	X Factor Finalists 2009 (2009)
Lady Marmalade	All Saints (1998)
	Christina Aguilera, Lil Kim, Mya & P!nk (2001)
Mambo No. 5	Lou Bega (1999)
	Bob the Builder (2001)
Against All Odds (Take A Look At Me Now)	Mariah Carey featuring Westlife (2000)
	Steve Brookstein (2005)

US NUMBER ONES BY DIFFERENT ARTISTS

Please Mr. Postman	The Marvelettes (1961)
	The Carpenters (1975)
The Loco-Motion	Little Eva (1962)
	Grand Funk (1974)
Go Away Little Girl	Steve Lawrence (1963)
	Donny Osmond (1971)
You Keep Me Hangin' On	The Supremes (1966)
	Kim Wilde (1987)
When a Man Loves a Woman	Percy Sledge (1966)
	Michael Bolton (1991)
I'll Be There	The Jackson 5 (1970)
	Mariah Carey (1992)
Venus	Shocking Blue (1970)
	Bananarama (1986)
Lean on Me	Bill Withers (1972)
	Club Nouveau (1987)
Lady Marmalade	Labelle (1975)
	Christina Aguilera, Lil Kim, Mya & P!nk (2001)

Above: Richard and Karen Carpenter.

FOREIGN LANGUAGE UK CHART-TOPPERS

Je T'aime ... Moi Non Plus	Jane Birkin & Serge Gainsbourg	French	Oct 11, 1969
Rock Me Amadeus	Falco	English/German	May 10, 1986
La Bamba	Los Lobos	Spanish	Aug 01, 1987
Livin' La Vida Loca	Ricky Martin	English/Spanish	Jul 17, 1999

FOREIGN LANGUAGE US CHART TOPPERS

Nel Blu Dipinto Di Blu (Volare)	Domenico Modugno	Italian	Sep 01, 1958
Sukiyaki	Kyu Sakamoto	Japanese	Jun 15, 1963
Dominique	The Singing Nun	French	Dec 07, 1963
Begin The Beguine (Volver A Empezar)	Julio Iglesias	English/Spanish	Dec 05, 1981
Rock Me Amadeus	Falco	English/German	Mar 29, 1986
La Bamba	Los Lobos	Spanish	Aug 29, 1987
Macarena (Bayside Boys Mix)	Los del Río	English/Spanish	Aug 03, 1996
Livin' La Vida Loca	Ricky Martin	English/Spanish	May 08, 1999

'Unchained Melody' has been Number One on four occasions by four different artists, with 'You'll Never Walk Alone', 'With A Little Help From My Friends', 'Spirit In The Sky' and 'Do They Know It's Christmas?' all clocking in three times.

MOST UK CHART SINGLES

Elvis Presley	173	Rod Stewart	59
Cliff Richard	135	Stevie Wonder	58
Michael Jackson	101	Queen	56
Elton John	87	Prince	55
David Bowie	71	The Rolling Stones	55
Madonna	68	The Beatles	54
Diana Ross	65	UB40	50
Status Quo	65		

Below: Frank Sinatra in 1953.

Presley's unrivalled haul of British hits began on May 12, 1956 when 'Heartbreak Hotel' marked his debut on the chart.

Above: Elvis at Graceland.

MOST UK CHART ALBUMS

Elvis Presley	113	Neil Young	39
Frank Sinatra	62	Neil Diamond	38
James Last	60	Status Quo	38
Cliff Richard	59	Shirley Bassey	37
Bob Dylan	52	The Beatles	37
The Rolling Stones	47	Van Morrison	36
David Bowie	42	Paul McCartney/Wings	35
Elton John	42	Iron Maiden	34
Diana Ross	42	The Shadows	31
Rod Stewart	39		

As co-founders of Britain's most enduring hard rock act, Francis Rossi and Alan Lancaster formed their first combo, The Spectres, in 1962 before name-changing to Status Quo in 1967. Their first charting album was *Piledriver* in 1972.

MOST US CHART SINGLES

Elvis Presley	123	The Rolling Stones	57
James Brown	92	Neil Diamond	57
Ray Charles	76	Dionne Warwick	56
Aretha Franklin	75	Madonna	55
The Beatles	72	Jackie Wilson	54
Elton John	65	Connie Francis	53
Fats Domino	57	The Temptations	53
Stevie Wonder	62	Ricky Nelson	52
The Beach Boys	56	Rod Stewart	51
Marvin Gaye	58		

Presley's remarkable US chart run started on March 10, 1956, also with 'Heartbreak Hotel'. It proved to be the first of five US number ones for Elvis that year alone.

Right: Johnny Mathis.

MOST US CHART ALBUMS

Elvis Presley	110	Lawrence Welk	38
Frank Sinatra	86	The Rolling Stones	42
Johnny Mathis	68	Neil Diamond	48
Willie Nelson	59	Johnny Cash	46
Bob Dylan	56	The Grateful Dead	46
Ray Conniff	50	Aretha Franklin	44
James Brown	50	Neil Young	44
The Temptations	50	Kenny Rogers/First Edition	42
The Beatles	48	Elton John	41
The Beach Boys	48	Henry Mancini	40
Mantovani	47		

Prolific pop crooner Johnny Mathis has recorded more than 100 albums in a career spanning more than 50 years from 1956's *Johnny Mathis* to *A Night To Remember* in 2008.

SIMULTANEOUS US/UK SINGLES CHART-TOPPERS

Oh Mein Papa	Eddie Calvert	Jan 09, 1954
Cherry Pink And Apple Blossom White	Perez Prado	May 07, 1955
Memories Are Made Of This	Dean Martin	Feb 18, 1956
Singing The Blues	Guy Mitchell	Jan 05, 1957
It's All In The Game	Everly Brothers	May 28, 1960
Can't Buy Me Love	The Beatles	Apr 04, 1964
A Hard Day's Night	The Beatles	Aug 01, 1964
Oh, Pretty Woman	Roy Orbison	Oct 10, 1964
Baby Love	The Supremes	Nov 21, 1964
I Feel Fine	The Beatles	Dec 26, 1964
You've Lost That Lovin' Feelin'	The Righteous Brothers	Feb 06, 1965
Get Off Of My Cloud	The Rolling Stones	Nov 06, 1965
We Can Work It Out	The Beatles	Jan 08, 1966
These Boots Are Made For Walkin'	Nancy Sinatra	Feb 26, 1966
Somethin' Stupid	Frank & Nancy Sinatra	Apr 15, 1967
Hello Goodbye	The Beatles	Dec 30, 1967
Get Back	The Beatles	May 24, 1969
Honky Tonk Women	The Rolling Stones	Aug 23, 1969
Bridge Over Troubled Water	Simon & Garfunkel	Mar 28, 1970
Maggie May	Rod Stewart	Oct 09, 1971
Without You	Nilsson	Mar 11, 1972
Tie A Yellow Ribbon Round The Ole Oak Tree	Dawn featuring Tony Orlando	Apr 21, 1973
Don't Go Breaking My Heart	Elton John & Kiki Dee	Aug 07, 1976
Night Fever	The Bee Gees	Apr 29, 1978
Three Times A Lady	The Commodores	Aug 19, 1978
I Will Survive	Gloria Gaynor	Mar 17, 1979
Call Me	Blondie	Apr 26, 1980
Woman In Love	Barbra Streisand	Oct 25, 1980
Down Under	Men At Work	Jan 29, 1983
Billie Jean	Michael Jackson	Mar 05, 1983
I Just Called To Say I Love You	Stevie Wonder	Oct 13, 1984
We Are The World	USA for Africa	Apr 20, 1985
(Everything I Do) I Do It For You	Bryan Adams	Jul 27, 1991
End Of The Road	Boyz II Men	Oct 31, 1992
I Will Always Love You	Whitney Houston	Dec 05, 1992
I'd Do Anything For Love (But I Won't Do That)	Meat Loaf	Nov 06, 1993
MMMBop	Hanson	Jun 07, 1997
Candle In The Wind 1997/ Something About The Way You Look Tonight	Elton John	Oct 11, 1997
Independent Women Part 1	Destiny's Child	Dec 02, 2000
Lady Marmalade	Christina Aguilera, Lil' Kim, Mya & P!nk	Jun 30, 2001
Dilemma	Nelly featuring Kelly Rowland	Oct 26, 2002
Lose Yourself	Eminem	Dec 14, 2002
Crazy In Love	Beyoncé featuring Jay-Z	Jul 12, 2003
Yeah!	Usher featuring Ludacris & Lil' John	Apr 10, 2004
Burn	Usher	Jul 17, 2004
SexyBack	Justin Timberlake	Sep 09, 2006
Viva La Vida	Coldplay	Jun 28, 2008
Just Dance	Lady Gaga featuring Colby O'Donis	Jan 17, 2009
Right Round	Flo Rida featuring Ke$ha	Mar 14, 2009
Poker Face	Lady Gaga	Apr 11, 2009
Boom Boom Pow	The Black Eyed Peas	May 23, 2009
I Gotta Feeling	The Black Eyed Peas	Aug 08, 2009

Above: Liverpool's finest chart-toppers.

SIMULTANEOUS CHART-TOPPERS

These acts share the rare distinction of topping the UK and US singles and albums charts at the same time.

	Single	Album	
The Beatles	A Hard Day's Night	A Hard Day's Night	Aug 1964
The Beatles	We Can Work it Out	Rubber Soul	Jan 1966
The Monkees	I'm A Believer	More Of The Monkees	Feb 1967
Simon & Garfunkel	Bridge Over Troubled Water	Bridge Over Troubled Water	Apr 1970
Rod Stewart	Maggie May	Every Picture Tells A Story	Oct 1971
The Bee Gees	Night Fever	Saturday Night Fever	May 1978
Men At Work	Down Under	Business As Usual	Jan 1983
Michael Jackson	Billie Jean	Thriller	Mar 1983
Beyoncé	Crazy In Love	Dangerously In Love	Jul 2003

Above: The Monkees were one of the original made-for-TV pop groups.

Only two years have witnessed a total of five singles simultaneously topping charts on both sides of the Atlantic: 1964 and 2009.

THE ARTISTS WITH THE LONGEST CHART SPANS ON THE UK SINGLES CHART

		Years-months-days
Nat King Cole	Nov 15, 1952–Dec 29, 2007	55-1-14
Perry Como	Jan 17, 1953–Dec 29, 2007	54-11-12
Bing Crosby	Nov 15, 1952–Dec 29, 2007	52-1-14
Elvis Presley	May 12, 1956–Dec 15, 2007	51-7-3
Cliff Richard & the Shadows	Oct 25, 1958–Sep 26, 2009	50-11-1
Andy Williams	Apr 20, 1957–Dec 27, 2007	50-8-7
Shirley Bassey	Feb 16, 1957–Aug 04, 2007	50-5-19
The Four Seasons	Oct 06, 1962–Mar 14, 2009	46-5-8
Bob Dylan	Mar 27, 1965–Jan 02, 2010	44-9-6
Frank Sinatra	Jul 10, 1954–Jan 30, 1999	44-6-20
Tom Jones	Feb 13, 1965–Apr 11, 2009	44-1-29
The Rolling Stones	Jul 27, 1963–Jun 02, 2007	43-10-6
Stevie Wonder	Feb 05, 1966–Sep 26, 2009	43-7-21
The Spencer Davis Group	Nov 07, 1964–Apr 12, 2008	43-5-6
Santana	Sep 28, 1974–Dec 30, 2006	42-3-2
Robin Gibb	Jul 12, 1969–Apr 11, 2009	40-3-1
Status Quo	Jan 27, 1968–Dec 27, 2008	40-10-0
Cat Stevens	Oct 22, 1966–Apr 07, 2007	40-5-16
The Kinks	Aug 15, 1964–Sep 25, 2004	40-1-10
Queen	Mar 09, 1974–Jan 02, 2010	35-9-23
T.Rex	May 11, 1968–Sep 22, 2007	39-4-11
Jackson 5	Jan 31, 1970–May 16, 2009	39-3-16
Cream	Oct 22, 1966–Dec 03, 2005	39-1-11
Nancy Sinatra	Jan 29, 1966–Oct 23, 2004	38-8-24
Slade	Jun 19, 1971–Jan 02, 2010	38-6-13
Johnny Cash	Jun 05, 1965–Nov 22, 2003	38-5-17
David Bowie	Sep 06, 1969–Dec 29, 2007	38-2-23
Wizzard	Dec 09, 1972–Jan 02, 2010	38-0-24
Michael Jackson	Feb 12, 1972–Dec 19, 2009	37-10-7
Neil Diamond	Nov 07, 1970–Jul 12, 2008	37-8-5
Paul McCartney	Feb 27, 1971–Jun 28, 2008	37-5-1
Engelbert Humperdinck	May 27, 1967–Jul 12, 2004	37-1-15
Elton John	Jan 23, 1971–Jan 05, 2008	36-11-13
Bill Withers	Aug 12, 1972–Jun 20, 2009	36-9-8
Cher	Aug 21, 1965–Jan 19, 2002	36-4-29
Lulu	May 16, 1964–Apr 15, 2000	35-10-30
Diana Ross	Jul 18, 1970–Feb 11, 2006	35-6-24
Queen	Mar 09, 1974–Dec 26, 2009	35-9-17
Tony Christie	Jan 09, 1971–Jul 08, 2006	35-5-29
Bobby Boris Pickett	Sep 01, 1973–Nov 15, 2008	35-2-14
Paul Simon	Feb 19, 1972–Jul 01, 2006	34-4-12
Abba	Apr 20, 1974–Aug 23, 2008	34-4-3
The Bee Gees	Apr 29, 1967–May 05, 2001	34-0-6
Mick Jagger	Nov 14, 1970–Nov 13, 2004	33-11-30
The Beatles	Oct 13, 1962–Apr 27, 1996	33-6-14
The Beach Boys	Aug 03, 1963–Mar 23, 1996	32-7-20
George Harrison	Jan 23, 1971–May 31, 2003	32-4-8
Lynyrd Skynyrd	Sep 11, 1976–Sep 20, 2008	32-0-9
John Lennon	Apr 03, 1971–Dec 29, 2007	31-7-26
The Who	Feb 20, 1965–Aug 03, 1996	31-5-14
Steve Harley & Cockney Rebel	May 11, 1974–Jul 09, 2005	31-1-28
The Wurzels	May 15, 1976–May 05, 2007	30-11-20
The Sex Pistols	Dec 11, 1976–Nov 03, 2007	30-10-21
Bob Marley & the Wailers	Sep 27, 1975–Dec 17, 2005	30-2-20
Kenny Rogers	Sep 17, 1977–Nov 03, 2007	30-1-17

THE ARTISTS WITH THE LONGEST CHART SPANS IN THE US SINGLES CHART

		Years-months-days
Elvis Presley	Mar 10, 1956–Oct 04, 2003	47-6-24
The Isley Brothers	Sep 26, 1959–Aug 16, 2003	43-10-21
Stevie Wonder	Aug 10, 1963–Apr 09, 2005	41-8-30
The Rolling Stones	May 02, 1964–Oct 04, 2003	39-5-2
Jeff Beck	Aug 02, 1969–May 19, 2007	37-9-17
Cher	Jul 03, 1965–May 11, 2002	36-10-8
Michael Jackson	Oct 30, 1971–Feb 23, 2008	36-3-24
Santana	Oct 25, 1969–Nov 19, 2005	36-0-24
Paul McCartney	Aug 14, 1971–Jul 14, 2007	35-11-0
Bruce Springsteen	Sep 20, 1975–Feb 21, 2009	33-5-1
Fleetwood Mac	Jan 31, 1970–Jun 07, 2003	33-4-7
Ray Charles	Nov 16, 1957–Mar 03, 1990	32-4-15
The Beatles	Jan 18, 1964–May 04, 1996	32-3-16
Mac McAnally	Jul 09, 1977–Apr 18, 2009	31-9-9
The Eagles	Jun 03, 1972–Nov 01, 2003	31-5-29
George Harrison	Nov 28, 1970–Feb 02, 2002	31-2-5
Daryl Hall & John Oates	Feb 09, 1974–Feb 05, 2005	30-11-27
The Bee Gees	May 27, 1967–Feb 07, 1998	30-8-11
Willie Nelson	Aug 30, 1975–Mar 04, 2006	30-6-4
Kenny Rogers	Mar 13, 1976–Jul 08, 2006	30-3-25
Little Richard	Jan 28, 1956–May 10, 1086	30-3-12
Jimmy Buffett	May 18, 1974–Aug 28, 2004	30-3-10
Elton John	Aug 15, 1970–Jul 29, 2000	29-11-17
Darlene Love	Apr 06, 1963–Jan 16, 1993	29-9-10
Roy Orbison	Jan 23, 1960–May 20, 1989	29-3-27
Dion	Oct 22, 1960–Sep 02, 1989	28-10-11
The Righteous Brothers	May 11, 1963–Mar 23, 1991	27-10-12
James Brown	Dec 20, 1958–Oct 25, 1986	27-10-5
The Beach Boys	Feb 17, 1962–Sep 09, 1989	27-6-23
The Everly Brothers	Jun 01, 1957–Nov 17, 1984	27-5-16
Rod Stewart	Jul 17, 1971–Nov 14, 1998	27-3-28
The Five Satins	Oct 13, 1956–Mar 27, 1982	25-5-14
Madonna	Oct 29, 1983–Aug 22, 2009	25-9-24
Prince	Nov 04, 1978–Mar 11, 2006	27-5-7
Aerosmith	Oct 20, 1973–Jun 09, 2001	27-7-20
U2	Apr 02, 1983–Mar 21, 2009	25-11-19
Janet Jackson	Dec 18, 1982–May 03, 2008	25-4-15
Whitney Houston	Jun 09, 1984–Oct 03, 2009	25-3-24
B.B. King	Mar 28, 1964–May 13, 1989	25-1-15

Elvis first charted with 'Heartbreak Hotel' in 1956 and then managed two more chart appearances with the song in 1971 and 1996.

Left: Nat King Cole.

The "King" of this list, Nat Cole, first charted in 1952 with 'Somewhere Along The Way' and most recently in 2007 with the annual chestnut, 'Christmas Song'.

SINGLES WHICH HAVE DEBUTED AT NUMBER ONE IN THE US

Michael Jackson	You Are Not Alone	Sep 02, 1995
Mariah Carey	Fantasy	Sep 30, 1995
Whitney Houston	Exhale (Shoop Shoop)	Nov 25, 1995
Mariah Carey & Boyz II Men	One Sweet Day	Dec 02, 1995
Puff Daddy & Faith Evans featuring 112	I'll Be Missing You	Jun 14, 1997
Mariah Carey	Honey	Sep 13, 1997
Elton John	Candle in the Wind 1997/ Something About the Way You Look Tonight	Oct 11, 1997
Céline Dion	My Heart Will Go On	Feb 28, 1998
Aerosmith	I Don't Want to Miss a Thing	Sep 05, 1998
Lauryn Hill	Doo Wop (That Thing)	Nov 14, 1998
Céline Dion & R. Kelly	I'm Your Angel	Dec 05, 1998
Clay Aiken	This Is the Night	Jun 28, 2003
Fantasia	I Believe	Jul 10, 2004
Carrie Underwood	Inside Your Heaven	Jul 02, 2005
Taylor Hicks	Do I Make You Proud	Jul 01, 2006
Britney Spears	3	Oct 24, 2009

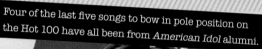

Four of the last five songs to bow in pole position on the Hot 100 have all been from *American Idol* alumni.

Above: American Idol, Carrie Underwood.

From 1952 (when UK chart compilation began) to around the mid-nineties, debuting at number one in the UK was a considerable and rare achievement. However, with dwindling sales and ever-creative, timed marketing campaigns by British record labels, this feat became commonplace and thereby meaningless: from 1996 to 2009, a staggering 322 records bowed in pole position. In the year 2000, 41 songs hit number one in their first week, more than all those combined from 1952 to 1994.

SINGLES WHICH HAVE DEBUTED AT NUMBER ONE IN THE UK (1952–95)

Jailhouse Rock	Elvis Presley	Jan 25, 1958
It's Now Or Never	Elvis Presley	Nov 05, 1960
The Young Ones	Cliff Richard & the Shadows	Jan 13, 1962
Can't Help Falling In Love/ Rock-A-Hula-Baby	Elvis Presley	Mar 03, 1962
Get Back	The Beatles	Apr 26, 1969
Cum On Feel The Noize	Slade	Mar 03, 1973
Skweeze Me, Pleeze Me	Slade	Jun 30, 1973
I Love You Love Me Love	Gary Glitter	Nov 17, 1973
Merry Xmas Everybody	Slade	Dec 15, 1973
Going Underground/ The Dreams Of Children	The Jam	Mar 22, 1980
Don't Stand So Close To Me	Police	Sep 27, 1980
Stand And Deliver	Adam & the Ants	May 09, 1981
Town Called Malice/Precious	The Jam	Feb 13, 1982
Beat Surrender	The Jam	Dec 04, 1982
Is There Something I Should Know?	Duran Duran	Mar 26, 1983
True	Spandau Ballet	Apr 30, 1983
Two Tribes	Frankie Goes To Hollywood	Jun 16, 1984
Do They Know It's Christmas?	Band Aid	Dec 15, 1984
Dancing In The Street	David Bowie & Mick Jagger	Sep 07, 1985
Let It Be	Ferry Aid	Apr 04, 1987
Ferry 'Cross The Mersey	The Christians, Holly Johnson, Paul McCartney, Gerry Marsden & Stock, Aitken & Waterman	May 20, 1989
Sealed With A Kiss	Jason Donovan	Jun 10, 1989
Let's Party	Jive Bunny & the Mastermixers	Dec 16, 1989
Do They Know It's Christmas?	Band Aid II	Dec 23, 1989
Bring Your Daughter To The Slaughter	Iron Maiden	Jan 05, 1991
Innuendo	Queen	Jan 26, 1991
The Fly	U2	Nov 02, 1991
Black Or White	Michael Jackson	Nov 23, 1991
Don't Let The Sun Go Down On Me	George Michael & Elton John	Dec 07, 1991
Bohemian Rhapsody/These Are The Days Of Our Lives	Queen	Dec 21, 1991
Abba-esque (EP)	Abba	Jun 13, 1992
Five Live (EP)	George Michael & Queen	May 01, 1993
Pray	Take That	Jul 17, 1993
Relight My Fire	Take That	Oct 09, 1993
Babe	Take That	Dec 18, 1993
Without You	Mariah Carey	Feb 19, 1994
Everything Changes	Take That	Apr 09, 1994
Saturday Night	Whigfield	Sep 17, 1994
Sure	Take That	Oct 15, 1994
Back For Good	Take That	Apr 08, 1995
Some Might Say	Oasis	May 06, 1995
Dreamer	Livin' Joy	May 13, 1995
Unchained Melody/ White Cliffs Of Dover	Robson Green & Jerome Flynn	May 20, 1995
Never Forget	Take That	Aug 05, 1995
Country House	Blur	Aug 26, 1995
Gangsta's Paradise	Coolio featuring LV	Oct 28, 1995
Boombastic	Shaggy	Sep 23, 1995
Fairground	Simply Red	Sep 30, 1995
I Believe/Up On The Roof	Robson Green & Jerome Flynn	Nov 11, 1995
Earth Song	Michael Jackson	Dec 09, 1995

Left: Cilla Black with her No. 1 disc, 'Anyone Who Had A Heart'.

THE FIRST ALL-BRITISH UK TOP TEN

These are the records which made up that historic top 10:

1	Anyone Who Had A Heart	Cilla Black
2	Bits And Pieces	The Dave Clark Five
3	Diane	The Bachelors
4	I Think Of You	The Merseybeats
5	Needles And Pins	The Searchers
6	Not Fade Away	The Rolling Stones
7	Little Children	Billy Kramer & the Dakotas
8	I'm The One	Gerry & the Pacemakers
9	Candy Man	Brian Poole & the Tremeloes
10	Boys Cry	Eden Kane

On March 7, 1964 the entire top 10 singles chart positions consisted – for the first time ever – of domestic recordings by UK artists. Indeed the highest-placed American act was Brenda Lee at the No. 13 with 'As Usual'. Below Ms. Lee were six more British acts: the only other American in the top 20 was Gene Pitney in the anchor position – ironically with a British song, 'That Belongs To Yesterday', written by Mick Jagger and Keith Richards. Perhaps most extraordinary about this top 10 is that the Beatles do not make an appearance.

CLOSE – BUT NO CIGAR: THE ALMOST ALL-BRITISH AMERICAN TOP TEN

1	Mrs. Brown You've Got A Lovely Daughter	Herman's Hermits
2	Count Me In	Gary Lewis & the Playboys
3	Ticket To Ride	The Beatles
4	The Game Of Love	Wayne Fontana & the Mindbenders
5	I Know A Place	Petula Clark
6	I'll Never Find Another You	The Seekers
7	Silhouettes	Herman's Hermits
8	I'm Telling You Now	Freddie & the Dreamers
9	The Last Time	The Rolling Stones
10	Cast Your Fate To The Wind	Sounds Orchestral

During the week ending May 8, 1965, the British invasion of American pop music was at its peak. Of the best-selling ten singles in the US, nine were of British origin, a record since unmatched. The sole American record was by Gary Lewis (son of comedian Jerry) at No. 2 with the follow-up to his million-seller 'This Diamond Ring'. The next highest-placed American artist, at No. 11, was Marvin Gaye with 'I'll Be Doggone'.

Right: Herman's Hermits.

Below: The Beatles in 1964.

THE FIRST TWENTY
MERSEYBEAT CHART HITS IN THE UK

		Charted	Reached
Love Me Do	The Beatles	Oct 13, 1962	21
Please Please Me	The Beatles	Jan 19, 1963	1
How Do You Do It?	Gerry & the Pacemakers	Mar 16, 1963	1
Some Other Guy	The Big Three	Apr 13, 1963	29
From Me To You	The Beatles	Apr 20, 1963	1
Do You Want To Know A Secret?	Billy J. Kramer & the Dakotas	May 04, 1963	1
If You Gotta Make A Fool Of Somebody	Freddie & the Dreamers	May 11, 1963	2
I Like It	Gerry & the Pacemakers	Jun 01, 1963	1
(Ain't That) Just Like Me	The Hollies	Jun 01, 1963	30
It's Too Late Now	The Swinging Blue Jeans	Jun 22, 1963	30
Sweets For My Sweet	The Searchers	Jun 29, 1963	1
By The Way	The Big Three	July 06, 1963	23
The Cruel Sea	The Dakotas	July 13, 1963	16
Twist And Shout (EP)	The Beatles	July 20, 1963	3
Bad To Me	Billy J. Kramer & the Dakotas	Aug 03, 1963	1
How Do You Do It	Gerry & the Pacemakers	Aug 03, 1963	36
I'm Telling You Now	Freddie & the Dreamers	Aug 16, 1963	2
Searchin'	The Hollies	Aug 31, 1963	16
Be My Girl	The Dennisons	Aug 31, 1963	46
She Loves You	The Beatles	Aug 01, 1963	1

A measure of the thoroughness with which the groups from the North-West corner of Britain (the Hollies were from Manchester but always regarded as a Merseybeat group) took over the UK singles charts during 1963 is that once 'Please Please Me' hit number one, a remarkable percentage of the singers listed here went all the way to the number one including Gerry & the Pacemakers and Billy J. Kramer & the Dakotas.

THE HIGHEST-PLACED ALBUMS IN THE UK SINGLES CHART

		Number	
With The Beatles	The Beatles	11	Dec 1963
Songs For Swinging Lovers	Frank Sinatra	12	Jul 1956
A Hard Day's Night	The Beatles	16	Aug 1964
Beatles For Sale	The Beatles	19	Jan 1965
Revolver	The Beatles	20	Aug 1965
Elvis Is Back	Elvis Presley	21	Jul 1960
Help!	The Beatles	22	Aug 1965
Sgt. Pepper's Lonely Hearts Club Band	The Beatles	24	Jun 1967
The Beatles (White Album)	The Beatles	24	Dec 1968
G.I. Blues	Elvis Presley	25	Dec 1960
The Rolling Stones	The Rolling Stones	25	Jan 1965
Rubber Soul	The Beatles	25	Dec 1965
Carousel	Soundtrack	26	Jul 1856
Lonnie Donegan Showcase	Lonnie Donegan	26	Jan 1957
Rock And Roll Stage Show	Bill Haley & His Comets	30	Nov 1956
Come Dance With Me	Frank Sinatra	30	May 1959

This list appears to be a contradiction in terms. UK album sales were fairly modest during the 1950s and much of the 1960s: although album charts existed, they were measuring a minority section of the market. Therefore, whenever the rare album sold in sufficient quantities to place it on a par with singles sales, it was included in the chart with the singles to show a comparison. The listing above includes every title to make the singles top 30 in this way.

Above: Original 50s rock and roll stars Bill Haley & His Comets.

Below: Erasure covered four Abba songs on their *Abba-esque* EP in 1992.

THE HIGHEST-PLACED EPS IN THE UK SINGLES CHART

		Number	
The Roussos Phenomenon	Demis Roussos	1	Jul 1976
Too Much Too Young Specials AKA Live	The Specials	1	Feb 1980
Abba-esque	Erasure	1	Jun 1992
Five Live	George Michael & Queen	1	May 1993
>Abort, Retry, Fail?	White Town	1	Jan 1997
All-Star Hit Parade	Various Artists	2	Jul 1956
Magical Mystery Tour	The Beatles	2	Dec 1967
Special Edition	Shakin' Stevens	2	Dec 1982
Crackers International	Erasure	2	Jan 1989
Four Bacharach & David Songs	Deacon Blue	2	Sep 1990
Everybody In The Place	The Prodigy	2	Jan 1992
Twist And Shout	The Beatles	3	Aug 1963
Four From Toyah	Toyah	4	Mar 1981
St. Valentine's Day Massacre	Motorhead/ Girlschool	5	Feb 1981
Nuff Vibes	Apache Indian	5	Aug 1993
Got Live If You Want It	The Rolling Stones	6	Jul 1965
Work Rest & Play	Madness	6	Apr 1980
The One In The Middle	Manfred Mann	7	Jul 1965
Extended Play	Bryan Ferry	7	Sep 1976
A Million Love Songs	Take That	7	Oct 1992
Nakasaki (I Need A Lover Tonight)	Ken Doh	7	Mar 1996
Legacy	Mansun	7	Jul 1998
The Golden Years	Motorhead	8	May 1980
Killer	Seal	8	Nov 1991
Welcome To The Cheap Seats	The Wonder Stuff	8	Feb 1992
All You Good People	Embrace	8	Nov 1997
Mrs. Robinson	Simon & Garfunkel	9	Feb 1969
Grandma's Party	Paul Nicholas	9	Jan 1977
The Music Of Torvill & Dean	Richard Hartley/ Michael Reed Orchestra	9	Apr 1984
King Of The Road	The Proclaimers	9	Dec 1990
Shortsharpshock	Therapy?	9	Mar 1993
Condemnation	Depeche Mode	9	Sep 1993
Hallowed Be Thy Name	Iron Maiden	9	Oct 1993
Kate Bush On Stage	Kate Bush	10	Oct 1979
3x3	Genesis	10	Jun 1982
On The Ropes	The Wonder Stuff	10	Sep 1993

EPs – essentially 7" extended-play releases usually containing four songs – were a familiar fixture in the 1950s and the early 60s in Britain (though less popular in the US). They were virtually killed off in the UK during the later 60s by the advent of budget albums, but had a renaissance in the mid-70s as deluxe singles. Five EPs have topped the UK singles chart.

BORN IN THE USA

In terms of where they were born, 37 different states in the US – plus the District of Columbia – have produced American chart-topping acts. Natives of Alaska, Colorado, Delaware, Idaho, Kansas, Maine, Montana, Nevada, New Hampshire, Oregon, South Dakota, Vermont and Wyoming unfortunately have yet to see one of their own top the US chart.

NO MATTER WHAT STATE I'M IN

Only solo artists and duo hits are included here and count for a point each: for example, The Everly Brothers – although there are two of them – get one point. If a solo artist has teamed up with another solo artist they score half a point.

New York	49	Maryland	4
California	27.5	Minnesota	4
Texas	22.5	Washington	3.5
New Jersey	17.5	District of Columbia	3
Georgia	15	Massachusetts	3
Pennsylvania	15	Arizona	2
Florida	12	Connecticut	2
Illinois	9.5	Iowa	2
Michigan	9.5	North Dakota	2
Tennessee	9	Nebraska	2
North Carolina	8	New Mexico	2
Mississippi	7.5	Virginia	2
Indiana	6	Rhode Island	1
Oklahoma	6	South Carolina	1.5
Arkansas	5	Hawaii	1.5
Louisiana	5	Kentucky	1.5
Missouri	5	Wisconsin	1.5
Alabama	4.5	Utah	1
Ohio	4.5	West Virginia	1

The strangest pairings are New Mexico, which provided John Denver and Staff Sgt. Barry Sadler and North Dakota, whose sole chart-toppers were Lawrence Welk and Bobby Vee.

Left: John Denver hails from Roswell, New Mexico.

NEW YORK TO LA

Brooklyn
Aaliyah • Neil Diamond • Jay-Z • Robert John • Carole King • Steve Lawrence • Barry Manilow • Nilsson • The Notorious B.I.G. • Eddie Rabbitt • Santo & Johnny • Neil Sedaka • Barbra Streisand

New York
Gregory Abbott • Christina Aguilera • Irene Cara • Mariah Carey • Harry Chapin • Terence Trent D'Arby • Bobby Darin • Sammy Davis Jr. • Dion • Lesley Gore • John Oates (of Hall & Oates) • Tab Hunter • Brian Hyland • Ja Rule • Alicia Keys • Lady Gaga • Cyndi Lauper • Jennifer Lopez • Bobby McFerrin • Johnny Rivers • John Sebastian • Carly Simon

Los Angeles
Paula Abdul • Herb Alpert • The Captain (of the Captain & Tennille) • Kim Carnes • Ke$ha • Johnny Horton • Siedah Garrett • Jan & Dean • Bill Medley • A Taste of Honey • Karyn White

13 acts hailed from Brooklyn, while another 22 were born in the other New York boroughs. In contrast, 11 acts were born in Los Angeles. Other major musical cities include 8 from Chicago, 7 from Detroit, 4 from New Orleans and 3 from Memphis.

Left: Brooklyn rapper, The Notorious B.I.G.

THE DARK SIDE

As with all professions, the music business experiences its own share of accidental deaths, murders, suicides, bizarre endings and tragedies. Given the seemingly high degree of free-spirited risk-taking long associated with a rock 'n' roll lifestyle – including the seductive and destructive qualities of alcohol and drugs – the death quotient is high – and high profile. An alarming number of artists who have gone too soon have committed suicide – many seemingly and tragically unable to cope with the unique pressures that celebrity and a small fortune can bring.

DEATH BY MISADVENTURE

Johnny Ace   **Dec 24, 1954**
American R&B star, accidentally shot himself with a .22 caliber revolver while reportedly playing Russian roulette backstage at the Houston Civic.

Johnny Burnette   **Aug 01, 1964**
Rockabilly pioneer drowned after his fishing boat was struck by a cabin cruiser in Clear Lake, California.

Brian Jones   **Jul 03, 1969**
Ex-Rolling Stones guitarist (he had quit the group the previous month), drowned in his swimming pool at Hartfield, Sussex. Although Jones had been battling drug and alcohol problems, the coroner's verdict was misadventure.

Les Harvey   **May 03, 1972**
Guitarist/singer in British rock band Stone the Crows, died from electrocution by handling an ungrounded microphone with wet hands during a gig in Swansea, Wales.

John Rostill   **Nov 26, 1973**
Bass player, songwriter and former member of The Shadows, electrocuted by electric guitar at his home recording studio in England.

Keith Relf   **May 14, 1976**
Lead singer and harmonica player for The Yardbirds, electrocuted while tuning his improperly earthed electric guitar at his London home.

Terry Kath   **Jan 23, 1978**
Founding member and guitarist with rock band Chicago, shot himself accidentally with a semiautomatic 9 mm pistol, playing Russian roulette in Woodland Hills, California. His last words were reportedly: "Don't worry, it's not loaded."

Sandy Denny   **Apr 21, 1978**
Lead singer of Fairport Convention, died of a cerebral hemorrhage in Wimbledon, London, four weeks after falling down a staircase while on vacation in Cornwall.

Dennis Wilson   **Dec 28, 1983**
Member of The Beach Boys, drowned at Marina del Rey, California, 28 December, 1983. He was buried at sea after the personal intervention of Ronald Reagan (burial at sea is usually reserved for naval personnel).

Jeff Porcaro   **Aug 05, 1992**
Founding member and drummer with American rock combo Toto, died in a gardening accident after inhaling too much insecticide while spraying his garden at his home in Los Angeles, California.

Randy California   **Jan 02, 1997**
Original member and guitarist for American rock group Spirit, drowned while trying to save his son, 12-year-old Quinn (who survived) in the ocean off Molokai, Hawaii.

Jeff Buckley   **May 29, 1997**
Burgeoning rock singer-songwriter – and the son of Tim Buckley – he accidentally drowned while swimming fully-clothed in Wolf River Harbor.

Michael Hutchence   **Nov 22, 1997**
INXS lead vocalist, following drug and alcohol consumption and in a state of depression, found dead with a black leather belt around his neck (possible autoerotic asphyxiation) in room 524 of the Sydney Ritz Carlton.

Sonny Bono   **Jan 05, 1998**
While skiing at the Heavenly Ski Resort near South Lake Tahoe, California, the singer, songwriter, producer and politician died from injuries sustained after hitting a tree.

Kirsty MacColl   **Dec 18, 2000**
British singer-songwriter died while diving with her sons on vacation in Cozumel, Mexico. MacColl was killed instantly after being hit by a speeding powerboat having managed to push her son, Jamie, out of the boat's path.

Ty Longley   **Feb 20, 2003**
Guitarist for heavy metal band Great White, Longley was among 100 people who perished in a fire at a Great White concert held at The Station nightclub in West Warwick, Rhode Island.

Spinal Tap drummers
Several dozen drummers for UK heavy metal act Spinal Tap have died over the past four decades from a variety of bizarre and often unexplained causes including vomit choking, a gardening accident and spontaneous human combustion.

Right: Rolling Stones guitarist
Brian Jones in 1964.

ALCOHOL DEATHS

THE TOP 10 UK FUNERAL SONGS

From a poll of 5,000 people, the top 10 most requested songs at funerals according to the Bereavement Register in Britain are:

1	Goodbye My Lover	James Blunt
2	Angels	Robbie Williams
3	(I've Had) The Time Of My Life	Bill Medley & Jennifer Warnes
4	Wind Beneath My Wings	Bette Midler
5	Pie Jesu from Andrew Lloyd Webber's Requiem	Sarah Brightman
6	Candle In The Wind	Elton John
7	With Or Without You	U2
8	Tears From Heaven	Eric Clapton
9	Every Breath You Take	The Police
10	Unchained Melody	The Righteous Brothers

Above: Led Zeppelin's John Bonham.

MISSING IN ACTION

Richey Edwards   Nov 23, 2008
Manic Street Preachers guitarist, disappeared on February 1, 1995; suspected suicide off the Severn Bridge in Wales. Officially "presumed dead" on November 23, 2008.

PRESCRIPTION DRUG DEATHS

Gram Parsons (singer-songwriter)	Morphine	Sep 19, 1973
Keith Moon (Who drummer)	Hemineverin	Sep 07, 1978
Gerald Levert (R&B singer)	Vicodin, Percocet, Darvocet	Nov 10, 2006
Jay Bennett (Wilco guitarist)	Fentanyl	May 24, 2009
Michael Jackson	Propofol, Lorazepam, Midazolam	Jun 25, 2009
DJ AM (Club DJ)	Oxycodone, Vicodin, Ativan, Klonopin, Xanax, Benadryl, Levamisole	Aug 28, 2009

Left: Gram Parsons in 1972.

NONPRESCRIPTION DRUG DEATHS

MURDERED MUSICIANS

Sam Cooke Dec 11, 1964
R&B icon Cooke was shot dead at the Hacienda motel, South Figueroa Street, Los Angeles by Bertha Franklin – the motel's manager – who claimed she was acting in self-defence.

King Curtis Aug 13, 1971
Curtis (Curtis Ousley), notable saxophone player (including several Coasters hits) was stabbed to death by Juan Montanez during a brawl in New York.

Al Jackson Jr. Oct 01, 1975
Drummer with legendary soul combo Booker T. & The M.G.s, shot five times in the back by an intruder at his home in Memphis, Tennessee.

John Lennon Dec 08, 1980
Shot dead outside the Dakota Building in New York by Mark David Chapman, who fired five bullets – one of which missed – from a Charter Arms .38 mm revolver.

Felix Pappalardi Apr 17, 1983
Rock producer, bassist and founding member of Mountain, shot dead by his wife Gail in their East Side apartment in Manhattan. She served time for "criminally negligent homicide," but continues to profess that the shooting was an accident.

Marvin Gaye Apr 01, 1984
R&B legend was shot dead by his father, Marvin Sr. – an apostolic church minister – at the family home in Los Angeles the day before his 45th birthday.

Carlton Barrett Apr 17, 1987
Drummer for legendary reggae group, The Wailers, shot twice in the head at his home in Kingston, Jamaica, allegedly by his wife's (Albertine) lover, Glenroy Carter. Albertine and Carter were convicted on conspiracy charges and sentenced to seven years.

Peter Tosh Sep 11, 1987
Jamaican reggae star, shot dead by ex-convict Dennis Lobban, one of three gang members who unsuccessfully demanded money from Tosh at his home in Kingston, Jamaica.

Don Myrick Jul 30, 1993
Earth Wind & Fire saxophonist, shot dead in his Palm District apartment in Los Angeles by police officer Gary Barbaro who was trying to serve Myrick with a search warrant for drug possession.

Rhett Forrester Jan 22, 1994
Lead vocalist with American heavy metal combo Riot, shot and killed during an attempted carjacking incident in Atlanta, Georgia. The crime remains unsolved.

Selena Mar 31, 1995
Mexican-American singer, the "Queen of Tejano Music", shot dead with one bullet in the back by Yolanda Saldivar – the president of Selena's fan club – during a row over missing business papers at the Days Inn hotel in Corpus Christi, Texas.

Tupac Shakur Sep 13, 1996
Rapper, died on September 13, 1996, from injuries sustained after being shot four times (from 12 fired bullets) while travelling in Death Row label boss Suge Knight's BMW 750iL sedan on Flamingo Road, Las Vegas.

The Notorious B.I.G. Mar 9, 1997
Larger-than-life rapper, shot by four bullets directed at the GMC Suburban vehicle in which he was travelling outside the Petersen Automotive Museum in Los Angeles.

Roger Troutman Apr 25, 1999
Lead singer of R&B/Funk quartet Zapp, shot dead by his older brother, band percussionist Larry – who then turned the gun on himself.

Jam-Master Jay Oct 20, 2002
Co-founder and DJ for legendary hip-hop group Run-DMC, shot dead by two assailants in a recording studio on Merrick Boulevard in Jamaica, Queens, New York.

Dimebag Darrell Abbot Dec 08, 2004
Guitarist with American Heavy Metal band Pantera, shot five times while performing onstage by crazed fan Nathan Gale during a Damageplan gig at the Alrosa Villa in Columbus, Ohio. Gale also killed three others and maimed seven.

Lucky Dube Oct 18, 2007
South Africa reggae star, shot and killed by three men during a carjacking incident in the Johannesburg suburb of Rosettenville, South Africa.

ROCK 'N' ROLL SUICIDE

Bobby Fuller Jul 18, 1966
Leader of Texas band, the Bobby Fuller Four, found dead in his car outside his Hollywood apartment in Los Angeles. Although recorded as a suicide, it is more likely that Fuller was a murder victim.

Joe Meek Feb 03, 1967
Notable British producer, shot himself in London, after killing his landlady Violet Shenton on the eighth anniversary of Buddy Holly's death.

Al Wilson Sep 03, 1970
Canned Heat singer-guitarist, barbiturate overdose, after reportedly attempting suicide twice before.

Paul Williams Aug 17, 1973
Founding member of Temptations, shot himself in the head near his car, age 34.

Graham Bond May 08, 1974
Founder of the British group Graham Bond Organization, died under a tube train at Finsbury Park station, North London.

Nick Drake Nov 25, 1974
Singer-songwriter, prescription drug overdose.

Pete Ham Apr 23, 1975
Badfinger vocalist, guitarist, songwriter, hung himself in his garage. With Tom Evans, the joint composer of Nilsson's global No. 1 hit 'Without You'.

Phil Ochs Apr 09, 1976
Folk singer-songwriter, by hanging in Queens, New York.

Donny Hathaway Jan 13, 1979
American R&B singer, plunged 15 floors to his death from the Essex House Hotel, New York, officially registered as suicide.

Ian Curtis May 18, 1980
Lead singer of Joy Division, he hung himself in his Manchester garage while listening to Iggy Pop's *The Idiot* album.

Tom Evans Nov 23, 1983
Badfinger vocalist, guitarist, songwriter, hanged himself on a willow tree in his garden; unable to get over the death of his song-writing partner Pete Ham, eight years earlier.

Richard Manuel Mar 04, 1986
The Band keyboardist/guitarist, by hanging at the Quality Inn in Winter Park, Florida, following a concert.

Roy Buchanan Aug 14, 1988
Rock/blues guitarist, by hanging in a jail cell in Fairfax County, Virginia.

Del Shannon Feb 08, 1990
Rock 'n' roll singer-songwriter, shot himself in Santa Clarita, California, following depression.

Kurt Cobain Apr 05, 1994
Nirvana lead vocalist, a single gun shot to the head, circa April 5, (body discovered April 8), 1994.

Phyllis Hyman Jun 30, 1995
R&B singer, prescription drug overdose, prior to a scheduled performance at Harlem's famed Apollo Theater.

Chris Acland Oct 17, 1996
Drummer for UK rock band Lush, by hanging at his parents' home in Burneside, Cumbria.

Faron Young Dec 10, 1996
Country music singer/songwriter at his home in Nashville from a single gunshot to the head following poor health.

Billy MacKenzie Jan 22, 1997
Associates lead singer, prescription overdose, found in the garden shed of his father's house in Auchterhouse, Scotland.

Wendy O. Williams Apr 06, 1998
Lead vocalist for the Plasmatics, single gun shot in woods near her home in Storrs, Connecticut.

Larry Troutman Apr 25, 1999
Shot himself after first killing his brother Roger Troutman.

Stuart Adamson Dec 16, 2001
Big Country lead vocalist, guitarist, self-strangulation at the Best Western Plaza hotel in Honolulu, Hawaii.

Jon Lee Jan 07, 2002
Original drummer for British rock group Feeder, by hanging using a metal dog chain at his home in Miami Beach.

Elliott Smith Oct 21, 2003
Singer/songwriter, of suspected self-inflicted stab wounds to the chest at an apartment in Echo Park, Los Angeles.

Gary Stewart Dec 16, 2003
Country singer-songwriter, single gun shot to the neck at his home in Fort Pierce, Florida, following the death of his wife, a month earlier.

Brad Delp Mar 09, 2007
Founding guitarist, vocalist of Boston, self-inflicted carbon monoxide poisoning from two charcoal grills.

Mark Linkous Mar 06, 2010
Frontman of Sparklehorse, self-inflicted rifle shot to the heart outside a friend's house in Knoxville, Tennessee.

Above: Kurt Cobain in 1993.

BANDS WITH REPLACEMENTS FOR DEAD MEMBERS

	Deceased	Replacement
The Rolling Stones	Brian Jones	Mick Taylor
AC/DC	Bon Scott	Brian Johnson
Chicago	Terry Kath	Donnie Dacus
The Who	Keith Moon	Kenney Jones
Def Leppard	Steve Clark	Vivian Campbell
The Who	John Entwistle	Pino Palladino
Led Zeppelin	John Bonham	Jason Bonham
Metallica	Cliff Burton	James Newsted
Queen	Freddie Mercury	Paul Rodgers
The Doors	Jim Morrison	Ian Astbury
INXS	Michael Hutchence	J.D. Fortune
The Charlatans	Rob Collins	Tony Rogers
Alice In Chains	Layne Staley	William DuVall

INXS selected its new lead singer – following the death of Michael Hutchence – via auditions on the CBS reality tv series, "Rock Star: INXS" in 2005. Many veteran R&B groups – such as The Temptations – have frequently replaced deceased or departing members with new talent.

PLATINUM & GOLD AWARDS

In order for any record to be certified, a record company must supply audited sales shipping data to support its application. Several labels over the years have chosen not to do this – most notably Motown Records, which in the 1960s never submitted the necessary paperwork. Dozens of million-plus selling records released by Motown were therefore never certified, including hits by The Supremes and Stevie Wonder. Their first official certified platinum album was *Natural High* by the Commodores in 1976. From the entire, historic Motown catalogue only 81 singles have ever been certified gold or platinum.

CERTIFICATION CRITERIA FOR US GOLD AND PLATINUM SINGLES AND ALBUMS

Gold Single
1958–89: 1,000,000 units
1989–present day: 500,000 units

Gold Album
1958–75: $1m in wholesale record sales
1975–89: $1m in wholesale record sales & 500,00 units
1989–present day: 500,000 units

Platinum Single:
1976–89: 2 million units
1989–present day: 1 million units

Platinum Album
1976–present day: 1 million units

Multi-Platinum Album
1984–present day: 2 million + units

Diamond Album
1999–present day: 10 million units

MOST US GOLD DISCS

Elvis Presley	82	Barry Manilow	24
Barbra Streisand	51	Rush	24
The Beatles	45	Chicago	23
The Rolling Stones	42	Prince	23
Neil Diamond	40	Hank Williams Jr.	23
Elton John	38	Alabama	22
George Strait	38	Willie Nelson	22
Bob Dylan	36	Bruce Springsteen	21
Frank Sinatra	34	AC/DC	20
Kenny Rogers	31	The Beach Boys	20
Reba McEntire	27	John Denver	20
Rod Stewart	26	Jefferson Airplane/	
Aerosmith	25	Starship	20
Eric Clapton	25	Santana	20
Kiss	24	James Taylor	20

MOST US PLATINUM DISCS

Elvis Presley	45	Pink Floyd	15
The Beatles	39	Alan Jackson	15
George Strait	33	Rush	14
Barbra Streisand	30	James Taylor	14
The Rolling Stones	28	The Doors	14
Elton John	26	Barry Manilow	13
Neil Diamond	21	John Denver	13
Alabama	20	Lynyrd Skynyrd	13
AC/DC	20	Linda Ronstadt	13
Kenny Rogers	19	Dave Matthews	
Reba McEntire	19	Band	13
Rod Stewart	18	Eric Clapton	12
Aerosmith	18	The Who	12
Chicago	18	Toby Keith	12
Led Zeppelin	18	John Mellencamp	12
Bruce Springsteen	17	Ozzy Osbourne	12
Madonna	17	Queen	11
Billy Joel	17	Kenny G	11
Bob Dylan	16	Frank Sinatra	10
Prince	16	Kiss	10
Willie Nelson	16	Santana	10
Garth Brooks	16	Johnny Cash	10
U2	16	Jimi Hendrix	10
Luther Vandross	15	The Isley Brothers	10

Right: Barbara Streisand in 1976.

In 1992, the RIAA – which certifies all gold and platinum awards in the US – began counting each disc in a multi-disc set (double album or boxed set) as an individual unit sale meaning, for example, that a double album certified as four-times platinum (normally 4 million units for a single disc album) has actually only sold 2 million units.

Gold certifications for record sales ("Gold Discs") were introduced in the US in March 1958 with Perry Como's 'Catch A Falling Star' becoming the first ever gold single for one million US units certified on March 14 that year – followed by the first Gold Album, the *Oklahoma!* film soundtrack in July.

MOST US MULTI-PLATINUM DISCS

Elvis Presley	24	Madonna	12
The Beatles	24	Billy Joel	12
Garth Brooks	15	Pink Floyd	12
Led Zeppelin	14	The Rolling Stones	11
George Strait	13	Neil Diamond	11
Barbra Streisand	13	U2	11
Elton John	12	Alabama	10
AC/DC	12	Rod Stewart	10
Aerosmith	12	Bruce Springsteen	10

ARTISTS TO HAVE SOLD IN EXCESS OF 50 MILLION ALBUMS IN THE US

The Beatles	171	Elton John	70	Van Halen	56.5
Garth Brooks	128	Michael Jackson	69.5	Whitney Houston	55
Elvis Presley	120	George Strait	68.5	U2	51.5
Led Zeppelin	111.5	Aerosmith	66.5	Kenny Rogers	51
The Eagles	100	The Rolling Stones	66	Céline Dion	50
Billy Joel	79.5	Madonna	64		
Pink Floyd	74.5	Bruce Springsteen	64		
Barbra Streisand	71.5	Mariah Carey	63		
AC/DC	71	Metallica	59		

These sales totals are only from certified sales.

THE JACKSON FAMILY

	Gold	Platinum
Michael Jackson	28	69
Janet Jackson	29	31
The Jacksons	8	6
The Jackson Five	2	1
Jermaine Jackson	1	1
Rebbie Jackson	1	0

Singles and albums combined.

The Jackson family has amassed 69 gold records and 108 platinum records between them.

MOST UK GOLD DISCS

Rod Stewart	31	UB40	18
Cliff Richard	30	Mike Oldfield	17
Elton John	28	The Beatles	16
Queen	28	Genesis	16
Madonna	27	James Last	16
Abba	25	Prince	16
Neil Diamond	21	Barbra Streisand	16
The Rolling Stones	21	Blondie	15
Status Quo	21	The Carpenters	15
David Bowie	20	Eric Clapton	15
Elvis Presley	20	Phil Collins	15
Diana Ross	19	Iron Maiden	15
Michael Jackson	18		

Above: Rod Stewart on *The Jay Leno Show* in 2009.

UK SALES THRESHOLDS FOR THE VARIOUS SILVER, GOLD AND PLATINUM DISCS

The current UK sales thresholds for the various Silver, Gold and Platinum discs are:

Singles		Albums	
Silver:	200,000 units	Silver:	60,000 units
Gold:	400,000 units	Gold:	100,000 units
Platinum:	600,000 units	Platinum:	300,000 units

In the UK albums certifications by the British Phonographic Industry (the BPI) began in April 1973 and were initially based on wholesale shipment revenues. This changed in January 1978 – when albums awards came into line with singles certifications, based solely on wholesale unit sales. Multi-platinum awards were introduced in February 1987.

MOST UK PLATINUM DISCS

Robbie Williams	59	Tina Turner	22
Madonna	54	Whitney Houston	21
Michael Jackson	52	Boyzone	20
Oasis	45	Meat Loaf	19
Simply Red	45	The Beatles	18
Queen	40	The Beautiful South	18
Elton John	37	The Eagles	18
Westlife	34	Shania Twain	18
Phil Collins	32	UB40	17
Take That	31	Dido	16
Coldplay	29	Eurythmics	16
Fleetwood Mac	29	Genesis	16
George Michael	28	Bryan Adams	15
Dire Straits	27	The Corrs	15
Céline Dion	25	Pink Floyd	15
Spice Girls	25	Chris Rea	15
Kylie Minogue	23	Snow Patrol	15
Abba	22	Travis	15

Left: Robbie Williams in 2009.

SONGWRITERS

Reliant upon songwriters throughout his entire career, Elvis Presley was well-placed to famously comment on the power of composition: "Without a song, the day would never end. Without a song, a man ain't got a friend. Without a song, the road would never bend, without a song." Although credited with co-writing several of his hits, Elvis didn't have any input into the compositions of any of those songs. In order to have the privilege of Elvis recording one of their songs, songwriters were prepared to give up a share of their ownership – a practice which continues to this day.

TOP 10 UK HITS PENNED BY BURT BACHARACH & HAL DAVID

		Peak Position	
The Story Of My Life	Michael Holliday	1	(Feb 15, 1958)
Magic Moments	Perry Como	1	(Mar 01, 1958)
Twenty Four Hours From Tulsa	Gene Pitney	5	(Jan 04, 1964)
Anyone Who Had A Heart	Cilla Black	1	(Feb 29, 1964)
Walk On By	Dionne Warwick	9	(May 09, 1964)
I Just Don't Know What To Do With Myself	Dusty Springfield	3	(Jul 25, 1964)
(There's) Always Something There To Remind Me	Sandie Shaw	1	(Oct 24, 1964)
Trains And Boats And Planes	Burt Bacharach	4	(Jun 26, 1965)
Make It Easy On Yourself	The Walker Brothers	1	(Sep 25, 1965)
Alfie	Cilla Black	9	(May 07, 1966)
Do You Know The Way To San Jose	Dionne Warwick	8	(Jun 08, 1968)
This Guy's In Love With You	Herb Alpert	3	(Aug 17, 1968)
I Say A Little Prayer	Aretha Franklin	4	(Sep 14, 1968)
I'll Never Fall In Love Again	Bobbie Gentry	1	(Oct 18, 1969)
Raindrops Keep Falling On My Head	Sacha Distel	10	(Mar 14, 1970)
(They Long To Be) Close To You	The Carpenters	6	(Oct 10, 1970)
Say A Little Prayer	Bomb the Bass featuring Maureen	10	(Dec 03, 1988)
Walk On By	Sybil	6	(Feb 17, 1990)
Four Bacharach & David Songs (EP)	Deacon Blue	2	(Sep 01, 1990)
Walk On By	Gabrielle	7	(Feb 01, 1997)

Pianist/composer Burt Bacharach and lyricist Hal David first met in 1957 at the Brill Building in New York and wrote over 100 songs together. Bacharach has also written hits with Peter Allen, Elvis Costello, Christopher Cross, Mack David, Neil Diamond, Bob Hilliard, Ray Parker Jr., Carole Bayer Sager and Barney Williams.

TOP 10 UK HITS PENNED BY DIANE WARREN

		Peak Position	
Rhythm Of The Night	DeBarge	4	(May 18, 1985)
I Get Weak	Belinda Carlisle	10	(Mar 26, 1988)
If I Could Turn Back Time	Cher	6	(Oct 28, 1989)
Love And Understanding	Cher	10	(Jul 27, 1991)
I'd Lie For You (And That's The Truth)	Meat Loaf	2	(Oct 28, 1995)
Not A Dry Eye In The House	Meat Loaf	7	(Feb 03, 1996)
Because You Loved Me	Céline Dion	5	(Jun 22, 1996)
Un-break My Heart	Toni Braxton	2	(Dec 21, 1996)
How Do I Live	LeAnn Rimes	7	(Mar 07, 1998)
I Don't Want To Miss A Thing	Aerosmith	4	(Oct 10, 1998)
From The Heart	Another Level	6	(Jun 12, 1999)
Could I Have This Kiss Forever	Whitney Houston/ Enrique Iglesias	7	(Oct 14, 2000)
Can't Fight The Moonlight	LeAnn Rimes	1	(Nov 25, 2000)
There You'll Be	Faith Hill	3	(Jun 30, 2001)

Inducted into the Songwriters Hall of Fame in 2001, Diane Warren is one of America's most prolific and successful female songwriters. Her maiden Top 10 composition was the 1983 Laura Branigan smash, 'Solitaire', the first of many power pop ballads which became Warren's signature. She has also penned hits with Bryan Adams, Walter Afansieff, Michael Bolton, Alice Cooper and Gloria Estefan among others.

Right: Diane Warren.

TOP 10 UK HITS
PENNED BY STOCK, AITKEN & WATERMAN

			Peak Position
Say I'm Your Number One	Princess	7	(Aug 31, 1985)
Showing Out	Mel & Kim	3	(Nov 22, 1986)
Respectable	Mel & Kim	1	(Mar 28, 1987)
Nothing's Gonna Stop Me Now	Samantha Fox	8	(Jun 20, 1987)
F. L. M.	Mel & Kim	7	(Jul 18, 1987)
Toy Boy	Sinitta	4	(Aug 22, 1987)
Never Gonna Give You Up	Rick Astley	1	(Aug 29, 1987)
Love In The First Degree/ Mr. Sleaze	Bananarama	3	(Oct 31, 1987)
Whenever You Need Somebody	Rick Astley	3	(Nov 07, 1987)
I Should Be So Lucky	Kylie Minogue	1	(Feb 20, 1988)
Together Forever (Lover's Leap Remix)	Rick Astley	2	(Mar 12, 1988)
That's The Way It Is	Mel & Kim	10	(Mar 12, 1988)
Cross My Broken Heart (Remix)	Sinitta	6	(Apr 02, 1988)
I Want You Back	Bananarama	5	(Apr 30, 1988)
Got To Be Certain	Kylie Minogue	2	(May 28, 1988)
The Harder I Try	Brother Beyond	2	(Sep 03, 1988)
Nothing Can Divide Us	Jason Donovan	5	(Sep 24, 1988)
He Ain't No Competition	Brother Beyond	6	(Nov 19, 1988)
Take Me To Your Heart	Rick Astley	8	(Dec 10, 1988)
Especially For You	Kylie Minogue & Jason Donovan	1	(Jan 07, 1989)
Too Many Broken Hearts	Jason Donovan	1	(Mar 11, 1989)
This Time I Know It's For Real	Donna Summer	3	(Mar 25, 1989)
I'd Rather Jack	Reynolds Girls	8	(Apr 01, 1989)
Hand On Your Heart	Kylie Minogue	1	(May 13, 1989)
I Don't Wanna Get Hurt	Donna Summer	7	(Jun 03, 1989)
You'll Never Stop Me Loving You	Sonia	1	(Jul 22, 1989)
Wouldn't Change A Thing	Kylie Minogue	2	(Aug 05, 1989)
I Just Don't Have The Heart	Cliff Richard	3	(Sep 02, 1989)
Every Day (I Love You More)	Jason Donovan	2	(Sep 16, 1989)
Je Ne Sais Pas Pourquoi	Kylie Minogue	2	(Oct 29, 1988)
Never Too Late	Kylie Minogue	4	(Nov 11, 1989)
When You Come Back To Me	Jason Donovan	2	(Dec 16, 1989)
Can't Shake The Feeling	Big Fun	8	(Dec 09, 1989)
Listen To Your Heart	Sonia	10	(Jan 13, 1990)
Happenin' All Over Again	Lonnie Gordon	4	(Feb 10, 1990)
Hang On To Your Love	Jason Donovan	8	(Apr 14, 1990)
Better The Devil You Know	Kylie Minogue	2	(May 19, 1990)
Step Back In Time	Kylie Minogue	4	(Nov 10, 1990)
What Do I Have To Do	Kylie Minogue	6	(Feb 16, 1991)
Shocked	Kylie Minogue	6	(Jun 08, 1991)
Especially For You	Denise & Johnny	3	(Dec 26, 1998)

Between 1986 and 1991, the SAW hit machine of British songwriters/producers Mike Stock, Matt Aitken and Pete Waterman virtually owned the UK singles chart. With a factory line of mostly catchy, uptempo, synth-driven pop/dance numbers, the trio either wrote and/or produced 13 British chart-toppers between 1985 – when they produced (but did not compose) Dead Or Alive's 'You Spin Me Round (Like A Record)' – to 1990's 'Tears On My Pillow' (Kylie Minogue – which, again, SAW only produced).

TOP 10 US HITS PENNED BY KARA DIOGUARDI

			Peak Position
Pieces Of Me	Ashlee Simpson	5	(Sep 18, 2004)
Rich Girl	Gwen Stefani featuring Eve	7	(Mar 05, 2005)
Ain't No Other Man	Christina Aguilera	6	(Jul 15, 2006)
No Boundaries	Kris Allen	1	(Dec 13, 2008)

American Idol judge Kara DioGuardi is one of the premier songwriters around today, with 36 Hot 100 credits to her name. Unlike songwriters from the old school, who either wrote on their own or with one other partner, DioGuardi's 36 hits have been shared with 60 other composers.

TOP 10 US HITS PENNED BY SEAN "PUFF DADDY"/"P. DIDDY"/"DIDDY" COMBS

			Peak Position
Peaches And Cream	112	4	(Jul 07, 2001)
Can't Nobody Hold Me Down	Puff Daddy (featuring Mase)	1	(Mar 22, 1997)
Hypnotize	Notorious B.I.G.	1	(May 03, 1997)
Honey	Mariah Carey	1	(Sep 13, 1997)
It's All About The Benjamins	Puff Daddy & the Family	2	(Jan 03, 1998)
What You Want	Mase (featuring Total)	6	(Mar 21, 1998)
Come With Me	Puff Daddy featuring Jimmy Page	4	(Jul 25, 1998)
Lookin' At Me	Mase featuring Puff Daddy	8	(Sep 19, 1998)
Love Like This	Faith Evans	7	(Dec 12, 1998)
All Night Long	Faith Evans featuring Puff Daddy	9	(Apr 03, 1999)
Satisfy You	Puff Daddy featuring R. Kelly	2	(Oct 30, 1999)
I Need A Girl (Part One)	P. Diddy featuring Usher & Loon	2	(May 25, 2002)
I Need A Girl (Part Two)	Diddy & Ginuwine featuring Loon, Mario Winans & Tammy Ruggieri P.	4	(Aug 03, 2002)
I Don't Wanna Know	Winans featuring P. Diddy & Enya Mario	2	(Apr 24, 2004)
Come To Me	Diddy featuring Nicole Scherzinger	9	(Nov 04, 2006)
Last Night	Diddy featuring Keyshia Cole	10	(Apr 14, 2007)

Rap impresario and hip-hop entrepreneur Combs has never been the sole writer of any of his hits, having collaborated with more than 150 other composers on his 49 US chart entries (some credited simply because of his sampling use of existing recordings).

PRODUCERS

Although a few top artists choose to produce their own recordings, the great majority of musicians need a skilled producer to bring their vocals and instrumentation to a coherent and commercially viable form. Production can include song selection, co-writing, enlisting session musicians and engineers, and supervising all stages of the recording, mixing and mastering. Over the years several top producers have started their own record labels, including Phil Spector (Philles), Clive Davis (Arista), Jimmy Iovine (Interscope), Dr. Dre (Aftermath) and Simon Cowell (SyCo).

TOP 10 UK HITS PRODUCED BY GEORGE MARTIN

Excluding those with the Beatles.

Song	Artist	Peak Position	Date
Splish Splash	Charlie Drake	7	(Sep 13, 1958)
Tie Me Kangaroo Down Sport	Rolf Harris	9	(Aug 20, 1960)
Goodness Gracious Me	Peter Sellers & Sophia Loren	4	(Dec 03, 1960)
Portrait Of My Love	Matt Monro	3	(Jan 21, 1961)
You're Driving Me Crazy	The Temperance Seven	1	(May 27, 1961)
A Hole In The Ground	Bernard Cribbins	9	(Mar 31, 1962)
Softly As I Leave You	Matt Monro	10	(Mar 31, 1962)
Right Said Fred	Bernard Cribbins	10	(Aug 04, 1962)
Sun Arise	Rolf Harris	3	(Dec 15, 1962)
How Do You Do It	Gerry & the Pacemakers	1	(Apr 06, 1963)
Do You Want To Know A Secret	Billy J. Kramer & the Dakotas	2	(Jun 01, 1963)
I Like It	Gerry & the Pacemakers	1	(Jun 22, 1963)
Bad To Me	Billy J. Kramer & the Dakotas	1	(Aug 24, 1963)
You'll Never Walk Alone	Gerry & the Pacemakers	1	(Nov 02, 1963)
I'll Keep You Satisfied	Billy J. Kramer & the Dakotas	4	(Nov 30, 1963)
I'm The One	Gerry & the Pacemakers	2	(Feb 08, 1964)
Anyone Who Had A Heart	Cilla Black	1	(Feb 29, 1964)
Little Children	Billy J. Kramer & the Dakotas	1	(Mar 21, 1964)
Don't Let The Sun Catch You Crying	Gerry & the Pacemakers	6	(May 09, 1964)
You're My World	Cilla Black	1	(May 30, 1964)
From A Window	Billy J. Kramer & the Dakotas	10	(Aug 22, 1964)
It's For You	Cilla Black	7	(Sep 05, 1964)
Walk Away	Matt Monro	4	(Nov 07, 1964)
Ferry 'Cross The Mersey	Gerry & the Pacemakers	8	(Jan 23, 1965)
You've Lost That Lovin' Feelin'	Cilla Black	2	(Jan 30, 1965)
I'll Be There	Gerry & the Pacemakers	15	(Apr 17, 1965)
Yesterday	Matt Monro	8	(Nov 06, 1965)
Love's Just A Broken Heart	Cilla Black	5	(Feb 05, 1966)
Alfie	Cilla Black	9	(May 07, 1966)
Don't Answer Me	Cilla Black	6	(Jul 02, 1966)
Lovers Of The World Unite	David & Jonathan	7	(Sep 10, 1966)
Step Inside Love	Cilla Black	8	(Apr 13, 1968)
Surround Yourself With Sorrow	Cilla Black	3	(Mar 29, 1969)
Conversations	Cilla Black	7	(Aug 16, 1969)
Something Tells Me (Something Is Going To Happen Tonight)	Cilla Black	3	(Jan 01, 1972)
Live And Let Die	Wings	9	(Jun 30, 1973)
Ebony And Ivory with additional vocals by Stevie Wonder	Paul McCartney	1	(Apr 24, 1982)
Say Say Say	Paul McCartney & Michael Jackson	2	(Nov 19, 1983)
Pipes Of Peace	Paul McCartney	1	(Jan 14, 1984)
No More Lonely Nights (Ballad)	Paul McCartney	2	(Oct 27, 1984)
We All Stand Together	Paul McCartney & the Frog Chorus	3	(Dec 22, 1984)
Something About The Way You Look Tonight/Candle In The Wind 1997	Elton John	1	(Sep 20, 1997)

Between 1963 and 65, Martin notched up 36 UK hit singles – including his most famous production work with The Beatles. Closing out this astonishing haul of hit production credits, Martin – who was knighted in 1996 – helmed the best-selling single of all time, worldwide: Elton John's 1997 ode to Princess Diana.

Above: Steve Lillywhite with punk singer Toyah Wilcox.

TOP 10 UK HITS PRODUCED BY STEPHEN STREET

		Peak Position	
Sheila Take A Bow	The Smiths	10	(May 02, 1987)
Suedehead	Morrissey	5	(Mar 05, 1988)
Everyday Is Like Sunday	Morrissey	9	(Jun 18, 1988)
Last Of The Famous International Playboys	Morrissey	6	(Feb 11, 1989)
Interesting Drug	Morrissey	9	(Apr 29, 1989)
There's No Other Way	Blur	8	(May 18, 1991)
Girls And Boys	Blur	5	(Mar 19, 1994)
Parklife	Blur	10	(Sep 03, 1994)
Country House	Blur	1	(Aug 26, 1995)
The Universal	Blur	5	(Nov 25, 1995)
Stereotypes	Blur	7	(Feb 24, 1996)
Charmless Man	Blur	5	(May 11, 1996)
Beetlebum	Blur	1	(Feb 01, 1997)
Song 2	Blur	2	(Apr 19, 1997)
On Your Own	Blur	5	(Jun 28, 1997)
Oh My God	The Kaiser Chiefs	6	(Mar 05, 2005)
Everyday I Love You Less And Less	The Kaiser Chiefs	10	(May 28, 2005)
I Predict A Riot/Sink That Ship	The Kaiser Chiefs	9	(Sep 03, 2005)
Boys Will Be Boys	The Ordinary Boys	3	(Feb 11, 2006)
Why Won't You Give Me Your Love	The Zutons	9	(Apr 15, 2006)
Hurry Up England – The People's Anthem	Sham 69 & the Special Assembly	10	(Jun 24, 2006)
Valerie	The Zutons	9	(Jul 01, 2006)
Ruby	The Kaiser Chiefs	1	(Mar 03, 2007)
Delivery	Babyshambles	6	(Sep 29, 2007)

TOP 10 UK HITS PRODUCED BY STEVE LILLYWHITE

		Peak Position	
Hong Kong Garden	Siouxsie & the Banshees	7	(Sep 16, 1978)
Games Without Frontiers	Peter Gabriel	4	(Mar 15, 1980)
New Year's Day	U2	10	(Feb 05, 1983)
Fields Of Fire (400 Miles)	Big Country	10	(Apr 16, 1983)
Chance	Big Country	9	(Oct 01, 1983)
Wonderland	Big Country	8	(Jan 28, 1984)
A New England	Kirsty MacColl	7	(Feb 23, 1985)
Fairytale Of New York	The Pogues featuring Kirsty MacColl	2	(Dec 26, 1987)
Even Better Than The Real Thing (Remix)	U2	8	(Jul 18, 1992)
The More You Ignore Me, The Closer I Get	Morrissey	8	(Mar 12, 1994)
Sweetest Thing	U2	3	(Oct 31, 1998)
Vertigo	U2	1	(Nov 20, 2004)
All Because Of You	U2	4	(Oct 22, 2005)

Grammy-Award winning British producer Steve Lillywhite – who helmed the first U2 album, *Boy* – has also been responsible for hits by Joan Armatrading, the Psychedelic Furs, Talking Heads, the Thompson Twins, Counting Crows, Razorlight and Crowded House.

British production maestro Stephen Street has accumulated more than 75 UK chart singles in his 23-year producing career. Following a short-lived attempt at performing as a member of early 80s ska/pop combo BIM, Street got his break in 1982 as an engineer in the Fallout Shelter Studio in the basement of Island Records.

Left: Producer George Martin in his studio.

Above: The Smiths in 1984.

TOP 10 US HITS PRODUCED BY JIMMY JAM & TERRY LEWIS

		Peak Position	
Tender Love	Force M.D.'s	10	(Apr 12, 1986)
What Have You Done For Me Lately	Janet Jackson	4	(May 17, 1986)
Nasty	Janet Jackson	3	(Jul 19, 1986)
When I Think Of You	Janet Jackson	1	(Oct 11, 1986)
Human	Human League	1	(Nov 22, 1986)
Control	Janet Jackson	5	(Jan 24, 1987)
Let's Wait Awhile	Janet Jackson	2	(Mar 21, 1987)
Diamonds	Herb Alpert	5	(Jun 20, 1987)
Monkey	George Michael	1	(Aug 27, 1988)
If It Isn't Love	New Edition	7	(Sep 17, 1988)
Miss You Much	Janet Jackson	1	(Oct 07, 1989)
Rhythm Nation	Janet Jackson	2	(Jan 06, 1990)
Escapade	Janet Jackson	1	(Mar 03, 1990)
Alright	Janet Jackson	4	(Jun 02, 1990)
Rub You The Right Way	Johnny Gill	3	(Aug 04, 1990)
Come Back To Me	Janet Jackson	2	(Aug 18, 1990)
Love Will Never Do (Without You)	Janet Jackson	1	(Jan 19, 1991)
Sensitivity	Ralph Tresvant	4	(Jan 26, 1991)
Romantic	Karyn White	1	(Nov 02, 1991)
The Best Things In Life Are Free	Luther Vandross & Janet Jackson	10	(Jun 13, 1992)
That's The Way Love Goes	Janet Jackson	1	(May 15, 1993)
If	Janet Jackson	4	(Sep 11, 1993)
Again	Janet Jackson	1	(Dec 11, 1993)
Because Of Love	Janet Jackson	10	(Mar 19, 1994)
Any Time, Any Place/ And On And On	Janet Jackson	2	(Jun 25, 1994)
On Bended Knee	Boyz II Men	1	(Dec 03, 1994)
You Want This/ 70's Love Groove	Janet Jackson	8	(Dec 24, 1994)
Scream/Childhood (from *Free Willy 2*)	Michael Jackson & Janet Jackson	5	(Jun 17, 1995)
Runaway	Janet Jackson	3	(Oct 21, 1995)
I'm Still In Love With You	New Edition	7	(Jan 11, 1997)
4 Seasons Of Loneliness	Boyz II Men	1	(Oct 04, 1997)
Together Again	Janet Jackson	1	(Jan 31, 1998)
I Get Lonely	Janet Jackson (featuring BLACKstreet)	3	(May 23, 1998)
Give It To You	Jordan Knight	10	(May 15, 1999)
Chanté's Got A Man	Chanté Moore	10	(Jun 12, 1999)
Thank God I Found You	Mariah Carey featuring Joe & 98 Degrees	1	(Feb 19, 2000)
Doesn't Really Matter	Janet	1	(Aug 26, 2000)
All For You	Janet	1	(Apr 14, 2001)
U Remind Me	Usher	1	(Jul 07, 2001)
Someone To Call My Lover	Janet	3	(Sep 01, 2001)

Iconic R&B production team Jimmy Jam and Terry Lewis first collaborated as members of the Minneapolis-based band Flyte Tyme in the early 80s. Interestingly, the duo helmed US chart-toppers for two non-R&B British acts, the Human League (1986) and George Michael (1988).

TOP 10 US HITS PRODUCED BY STARGATE

		Peak Position	
So Sick	Ne-Yo	1	(Mar 18, 2006)
Unfaithful	Lionel Richie	6	(Jul 22, 2006)
Sexy Love	Ne-Yo	7	(Sep 23, 2006)
Irreplaceable	Beyoncé	1	(Dec 16, 2006)
Walk Away (Remember Me)	Paula Deanda featuring the Dey	18	(Jan 06, 2007)
Beautiful Liar	Beyoncé & Shakira	3	(Apr 07, 2007)
Because Of You	Ne-Yo	2	(May 19, 2007)
Hate That I Love You	Rihanna featuring Ne-Yo	7	(Dec 22, 2007)
Tattoo	Jordin Sparks	8	(Dec 29, 2007)
With You	Chris Brown	2	(Feb 16, 2008)
Don't Stop The Music	Rihanna	3	(Feb 16, 2008)
Take A Bow	Rihanna	1	(May 24, 2008)
Closer	Ne-Yo	7	(Sep 27, 2008)
Miss Independent	Ne-Yo	7	(Dec 13, 2008)

Stargate is the production moniker for Norwegian duo Tor Erik Hermansen and Mikkel Storleer Eriksen, whose catchy pop/hip-hop sheen underpinned chart success for major American acts during the noughties. In 2010 they launched a New York-based record label StarRoc in partnership with rap mogul Jay-Z.

Above: Tor Erik Hermansen and Mikkel Storleer Eriksen.

Left: Jimmy Jam and Terry Lewis.

TOP 10 US HITS
PRODUCED BY TIMBALAND

		Peak Position	
Pony	Ginuwine	6	(Nov 23, 1996)
Make It Hot	Nicole featuring Missy "Misdemeanor" Elliott & Mocha	5	(Aug 01, 1998)
Hot Boyz	Missy "Misdemeanor" Elliott featuring Nas, Eve & Q-Tip	5	(Jan 08, 2000)
Try Again	Aaliyah	1	(Jun 17, 2000)
Get Ur Freak On	Missy "Misdemeanor" Elliott	7	(Jun 30, 2001)
Oops (Oh My)	Tweet	7	(May 04, 2002)
Work It	Missy "Misdemeanor" Elliott	2	(Nov 16, 2002)
Cry Me A River	Justin Timberlake	3	(Feb 01, 2003)
Gossip Folks	Missy "Misdemeanor" Elliott featuring Ludacris	8	(Mar 08, 2003)
Dirt Off Your Shoulder	Jay-Z	5	(Apr 10, 2004)
Promiscuous	Nelly Furtado featuring Timbaland	1	(Jul 08, 2006)
SexyBack	Justin Timberlake	1	(Sep 09, 2006)
My Love	Justin Timberlake featuring T.I.	1	(Nov 11, 2006)
Say It Right	Nelly Furtado	6	(Dec 23, 2006)
Say It Right	Nelly Furtado	1	(Feb 24, 2007)
What Goes Around … Comes Around	Justin Timberlake	1	(Mar 03, 2007)
Give It To Me	Timbaland featuring Nelly Furtado & Justin Timberlake	1	(Apr 21, 2007)
Summer Love	Justin Timberlake	6	(Jun 09, 2007)
The Way I Are	Timbaland featuring Keri Hilson	3	(Aug 25, 2007)
Make Me Better	Fabolous featuring Ne-Yo	8	(Aug 25, 2007)
Ayo Technology	50 Cent featuring Justin Timberlake & Timbaland	5	(Sep 29, 2007)
Apologize	Timbaland Presents OneRepublic	2	(Nov 10, 2007)
Give It Up To Me	Shakira featuring Lil Wayne	1	(Nov 28, 2009)

Above: Timbaland in 2010.

In recent years, Timothy Zachery Mosley – aka Timbaland – has branched out from his traditional rap/R&B fare, producing projects for the likes of ex-Soundgarden frontman Chris Cornell ('Scream', 2009) and, amazingly, Azerbaijani's 2010 Eurovision Song Contest entry.

Right: Timbaland with
Nelly Furtado in 2008.

MTV
MUSIC TELEVISION™

ROCK PRESS

Although the music trade publication *Billboard* began publication in 1894 in Cincinnati (in its early years carrying news of bill-posting and general live entertainment), the first weekly music paper for musicians of the day was *Melody Maker* which bowed in 1926 in the UK (lasting until 2000). The venerable and still-published *New Musical Express* first hit newsstands in 1952 – and with the monthly *Q* and *Mojo* magazines – remains a must-read for British rock fans. In the US, the longest-running music consumer magazine is *Rolling Stone*, still going strong after more than forty years.

TIME MAGAZINE

Over the last few years, the revered weekly American news magazine *Time* has published dozens of Top 10 and Top 100 lists on subjects ranging from the top crime stories to top novels. Assembled by staff of its Arts & Entertainment department, *Time* frequently includes some interesting music lists:

TIME MAGAZINE'S TOP 10 MUSIC FESTIVAL MOMENTS

1	The Flaming Lips	SXSW	2006
2	Bob Dylan	The Newport Folk Festival	1965
3	Jimi Hendrix	The Monterey Pop Festival	1967
4	The Who	Woodstock	1969
5	The Rolling Stones	Altamont	1969
6	U2	Live Aid	1985
7	Woodstock		1999
8	Rage Against The Machine	Lollapalooza	1993
9	Jay-Z	Glastonbury	2008
10	M.I.A.	Bonnaroo	2008

TIME MAGAZINE'S TOP 10 MTV MOMENTS

1 Video Killed The Radio Star
2 Michael Jackson's "Thriller" premières
3 Yo! MTV Raps
4 Boxers Or Briefs?
5 Beavis And Butt-head
6 Nirvana Unplugs
7 Seven Strangers Picked To Live In A House
8 These Walls Look Like Candy
9 Farewell, TRL
10 Snooki Gets Punched

Below Left: Jimi Hendrix plays Monterey in 1969 .

TIME MAGAZINE'S TOP 10 BAND BREAKUPS

1 The Beatles	6 The Dorsey Brothers
2 The Sex Pistols	7 The Smashing Pumpkins
3 The Supremes	8 Blondie
4 The Pixies	9 Talking Heads
5 Oasis	10 N.W.A.

No surprise at number one, but Talking Heads went on a hiatus in 1991 which shows no sign of ending. Frontman David Byrne's eclectic solo career includes the 2010 collaboration with Fatboy Slim: 'Here Lies Love'.

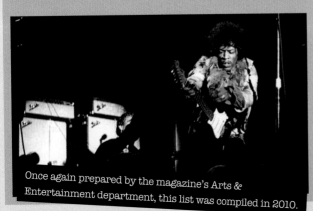

Once again prepared by the magazine's Arts & Entertainment department, this list was compiled in 2010.

Q MAGAZINE

First published in 1986, Q magazine has consistently remained Britain's most popular and authoritative monthly music digest for more than 20 years. It regularly publishes well-researched and provocative "best-of" lists, which provoke much discussion and debate among its loyal readers.

Below: Kasabian.

Q MAGAZINE'S ALBUMS OF THE 2000S

1	Back To Black	Amy Winehouse	2007
2	Is This It	The Strokes	2001
3	Whatever People Say I Am, That's What I'm Not	Arctic Monkeys	2006
4	Elephant	The White Stripes	2003
5	Viva La Vida Or Death And All His Friends	Coldplay	2008
6	Funeral	Arcade Fire	2006
7	American Idiot	Green Day	2004
8	The Blueprint	Jay-Z	2001
9	Kid A	Radiohead	2000
10	American IV – The Man Comes Around	Johnny Cash	2004

Q RECORDINGS OF THE YEAR – 2009

1	West Ryder Pauper Lunatic Asylum	Kasabian
2	Lungs	Florence + the Machine
3	It's Blitz	Yeah Yeah Yeahs
4	Merriweather Post Pavilion	Animal Collective
5	Journal For Plague Lovers	The Manic Street Preachers
6	Humbug	Arctic Monkeys
7	The Resistance	Muse
8	It's Not Me, It's You	Lilly Allen
9	No Line On The Horizon	U2
10	Wolfgang Amadeus Phoenix	Phoenix
11	Kingdom Of Rust	The Doves
12	Everything Is New	Jack Penate
13	Veckatimest	Grizzly Bear
14	What Will We Be	Devendra Banhart
15	Tongue 'N Cheek	Dizzee Rascal
16	Walking On A Dream	Empire of the Sun
17	21st Century Breakdown	Green Day
18	The Boy Who Knew Too Much	Mika
19	Monsters Of Folk	Monsters of Folk
20	Fever Ray	Fever Ray

Named after a mental health institution in Yorkshire, the list-topping third studio outing by British alt-rockers Kasabian, 'West Ryder Pauper Lunatic Asylum' was also nominated for the prestigious Mercury Music Prize in 2009.

Q READERS' BEST BRITISH ALBUMS

In the May 2008 edition of Q, the magazine's readers voted on its all-time favourite albums. Here is the top 10:

1	Definitely Maybe	Oasis
2	(What's The Story) Morning Glory?	Oasis
3	OK Computer	Radiohead
4	Revolver	The Beatles
5	The Stone Roses	The Stone Roses
6	Sgt. Pepper's Lonely Hearts Club Band	The Beatles
7	London Calling	The Clash
8	Under The Iron Sea	Keane
9	Dark Side Of The Moon	Pink Floyd
10	Urban Hymns	The Verve

The first album by Britpop heroes Oasis, *Definitely Maybe*, was released in 1994 when it became the fastest-selling album to date in the UK. Eventually shifting more than eight million copies worldwide, all of its 11 tracks were written by Noel Gallagher.

NEW MUSICAL EXPRESS

The *New Musical Express* was first published on March 7, 1952 in the UK and remains Britain's longest-running weekly music paper. Immensely popular during the 1960s, the *N.M.E.* arguably had its hey-day during the last half of the 1970s with its insightful and provocative coverage of the punk revolution, led by top scribes Tony Parsons and Julie Burchill.

NME ALBUMS OF THE YEAR

Since 1974, the journalists at the *New Musical Express*, have picked their top albums of the year:

Year	Album	Artist
1974	Pretzel Logic	Steely Dan
1975	Blood On The Tracks	Bob Dylan
1976	Desire	Bob Dylan
1977	Heroes	David Bowie
1978	Darkness On The Edge Of Town	Bruce Springsteen
1979	Fear Of Music	Talking Heads
1980	Closer	Joy Division
1981	Nightclubbing	Grace Jones
1982	Midnight Love	Marvin Gaye
1983	Punch The Clock	Elvis Costello
1984	The Poet II	Bobby Womack
1985	Rain Dogs	Tom Waits
1986	Parade	Prince & the Revolution
1987	Yo! Bum Rush the Show	Public Enemy
1988	It Takes A Nation Of Millions To Hold Us Back	Public Enemy
1989	3 Feet High And Rising	De La Soul
1990	Pills 'n' Thrills And Bellyaches	The Happy Mondays
1991	Nevermind	Nirvana
1992	Copper Blue	Sugar
1993	Debut	Björk
1994	Definitely Maybe	Oasis
1995	Maxinquaye	Tricky
1996	Odelay	Beck
1997	Ladies And Gentlemen We Are Floating In Space	Spiritualized
1998	Deserter's Songs	Mercury Rev
1999	The Soft Bulletin	The Flaming Lips
2000	Rated R	Queens of the Stone Age
2001	Is This It	The Strokes
2002	A Rush Of Blood To The Head	Coldplay
2003	Elephant	The White Stripes
2004	Franz Ferdinand	Franz Ferdinand
2005	Silent Alarm	Bloc Party
2006	Whatever People Say I Am, That's What I'm Not	Arctic Monkeys
2007	Myths Of The Near Future	Klaxons
2008	Oracular Spectacular	MGMT
2009	Primary Colours	The Horrors

THE NME GREATEST ALBUMS OF THE DECADE

The magazine published its Top 100 albums list for those titles released between January 2000 and December 2009, as selected by a panel of past and present *NME* staffers and invited musicians/music industry figures. Here is the top 10:

1	Is This It	The Strokes
2	Up The Bracket	Libertines
3	Xtrmntr	Primal Scream
4	Whatever People Say That's What I'm Not	Arctic Monkeys
5	Fever To Tell	Yeah Yeah Yeahs
6	Stories From The City, Stories From The Sea	PJ Harvey
7	Funereal	Arcade Fire
8	Turn On The Bright Lights	Interpol
9	Original Pirate Material	The Streets
10	In Rainbows	Radiohead

Is This It was the much-lauded 2001 debut album by garage rock revivalists, the Strokes. A five-member band hailing from New York, its rhythm guitarist, Albert Hammond Jr., is the son of 'It Never Rains In Southern California' hit singer-songwriter, Albert Hammond.

THE NME TRACKS OF THE DECADE (2000-09)

Here is the top 10:

1	Crazy In Love	Beyoncé
2	Time To Pretend	MGMT
3	Hard To Explain	The Strokes
4	Paper Planes	Mia
5	Hey Ya!	OutKast
6	House Of Jealous Lovers	The Rapture
7	Golden Skans	The Klaxons
8	Out Of Time	Blur
9	Rebellion (Lies)	Arcade Fire
10	A Certain Romance	Arctic Monkeys

Beyoncé's global smash, 'Crazy In Love' was originally created by co-producer Rich Harrison as 'Crazy Right Now.' Future husband Jay-Z's featured rap was written by the hip-hop star in 10 minutes.

ROLLING STONE MAGAZINE

Long-revered as America's most durable and beloved music magazine, *Rolling Stone* was founded by University of California dropout Jann Wenner and music critic Ralph J. Gleason in 1967, with its first publication hitting the streets on November 9.

ROLLING STONE MAGAZINE'S SONGS OF THE 2000S

Rolling Stone published a Top 100 list. Here is the Top 10:

1	Crazy	Gnarls Barkley	2006
2	99 Problems	Jay-Z	2004
3	Crazy in Love	Beyoncé featuring Jay-Z	2003
4	Hey Ya!	OutKast	2003
5	Paper Planes	M.I.A.	2008
6	Seven Nation Army	The White Stripes	2003
7	Maps	Yeah Yeah Yeahs	2004
8	Rehab	Amy Winehouse	2007
9	Beautiful Day	U2	2001
10	Stan	Eminem	2000

'Crazy' was the debut hit collaboration between producer/ musician Danger Mouse and vocalist/rapper Cee-Lo – known together as Gnarls Barkley. The global smash was also voted Song of the Year by *Rolling Stone* in 2006, won a Grammy for Best Urban/Alternative Performance and an MTV Europe Music Award for Best Song.

ROLLING STONE MAGAZINE'S ALBUMS OF THE 2000S

Rolling Stone published a Top 100 list. Here is the Top 10:

1	Kid A	Radiohead	2000
2	Is This It	The Strokes	2001
3	Yankee Hotel Foxtrot	Wilco	2002
4	The Blueprint	Jay-Z	2001
5	Elephant	The White Stripes	2003
6	Funeral	Arcade Fire	2004
7	The Marshall Mathers LP	Eminem	2000
8	Modern Times	Bob Dylan	2006
9	Kala	M.I.A.	2007
10	The College Dropout	Kanye West	2004

Their fourth album release, Radiohead's *Kid A* was intermittently recorded over a 16-month period between January 1999 and April 2000 in France, Denmark and England, and was produced by Nigel Goodrich. Hitting number one on both sides of the Atlantic, the 50-minute opus also topped *The Times* British newspaper's Top 100 Best Pop Albums of the Noughties list.

ROLLING STONE MAGAZINE'S TOP 30 SONGS OF ALL TIME

Below: Bob Dylan.

In its December 2004 issue, *Rolling Stone* published a list of its all-time Top 500 songs. The following are the Top 30:

1	Like A Rolling Stone	Bob Dylan
2	Satisfaction	The Rolling Stones
3	Imagine	John Lennon
4	What's Going On	Marvin Gaye
5	Respect	Aretha Franklin
6	Good Vibrations	The Beach Boys
7	Johnny B. Goode	Chuck Berry
8	Hey Jude	The Beatles
9	Smells Like Teen Spirit	Nirvana
10	What'd I Say	Ray Charles
11	My Generation	The Who
12	A Change Is Gonna Come	Sam Cooke
13	Yesterday	The Beatles
14	Blowin' In The Wind	Bob Dylan
15	London Calling	The Clash
16	I Want To Hold Your Hand	The Beatles
17	Purple Haze	Jimi Hendrix
18	Maybellene	Chuck Berry
19	Hound Dog	Elvis Presley
20	Let It Be	The Beatles
21	Born To Run	Bruce Springsteen
22	Be My Baby	The Ronettes
23	In My Life	The Beatles
24	People Get Ready	The Impressions
25	God Only Knows	The Beach Boys
26	A Day In The Life	The Beatles
27	Layla	Derek & the Dominos
28	(Sittin' On) The Dock Of The Bay	Otis Redding
29	Help!	The Beatles
30	I Walk the Line	Johnny Cash

Dylan's 'Like A Rolling Stone' was nailed after 21 takes, recorded over a two-day session in Columbia Records' Studio A, Manhattan, in June 1965.

Although the music industry today is dominated by just four major companies – SonyBMG, Warner Music, Universal and EMI – rock history's evolution is hallmarked by the rise and success of enormously influential small, independent labels. Some like Sun Records in Memphis and Stiff Records in London came and went (their catalogues subsequently swallowed by the majors), while others such as A&M (co-founded in a garage by Herb Alpert), Island (founded by Chris Blackwell) and Virgin (started by Richard Branson) became longstanding large labels in their own right.

THE FIRST TEN SINGLES
ON THE STIFF LABEL (UK RELEASES)

So It Goes/Heart Of The City	Nick Lowe	BUY 1 1976
Between The Lines/ Spoiling For A Food Fight	Pink Fairies	BUY 2 1976
All Aboard/Cincinnati Fatback	Roogalator	BUY 3 1976
Styrofoam/Texas Chainsaw Massacre Boogie	Tyla Gang	BUY 4 1976
Boogie On The Street/ Caravan Man	The Lew Lewis Band	BUY 5 1976
New Rose/Help	The Damned	BUY 6 1976
Another World/Blank/Generation/ You Gotta Lose	Richard Hell & the Voidoids	BUY 7 1976
Silver Shirt/This Is The World	Plummet Airlines	BUY 8 1976
Leavin' Here/White Line Fever	**Motorhead**	BUY 9 1977
Neat Neat Neat/Stab Your Back/ Singalongs Scabies	The Damned	BUY 10 1977

Formed by Jake Riviera and Dave Robinson in 1976, the London-based Stiff Records signed a succession of noteworthy New Wave and punk acts during the dawn of punk. With a BUY catalogue prefix assigned to its singles releases, Stiff also had fun with its marketing slogans, which included "The World's Most Flexible Record Label", "If It Ain't Stiff, It Ain't Worth a F#*@" and "If They're Dead, we'll sign them".

THE FIRST 20 ITEMS RELEASED
ON THE FACTORY LABEL

The Factory (Club No. 1)	Various Artists	FAC 1	Event Poster
A Factory Sample	Various Artists: Cabaret Voltaire, Joy Division, Durutti Column, John Dowie	FAC 2	Double Single
The Factory (Club No. 2)	Various Artists	FAC 3	Event Poster
The Factory December (Club No. 3)	Various Artists	FAC 4	Tony Wilson
All Night Party	A Certain Ratio	FAC 5	Single
Electricity	Orchestral Manoeuvres in the Dark	FAC 6	Single
Stationery	Factory note paper	FAC 7	
Menstrual egg timer design	Linder Sterling	FAC 8	Concept
The Factory Flick	Various Artists	FAC 9	Film
Unknown Pleasures	Joy Division	FACT 10	Album
Joy Division, Various Artists Posters		FACT 10+4	
English Black Boys	X-o-dus	FAC 11	Single
Time Goes By So Slow	The Distractions	FAC 12	Single
Transmission	Joy Division	FAC 13	Single
Transmission Factory logo	Joy Division, Factory Records	FAC 13T	T-shirt
The Return Of The Durutti Column	Durutti Column	FACT 14	Album
Testcard	Martin Hannett	FACT 14	Flexi-disc
Zoo Meets Factory Halfway, Leigh Festival	Various Artists	FAC 15	Poster
The Graveyard And The Ballroom album	A Certain Ratio	FACT 16	Cassette
Sex Machine	Crawling Chaos	FAC 17	Single
Girls Don't Count	Section 25	FAC 18	Single
Hard To Be An Egg	John Dowie	FAC 19	Single

Unique UK post-punk label Factory Records was formed in 1978 in Manchester, England by local television presenter Tony Wilson and band manager Alan Erasmus. Rarely signing formal contracts with their artists, the label used a catalogue number release format (FAC or FACT), which included non-music related items, including company notepaper (FAC 7) and even a lawsuit (FAC 61). The number FAC 501 in 2007 was allocated to the funeral of co-founder Wilson and his plaque.

THE FIRST TEN
ALBUMS ON THE VIRGIN LABEL

Tubular Bells	Mike Oldfield	V2001	1973
Radio Gnome Invisible, Part 1: The Flying Teapot	Gong	V2002	1973
Manor Live	Various	V2003	1973
Faust 4	Faust	V2004	1973
The Henry Cow Legend	Henry Cow	V2005	1973
Beans And Fatback	Link Wray	V2006	1973
Radio Gnome Invisible, Part 2: Angel's Egg	Gong	V2007	1973
The Hatfield And The North Album	Hatfield And The North	V2008	1974
Busy Corner	Chili Charles	V2009	1974
Phaedra	Tangerine Dream	V2010	1974

Serial entrepreneur Richard Branson's all-encompassing Virgin empire began with the establishment of the Virgin Records and Tapes store in London 1971. The following year he formed the Virgin Records label and took a gamble on signing progressive rock multi-instrumentalist Mike Oldfield.

Right: George Harrison in 1968.

THE FIRST 20 ALBUMS
RELEASED ON THE APPLE LABEL

Wonderwall Music	George Harrison	SAPCOR 1	1968
The Beatles	The Beatles	PCS 7067/68	1968
Unfinished Music No. 1: Two Virgins	John Lennon & Yoko Ono	SAPCOR 2	1968
James Taylor	James Taylor	SAPCOR 3	1968
Under The Jasmine Tree	The Modern Jazz Quartet	SAPCOR 4	1968
Yellow Submarine	The Beatles	PCS 7070	1969
Postcard	Mary Hopkin	SAPCOR 5	1969
Is This What You Want?	Jackie Lomax	SAPCOR 6	1969
Maybe Tomorrow (released only in Japan, Italy and Germany)	The Iveys	SAPCOR 8	1969
That's The Way God Planned It	Billy Preston	SAPCOR 9	1969
Abbey Road	The Beatles	PCS 7088	1969
Space	The Modern Jazz Quartet	SAPCOR 10	1969
Wedding Album	John Lennon & Yoko Ono	SAPCOR 11	1969
Live Peace In Toronto 1969	Plastic Ono Band	CORE 2001	1969
Magic Christian Music	Badfinger	SAPCOR 12	1970
Sentimental Journey	Ringo Starr	PCS 7101	1970
McCartney	Paul McCartney	PCS 7102	1970
Let It Be	The Beatles	PXS 1	1970
Doris Troy	Doris Troy	SAPCOR 13	1970
Encouraging Words	Billy Preston	SAPCOR 14	1970

The Beatles' members formed their own Apple Records label in 1968 – and its first 20 album releases reveal both a diverse roster of many successful non-Beatles artists – including debuts by James Taylor and Badfinger – and also documents the dissolution of the band, with group albums interspersed in between the first solo projects by each Beatle.

THE FIRST 20 SINGLES
RELEASED ON THE SUB POP LABEL

Sub Pop Cassette 'Zine 5, 1980	Various Artists	SP 005	1974
Sub Pop Cassette 'Zine 7, 1982	Various Artists	SP 007	1974
Sub Pop 100	Various Artists	SP 010	1990
Dry As A Bone/Rehab Doll	Green River	SP 011	1988
Screaming Life	Soundgarden	SP 012	1991
Two Way Street/Six Foot Under	Blood Circus	SP 013	1992
Guts/Trapped	Swallow	SP 014	1992
Rehab Doll	Green River	SP 015	1992
Clear Black Paper	Fluid	SP 016	1988
Fopp	Soundgarden	SP 017	1992
Touch Me I'm Sick/ Sweet Young Thing	Mudhoney	SP 018	1992
Ritual Device/Daisy	Tad	SP 019	1992
Hit It Or Quit It	Girl Trouble	SP 020	1992
Superfuzz Bigmuff	Mudhoney	SP 021	1992
Primal Rock Therapy	Blood Circus	SP 022	1993
Love Buzz/Big Cheese	Nirvana	SP 023	1988
Swallow	Swallow	SP 024	1993
Sub Pop 200	Various	SP 025	1992
Halloween/Touch Me I'm Sick	Mudhoney/ Sonic Youth	SP 026	1988
God's Balls	Tad	SP 027	1993
Strychnine/Drug Machine/ What's So Funny	Flaming Lips	SP 028	1993
Chess And Crimes/Sunday Time	Les Thugs	SP 029	1993

Left: Metal band Soundgarden reformed in 2010

Founded by Jonathan Poneman and Bruce Pavitt in 1986 in Seattle, Sub Pop became synonymous with the Grunge rock genre which burst forth from that city in the late 80s. Home to pioneering acts including Soundgarden, Mudhoney and Nirvana, Sub Pop continues today signing the likes of popular alt-rockers the Postal Service, Fleet Foxes and The Shins.

MTV
MUSIC TELEVISION

This section of the book is dedicated to lists that wouldn't quite fit any criteria – and they are all the more unique for it. We cover all subjects here, from video games to expensive videos and from memorabilia to Jewish composers of Christmas Songs. Add in the Vatican's recommended listening in these "difficult times" and you have a mixture of fun, fascinating and downright odd information that defies categorization – hence "Pop Pourri".

THE TOP 20 MOST EXPENSIVE MUSIC VIDEOS EVER PRODUCED

1	Michael Jackson & Janet Jackson	Scream	Mark Romanek	1995	$7,000,000
2	Madonna	Die Another Day	Traktor	2002	$6,100,000
3	Madonna	Express Yourself	David Fincher	1989	$5,000,000
4	Madonna	Bedtime Story	Mark Romanek	1995	$5,000,000
5	Guns N' Roses	Estranged	Andy Morahan	1993	$4,000,000
6	Puff Daddy (featuring Notorious B.I.G & Busta Rhymes)	Victory	Marcus Nispel	1998	$2,700,000
7	MC Hammer	Too Legit to Quit	Rupert Wainwright	1991	$2,500,000
8	Mariah Carey (featuring Jay-Z)	Heartbreaker	Brett Ratner	1999	$2,500,000
9	Busta Rhymes (featuring Janet Jackson)	What's It Gonna Be?!	Hype Williams & Busta Rhymes	1999	$2,400,000
10	Celine Dion	It's All Coming Back to Me Now	Nigel Dick	1996	$2,300,000
11	Michael Jackson	Bad	Martin Scorsese	1987	$2,200,000
12	Backstreet Boys	Larger Than Life	Joseph Kahn	1999	$2,100,000
13	Will Smith	Miami	Wayne Isham	1998	$2,000,000
14	Missy Elliott	She's a Bitch	Hype Williams	1999	$2,000,000
15	George Michael	Freeek!	Joseph Kahn	2004	$2,000,000
16	Ayumi Hamasaki	My Name's Women	Wataru Takeishi	2005	$2,000,000
17	Ayumi Hamasaki	Fairyland	Wataru Takeishi	2005	$2,000,000
18	TLC	Unpretty	Paul Hunter	1999	$1,600,000
19	Ayumi Hamasaki	Green	Wataru Takeishi	2008	$1,600,000
20	Michael Jackson	Black or White	John Landis	1991	$1,500,000

Michael and Janet Jackson's expensive 1995 collaborative anti-media intrusion video, *Scream*, was mostly filmed in black and white on a 13-piece stage set and took four weeks to produce. Janet reprised her performance in the clip at the 2009 MTV Video Music Awards in tribute to her recently deceased brother.

Above: Madonna in the James Bond movie *Die Another Day*.

GUITAR HERO VIDEO GAMES

The "Guitar Hero" video game franchise – begun by Activision in 2005 – hit $1 billion in US retail sales after just two years.

ROCK BAND VIDEO GAMES

		Release date
1	Rock Band	Nov 20, 2007
2	Rock Band Track Pack Vol. 1	Jul 15, 2008
3	Rock Band 2	Sep 14, 2008
4	AC/DC Live – Rock Band Track Pack	Nov 02, 2008
5	Rock Band Track Pack Vol. 2	Nov 18, 2008
6	Rock Band Track Pack – Classic Rock	May 19, 2009
7	Rock Band Unplugged	Jun 09, 2009
8	Rock Band Country Track Pack	Jul 21, 2009
9	The Beatles – Rock Band	Sep 09, 2009
10	Rock Band Mobile	Sep 16, 2009
11	Rock Band Metal Track Pack	Sep 22, 2009
12	Rock Band iPhone	Oct 19, 2009
13	Lego Rock Band	Nov 03, 2009
14	Green Day – Rock Band	Jun 08, 2010

The "Rock Band" video game series was launched by Harmonix Music Systems and MTV Games in 2007.

The influential monthly magazine *Record Collector* compiled an extensive list of the most valuable records in the UK in their December 2004 issue. Twenty-nine records were valued at £2,000 or more. They were:

£100,000	The Quarry Men	That'll Be the Day/In Spite Of All the Danger (1958 acetate)
£10,000	The Quarry Men	That'll Be the Day/In Spite Of All the Danger (1981 private reissue)
£10,000	The Beatles	The Beatles (White Album (numbered 110)
£5,000– £5,500	The Sex Pistols	God Save the Queen (A&M, some with press release)
£5,000	Queen	Bohemian Rhapsody (blue vinyl + press pack)
£3,250	Ron Hargrove	Latch On (MGM 7")
£3,000	John's Children	Midsummer Night's Dream (Track withdrawn 7")
£3,000	John Lennon/Yoko Ono	Unfinished Music No 1: 2 Virgins (LP)
£3,000	The Crows	Gee (Columbia 7")
£3,000	The Beatles	Abbey Road (export issue, yellow & black labels: Decca)
£3,000	David Bowie	Space Oddity (unreleased pic sleeve Philips 7")
£3,000	The Beatles	Please Please Me (black & gold label, stereo)
£3,000	The Beatles	Love Me Do (7" demo)
£2,600	Bobby Charles	See You Later Alligator (London 7" 1956)
£2,500	T. Rex	Ride a White Swan/Summertime Blues/Jewel (Octopus unreleased 7")
£2,000	Marc Bolan	Hard on Love (2-sided acetate of unreleased LP)
£2,000	Willie Dixon & the Allstars	Walking the Blue/Crazy for My Baby (London 7")
£2,000	The Plastic Ono Band	You Know My Name/What's the New Mary Jane (unreleased 7")
£2,000	The Chords	Sh Boom (Life Could Be A Dream) (Columbia 7" 1954)
£2,000	The Bread & Beer Band (with Elton John)	Bread & Beer Band (Rubbish LP 1969)
£2,000	The Beatles	Yellow Submarine (export LP, Odeon sticker on Apple sleeve)
£2,000	U2	Rattle & Hum (CD, LP & Cass flight case promo)
£2,000	Pink Floyd	Arnold Layne/Candy & a Currant Bun (demo, in promo p/s)
£2,000	Pink Floyd	Apples & Oranges/Paintbox (demo, in promo p/s)
£2,000	Pink Floyd	See Emily Play (demo, in promo p/s)
£2,000	Pink Floyd	It Would Be So Nice/Julia Dream (7" demo, in promo p/s)
£2,000	The Beatles	Golden Discs (unreleased, 2 x 1-sided test pressings)
£2,000	Jackie Lee Cochran	Ruby Pearl (Brunswick 7")
£2,000	Billy Nichols	Would You Believe (withdrawn Immediate LP)

ROCK MUSICALS ON STAGE

Grease		1972
Elvis	Elvis Presley	1977
Chess	Tim Rice, Björn Ulvaeus, Benny Andersson	1984
Leader Of The Pack	Ellie Greenwich & others	1984
The Iron Man	Pete Townshend	1989
Five Guys Named Moe	Louis Jordan	1990
Tommy	The Who	1993
Randy Newman's Faust	Randy Newman	1993
Buddy: The Buddy Holly Story	Buddy Holly	1995
The Lion King	Elton John/Tim Rice	1997
Quadrophenia	The Who	1998
Saturday Night Fever	The Bee Gees	1998
The Boy From Oz	Peter Allen	1998
Mamma Mia!	Abba	1999
Aida	Elton John/Tim Rice	2000
Movin' Out	Billy Joel	2002
We Will Rock You	Queen	2002
Our House	Madness	2002
Tonight's The Night	Rod Stewart	2003
Cliff – The Musical	Cliff Richard	2003
Good Vibrations	Brian Wilson/ Beach Boys	2005
Jersey Boys	Four Seasons	2005
Billy Elliot	Elton John	2005
All Shook Up	Elvis Presley	2005
Ring Of Fire	Johnny Cash	2006
Love	Beatles/ Cirque du Soleil	2006
Hot Feet	Earth Wind & Fire	2006
The Times They Are A-Changin'	Bob Dylan	2006
Daddy Cool	Boney M	2006
Never Forget	Take That	2007
Slide	Beautiful South	2007
Spring Awakening	Duncan Sheik	2007
All The Fun Of The Fair	David Essex	2008
Thriller – Live	Jackson 5/ Michael Jackson	2009
American Idiot	Green Day	2010
Spider-Man: Turn Off The Lights	Bono/The Edge	2010

Left: American punk trio Green Day.

With its official Broadway opening much-delayed, the *Spider-Man: Turn Off The Lights* musical was rescheduled to open in autumn 2010. Directed by Tony Award-winning *The Lion King* helmer, Julie Taymor, the comic book hero's theatrical bow features music and lyrics by U2's Bono and The Edge.

MTV MUSIC TELEVISION

THE SEX PISTOLS
BEFORE AND AFTER

Sex Pistols albums released by seminal lineup of Johnny Rotten, Sid Vicious, Steve Cook and Paul Jones:

1977   Never Mind The Bollocks, Here's the Sex Pistols

Sex Pistols albums released after their dissolution in 1978:

1979	The Great Rock 'n' Roll Swindle
1979	Some Product – Carri on Sex Pistols
1980	Flogging a Dead Horse
1980	Sex Pack
1985	Anarchy in the UK – Live At The 76 Club
1992	Kiss This
1996	Filthy Lucre Live
2002	Jubilee
2002	Sex Pistols (boxed set)
2005	Raw And Live
2007	Agents Of Anarchy
2008	Live & Filthy

Above: The Sex Pistols in 1976.

With only one original studio album to its iconic name, the Sex Pistols – featuring Rotten, Cook and Jones – have reunited for three tours since 1996.

JEWISH COMPOSERS
OF TEN ICONIC CHRISTMAS SONGS

White Christmas	Irving Berlin
Winter Wonderland	Felix Bernard
Rockin' Around The Christmas Tree	Johnny Marks
The Christmas Song	Mel Tormé
Sleigh Ride	Mitchell Parish
Rudolph The Red Nosed Reindeer	Johnny Marks
Let It Snow	Sammy Cahn, Jule Styne
I'll Be Home For Christmas	Walter Kent, Buck Ram
A Holly Jolly Christmas	Johnny Marks
Silver Bells	Jay Livingston, Ray Evans

THE VATICAN'S TOP TEN MUST-HAVE RECORD ALBUMS

1	Revolver	The Beatles
2	If I Could Only Remember My Name	David Crosby
3	Dark Side of the Moon	Pink Floyd
4	Rumours	Fleetwood Mac
5	The Nightfly	Donald Fagen
6	Thriller	Michael Jackson
7	Graceland	Paul Simon
8	Achtung Baby	U2
9	(What's The Story?) Morning Glory	Oasis
10	Supernatural	Carlos Santana

The official Vatican newspaper journal, *L'Osservatore Romano* unexpectedly issued the above list and explanation in February 2010: "A little handbook of musical resistance could be useful during this time of the year in which, in addition to having put up with the rigours of winter, we have to endure a rising tide of musical festivals. So as not to be totally overwhelmed, and to remember that an alternative exists, our modest guide can point you on the road to good music."

NOTABLE ALBUMS RECORDED
AT ABBEY ROAD STUDIOS

Located at 3, Abbey Road, St. John's Wood in North London, the legendary recording studio was purchased by EMI in 1929 for £100,000 (which briefly put it up for sale in February 2010 before public outrage changed their mind).

ACTORS MOONLIGHTING AS MUSICIANS

FAMOUS MUSICIAN MARRIAGES

	Year	Status
Tina Turner + Ike Turner	1962	divorced
Michelle Phillips + John Phillips	1962	divorced
Cher + Sonny	1964	divorced
Ronnie Spector + Phil Spector	1968	divorced
Tammy Wynette + George Jones	1969	divorced
Syreeta + Stevie Wonder	1970	divorced
Rita Coolidge + Kris Kristofferson	1973	divorced
Cher + Greg Allman	1975	divorced
Jackie DeShannon + Randy Edelman	1976	
Gloria Estefan + Emilio Estefan	1978	
Patti Smith + Fred "Sonic" Smith (MC5)	1980	
Donna Summer + Bruce Sudano (producer)	1980	
Joni Mitchell + Larry Klein (producer)	1982	divorced
Janet Jackson + James DeBarge	1984	divorced
Cait O'Riordan (Pogues) + Elvis Costello	1986	divorced
Carly Simon + James Taylor	1987	divorced
Patti Scialfa + Bruce Springsteen	1991	
Edie Brickell + Paul Simon	1992	
Courtney Love + Kurt Cobain	1992	
Whitney Houston + Bobby Brown	1992	divorced
Shania Twain + Robert John 'Mutt' Lange	1993	divorced
Mariah Carey + Tommy Mottola (Sony boss)	1993	divorced
Lisa Marie Presley + Michael Jackson	1994	divorced
Faith Hill + Tim McGraw	1996	
Aimee Mann + Michael Penn	1997	
Meg White + Jack White	2000	divorced
Gwen Stefani + Gavin Rossdale (Bush)	2002	
Diana Krall + Elvis Costello	2003	
Natalie Imbruglia + Daniel Johns (Silverchair)	2003	divorced
Jennifer Lopez + Marc Anthony	2004	
Allison Moorer + Steve Earle	2005	
Kelis + Nas	2005	divorced
Trisha Yearwood + Garth Brooks	2005	
Avril Lavigne + Deryck Whibley (Sum 41)	2006	
Beyoncé Knowles + Jay Z	2008	
Laurie Anderson + Lou Reed	2008	

FAMOUS MUSICIAN AND THEIR MUSICIAN DAUGHTERS/SONS

Dhani Harrison (thenewno2)	George Harrison
Joseph Sumner (Fiction Plane)	Sting
Miley Cyrus	Billy Ray Cyrus
Trace Cyrus (Metro Station)	Billy Ray Cyrus
Cosby Loggins	Kenny Loggins
Harper Simon	Paul Simon
Chesney Hawkes	Chip Hawkes (The Tremeloes)
Shelly & Karen Poole (Alisha's Attic)	Brian Poole (& The Tremeloes)
Wolfgang Van Halen	Eddie Van Halen
Gunnar and Matthew Nelson (The Nelsons)	Rick Nelson
Jakob Dylan (The Wallflowers)	Bob Dylan
Elijah Blue Allman (Deadsy)	Gregg Allman and Cher
Sean Lennon	John & Yoko Lennon
Julian Lennon	John Lennon
Kelly Osbourne	Ozzy Osbourne
Sean Stewart	Rod Stewart
Lisa Marie Presley	Elvis Presley
Dweezil Zappa	Frank Zappa
Hank Williams Jr.	Hank Williams
Hank Williams III	Hank Williams Jr.
Ben Taylor	James Taylor & Carly Simon
Rufus Wainwright	Kate McGarrigle & Loudon Wainwright III
Martha Wainwright	Kate McGarrigle & Loudon Wainwright III
Justin Townes Earle	Steve Earle
Shooter Jennings	Waylon Jennings
Jeff Buckley	Tim Buckley
Rosanne Cash	Johnny Cash
Zak Starr	Ringo Starr
Stephen, Ziggy, Damian, Julian, Ky-Mani Marley	Bob Marley

More than half of the rock star marriages listed ended in divorce.

Below: Bob Marley with his son Ziggy.

Though not a musician, David Bowie's son, Duncan Jones directed the 2009 BAFTA Award-winning film, *Moon.*

HARD ROCK CAFE'S TOP 10 COOLEST PIECES OF MEMORABILIA ACQUIRED IN 2009

With a well-deserved reputation as one of the world's most knowledgeable and thorough collectors of rock and pop memorabilia – which it uses to adorn the walls of its restaurants around the globe – the Hard Rock Cafe issued two press releases in 2009 regarding both their recent most-prized acquisitions – and those still on its future wish-list:

1) SNOOP DOGG'S PIMP COAT – We just picked up a floor-length, baby-blue leather trench coat that the smoothest rapper since Rakim wore in the film *Starsky and Hutch*. This coat is so over-the-top that it will quickly become your favorite thing ever.

2) STEVIE NICKS' THIGH-HIGH BOOTS – Check out these bad boys. Stevie wore them during Fleetwood Mac's *Tango in the Night* tour in '89. When she put these boots on, Ms. Nicks was still only about 5' 6". Stevie may not be the tallest girl at the prom, but she's definitely the queen.

3) THE KING'S CIGAR LIGHTER – In 2009, we were able to spark out stories with Elvis' personal cigar lighter. It's solid silver and has the initials "EAP" engraved on it. If we have to explain what those initials stand for, you're reading the wrong book.

4) ROBERT LANG STUDIO DOOR – Here's the graffiti-covered door from legendary Seattle studio Robert Lang Recorders. Nirvana did one of their very last sessions there, and Kurt took the opportunity to doodle on this door. His drawing of a little dude is in the upper left-hand corner.

5) CARLOS SANTANA'S CUSTOM PEAVEY GUITAR – Though Carlos is the poster boy for PRS guitars, Peavey handmade an absolute stunner for him. It's a gorgeous flame-maple number that will drop your jaw when you see it. We can't figure out why Carlos parted with it, but his loss is your gain.

6) EDDIE VAN HALEN'S SPEAKER CABINETS – This was a great find. Eddie brutalized these cabinets during Van Halen's 2004 world tour.

7) NEIL YOUNG'S TAKAMINE 12-STRING – When Neil played our annual Hard Rock Calling show in Hyde Park this year, he was gracious enough to give us his 12-string acoustic. Needless to say, we were blown away. It's almost impossible to get instruments from Neil's arsenal, so this was a very special acquisition.

8) KRIST NOVOSELIC'S IBANEZ BASS – In 2010 we're opening a brand new cafe in one of America's most storied rock 'n' roll towns: Seattle. This is equally exciting and daunting. Exciting for obvious reasons, daunting because in a city like Seattle you had better come correct. We've collected a number of great pieces from the town's history and this is one of the best. It's Nirvana bassist Krist Novoselic's Ibanez Black Eagle bass. This machine saw tons of action during Nirvana's heyday and will have a place of honour in our new cafe.

9) KURT COBAIN'S AUNT'S OVATION ACOUSTIC – Here's another piece of Seattle history. Kurt's aunt was/is a musician, and this Ovation acoustic was the first really decent instrument he ever played. We also acquired video of Kurt playing this axe in his aunt's house just prior to Nirvana's rise to world dominance.

10) JUAN ALDERETE'S FENDER BASS – Though these lists are by nature subjective, we think the coolest thing we acquired in '09 is this battered Fender Precision. It was used by Mars Volta bassist Juan Alderete on every album and tour since 2003's *Deloused*. Mars Volta is easily one of the best, most original, most exciting groups to emerge in the 21 century, so it's fitting that we close out our first decade paying tribute to this group's greatness. We're convinced that original memorabilia from the Mars Volta will eventually be as important as stuff from rock greats like Hendrix. They're just that good.

TOP TEN PIECES OF MEMORABILIA THE HARD ROCK CAFE WOULD LOVE TO GET THEIR HANDS ON

"Even though we have by far the largest collection of rock artifacts the world has ever seen, there are still tons of pieces we'd love to add to the party. Maybe we'll get lucky in 2010 and pick up some of these pop culture artifacts, or maybe we're just pulling your leg about these pieces. You decide. They are:

1) JACK WHITE'S GRETSCH WHITE PENGUIN – Jack is one of the very few people who owns a vintage Gretsch White Penguin guitar. We want it. Come on, Jack, hook us up.

2) LARRY BLACKMON'S RED CODPIECE FROM THE "WORD UP" VIDEO – You've got to be a special kind of guy to have the balls to wear a fire-engine-red codpiece in your big MTV opus. Larry Blackmon stepped into the pop culture stratosphere with Cameo's "Word Up" video and his crimson codpiece. We want the thing.

3) SHOCK G'S GROUCHO NOSE FROM "HUMPTY DANCE" – There was something really, really cool about Digital Underground's Shock G hitting the rap scene with an inane Groucho nose/glasses combination in the video for "Humpty Dance" – especially considering it was the heyday of oh-so-serious militant gangsta rap. We've got to have it.

4) OLIVIA NEWTON JOHN'S HEADBAND FROM THE "PHYSICAL" VIDEO – One of the most popular New Year's resolutions is to start hitting the gym and getting more physical. We're convinced that if we had Olivia's headband on display, we'd inspire millions to get healthy.

5) RICK JAMES' RICKENBACKER BASS – The late, great Rick James was everything a funky rock star should be. You know it, we know it. He was also a kick-ass bass player. We want the white Rickenbacker 4001 he played in the "Super Freak" video and is holding on the cover of Street Songs. On an unrelated note, what do you think happened to the girls in this video? They seem like such wholesome, lovely ladies.

6) OVERALLS FROM THE "COME ON EILEEN" VIDEO – Nothing says "dubious '80s video fashion choice" more than the dirty overalls from Dexy's Midnight Runners' "Come on Eileen" clip. We're on the hunt for them.

7) EVERY SINGLE COPY OF AUTO TUNE SOFTWARE ON THE PLANET – We want this not to display, but to burn. It would be our good deed for the decade and the mountain of good Karma we'd get is always handy to have around.

8) GERARDO'S HAIR EXTENSIONS – "Rico Suave" was the greatest song ever recorded. It's better than anything by Dylan, the Beatles, Cobain – you name it, "Rico Suave" is better. It's just so damn deep. In the video, Gerardo's asinine hair extensions seem to come and go as they please. Now you see 'em, now you don't. We want them.

9) TONY IOMMI'S FINGERTIPS – We're not talking about the metal and leather thimbles he uses on his missing digits, we're looking for the actual disembodied fingertips that he lost in an industrial accident in '66. We'd keep them in a jar of formaldehyde and show them to our "special" guests.

10) BUST OF LIONEL RICHIE – The single greatest piece of memorabilia possible – the Holy Grail – is the clay bust from Lionel Richie's 'Hello' video. Everything about it is awesome – especially the fact that it's an oversized noggin that looks nothing like Lionel Richie. We realize that it has probably returned to the raw clay state from whence it came, but maybe we'll get lucky. Be assured that if we ever find it, it will have a place of honour in our collection complete with high-security laser alarms, fancy lighting, and a perpetual tape loop of this video."

THE TEN MOST SAMPLED SONGS OF ALL-TIME

1	Funky Drummer	James Brown	197
2	Sing a Simple Song	Sly & the Family Stone	128
3	Impeach the President	The Honey Drippers	117
4	Think (About It)	Lyn Collins	112
5	Funky President	James Brown	101
6	Synthetic Substitution	Melvin Bliss	94
7	Atomic Dog	George Clinton	80
8	N.T.	Kool & the Gang	74
9	The Payback	James Brown	67
10	Nautilus	Bob James	62

The legendary "Funky Drummer" beat track has been sampled in no less than four Run-DMC songs – and eight recordings by Public Enemy.

THE TEN MOST SAMPLED ARTISTS OF ALL-TIME

1	James Brown	922
2	Kool & the Gang	294
3	Parliament	280
4	Sly & the Family Stone	255
5	The J.B.s	198
6	Bob James	191
7	Funkadelic	186
8	Isaac Hayes	183
9	Lyn Collins	146
10	Ohio Players	136

Above: The much-sampled James Brown in 1981.

According to www.the-breaks.com, James Brown remains the undisputed king of the samples. In addition to his own total, vintage recordings by both the J.B.s (his backing band) and Lyn Collins (whom he produced) also feature prominently in these lists.

TEN ALUMNI OF THE BERKLEE COLLEGE OF MUSIC

The esteemed Berklee College of Music was founded in 1945 in Boston, USA, and is widely regarded as the top music academy in the country.

Paula Cole • Gavin DeGraw • Melissa Etheridge • Bruce Hornsby • Keith Jarrett • Quincy Jones • Diana Krall • John Mayer • Aimee Mann • Brad Whitford and Joey Kramer (Aerosmith)

TEN ALUMNI OF THE BRIT SCHOOL

The Brit School of the Performing Arts and Technology in Croydon, south London, has produced several famous music chart-toppers over the years.

Adele • The Feeling • Imogen Heap • The Kooks • Leona Lewis • Katie Melua • Kele Okereke • Katy Pedwent • Amy Winehouse • Jessie Ware (?)

TOP GUITARISTS WHO USE OR HAVE USED THE GIBSON LES PAUL GUITAR

Duane Allman	(The Allman Brothers)
Billie Joe Armstrong	(Green Day)
Peter Frampton	
Ace Frehley	(Kiss)
Peter Green	(Fleetwood Mac)
Paul Kossoff	(Free)
Bob Marley	
Gary Moore	
Jimmy Page	(Led Zeppelin)
Joe Perry	(Aerosmith)
Les Paul	
Randy Rhoads	(Ozzy Osbourne)
Keith Richards	(The Rolling Stones)
Slash	(Guns N' Roses)
Neil Young	

Originally created in 1952 – and also a solid body electric guitar – the Gibson Les Paul was designed by Gibson Guitar Corporation's boss, Ted McCarty, together with legendary guitarist/inventor Les Paul. In addition to the various natural wood finishes made available over the years, the Gibson Les Paul has been sold in Vintage Sunburst, Ebony, Wine Red, Honey Burst, Arctic white and Heritage Cherry Sunburst.

TOP GUITARISTS WHO USE OR HAVE USED THE GIBSON SG GUITAR

Mick Box	(Uriah Heep)	Frank Marino	(Mahogany Rush)
Eric Clapton		Sister Rosetta Tharpe	
Elliot Easton	(The Cars)	Pete Townshend	(The Who)
Jerry Garcia	(The Grateful Dead)	Derek Trucks	(The Allman
Jimi Hendrix		Brothers	
Tony Iommi	(Black Sabbath)	Thom Yorke	(Radiohead)
Robby Krieger	(The Doors)	Angus Young	(AC/DC)
Daron Malakian	(System of a Down)	Frank Zappa	

Advertised as having "the fastest neck in the world", the Gibson SG Guitar was launched in 1961. Several variations of the iconic solid axe have been produced over the decades, its body using mahogany, maple and birch laminate woods.

Left: Beyoncé.

THE RICHEST AMERICAN ROCK STARS UNDER 30, 2009

	millions
Beyoncé	$87
Britney Spears	$35
Miley Cyrus	$25
The Jonas Brothers	$25
Jessica Simpson	$20
Lil' Wayne	$18
Taylor Swift	$18
Rihanna	$15
T-Pain	$15
Carrie Underwood	$14

According to *Forbes* magazine, Beyoncé, in addition to her music and film income, earned a pretty penny from endorsements and sponsors including Giorgio Armani, Nintendo, Crystal Geyser, L'Oréal and General Mills.

THE RICHEST MALE HIP-HOP MOGULS IN 2009

	millions

One-year earnings between June 2008–June 2009, as estimated by *Forbes* magazine.

	millions
Edgar Bronfman, Jr.	£1,640
Clive Calder	£1,300
Lord Lloyd-Webber	£700
Sir Cameron Mackintosh	£635
Sir Paul McCartney	£475
Simon Fuller	£350
Sir Mick Jagger	£190
Sir Elton John	£185
Sting	£180
Keith Richards	£175

The Sunday Times announces these figures annually, based on estimated total wealth. Although not a household name, South African-born Clive Calder made a bundle as co-founder of the Zomba Group, whose labels include Jive Records – which he sold in 2002 for $2.74 billion to Germany's BMG corporation.

Left: Clive Calder with Justin Timberlake in 2009.

THE HIGHEST-EARNING ROCK STARS, 2009

	millions
U2	$109
Bruce Springsteen	$58
Madonna	$47
AC/DC	$44
Britney Spears	$39
P!nk	$36
The Jonas Brothers	$34
Coldplay	$27
Kenny Chesney	$26
Metallica	$25

Estimated income by *Billboard* magazine for the year 2009, the criteria includes tour revenue and record sales (but not songwriter performance royalties or merchandising and sponsorship deals).

Above: U2's Bono and Adam Clayton in 2009.

This historic event was held in the bitter cold on January 18, 2009 at the Lincoln Memorial in Washington, DC.

Bruce Springsteen	The Rising
Mary J. Blige	Lean On Me
Jon Bon Jovi & Bettye LaVette	A Change is Gonna Come
James Taylor, John Legend, Jennifer Nettles,	
Arnold McCuller and Caroline Taylor	Shower The People
John Mellencamp	Pink Houses
Josh Groban, Heather Headley &	
the Gay Men's Chorus of Washington	My Country, 'Tis of Thee
Herbie Hancock, will.i.am & Sheryl Crow	One Love
Garth Brooks & the Inaugural Celebration Chorus	American Pie, Shout, We Shall Be Free
Usher, Stevie Wonder and Shakira	Higher Ground
U2	Pride (In the Name of Love), City of Blinding Lights
Pete Seeger, Bruce Springsteen,	
Tao Rodríguez-Seeger &	
the Inaugural Celebration Chorus	This Land Is Your Land
Beyoncé & entire ensemble	America the Beautiful

SUPERBOWL HALF-TIME PERFORMERS

XXV	New Kids on the Block	1991
XXVI	Gloria Estefan	1992
XXVII	Michael Jackson	1993
XXVIII	Clint Black, Tanya Tucker, Travis Tritt, The Judds	1994
XXIX	Teddy Pendergrass, Tony Bennett, Arturo Sandoval,	
	Miami Sound Machine	1995
XXX	Diana Ross	1996
XXXI	The Blues Brothers, ZZ Top, James Brown	1997
XXXII	Boyz II Men, Smokey Robinson, Martha Reeves,	
	The Temptations, Queen Latifah	1998
XXXIII	Chaka Khan, Gloria Estefan, Big Bad Voodoo Daddy,	
	Stevie Wonder	1999
XXXIV	Phil Collins, Christina Aguilera, Enrique Iglesias, Toni Braxton	2000
XXXV	Aerosmith, *NSync, Britney Spears, Nelly, Mary J. Blige	2001
XXXVI	U2	2002
XXXVII	Shania Twain, No Doubt, Sting	2003
XXXVIII	Janet Jackson, Justin Timberlake, P. Diddy, Nelly, Kid Rock	2004
XXXIX	Paul McCartney	2005
XL	The Rolling Stones	2006
XLI	Prince	2007
XLII	Tom Petty & the Heartbreakers	2008
XLIII	Bruce Springsteen & the E. Street Band	2009
XLIV	The Who	2010

From the first Superbowl in 1967 up until 1991 the half-time show at the annual Superbowl was performed by college marching bands, drill teams and veteran comedians. Following New Kids on the Block's performance at Superbowl XXV, however, each subsequent year has seen a succession of major music acts booked to play what has become one of the most prestigious gigs on the entertainment calendar.

NOTABLE US PRESIDENTIAL CAMPAIGN SONGS

Upon discovering that politicians were using their songs on the campaign trail without permission, several high-profile artists have demanded they stop doing so including Bruce Springsteen, who asked Ronald Reagan to stop using 'Born In The USA' in 1980; and Tom Petty who threatened to sue the George W. Bush campaign if it continued exploiting 'I Won't Back Down'.

MTV
MUSIC TELEVISION™

INDEX

ACKNOWLEDGEMENTS

The authors would like to acknowledge and thank the following sources:

Activision, Agency for Confirmations and Registration of Sightings of the King (ACRSK), AllMusicCharts.com, American Academy of Motion Picture Arts and Sciences, American Film Institute (AFI), American Music Awards, AOL, Apple Inc., Arbitron, Australian Recording Industry Association (ARIA), BASCA, Billboard, British Association of Record Dealers (BARD), British Broadcasting Corporation (BBC), British Phonographic Industry (BPI), Broadcast Music Inc. (BMI), Canadian Academy of Recording Arts and Sciences, Canadian Music Hall of Fame, Channel 4, Collectibles Today, Crowley Broadcast Analysis, Dick Clark Productions, ECHO Deutscher Musikreis, Eurovision, Federazione Industria Musicale Italiana (FIMI), Forbes, Fox Television, Hard Rock Café, Harmonix Music Systems, International Federation of the Phonographic Industry (IFPI), Irish Recorded Music Association (IRMA), Kerrang!, ledzeppelin.com, Media Control AG, Media Control GfK International, MTV, MTV Europe, MTV Games, Music & Media, Music Information Database, Music of Black Origin Awards (MOBO), National Academy of Recordings Arts & Sciences (NARAS), National Endowment for the Arts, National Football League, NBC Television, New Musical Express, Nielsen Music Control, Nielsen Soundscan, Nordoff-Robbins Music Therapy Centre, The Official Charts Company (OCC), PRS for Music, Phonographic Performance Limited (PPL), Planet Rock, Productores de Musica de Espana (PROMUSICAE), Q Magazine, Radio 538, RAJAR, Record Collector, Recording Industry Assocation of America (RIAA), Recording Industry Association of Japan (RIAJ), Recording Industry Association of New Zealand (RIANZ), Rock and Roll Hall of Fame, Rolling Stone, Royal Swedish Academy of Music, Songwriters Hall of Fame, Soul Train, Swedish Grammis, SYCOtv, Syndicat National de l'Edition Phonographique (SNEP), Thames Television, Time, UK Music Hall of Fame, Vevo, Visible Measures, World Music Awards, YouTube.

Thanks to:
Russell Ash, Pete Compton, Lisa Elliott, Jessica Ellis, Roland Hall, Barney Hooper, Anna Loynes, Wellesley Marsh, Abena Mills and finally, thanks and love to Abby Rose.